Joe Feddersen

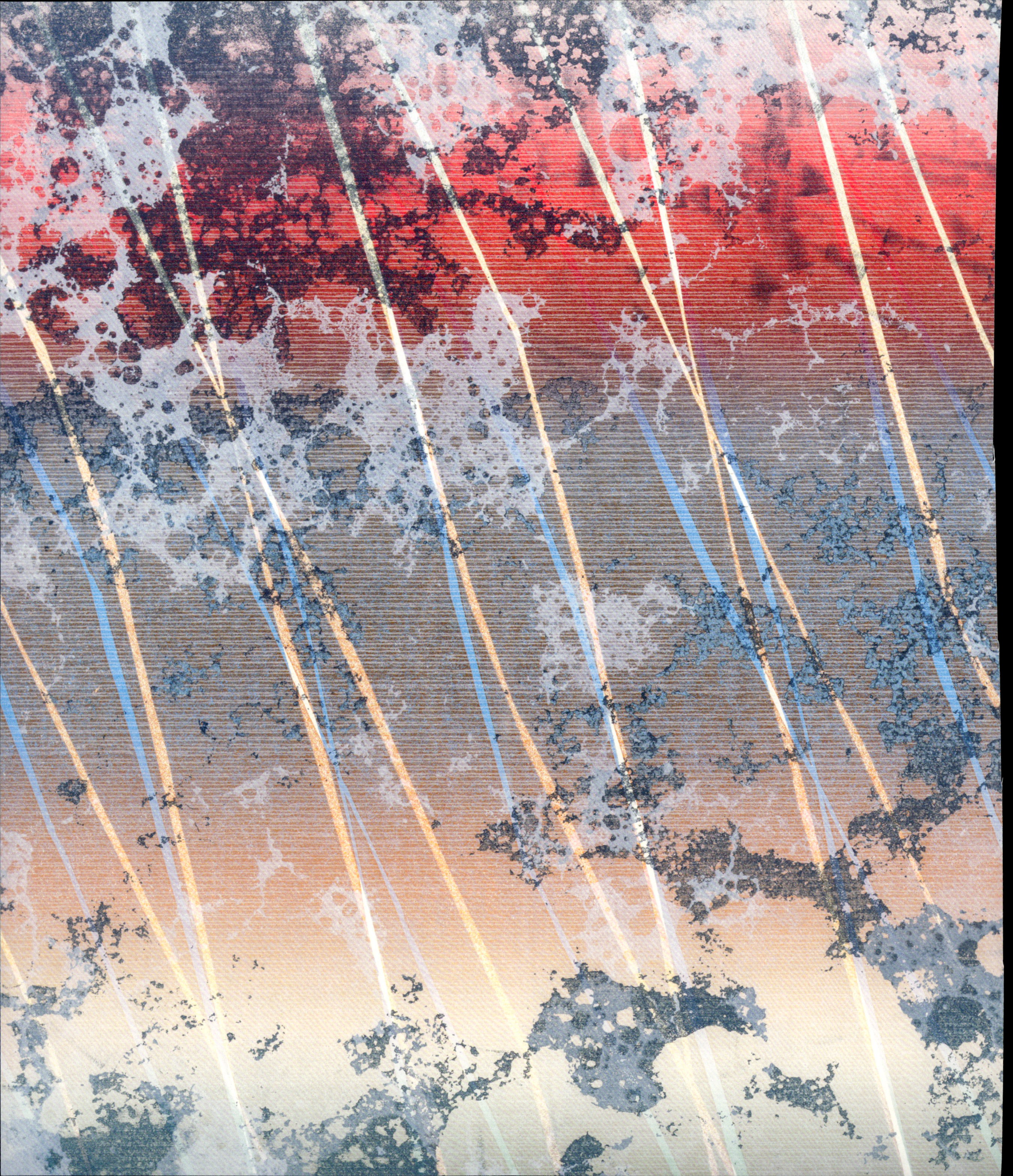

Joe Feddersen

Earth, Water, Sky

Edited by
heather ahtone and Rachel Allen

With contributions by
Victor A. Charlo, Miles R. Miller,
Anya Montiel, Ramona Wilson,
and Elizabeth A. Woody

Northwest Museum of Arts and Culture
Spokane, Washington

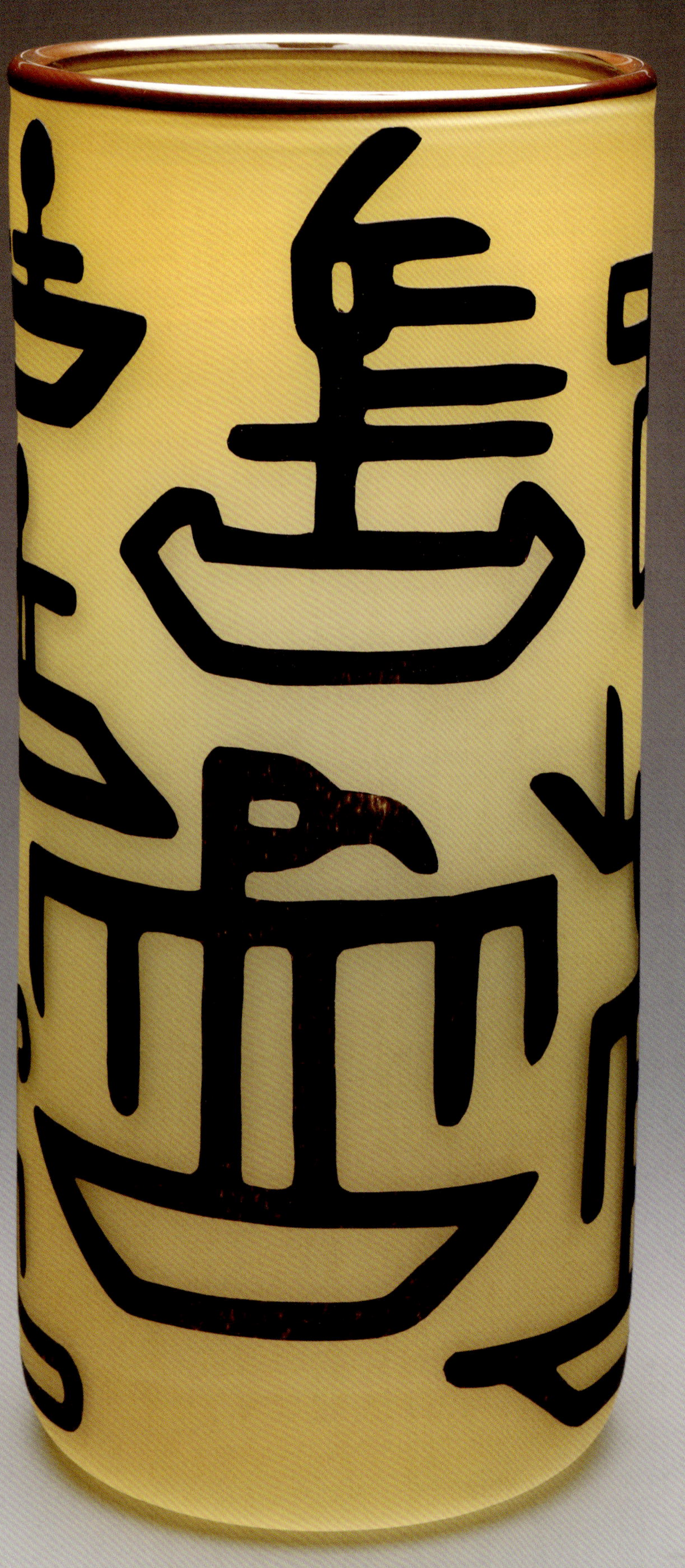

Contents

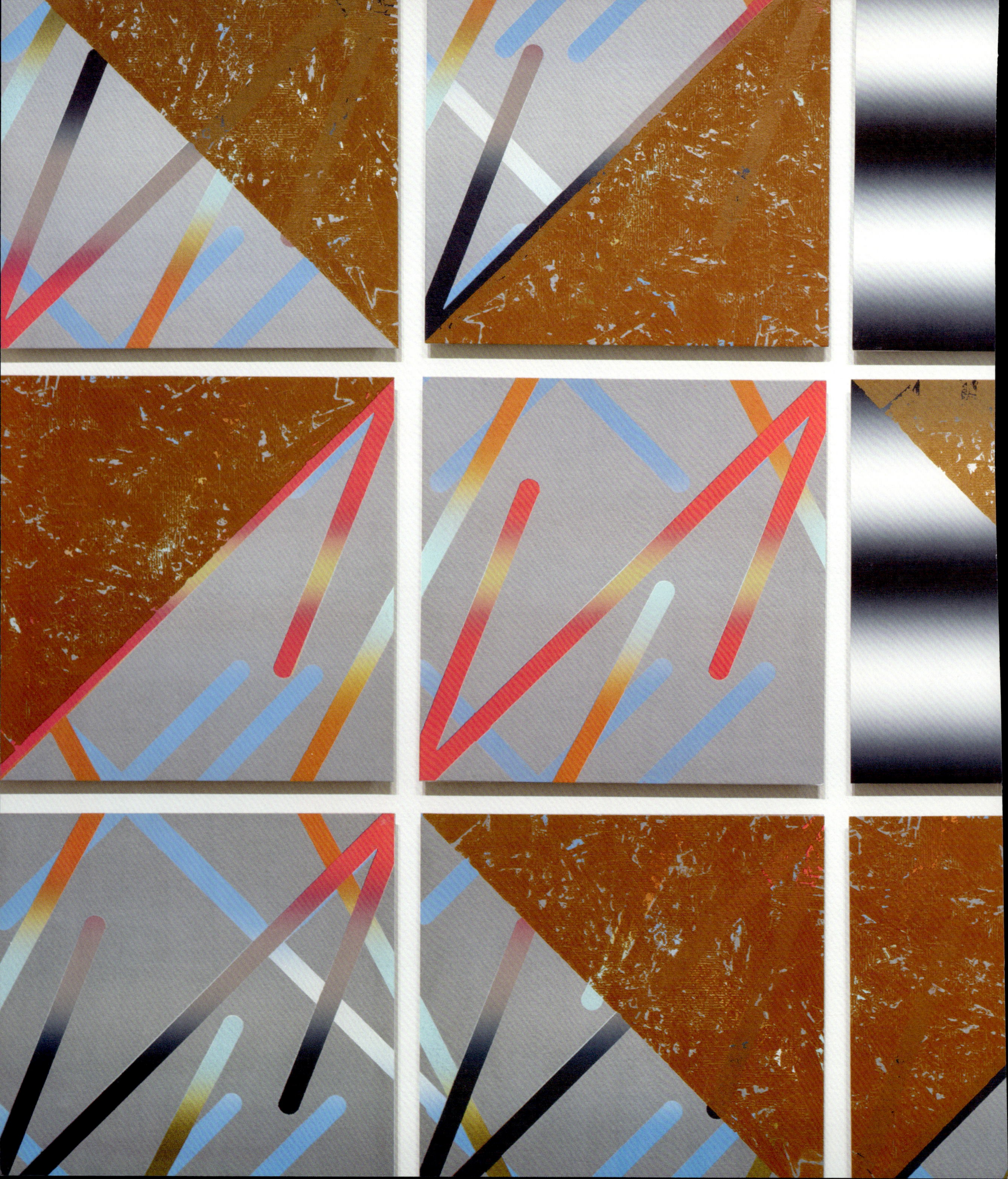

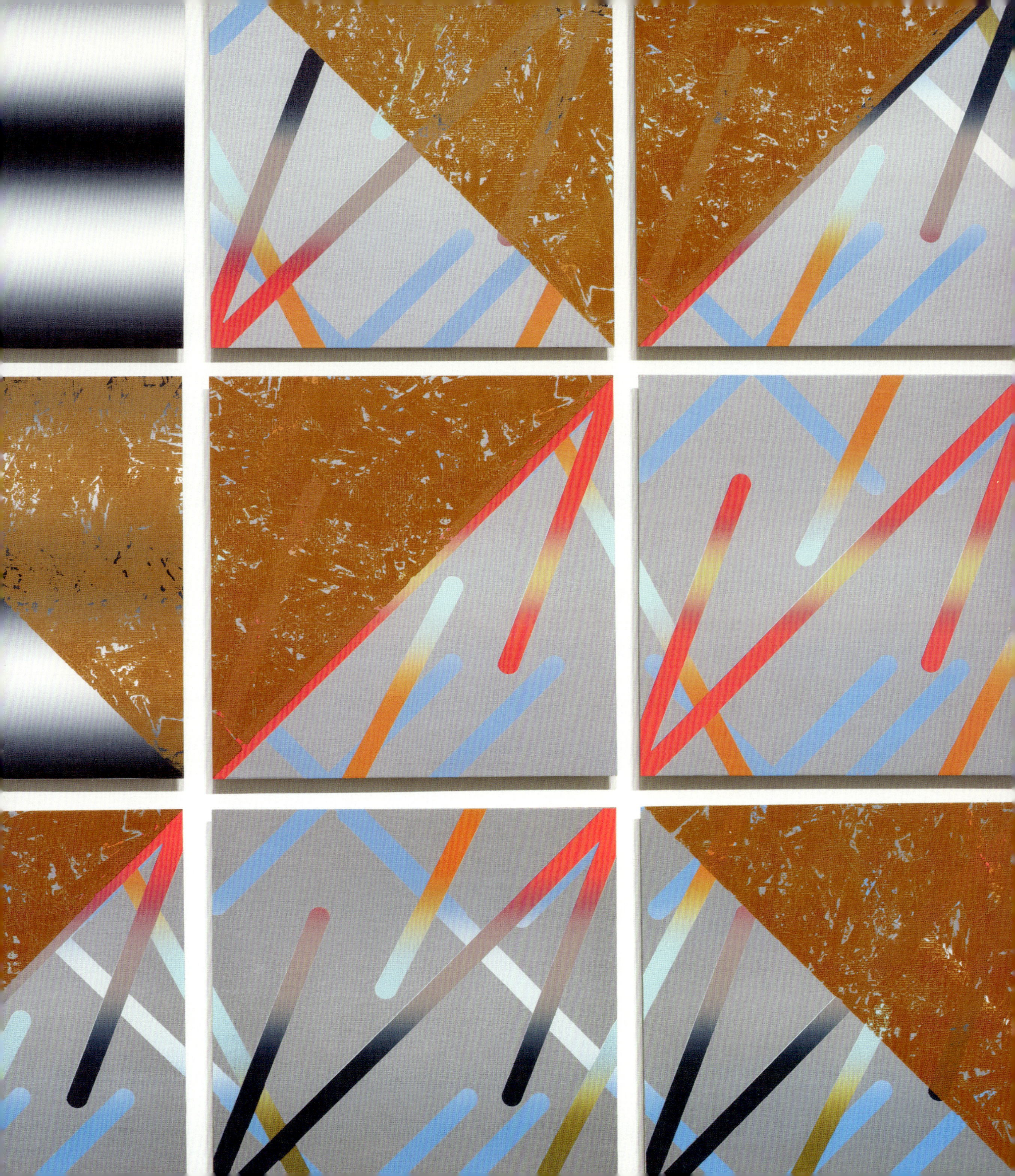

Director's Foreword

The Northwest Museum of Arts and Culture (the "MAC") is thrilled to publish this catalogue on the occasion of the exhibition *Joe Feddersen: Earth, Water, Sky*. The MAC is a regional museum with a significant permanent collection of historic art and material culture from Plateau Native Nations. Joe's work as a contemporary artist helps us think and reflect on Plateau life, artmaking, and community in the twenty-first century.

I met Joe for the first time at his home studio after he had recently retired as an art professor at The Evergreen State College in Olympia, Washington, and had moved back to his hometown of Omak. At the time I was new in my position as executive director of the MAC and meeting a number of regional artists. Joe welcomed me into his home, and we talked for hours about his work, his friends' and colleagues' work, as well as the books in his extensive library. There was a small gallery in the home installed with work by him and his many artist friends from over the decades. I took from this visit the idea that this house reflected a long and fruitful career filled with thoughtful experimentation, exploration, and perhaps most importantly, friendships and creative partnerships.

As a career retrospective became a topic of discussion between Joe and me, I imagined that the time was ideal for the MAC to work with Joe to organize this exhibition. The MAC is in the city of Spokane, which is the largest in the Plateau, a region centered between the Cascade Range to the west and the Rocky Mountains to the east. Unlike other artistic regions of the country, the Plateau is lesser known, even though it has been a fertile territory for many artists. With a foundation of Plateau-Native artists stretching back for millennia, the twentieth century ushered in some key modern artists, including Clyfford Still, Ed Kienholz, and Jaune Quick-to-See Smith. Joe fits into this long trajectory of artists making significant creative contributions on a national scale. The timing of this exhibition is also important. Over the past decade, Joe's work has been collected by many nationally renowned museums, and he is routinely included in contemporary Indigenous survey exhibitions. He enjoys a wide audience of collectors, curators, and fellow artists at a time when American art is being reassessed to include and embrace artists from a more diverse range of backgrounds and cultures.

This exhibition represents a new era at the MAC of initiating critical scholarship, honoring the important contributions of Indigenous artists from the region, and partnering with other museums across the country. As defined in our strategic plan, we aim to elevate the arts and stories of the Plateau beyond this region. As such, we're thrilled that this exhibition will travel to several museums around the country, where other audiences will be able to appreciate and understand Joe's creative journey. It is a timely pivot for this museum as we explore future projects and exhibitions that will elevate and celebrate the creativity in this region on a broader scale.

Joe Feddersen: Earth, Water, Sky represents the incredible efforts of co-curators heather ahtone, director of curatorial affairs at the First Americans Museum in Oklahoma City, and Rachel Allen, special projects curator at the MAC. Their combined effort to select an extraordinary group of works reflecting Joe's long career and to bring together a team of writers and designers who have thoughtfully honored this body of work has elevated this project. I am grateful for the spirit of collaboration of this team, which stretches across the country, and I appreciate their time and efforts to travel to Spokane to make this a successful project. And to the incredible MAC staff who have worked behind the scenes to ensure the project's success, I offer my deepest thanks.

I am also grateful to the American Indian Cultural Council (AICC) at the MAC, representing the Spokane Tribe of Indians, the Confederated Tribes of the Colville Reservation, the Coeur d'Alene Tribe, and the Kalispel Tribe of Indians. Their advice and participation in developing this exhibition was important to its success. Peter Sanburn, chair of the board of trustees (2022–24), was supportive and encouraging at every stage of this project. The MAC Foundation, chaired by Donna Weaver, was critical in providing support for curatorial travel and many of the expenses required for this project to succeed. Longtime MAC supporters Mary and Cheney Cowles, who appreciate and understand the importance of research and scholarship, provided significant support for the exhibition catalogue. This exhibition and catalogue project is made possible through major support from the Henry Luce Foundation, the Terra Foundation for American Art, and The Andy Warhol Foundation for the Visual Arts. This project is also supported in part by the National Endowment for the Arts.

And finally, I am deeply thankful to Joe Feddersen for his continued trust in the MAC and unwavering support of our Plateau art initiatives. Thanks, Joe.

Wesley Jessup
Executive Director,
Northwest Museum of Arts and Culture

Acknowledgments

At the center of this project is Joe Feddersen, not just because his art is the subject of this monograph, but because from him extends a dense network of relationships that Joe has cultivated over his lifetime. The very first piece of advice Joe gave me was to meet two people each month. He explained that he followed this rule in his career and encouraged his students to do the same. Joe understands the value of relationships, and I have met more than two people per month while working with him. Anyone who knows Joe understands that you do not cross paths with him; you make friends. His calming presence, subtle humor, and generous spirit make time spent with him as special as each work of art he creates. I am honored and humbled to be welcomed into his world of beautiful art and cherished friendships. Thank you, Joe Feddersen.

Because of Joe, I have the pleasure to work with heather ahtone, director of curatorial affairs at the First Americans Museum in Oklahoma City. Her involvement was essential from the start. This project could not have happened without her curatorial leadership, thoughtful writing contributions, and network of relationships. On top of being an accomplished curator and thoughtful scholar, heather is a generous mentor. From her I have learned about working with artists, managing large projects, and moving through the world with clear intention. I have observed her care with artists and enjoyed our conversations on long drives. She looks out for me personally and professionally beyond this project, and I am forever grateful.

Anya Montiel, curator at the National Museum of the American Indian and another friend to Joe, generously devoted time to several interviews for this book. Thank you for your care in doing this work. To her interviewees, your words contribute perhaps the most critical representations of Joe: as a fellow artist, friend, colleague, teacher, and uncle. Thank you for your time and beautiful words, Corwin "Corky" Clairmont, Carly Feddersen, Erin Genia, Alex McCarty, William Passmore, and Kay WalkingStick. Alex, a kind person and generous artist, will be deeply missed. To the poets who graciously agreed to share your thoughtful words in this book, my sincere thanks: Victor A. Charlo, Miles R. Miller, Ramona Wilson, and Elizabeth A. Woody. Joe deeply respects your work, and each contribution makes a compelling complement to his art that spurs deeper reflection and connection.

The network of people behind this project extends to additional colleagues, researchers, mentors, and friends. Rebecca Dobkins, professor emerita and curator of Native American art at the Hallie Ford Museum of Art at Willamette University, curated Joe's last career survey. Thank you for your past research, unwavering support of this project, and conversations about research directions. Her colleague, John Olbrantz Curator of Collections and Exhibitions Jonathan Bucci, kindly opened the collection to us for research and photography. Thank you so much, Jonathan, for your flexible scheduling and time spent aiding this project. Thank you, Elayne Silversmith of the Vine Deloria, Jr. Library at the National Museum of the American Indian, for your research support. To the vibrant and generous Association of Print Scholars community, thank you for thinking with me about media lines and unique prints, particularly Danielle Canter, Shelley Langdale, and Ben Levy. Thank you to my new kindred print colleague, Susanne Meurer of the University of Western Australia, for your support and advice. Thank you, Charles Froelick, for your critical support in the project's early stages. To my University of Delaware cohort and fellow paddlers on this PhD journey, thank you for your PDF requests, salient feedback, and generous friendship: Yoo Jin Choi, Julia Hamer-Light, Thomas Price, and Dakota Stevens. To my kind and steadfast PhD advisor, Jessica Horton, thank you for your understanding, flexibility, phone calls, intelligent advice, and friendship. Karen Kramer, The Stuart W. and Elizabeth F. Pratt Curator of Native American and Oceanic Art and Culture at the Peabody Essex Museum, provides continual mentorship to me. I would not be a curator if it were not for her ushering me through the door. My dearest thanks, KK. It is an honor to offer my deep thanks to generous mentors: Jennifer Himmelreich, Sarah Chasse, and Rochelle Kulei Nielsen. To my past colleagues from other museums, thank you for sharing resources and advice: Kathy Fredrickson, Hannah Silbert, Rebecca Bednarz, and Claire Blechman. I have also learned so much from Joe's friends. To Corky Clairmont, Linda King, and Cappy Thompson, thank you for your time, hospitality, and wisdom. And to Joe's sisters, Yvonne and Vicki, thank you for the fun time we spent together while away from my sisters. There have been numerous artists, scholars, curators, and authors who have supported Joe throughout his career. This project stands bolstered by that work; thank you all.

This exhibition and publication would not have been possible without generous lenders parting with cherished artworks. Thank you to the private collectors who support Joe and this project: Kym Aughtry, Bill R. Roulette and Laura L. De Simone, Judith Kovacs, and Preston Singletary. Thank you, Jordan Schnitzer and the Jordan Schnitzer

Family Foundation in Portland, Oregon, for lending, supported by Michael Whittington and Catherine Malone. Additionally, my deepest gratitude to the wonderful staff at these institutions: the Hallie Ford Museum of Art at Willamette University, Salem, Oregon; the Washington State Arts Commission, Olympia; Missoula Art Museum, Montana; Eiteljorg Museum of American Indians and Western Art, Indianapolis; High Desert Museum, Bend, Oregon; Colville Tribal Museum, Confederated Tribes of the Colville Reservation, Coulee Dam, Washington; and the Crow's Shadow Institute of the Arts, Pendleton, Oregon. My deepest gratitude to Joe Feddersen and Dawna Holloway of studio e gallery for lending work as well. And thank you, Dawna, for your crucial support of this project and the generous help you gave to me.

It is an honor to work with leadership at the MAC, which had the vision to bring this ambitious project together. To Wesley Jessup, instigator of the project and fierce advocate for contemporary Plateau artists, thank you for your leadership and vision and for assembling this wonderful team. I am deeply grateful to our museum board of trustees, which has supported this project; thank you, Peter Sanburn, Janet Durnford, Matthew Henshaw, Jeanie Louie, Debra Schultz, Frank Velázquez, Gayle Terry, Michael Dunn, Steve Duvoisin, Jason Brown, Lukus Collins, Greg Hesler, and Laurie Arnold. I am also deeply grateful for the support from the MAC Foundation: Donna Weaver, Greer Bacon, Pati Dahmen, Patty Dicker, Michael Flannery, Maureen Green, Scott LaPlant, and Mike Ormsby. Thank you, Joyce Perkins, for your steadfast organization, communication, and generous attitude. I am also so grateful to Debra Schultz and Penn Fix, Dean Lynch and Michael Flannery, and Laurie Arnold for so generously welcoming me to the Spokane community. I am humbled by the collaborative work the American Indian Cultural Council has done through the years, and to those currently serving, thank you: Karen Condon, Francis Cullooyah, Jeanie Louie, Cindy Marchand, John Matt, Annette Pierre, Neeka Somday, and Leona Stanger.

Of course, this project could not have happened without the expert implementation of the MAC staff, and I am grateful for each of their critical contributions. To the unflappable director of exhibitions and collections Kayla Tackett, thank you for your leadership and unwavering support. Thank you, exhibitions registrar Natalie Wadle, who kept everything together with cheerful spirit. Thank you for your expertise and for generously sharing your collections, American Indian Collection curator Tisa Matheson (Nimiipuu), collections curator Brooke Shelman Wagner, and Johnston-Fix Curator of Archives and Special Collections Anna Harbine; it is an honor to work with all of you. Thank you, John Fullmer, exhibitions and collections technician, for always coming through with help at the right moment. To collections database project manager Theo Courtney, thank you for sharing your expertise and spreadsheet templates. Thank you John Richardson, facilities manager and exhibitions preparator, for your diverse support of the building and execution of the exhibition. Thank you, Tammy Gabbert of Art Source, for your exhibition expertise and support. Thank you, associate curator Anne-Claire Mitchell, for your crucial and holistic support of this project. Thank you, Jack Gassen and all those who contribute to Exhibitions and Collections.

I am deeply grateful to chief operating officer Renee Webber for her leadership, efficiency, and thoughtful collaboration. To her team, I offer my gratitude for your critical support in operating the museum. IT system admin John Leberman made my work possible through his unwavering (sometimes daily!) IT support, and I am deeply grateful. Visitor operations manager Kate Rau not only facilitates a friendly entry experience for our visitors and incredible retail selections but also has a warm and helpful demeanor with her colleagues. Thank you, and good luck on your next chapter, Kate! Welcome, visitor services manager Jordan Crowder. Her incredible team, led by Kelly Robbins, could not be more outstanding to everyone they meet; thank you, Athaylia Begay, Andrew Acuna, Alyssa Greninger, and Anna Cantu. To maintenance mechanic Levi Lounder, who is working rain or shine or weekend, thank you. Thank you, custodians Brett Turner and Jack Allard, for not only your support but your persistent kindness. To the awesome security team, Allen Eaker and Joel Salter, I am so grateful for your flexibility, your generous attitudes, and for always being the first to help. You all make working at the MAC more efficient and enjoyable.

To chief marketing officer Marit Fischer, thank you for your expert leadership and thoughtful approach. It is a delight and honor to work with you and your team. Thank you, graphic designer Jessie Bart, for your beautiful designs and easy collaboration. Thank you, Carol Summers, for looking forward to championing our new initiatives. I am also grateful to the education team, led by thoughtful director of education Rob Worstell. Amanda Gardner, thank you for coordinating adult programs and events with Erik Ness. Thank you, Ellen Postlewait, for your productive ideas and fruitful collaboration as interpretation manager. Congrats on your new role as curator of history and Campbell House! Thank you, volunteer coordinator Linda Strong, for sustaining and leading such a delightful group of volunteers. To our loyal and generous volunteers, I am so grateful for your support of the MAC—we could not do this work without you! Thank you, Lindsey Newton, for teaching our groups to think through art with Visual Thinking Strategies, and Noe Yoder, for facilitating such great experiences for our young visitors. I am also grateful for the education work of Josh Watkins and Leighton Kittleman. Thank you,

Shawn Gunnier, for hitting the ground running with enthusiasm and initiative to engage with our communities.

To our finance team, chief financial officer Francis Langston, supported by Anita Guidry, I offer my thanks for your steadfast and efficient work on this project. I am grateful for the leadership of chief development officer Anna Bresnahan and her team: Carolyn Black, Will Simons, Amada Souza, and Cheree LaPierre. It is a delight to collaborate with all of you. Thank you, HR liaison Kristin Howard, for all your efforts to support the staff. I offer my sincere thanks to executive assistant Melissa Allard, who has been a beacon of encouragement, efficient support, and quick thinking since I first worked with the MAC in 2021. Thank you, Melissa, and to those who were so welcoming when I first met the MAC three years ago: Betsy Godlewski, Carolyn Black, Anita Guidry, Brooke Shelman Wagner, Carol Summers, and Allen Eaker. It is a privilege to have MAC staff as colleagues, and I thank you all for your efforts to ensure the success of this project.

Outside the museum, this project was made possible by numerous partnerships and collaborators. Thank you, Ed Marquand and Adrian Lucia, for getting us started with Marquand Books. I am deeply grateful to Kestrel Rundle for your project management, flexibility, and calm during this book project. Thank you, Melissa Duffes, for your editorial expertise and flexibility. And thank you, Ryan Polich and Jeremy Linden, for a book design that offers a gorgeous platform for Feddersen's work. I am deeply grateful to everyone at Marquand Books who has touched this project and ensured its success. Thank you.

To Keri Healey, thank you so much for your amazing project management, organization, and writing expertise for grant applications. To Dean Davis, thank you so much for the gorgeous photography that fills this book. I am also grateful to Mark Meyer, who provided excellent assistance with photography along with a calming presence. Thank you both for your enthusiasm, patience, flexibility, and willingness to work in multiple locations. To our exhibition graphic designer, Kevin Coochwytewa, I am deeply grateful for your sophisticated and joyful design, which bolsters Joe's love for his home. Thank you, Alex Mann, for your flexible, meticulous, and thoughtful design work. To Yvonne Lever and Scott Jones from Atlas, thank you for rising to the occasion for this complex fabrication project and engineering a beautiful exhibition design. Thank you, Jerry Judd of Perception Plastics, for your fabrication expertise and long-standing commitment to the MAC. Thank you, Holly Swanson of Spokane Gallery and Framing, for your high-quality and expeditious work. Thank you, Eric-Alain Parker, for contributing your creative insights and problem solving skills at critical moments. I am deeply grateful to all of the creative minds who ensured the beauty and success of this book and exhibition.

Joe Feddersen: Earth, Water, Sky was made possible through major support from the Henry Luce Foundation, Terra Foundation for American Art, and The Andy Warhol Foundation for the Visual Arts. I am so honored that each of them believed in the MAC and this project, and I am grateful to their philanthropic leadership, which expands the definitions of American art. This project is also supported in part by the National Endowment for the Arts, and I am thankful for this national recognition, which sheds light not only on Joe Feddersen's powerful work, but on Indigenous artistic leadership in the Plateau.

Joe Feddersen's works of art celebrate his joy in the land, waters, and skies of his home, and Joe revels in all of his relationships. I am so grateful to Joe's friends, family, and extended network, as you are all integral to who Joe is as an artist and friend. Thank you for sharing with the MAC through Joe and your many contributions. I am also deeply grateful to my family, who, like Joe, continually teach me about joy.

Rachel Allen
(Nimiipuu [Nez Perce])
Special Projects Curator,
Northwest Museum of Arts and Culture

Artist Acknowledgments

The creation of visual arts has never been a solitary experience for me. I have been blessed with the support of many, including family members, dear friends, and a vibrant, active arts community. It is my hope that this book and exhibition will be considered as a celebration of community and the land of my ancestors.

Early in my career, I found support from within my family. My parents, Jenny and Ted Feddersen, encouraged my inquiry into the arts. My siblings, Anthony, Yvonne, Vicki, and Lincoln, also often offered support, as did my nieces and nephew, Robin, Kristen, Carly, RYAN!, Michelle, and William.

I am truly indebted to all the people offering kind words and support, especially the educators: H. H. Hall, Daryl Dietrich, Rae Dana, Robert Graves, Ruth Allen, Scott Bailey, Vi taqʷšəblu Hilbert, Glen Alps, and Dean Meeker.

And my fellow artists, colleagues, and friends: Corky Clairmont, Linda King, Cappy Thompson, Truman Lowe, Jaune Quick-to-See Smith, Neal Ambrose-Smith, Marwin Begaye, Ric Gendron, Peter Jemison, Lillian Pitt, Elizabeth Woody, George Longfish, Larry Beck, Ron Carraher, Judith A. Kovacs, James Lavadour, Conrad House, Kay WalkingStick, Rick Bartow, Jim Schoppert, Gail Tremblay, Lawney Reyes, Marvin Oliver, Karl Leonard, Linda Lomahaftewa, Anne Appleby, George Cramer, Cris Bruch, Anthony Benson, Tim Marr, Bob Seng, Lisa Hines, Miles Miller, Randy Mundt, Bill Ransom, Tom Johnston, Ann Friedman, Michael Gibbons, Mike Marchand, Ken Vander Stoep, Ann Kier, Lynnette Miller, Maggie Smith, Randy Miller, Tom Miller, Todd Clark, Ben Cobb, Julie Edwards, Preston Singletary, Joe Benvenuto, Gabe Feenan, Kristin Elliott, Sarah Gilbert, Dan Friday, Elaine Timentwa Emerson, Laurie Meeker, Carol Minugh, Barbara Brotherton, Barbara Earl Thomas, Eliot Aust, Gloria Garcia, Melissa Bob, Nora Naranjo Morse, Melanie Yazzie, Britt Rynearson, Derek Bruno, Mack McFarland, Karen Goulet, Lara Evans, Lucia Harrison, Susan Aurand, Anya Montiel, Letitia Chambers, Laura Mullen, Erin Younger, Melissa Feldman, Rebecca Dobkins, Michael Holloman, Laura VerMeulen, Kirby Stanton, Tina Kuckkahn, Marilyn Frasca, Kym Aughtry, Bill Avery, Linda Hutchins, Johanna Nitzke,

Susan Platt, James Bailey, Bernie Whitebear, Dominic Nieri, Tamar Benzikry, Jim Holiday, Sidney Herness, John Wesley, Stephanie Stebich, Dorene Red Cloud, Jim Denomie, Arnie Marchand, Jackie Cook, Mario Caro, Jennifer Complo McNutt, Amy Adams, Dawna Holloway, Marilyn Butler, Jan Cicero, Lynn McAllister, Elizabeth Leach, Charles Froelick, Jeffrey Moose, Wilder Schmaltz, Cathy Denning, Margery Aronson, Jordan Schnitzer, Michelle Jack, and Alex McCarty.

I am forever indebted to heather ahtone and to the staff of the MAC and appreciate all the hard work and dedicated commitment to the arts: Wesley Jessup, Rachel Allen, Brooke Wagner, Tisa Matheson, Kayla Tackett, Natalie Wadle, John Fullmer, Tammy Gabbard, John Richardson, Melissa Allard, Marit Fischer, Jessie Bart, Rob Worstell, Amanda Gardner, Ellen Postlewait, Erik Ness, Renee Webber, Kate Rau, Kelly Robbins, Athaylia Begay, Allen Eaker, and Joel Salter.

Joe Feddersen
(Confederated Tribes of
the Colville Reservation)

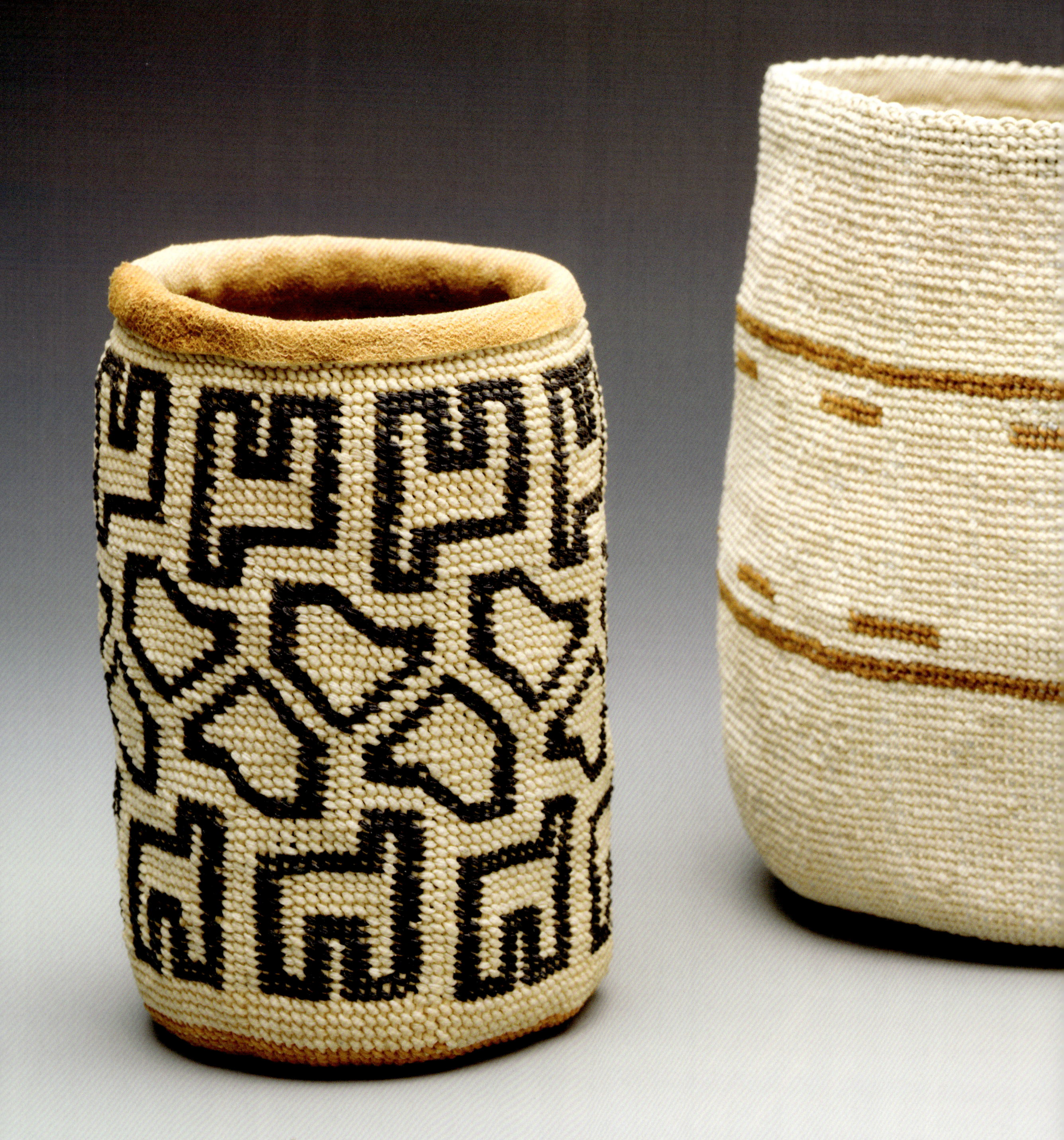

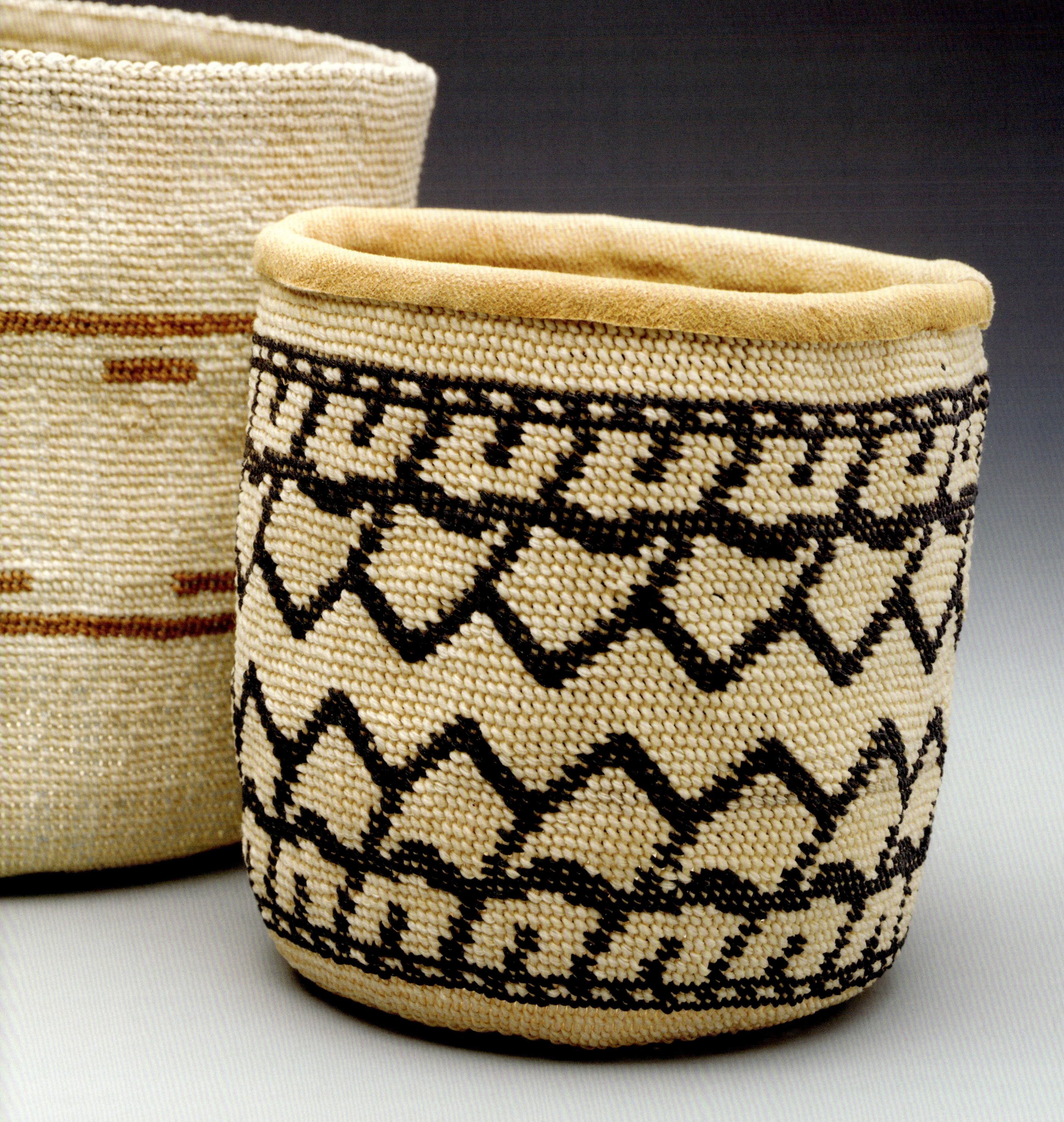

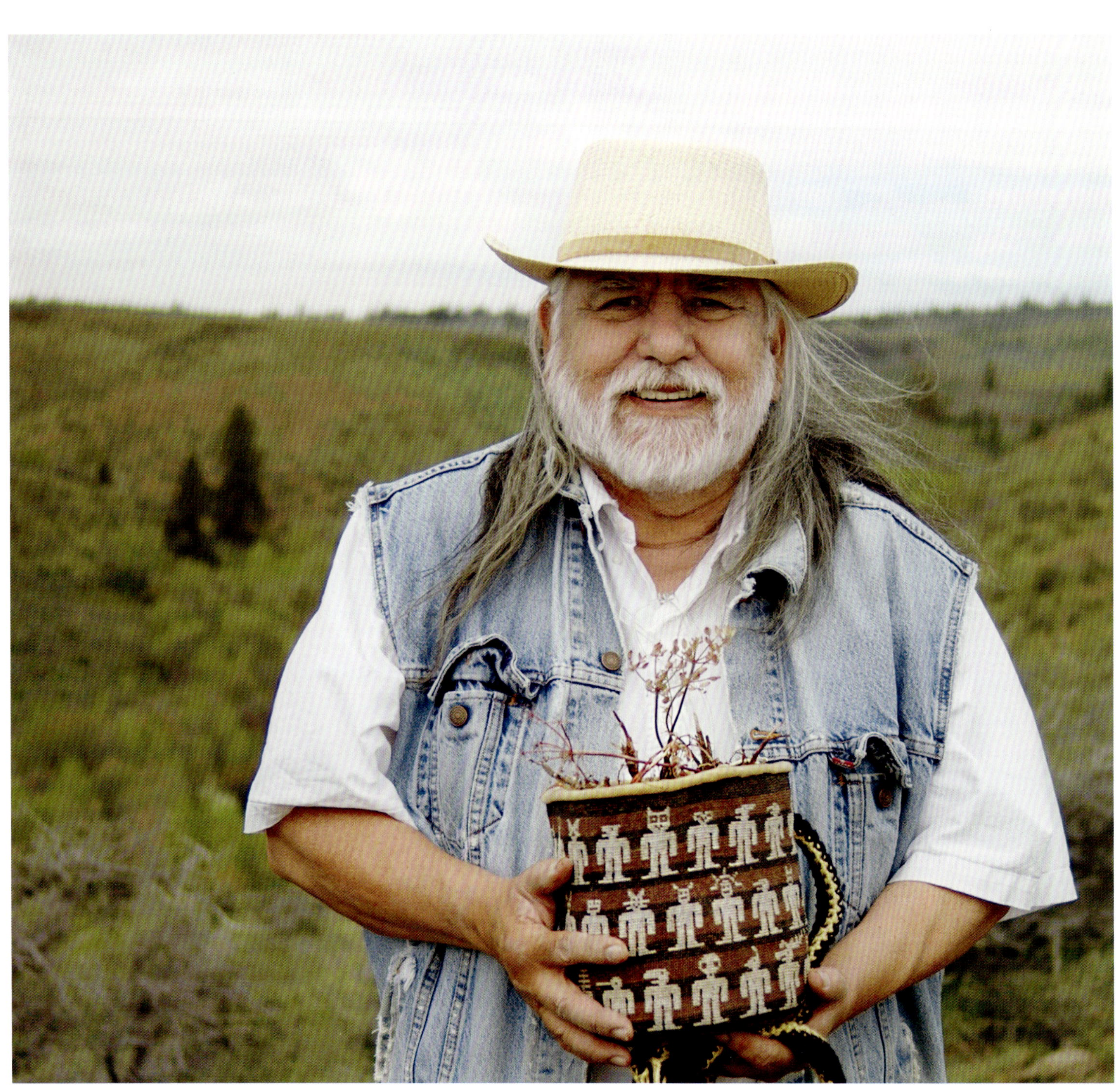

A Landscape of Relations

heather ahtone and Rachel Allen
with Interviews by Anya Montiel

Joe Feddersen's (b. 1953) impact stretches in many directions across various terrains. From Washington State, he formed close connections in his hometown of Omak, in the Seattle art community, and as faculty at The Evergreen State College, Olympia. Those relationships became the foundation of larger networks in the Northwest, across the United States, and as far as New Zealand. Tracing his career across these six regions, Feddersen emerges as an artistic leader whose legacy is marked by his relationships. He continues to be a relative to his home communities, a storyteller through his artwork, a generous mentor to his students, an advocate of Northwest and Plateau artists, a dear friend, and an eager collaborator. Rather than a chronological accounting of his life, these pages offer a brief look into the network of relations Feddersen has cultivated across the landscapes he depicts in his art.

When he retired from Evergreen, I think he was looking forward to moving back to Omak, to his tribal community. To work with the elders and other people in his community. It also was a great enrichment for him, to utilize very specific things about his community in his artwork. You could see his artwork flourish. Joe's work often talks about community as well. The community and land, and the story that is contained within the landscape. I think that's why we are as close as we are, because we foster a similar attitude about community, landscape, and place. That's who we are as tribal people.[1]

—Corwin "Corky" Clairmont
(Confederated Salish and Kootenai Tribes), artist

We go to secondhand stores together. He is always looking for textures that he can incorporate into his prints and what those textures can communicate. It is fascinating how he can pick up a doily or textured mat and point out mountain designs on it. He sees them everywhere.[2]

—Carly Feddersen
(Okanagan and Arrow Lakes
[Colville Confederated Tribes]), artist and niece

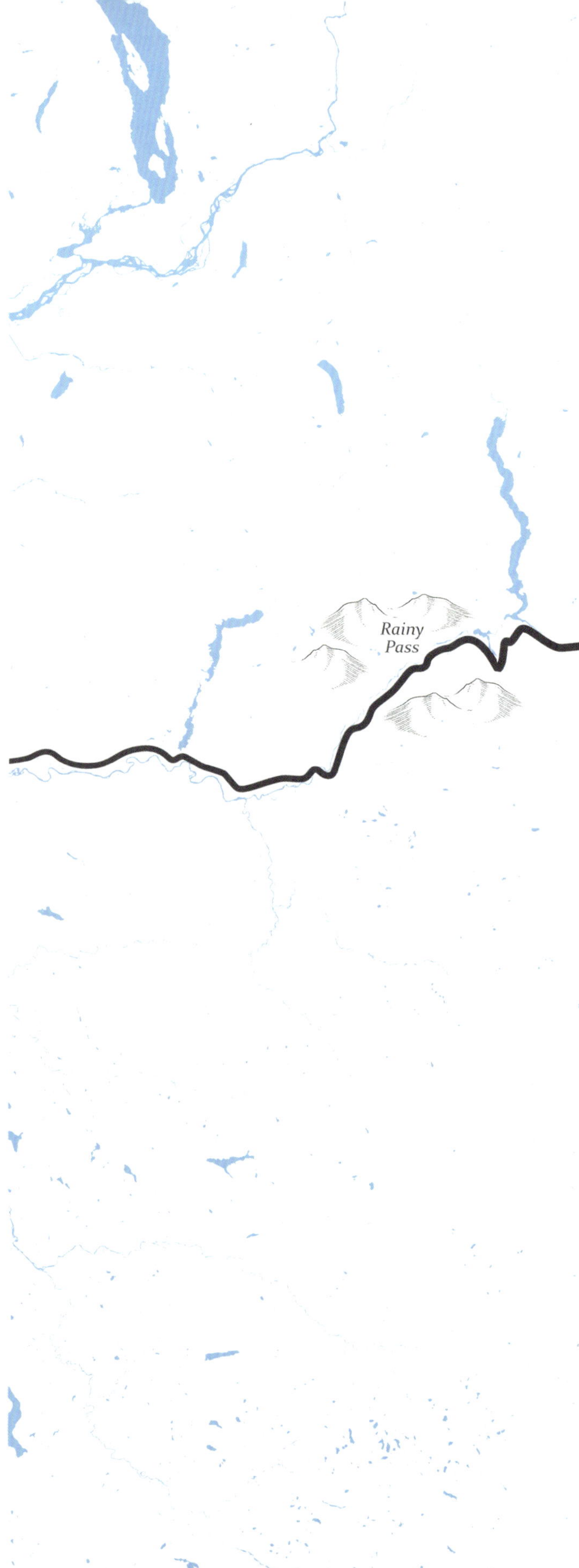

A RELATIVE

Upon retirement from The Evergreen State College in 2009, emeritus faculty member Joe Feddersen returned to his hometown of Omak, Washington. "I really enjoy being home. I was gone for so long," Feddersen explains; "it's such a wonderful feeling to be in a room surrounded by your people. Part of that's from my grandmother. My grandmother always said, 'Come home, you're needed. You need to be part of your people.'"[3] Feddersen is a citizen of the Confederated Tribes of the Colville Reservation, and his cultural background ties him to Okanagan and Arrow Lakes communities that straddle the Canada–United States border. Feeling like a guest everywhere else, Feddersen belongs with his relations. He immerses himself in the community, spending time with family, meeting long-standing friends, mentoring high school students, teaching workshops, and attending events.

For Feddersen, home is not just the town of Omak but also the surrounding landscape. From the praying mantis visiting his front door to plein air painting excursions with his nieces, he revels in the lively and diverse ecology of the region. Medicinal lakes, annual Canoe Journeys, and recovering wildlife populations weave their way into the artmaking at his home studio. Feddersen's deep-seated connection to this place is matched only by his responsibility to it. He remains committed to his community.

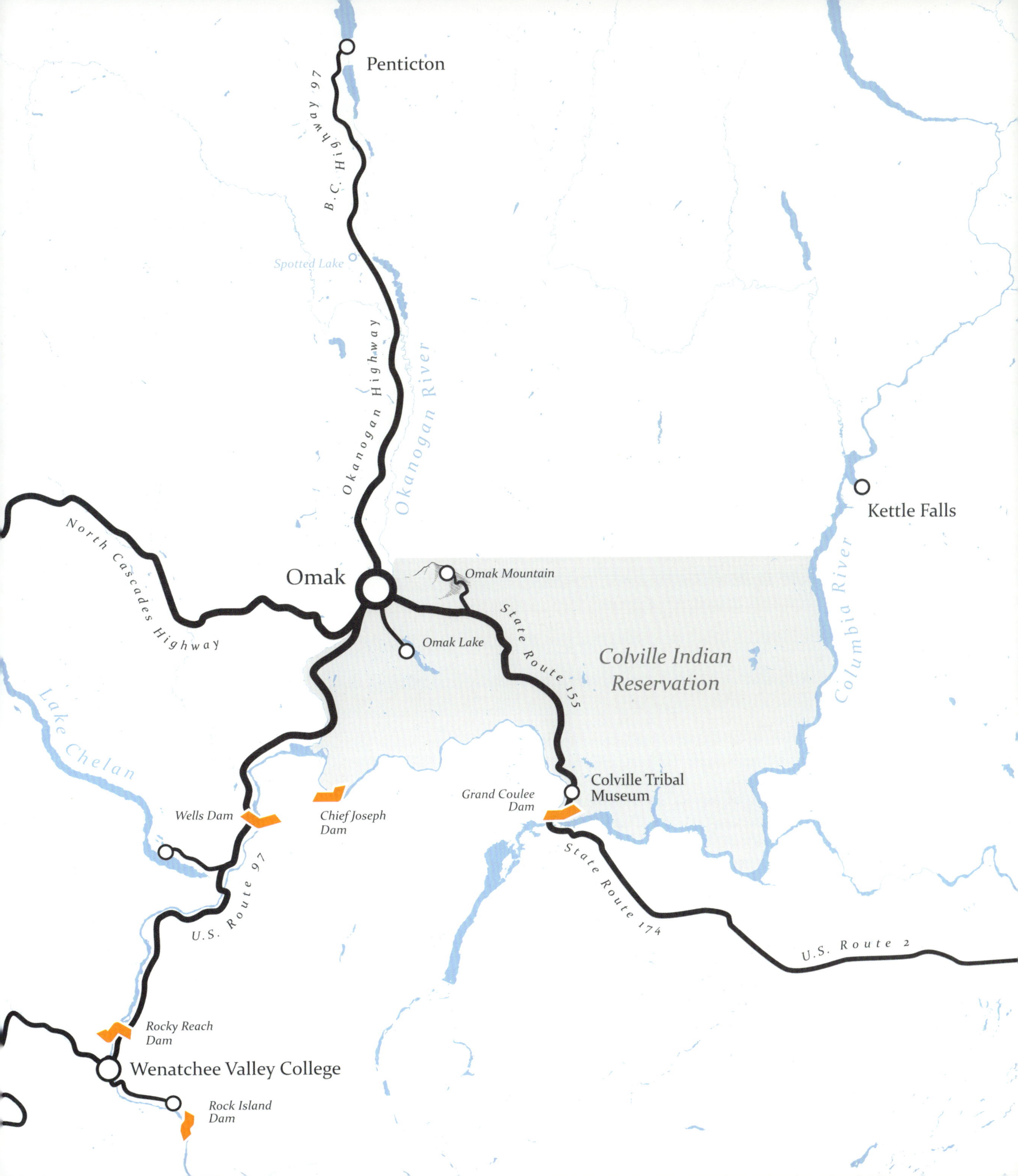

Penticton
B.C. Highway 97
Spotted Lake
Okanogan Highway
Okanogan River
Kettle Falls
North Cascades Highway
Omak
Omak Mountain
Omak Lake
State Route 155
Colville Indian Reservation
Columbia River
Lake Chelan
Wells Dam
Chief Joseph Dam
Grand Coulee Dam
Colville Tribal Museum
State Route 174
U.S. Route 97
U.S. Route 2
Rocky Reach Dam
Wenatchee Valley College
Rock Island Dam

I see a lot of storytelling in his work. It inspires me when he takes our stories and keeps them going by adding new characters and making them continuous and contemporary. He's not replicating old work. It is about continuing the tradition by innovating, creating new work. He does that beautifully.[4]

—Carly Feddersen
(Okanagan and Arrow Lakes [Colville Confederated Tribes]), artist and niece

You can judge someone not by the number of friends they have but by the quality. Joe's friends are some of the highest-quality people.[5]

—William Passmore
(Okanagan and Arrow Lakes [Colville Confederated Tribes]), artist and nephew

A STORYTELLER

After completing his program at Wenatchee Valley College and working at dams near his home, Feddersen pursued a BFA at the University of Washington. There, he studied with Ron Carraher (Colville Confederated Tribes, b. 1935), Glen Alps (1914–1996), and Vi taqʷšəblu Hilbert (Upper Skagit, 1918–2008). As a language and culture teacher, Hilbert encouraged Feddersen's artistic narratives. So impressed, she stated, "Joe, you're not an artist, you're a storyteller."[6]

By the early 1980s, Feddersen had entered an active Native art scene in Seattle. In 1977 the United Indians of All Tribes, led by Bernie Whitebear (Colville Confederated Tribes, 1937–2000), opened Daybreak Star Indian Cultural Center, which would house Sacred Circle Gallery, a critical hub for contemporary Native arts. Whitebear's older brother Lawney Reyes (Colville Confederated Tribes, 1931–2022) curated the Seafirst Corporation collection, acquiring Native art from Feddersen and others.

Through gallery networks, Feddersen developed close friendships with fellow emerging artists Rick Bartow (Mad River Band of Wiyot Indians, 1946–2016) and Lillian Pitt (Warm Springs, Wasco, Yakama, b. 1944). At the same time, he met artist mentors that would become lifelong friends: Jaune Quick-to-See Smith (Confederated Salish and Kootenai Tribes, b. 1940), George Longfish (Seneca and Tuscarora, b. 1942), Truman Lowe (Ho-Chunk, 1944–2019), Larry Beck (Inuit-Chanagmiut, 1938–1994), and Ric Glazer-Danay (Mohawk [Kahnawake], b. 1942). Later, Feddersen forged collaborative friendships with glass artists Cappy Thompson (b. 1952) and Preston Singletary (Tlingit, b. 1963). Feddersen frequently visits friends in Seattle and credits Quick-to-See Smith with forty years of support and advice.

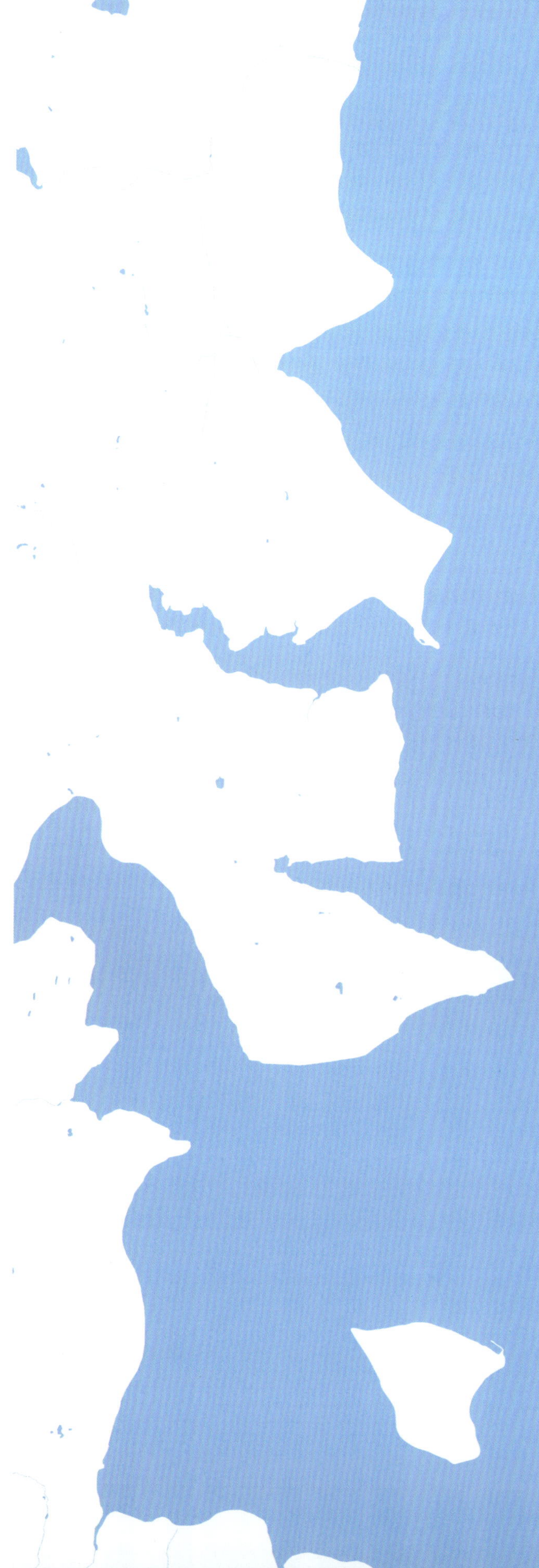

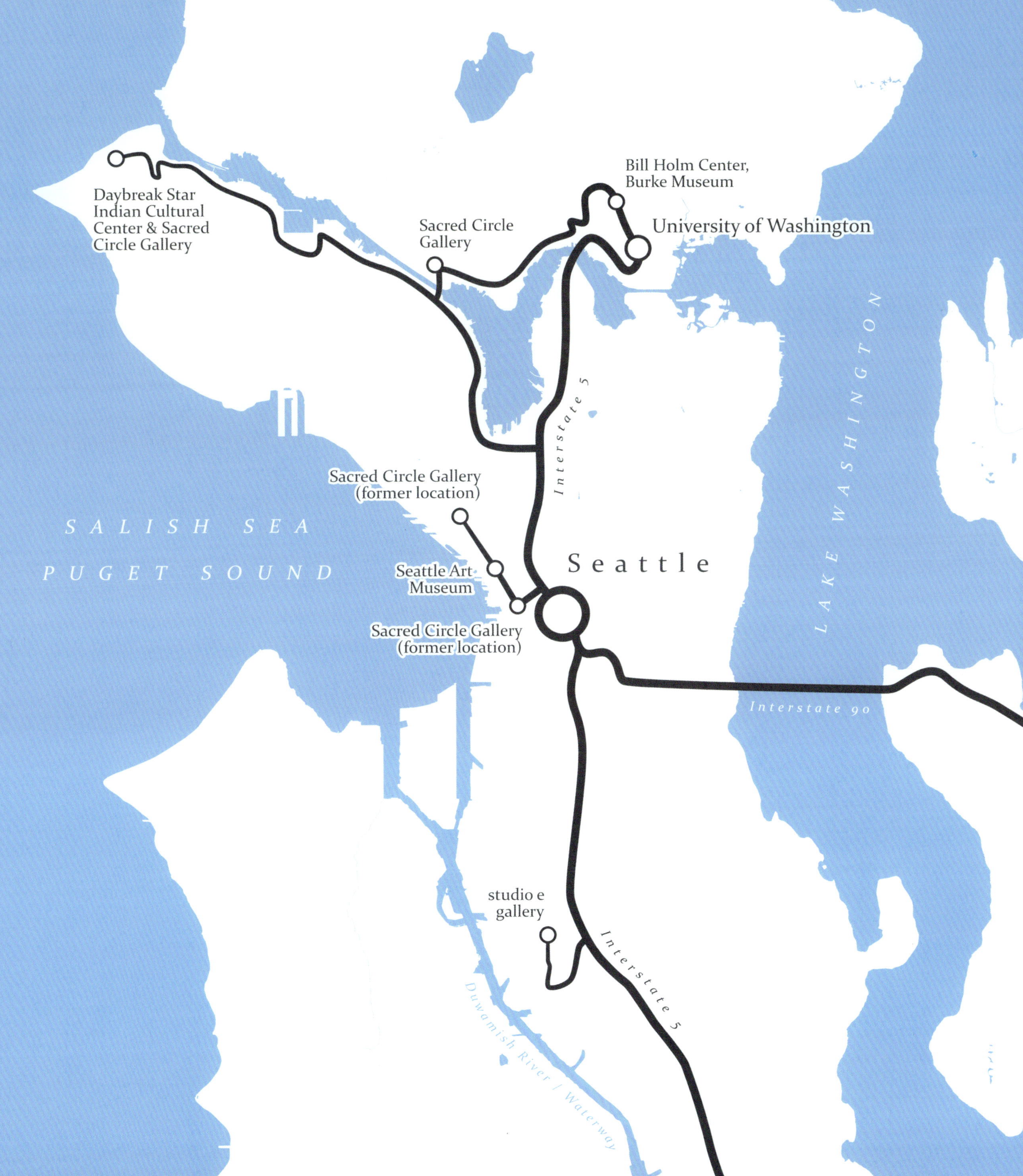

Daybreak Star
Indian Cultural
Center & Sacred
Circle Gallery
Sacred Circle
Gallery
Bill Holm Center,
Burke Museum
University of Washington
Interstate 5
Sacred Circle Gallery
(former location)
SALISH SEA
PUGET SOUND
Seattle Art
Museum
Seattle
Sacred Circle Gallery
(former location)
LAKE WASHINGTON
Interstate 90
studio e
gallery
Interstate 5
Duwamish River / Waterway

He really has a gift, and as a teacher, he shares his gift with others and shows his students how to realize their own vision. Often, he is asked what he is most proud of, and he says his students.[7]

—Erin Genia
(Sisseton-Wahpeton Oyate), artist and former student

I was hired at Evergreen as the 3D Indigenous arts faculty. I teach wood carving and Native American Studies. I also teach in the printmaking studio. I teach serigraphy and relief prints (wood cuts, linocuts, and monotypes). I have the opportunity to teach in a Native American Studies program and to teach printmaking. I am passing on what I learned from Joe.[8]

—Alex McCarty
(Makah), faculty, The Evergreen State College; artist; and former student

MUD BAY

A MENTOR

Eager to return to the Northwest upon completing his graduate studies in 1989, Feddersen joined the art faculty at The Evergreen State College in Olympia, Washington. Artist and writer Gail Tremblay (1945–2023) had been teaching there since earlier in the decade. Reuniting with Seattle friends, a cohort of Feddersen, Tremblay, Lillian Pitt, and Larry Beck supported each other, expanding their networks to artists such as Elizabeth A. Woody (Navajo Nation, Yakama Nation, Confederated Tribes of Warm Springs, b. 1959), James Lavadour (Walla Walla, b. 1951), Philip Cash Cash (Cayuse and Nez Perce, b. 1960), and Conrad House (Navajo and Oneida, 1956–2001).

Feddersen enjoyed supporting his students during his twenty-year teaching career at Evergreen. As with his mentors, many became colleagues and friends. Former student Alex McCarty (Makah, 1978–2024) was faculty at Evergreen and worked with Feddersen on preparations for the Paimārire Fiber Arts Studio, which opened in 2018. Paimārire expanded the Indigenous Arts Campus at Evergreen, which includes the "House of Welcome" Longhouse Education and Cultural Center and the Pay3q'ali Carving Studio (where McCarty also advised). One of Feddersen's first students, Dawna Holloway, represents his work at studio e gallery in Seattle.

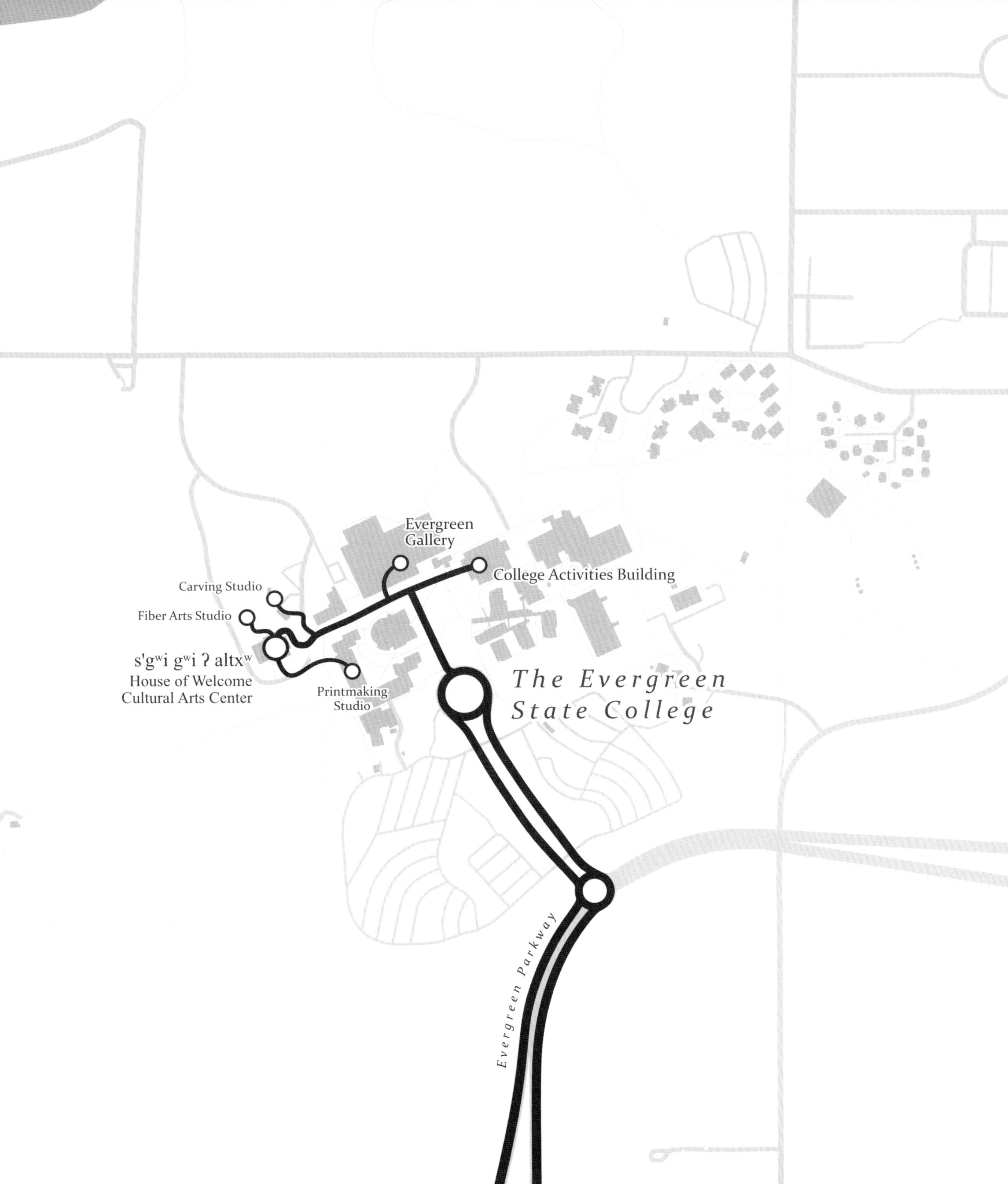
Evergreen
Gallery
College Activities Building
Carving Studio
Fiber Arts Studio
s'gʷi gʷi ʔ altxʷ
House of Welcome
Cultural Arts Center
Printmaking
Studio
The Evergreen
State College
Evergreen Parkway

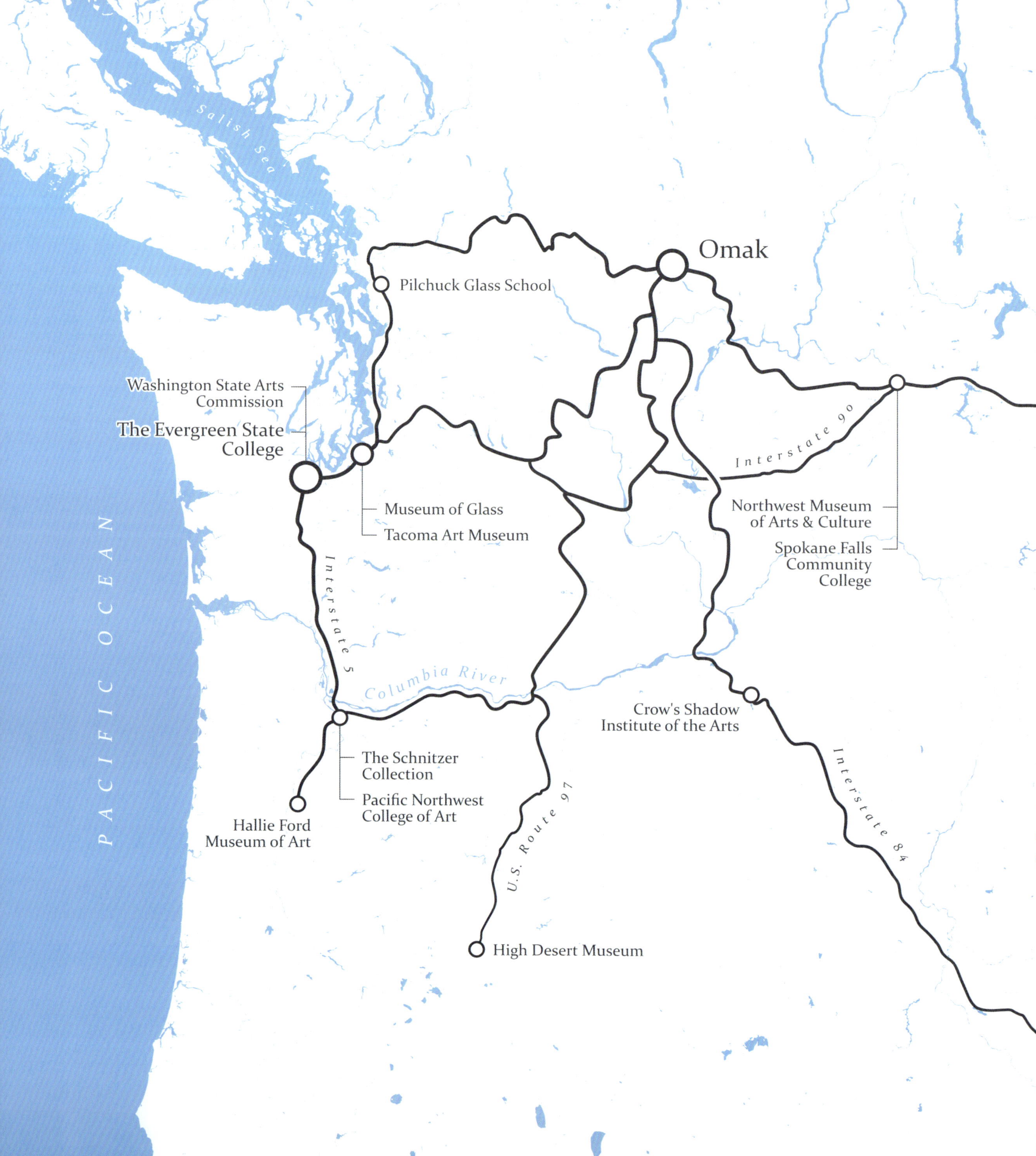
Salish Sea
Omak
Pilchuck Glass School
Washington State Arts Commission
The Evergreen State College
Museum of Glass
Tacoma Art Museum
Interstate 90
Northwest Museum of Arts & Culture
Spokane Falls Community College
PACIFIC OCEAN
Interstate 5
Columbia River
Crow's Shadow Institute of the Arts
The Schnitzer Collection
Pacific Northwest College of Art
Hallie Ford Museum of Art
U.S. Route 97
Interstate 84
High Desert Museum

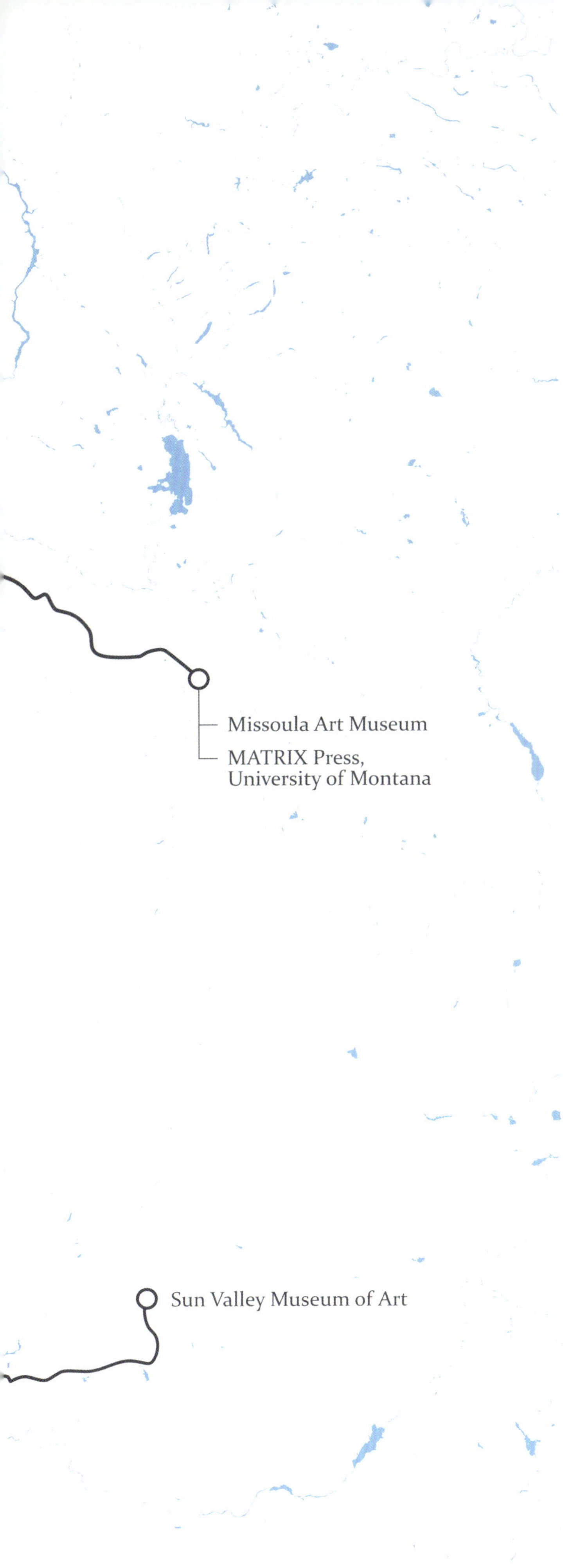

Joe has been such an inspiration to many people. When you visit his studio, it's not about seeing his work. He will get you involved in artmaking. He is a great pusher of other artists, wanting them to do the best they can. He is a brother to many artists. We always support each other as much as we can.[9]

—*Corwin "Corky" Clairmont (Confederated Salish and Kootenai Tribes), artist*

He has been very encouraging of my own creativity. I drew this little sketch when I was a kid and showed it to him. He didn't belittle it. That was really nice. I still remember that.[10]

—*William Passmore (Okanagan and Arrow Lakes [Colville Confederated Tribes]), artist and nephew*

Missoula Art Museum

MATRIX Press, University of Montana

Sun Valley Museum of Art

AN ADVOCATE

Beyond Evergreen, Feddersen grew his career in all directions. He gained gallery representation in Portland and participated in numerous artist residencies. A 2005 exhibition at the Northwest Museum of Arts and Culture, *Land Mark*, showcased his monumental *Okanagan IV* (2003) print installation. The Hallie Ford Museum of Art at Willamette University, Salem, Oregon, organized his 2008 career retrospective, *Vital Signs*, curated by Rebecca Dobkins. In 2023 the High Desert Museum in Bend, Oregon, commissioned Feddersen to weave a basket for the spring root harvest before exhibiting in *Creations of Spirit*.

Committed to Northwest and Plateau peoples, Feddersen constantly champions Native artists. "And that's been really important to me, especially lately, that I want to do these projects that bring artists together and create community, rather than being so individualistic and about yourself and your own career. It's about helping others, being [a leader], you know, hopefully encouraging others," explains Feddersen.[11] This includes involvement with the Northwest Native American Basketweavers Association and other weaving communities. In 2014 he organized *Terrain: Plateau Native Art & Poetry*, a folio of prints and poetry by Plateau artists from all career stages. Fifteen of the folios were donated to museum collections. Feddersen continues to contribute works of art by Plateau artists to museums and collections across the country.

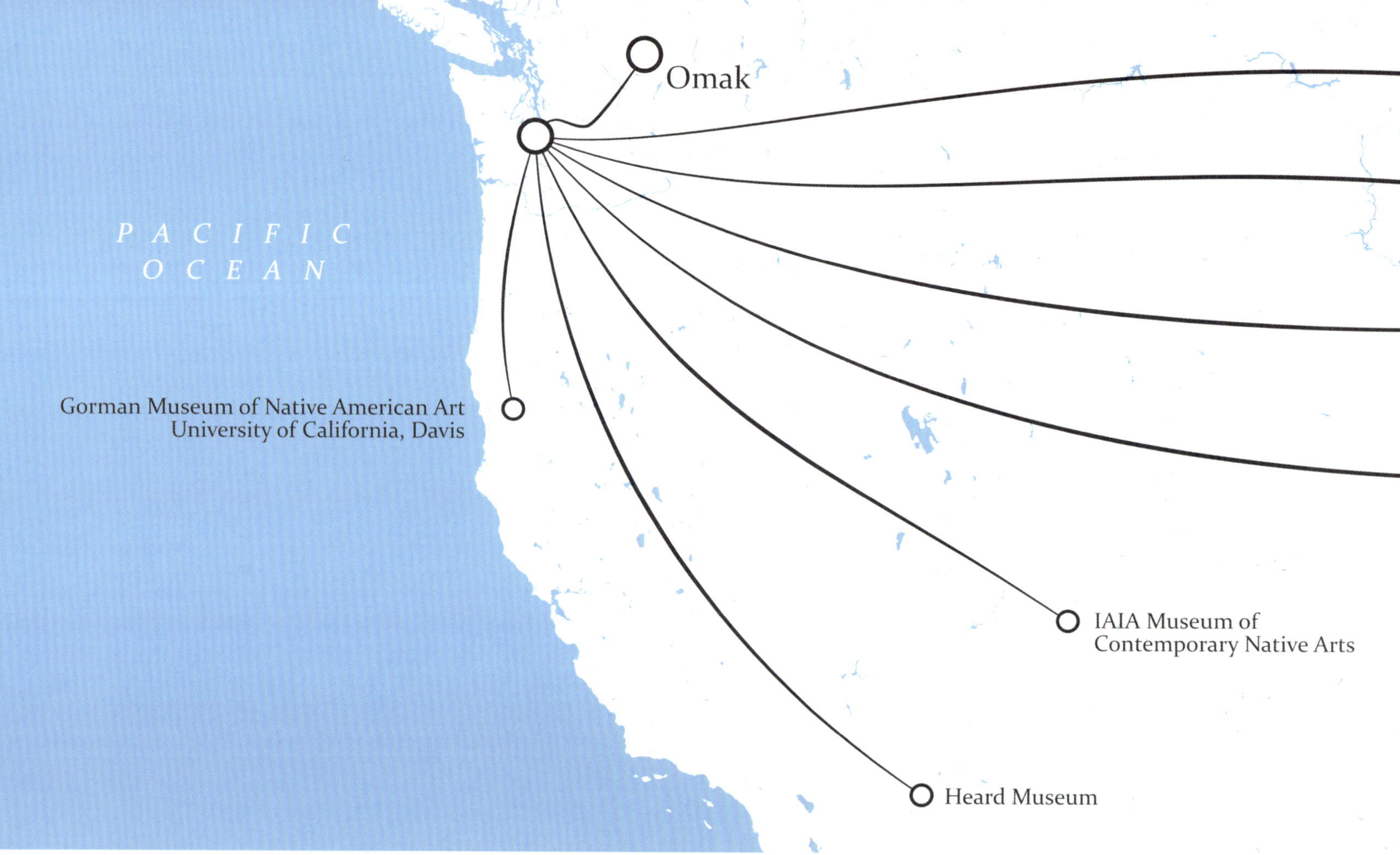

He is a dear friend, a wonderful artist, and he's smart as a whip. After my first husband died in 1989, Joe called me. He telephoned me but said nothing. I said nothing. There wasn't anything to say. Joe, in saying so little, expressed more in that moment about how I was feeling. He really understood my grief.[12]

—Kay WalkingStick
(Cherokee Nation), artist

Joe is a genuine, good human being. He's thoughtful. He wants tribal people to succeed, especially in the arts. The arts are a way we communicate best about who we are.[13]

—Corwin "Corky" Clairmont
(Confederated Salish and Kootenai Tribes), artist

His humor is all over his work. It is everywhere. It is the way he is.[14]

—Carly Feddersen
(Okanagan and Arrow Lakes [Colville Confederated Tribes]), artist and niece

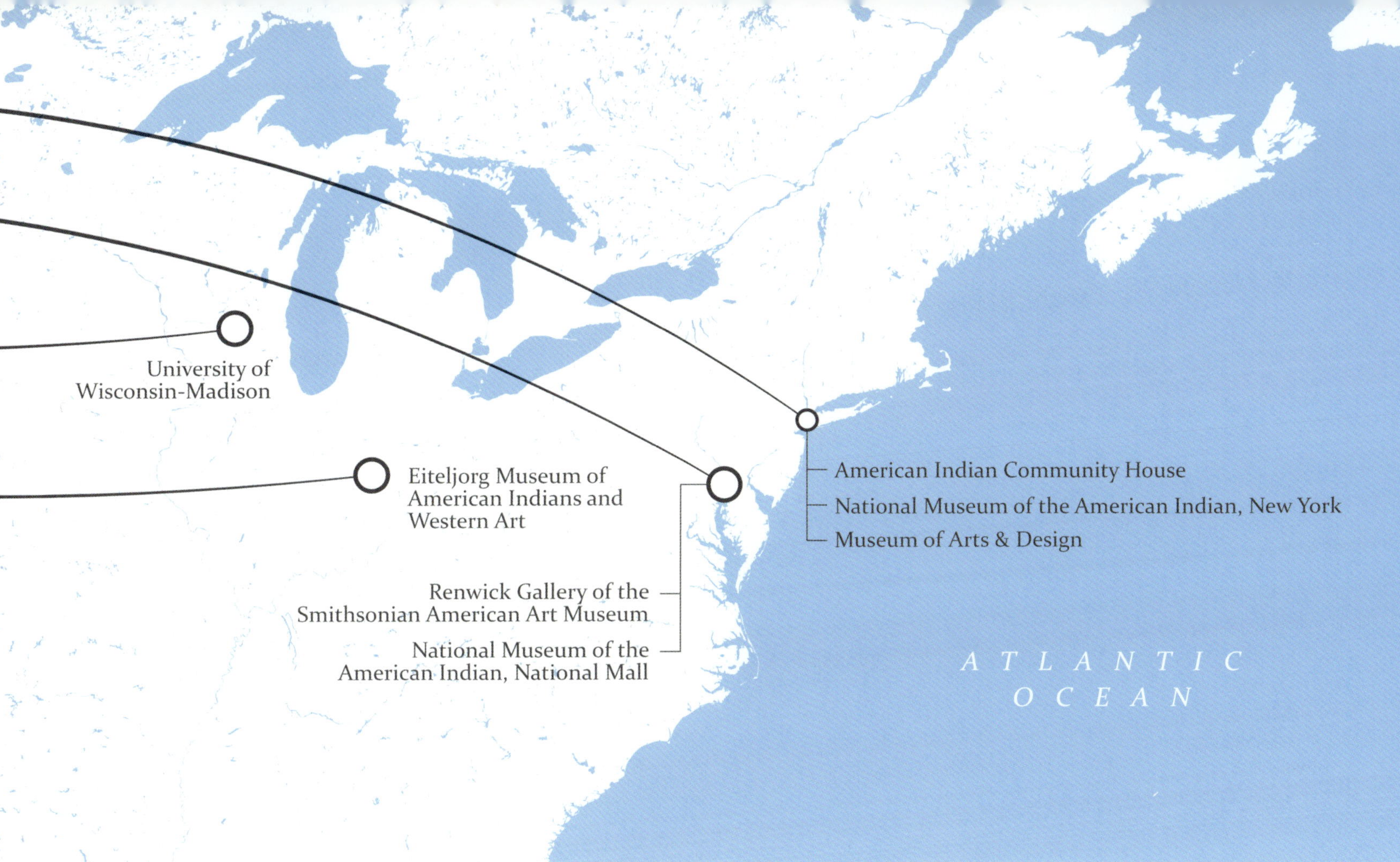

A FRIEND

Early on, venues such as the Gorman Museum of Native American Art at the University of California, Davis, and the American Indian Contemporary Arts Gallery in San Francisco proved critical in supporting Feddersen and his contemporaries. Feddersen's mentors, such as Jaune Quick-to-See Smith and George Longfish, "set the pace. They set the tone . . . they helped everybody, and they were generous."[15] In 1987 Feddersen, Lillian Pitt, Larry Beck, and others participated in the Third Biennial Native American Fine Arts Invitational at the Heard Museum, Phoenix. That same year, Feddersen began studying with Truman Lowe at the University of Wisconsin–Madison. Over the next decade, Feddersen exhibited in numerous galleries, including the American Indian Community House in New York City. Quick-to-See Smith curated his work into exhibitions such as *Our Land/Ourselves: American Indian Contemporary Artists* (1991). In 2001 Feddersen joined the second cohort of the prestigious Eiteljorg Contemporary Art Fellowship at the Eiteljorg Museum of American Indians and Western Art in Indianapolis.

The following years brought Feddersen's work into additional museum holdings and exhibitions nationwide. *Sharing Honors and Burdens: Renwick Invitational 2023* showcased Feddersen's work at the Renwick Gallery of the Smithsonian American Art Museum in Washington, DC, the preeminent center for American craft in the US. Looking back on his mentorship, Feddersen reflects: "I think that I aspire to be as generous as they were—to help other artists and to promote people. . . . I try to create a community rather than a business."[16]

> Joe has this curiosity. It's an exploration. He is enjoying it through the process. He says, "You have these prints that are the result of this exploration, through different ideas. The fun part is the making." It is about the process for Joe. He taught me that as well. When you have an idea, it becomes a research inquiry. That's what being an artist is all about. It is about having that fascination, those questions that you want to answer. It makes the work meaningful to you, and it will be meaningful to viewers as well.[17]
>
> —*Alex McCarty*
> *(Makah), faculty, The Evergreen State College;*
> *artist; and former student*

> Joe is a person who continuously creates. He's continuously curious, growing, and learning.[18]
>
> —*RYAN! Feddersen*
> *(Okanagan and Arrow Lakes [Colville*
> *Confederated Tribes]), artist and niece*

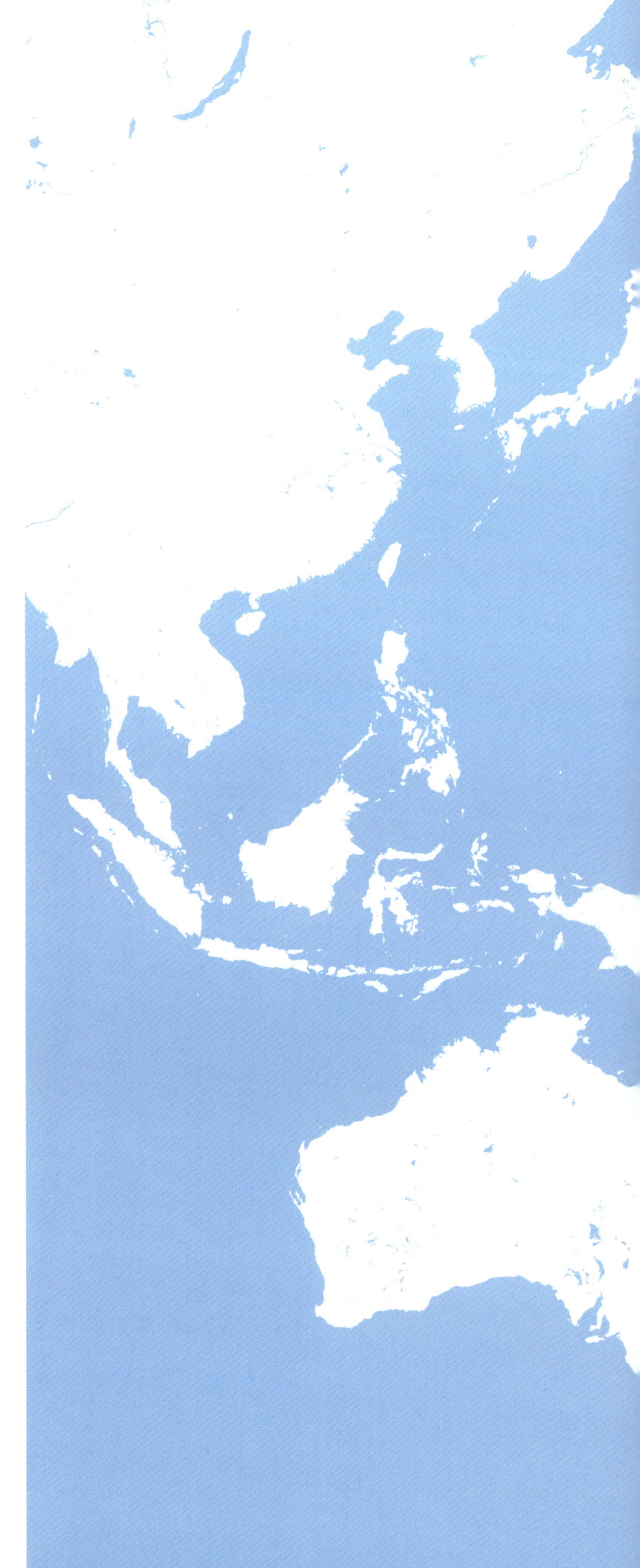

A COLLABORATOR

Founder of the Native American studies program in 1972, Mary Ellen Hillaire's (Lummi Nation, 1927–1982) impact on the philosophy of The Evergreen State College community remains palpable. When Feddersen came to Evergreen, he extended her legacy by inviting artists of various backgrounds to work with his students. In 1995 the s'gʷi gʷi ʔ altxʷ (House of Welcome) Longhouse Education and Cultural Center opened to support Indigenous arts by hosting local and international communities. With this culturally congruent infrastructure, opportunities grew for cross-cultural exchange. The first International Gathering of Indigenous Visual Artists of the Pacific Rim took place the same year in Rotorua, New Zealand. Feddersen and Longhouse director Tina Kuckkahn-Miller attended a subsequent Gathering. In 2001 the Longhouse hosted the first Pacific Rim Gathering in the US, with Feddersen serving as a lead artist. Artists from the continental US, Hawaii, Alaska, Canada, Samoa, and New Zealand learned from each other and exchanged ideas. The Longhouse hosted another Gathering in 2017, *Tears of Duk'Wibahl.*

In 2006 a partnership between the Longhouse and Te Waka Toi/ Creative New Zealand initiated a twelve-week artist-in-residence program for Māori artists at Evergreen. The program expanded into a biennial exchange in 2009, and Feddersen participated as the visiting artist to New Zealand in 2011. The Gatherings and exchanges fostered fruitful collaborations, such as the Paimārire Fiber Arts Studio at Evergreen, modeled after Māori meeting houses. Feddersen's support of Indigenous artists transcends continents, enriching the greater Indigenous Pacific community.

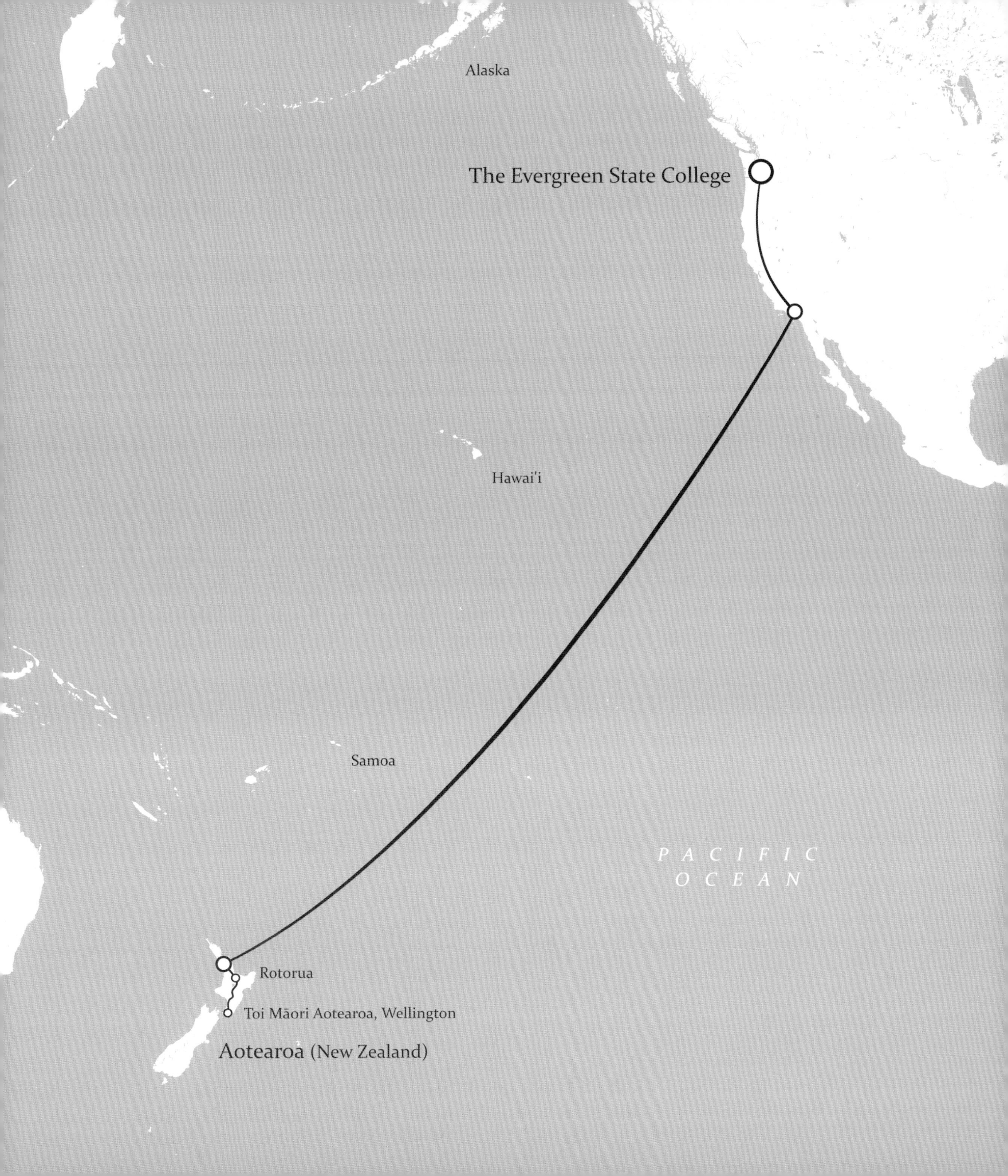

Alaska

The Evergreen State College

Hawai'i

Samoa

PACIFIC
OCEAN

Rotorua

Toi Māori Aotearoa, Wellington

Aotearoa (New Zealand)

Notes

1. Corwin Clairmont, interview by Anya Montiel, Jan. 16, 2023.

2. Carly Feddersen, interview by Anya Montiel, Jan. 20, 2023.

3. Joe Feddersen, conversation with heather ahtone and Rachel Allen, Feb. 19, 2023.

4. Carly Feddersen, interview.

5. William Passmore, interview by Anya Montiel, Jan. 18, 2023.

6. "Joe Feddersen: These Are My Stories." Smithsonian American Art Museum, May 12, 2023. Video, 0:01:23, https://www.youtube.com/watch?v=gFLCqtwchFE.

7. Erin Genia, interview by Anya Montiel, Jan. 31, 2023.

8. Alex McCarty, interview by Anya Montiel, Jan. 24, 2023.

9. Corwin Clairmont, interview.

10. William Passmore, interview.

11. Oral history interview with Joe Feddersen, Apr. 29 and May 6, 2021. Archives of American Art, Smithsonian Institution.

12. Kay WalkingStick, interview by Anya Montiel, Jan. 13, 2023.

13. Corwin Clairmont, interview.

14. Carly Feddersen, interview.

15. Joe Feddersen, conversation.

16. Joe Feddersen, conversation.

17. Alex McCarty, interview.

18. Mack McFarland and RYAN! Feddersen, "Two Generations: Joe Feddersen & Wendy Red Star," in *Cross-Platform Curation* (Ashland, OR: Schneider Museum of Art, 2020), 33.

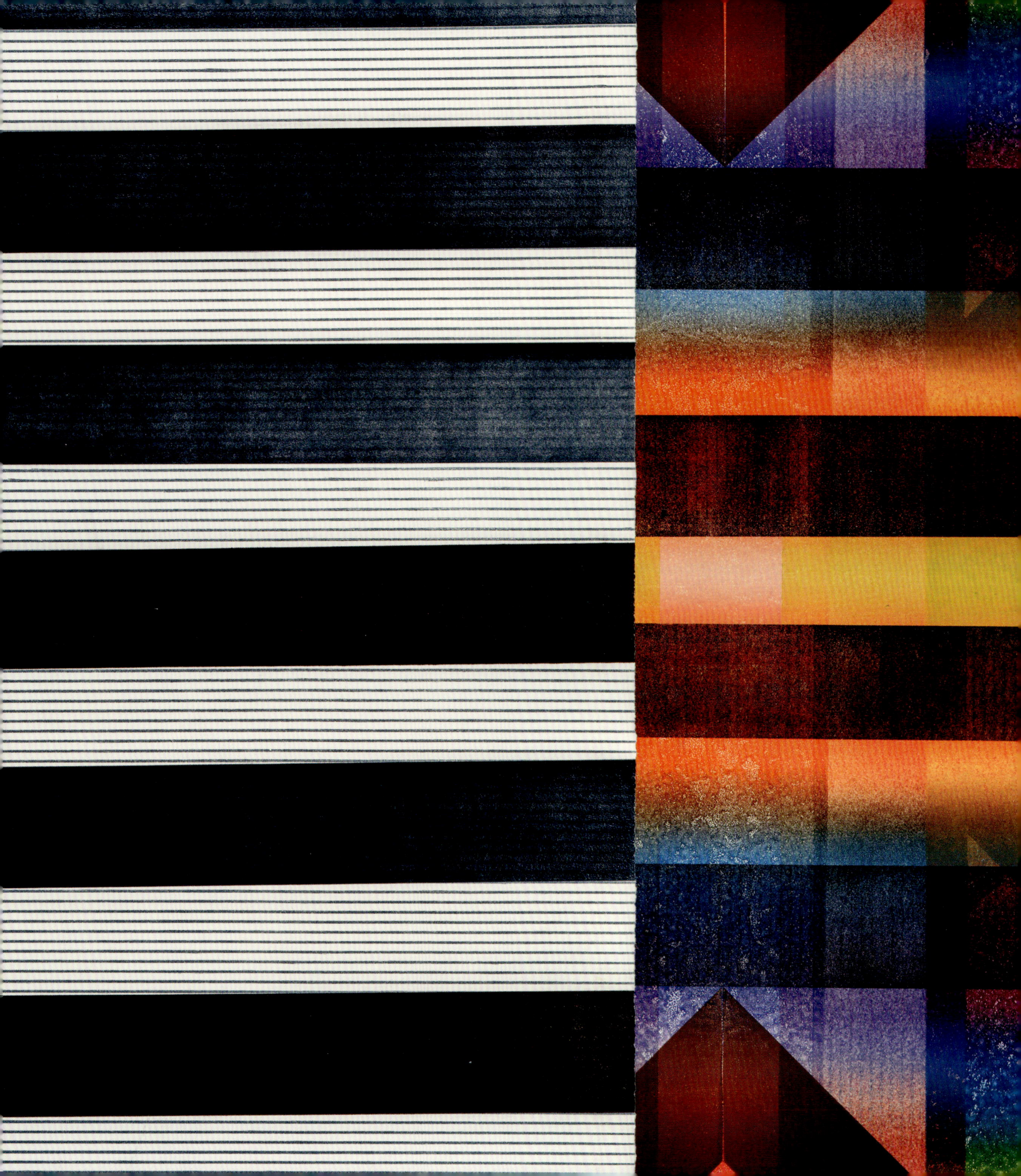

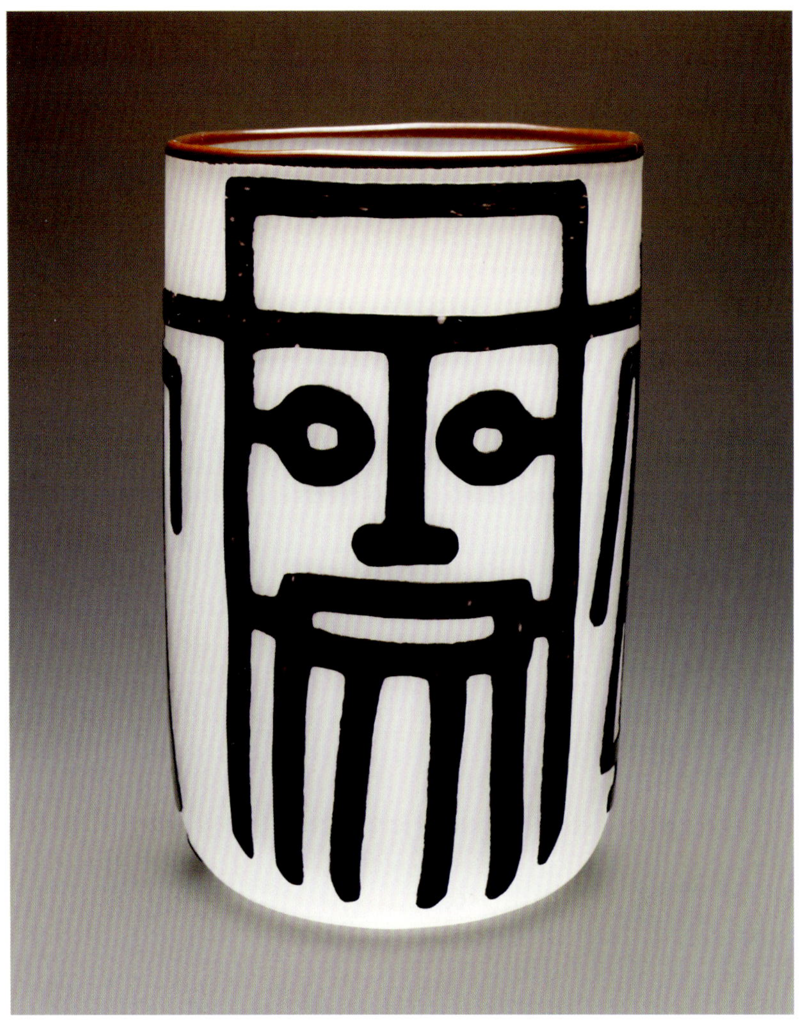

Plate 1
Self Portrait, 2023
Sandblasted blown glass
12½ × 7 × 7 in.
(31.8 × 17.8 × 17.8 cm)

Plate 2
Self Portrait #10, 1983
Photomontage
9½ × 12 in.
(24.1 × 30.5 cm)

Untitled (back of head), 1983
Photograph
7½ × 9½ in.
(19.1 × 24.1 cm)

Self Portrait #1, 1983
Photograph
9½ × 8 in.
(24.1 × 20.3 cm)

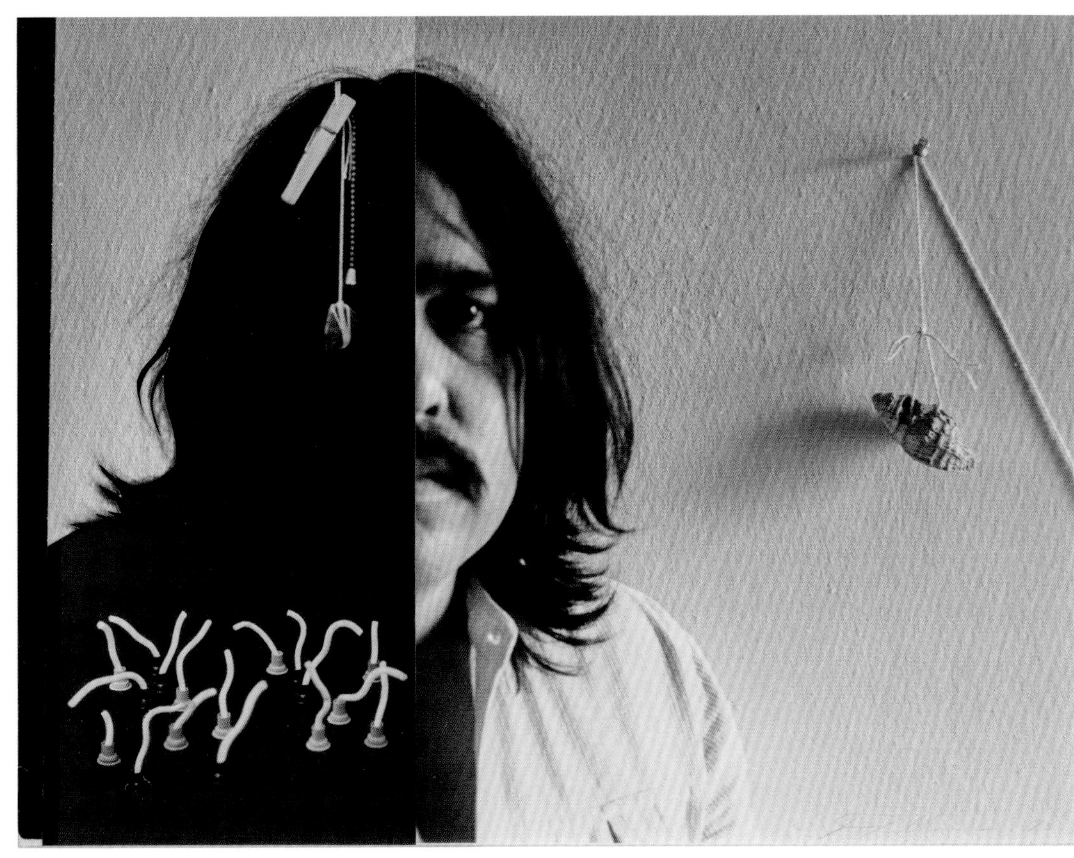

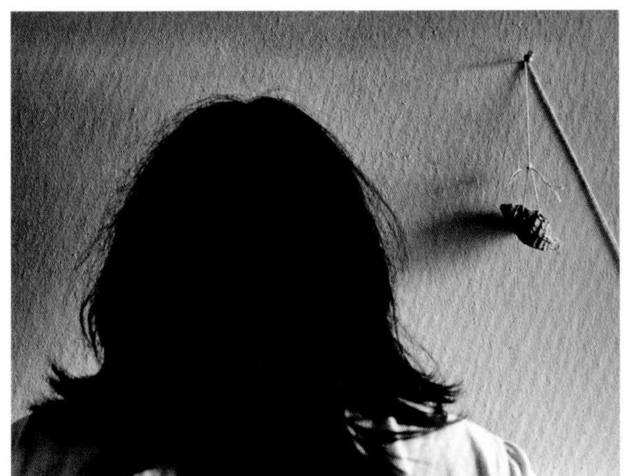

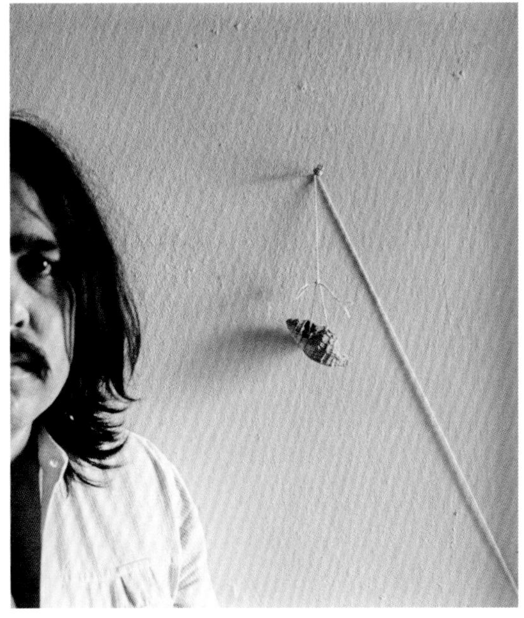

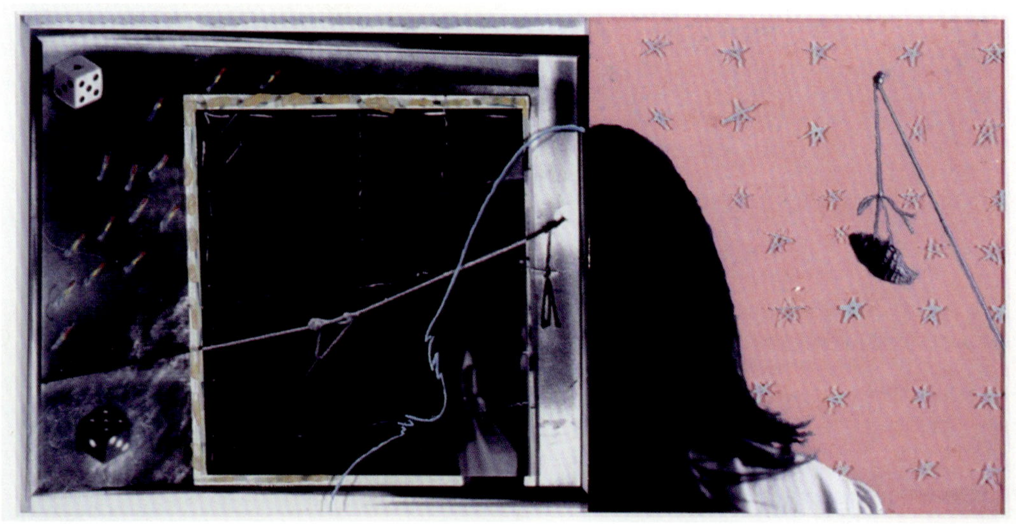

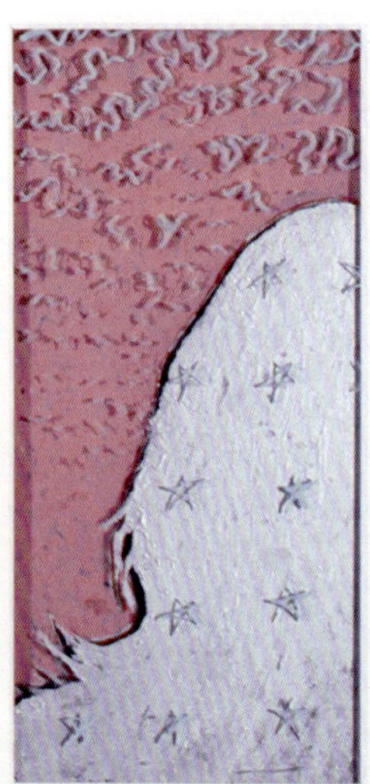

Plate 3
Self Portrait #6, 1984
Collage of photography, paint, and glass
16 × 24 in. (40.6 × 61 cm)

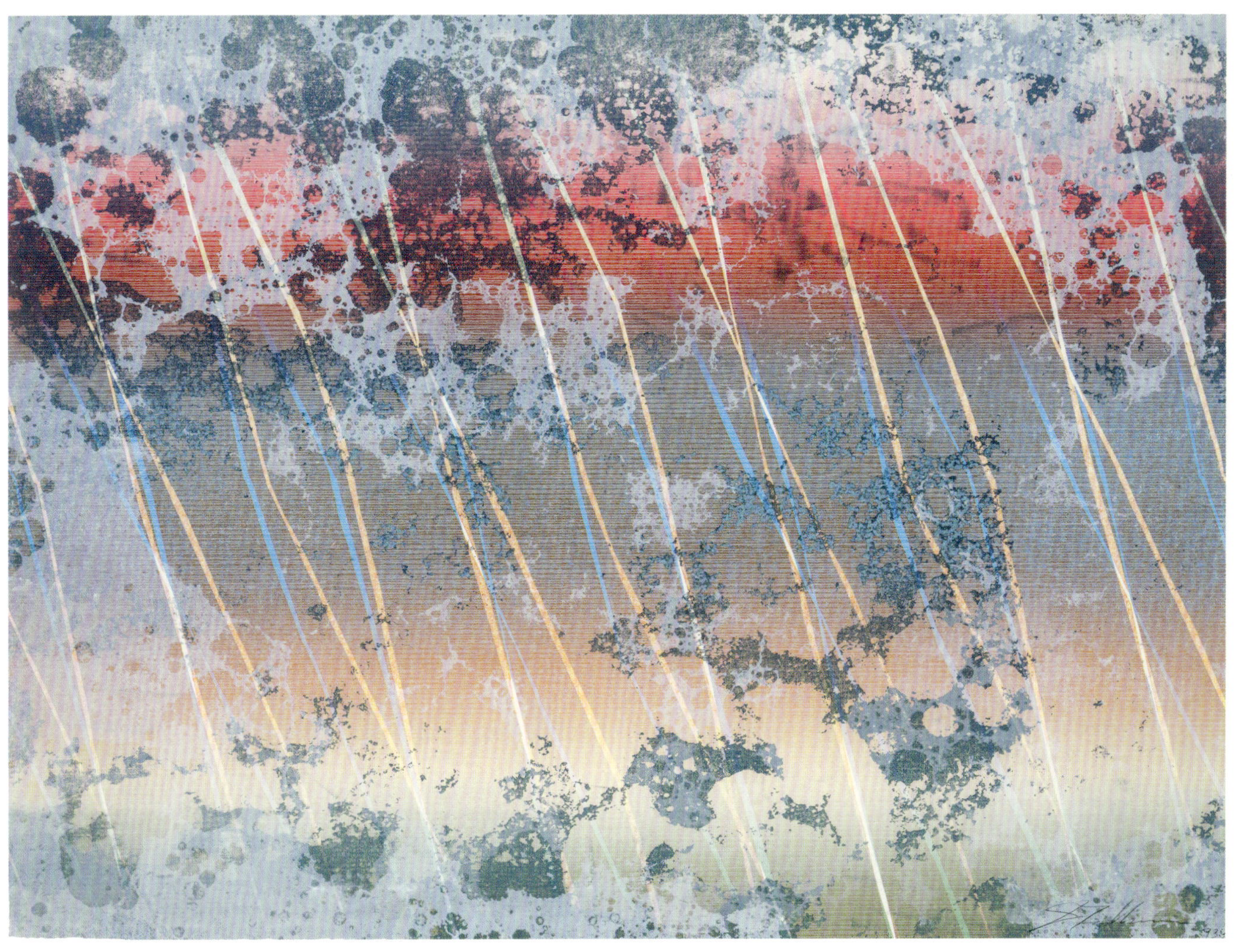

Plate 4
Rainscape, 1993
Linocut monoprint
18½ × 23½ in. (47 × 59.7 cm)

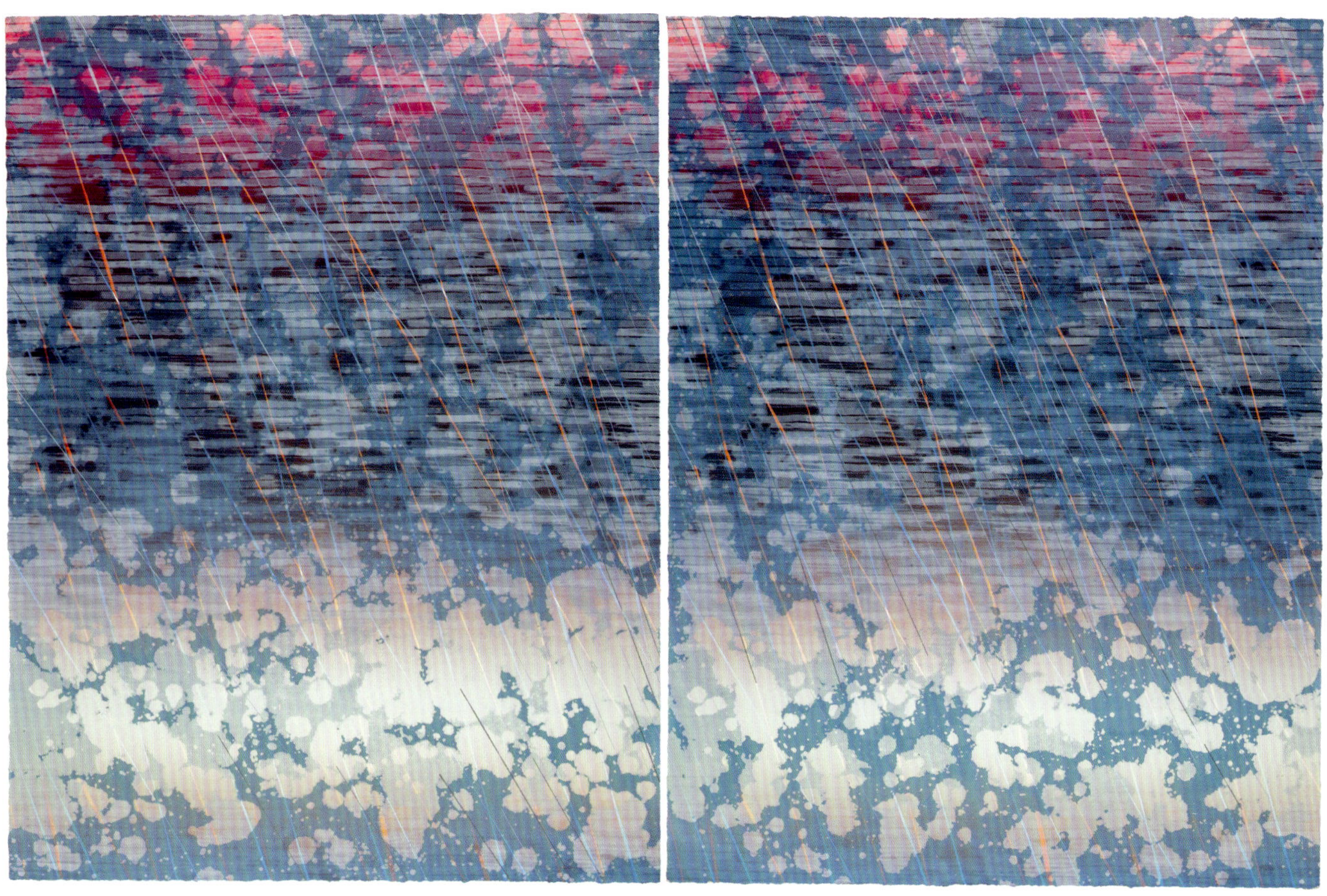

Plate 5
Rainscape #2, 1983
Lithograph
Each: 44 × 33 in.
(111.8 × 83.8 cm)

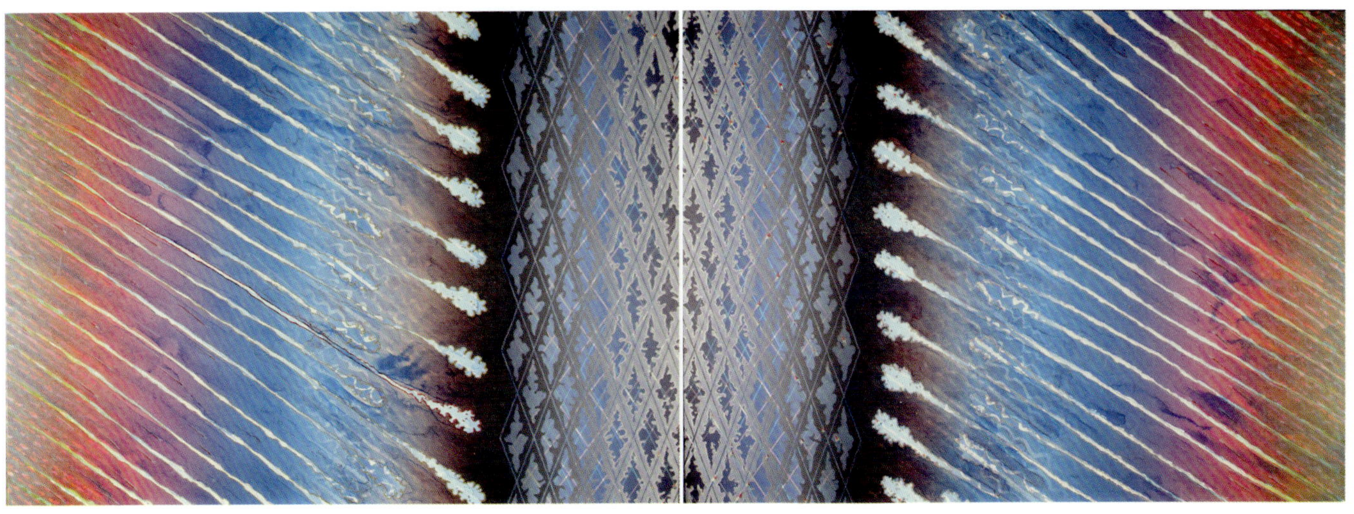

Plate 6
Sheltered from Nightrain,
1984
Lithograph
33 × 90 in. (83.8 × 228.6 cm)

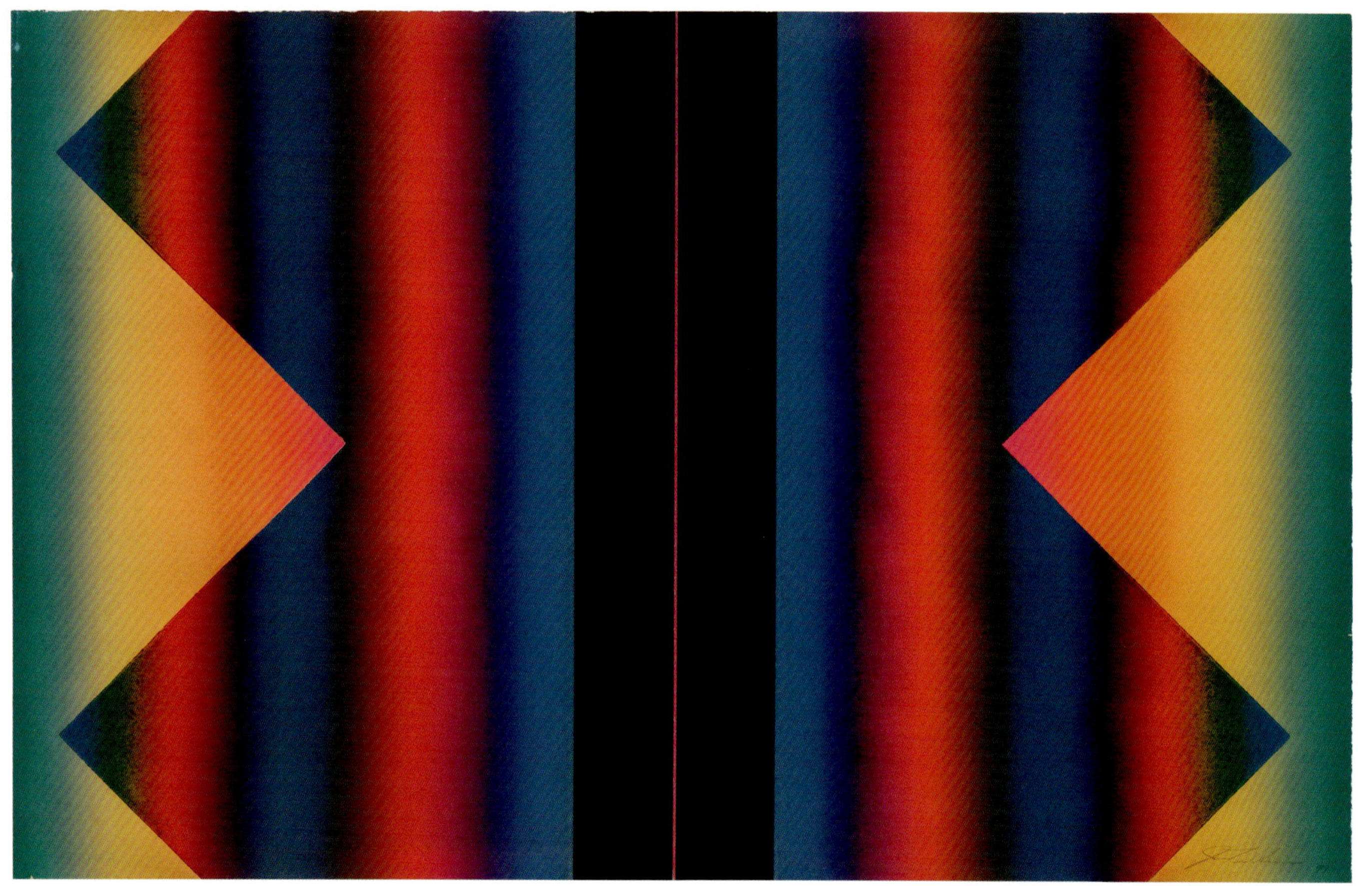

Plate 7
Blanket Series 5, 1991
Monotype
25½ × 38½ in. (64.8 × 97.8 cm)

Plate 8
Stripes, 2021
Blown glass
11½ × 9½ × 9½ in.
(29.2 × 24.1 × 24.1 cm)

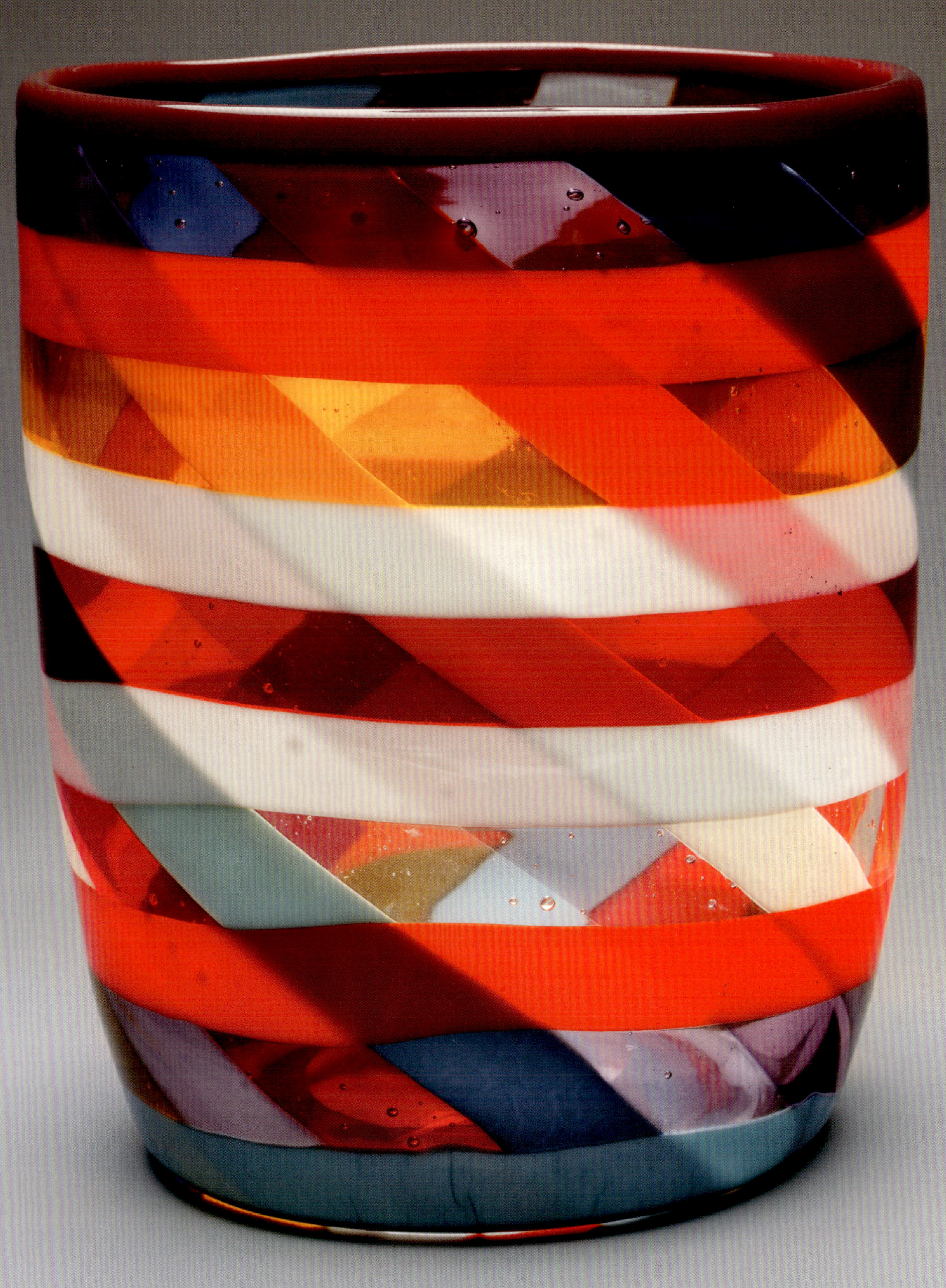

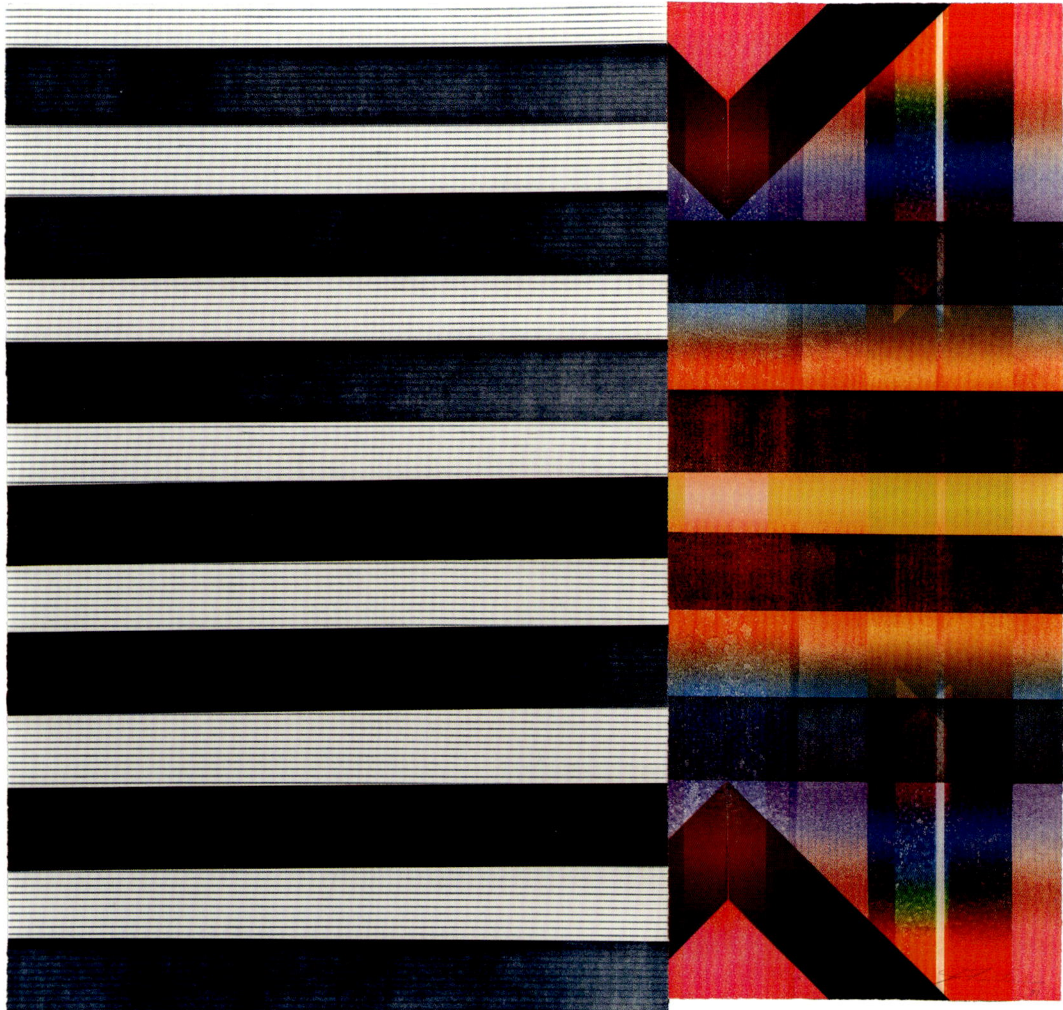

Plate 9
Two Blankets I, 1990
Relief monoprint
35½ × 37 in. (90.2 × 94 cm)

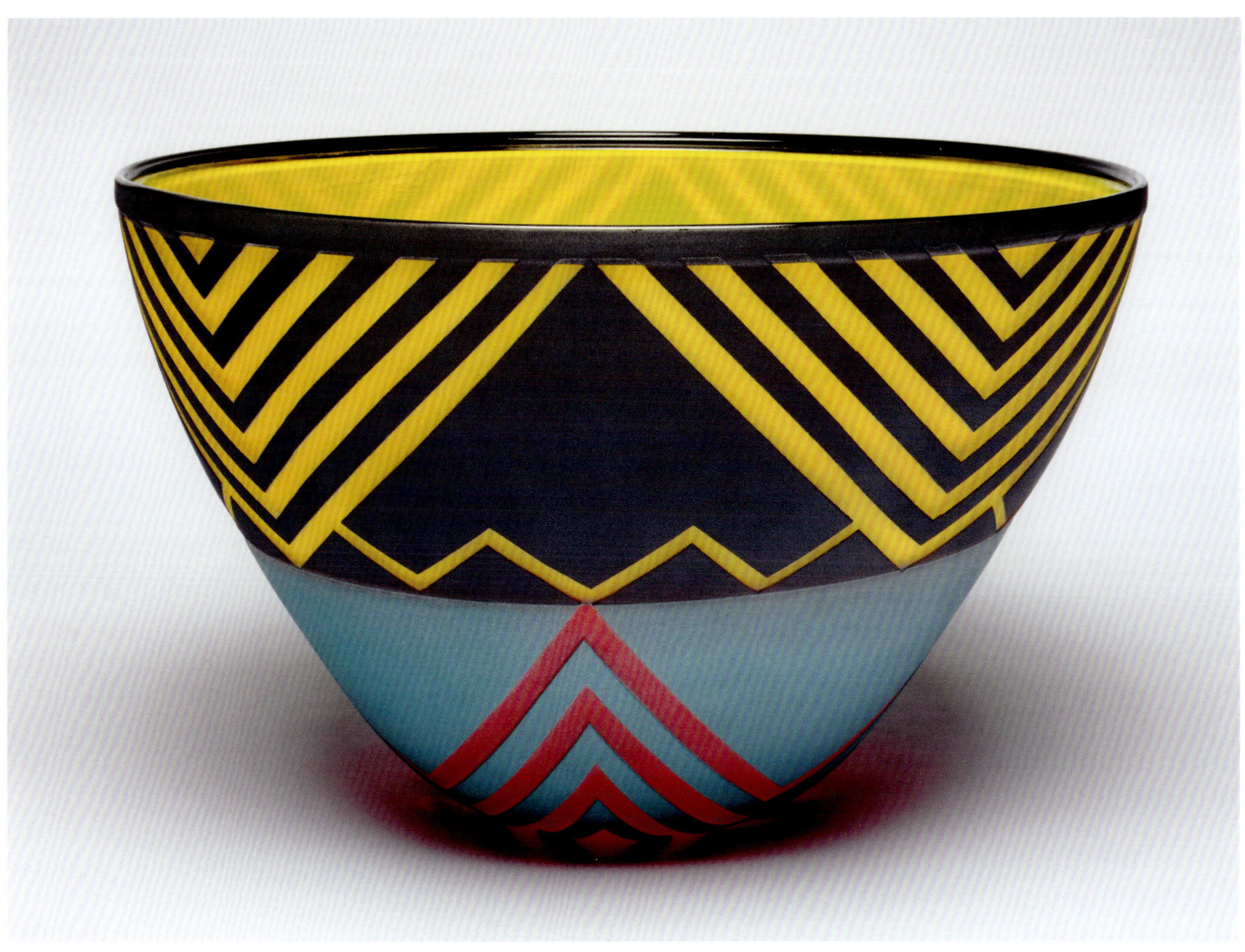

Plate 10
Stealth, 2006
Sandblasted blown glass
10 × 16 × 16 in.
(25.4 × 40.6 × 40.6 cm)

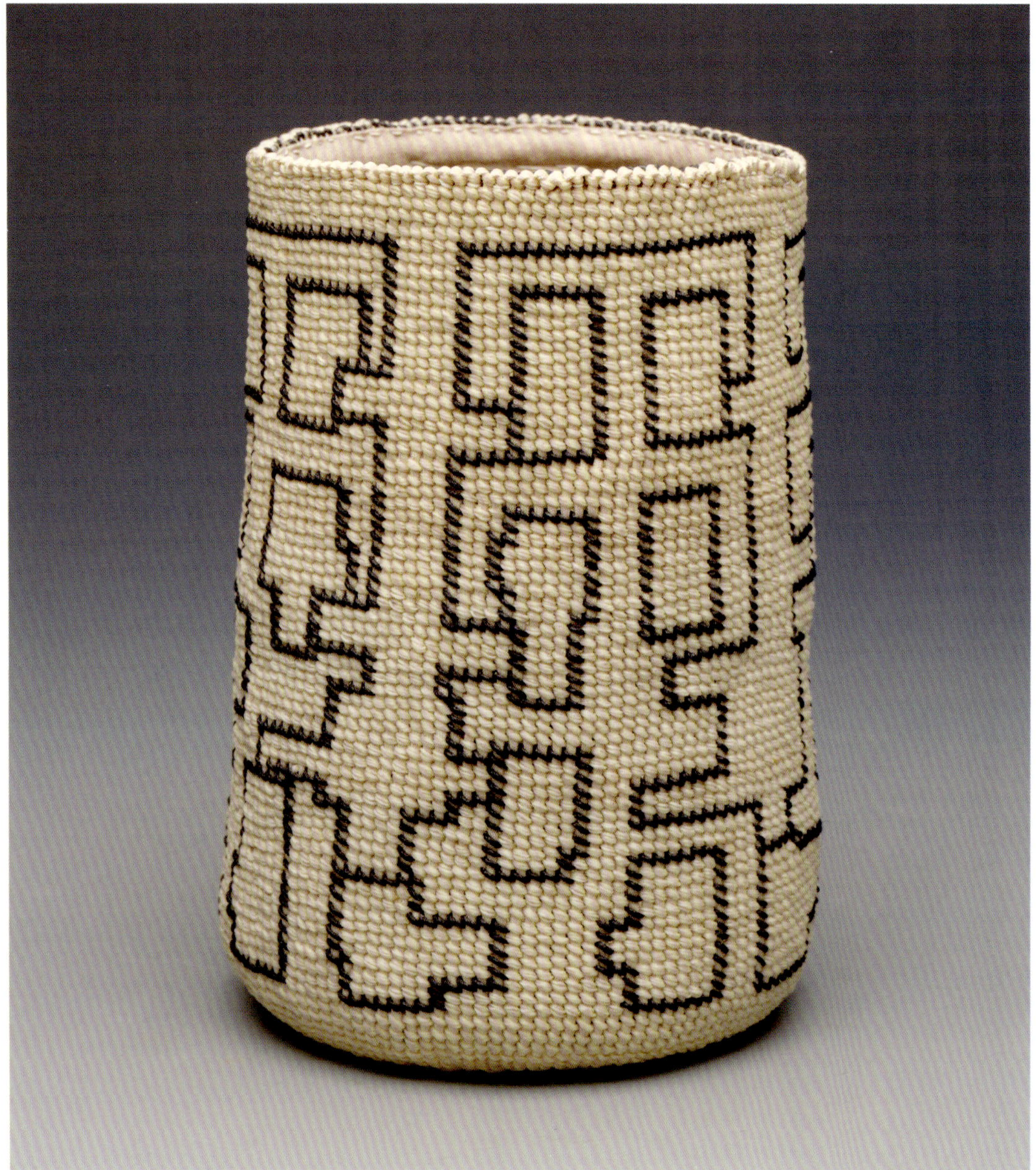

Plate 11
Cul-de-sac, 2002
Waxed linen, bias tape, and thread
6½ × 4½ × 4½ in.
(16.5 × 11.4 × 11.4 cm)

Plate 12
Wyit View, 2003
Lithograph
40 × 30 in.
(101.6 × 76.2 cm)

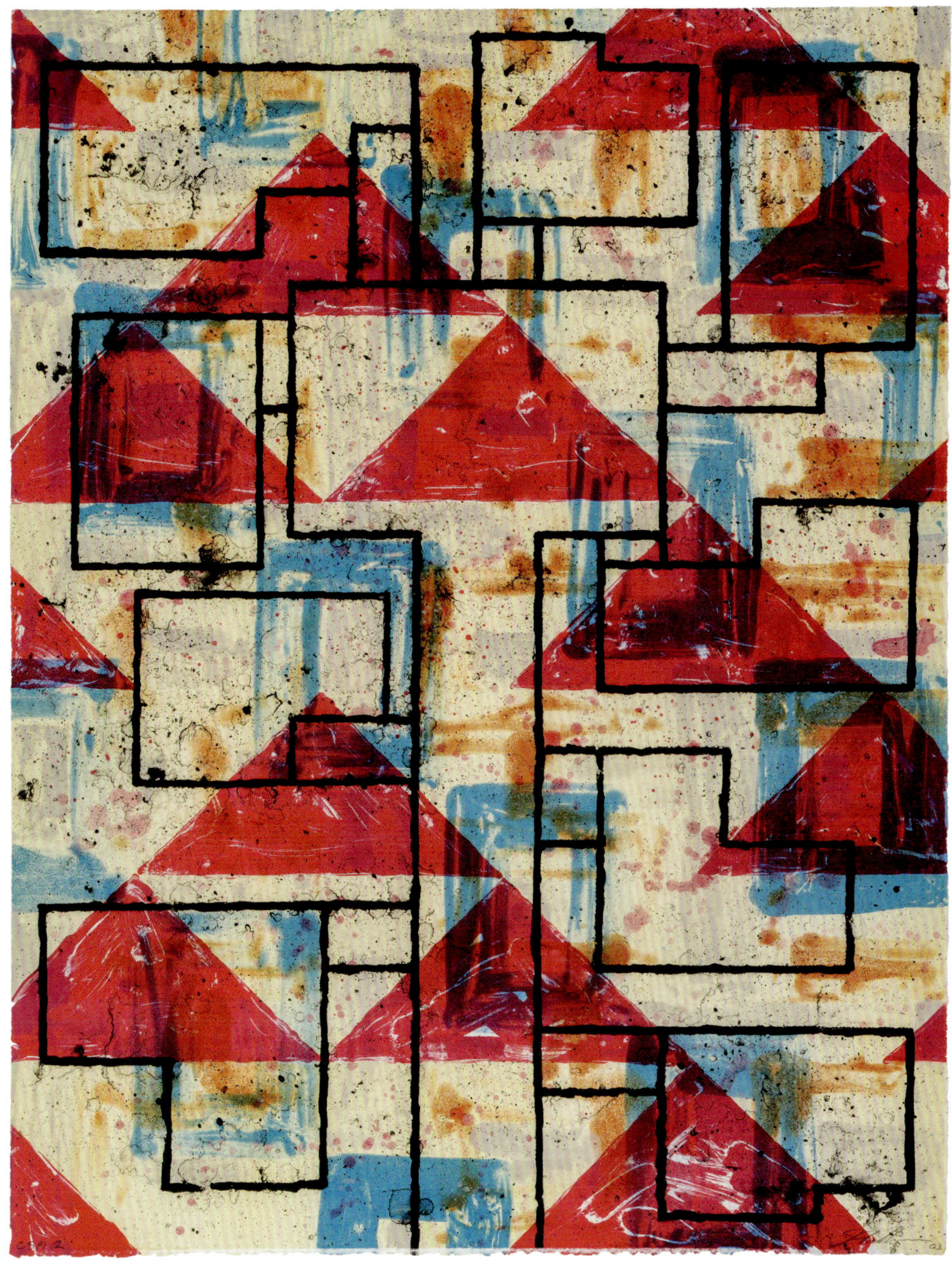

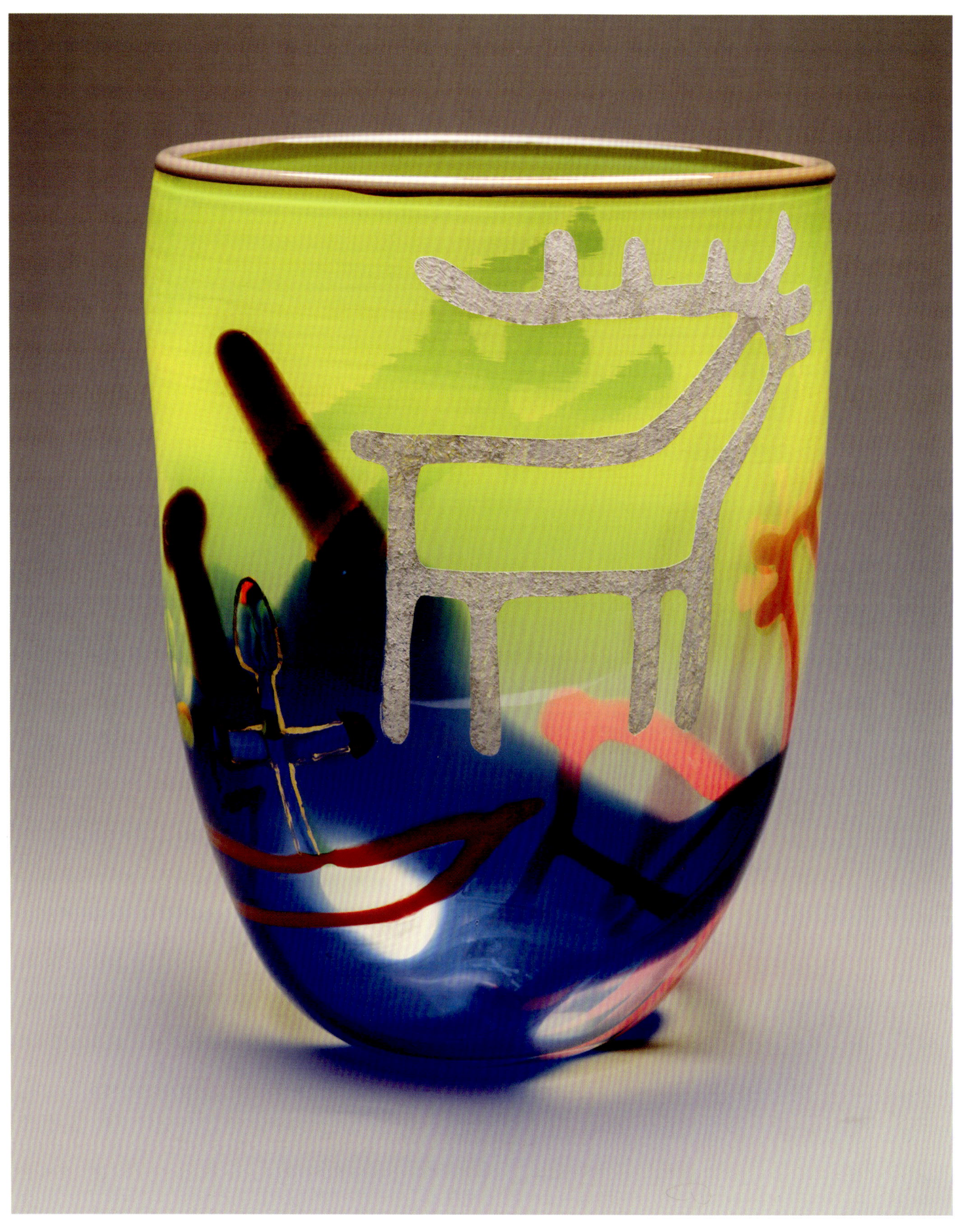

Plate 13
Floating By, 2020
Blown glass with enamel
13 × 9¾ × 9¾ in.
(33 × 24.8 × 24.8 cm)

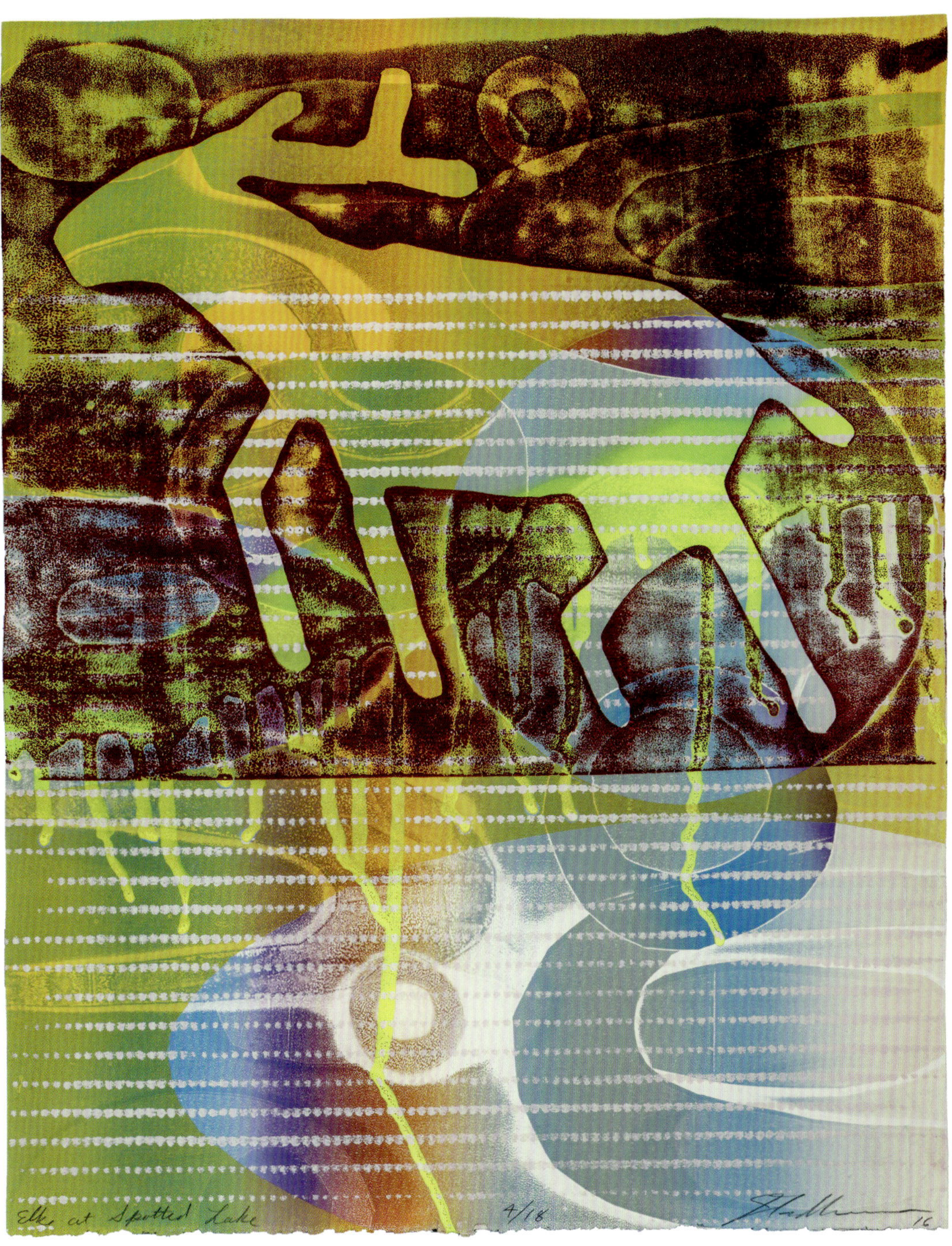

Plate 14
Elk at Spotted Lake, 2016
Relief monoprint with
spray paint
19 × 14¾ in.
(48.3 × 37.5 cm)

Rebellion

Chokecherry leaves are red,
money trees quake a young grasshopper green.
Bark dazzles you like the snow vest
on Dancing Boy as apples are good as gone
outside the kitchen window
beyond right through that narrow passage.

Jocko, who is going to teach me to dance?
Should I ask the dancing boy to show me?
Knees bent, legs raised, arm up, ribbons
flowing in the wind , eagle feathers, dancing, dancing.
They ask me to go to Wounded Knee
but I say I am helper here at home,
have to tend to the garden.
They agree, for people have died at Wounded Knee,
and it is time that they come home.

I am home, that is all the wisdom I need to know:
White bird dancing.
Everyone should have a place at least once
in their life that is secure, where they can
come and go as freely as they want.
Break camp, Dancing Boy, you have the mountain,
sing me your song, teach me your dance.

Victor A. Charlo - Salish

Victor A. Charlo, "Rebellion," in *Terrain: Plateau Native Art & Poetry*, ed. Joe Feddersen, 2014

Plate 15
Drizzle, 2016
Relief and stencil monoprint with collage, staples, and spray paint
20½ × 18 in.
(52.1 × 45.7 cm)

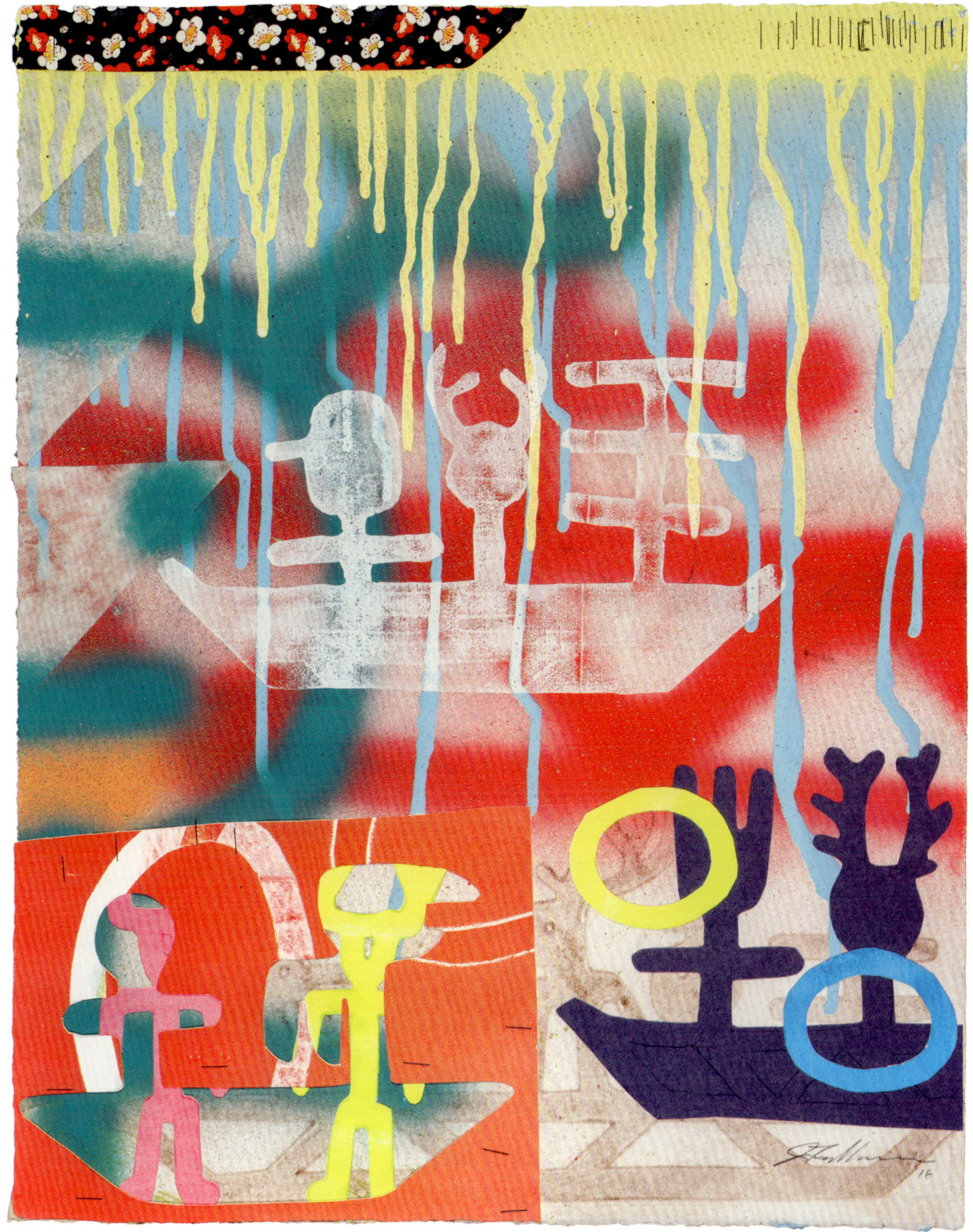

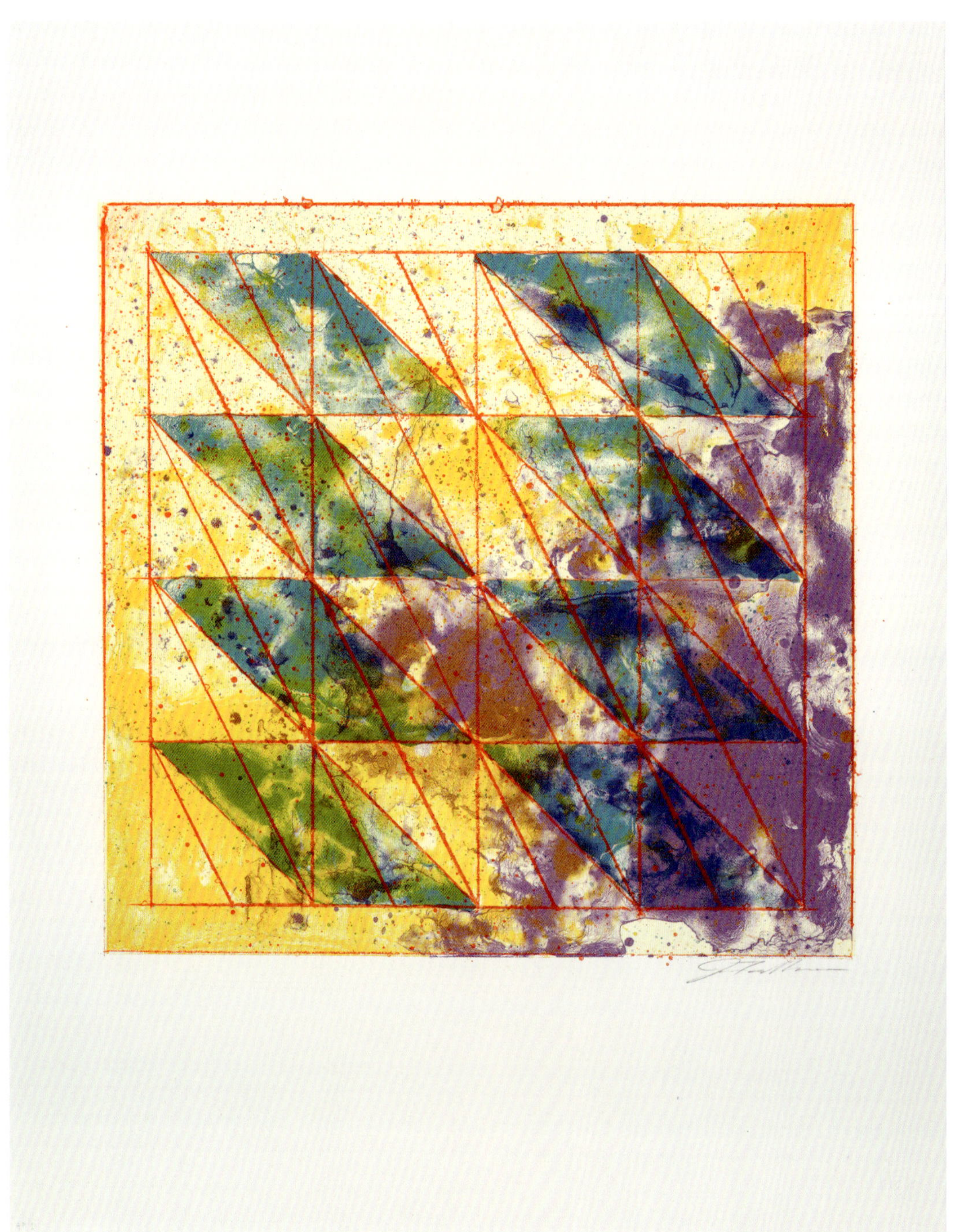

Plate 16
Plateau Geometrics, 2001
Lithograph
Sheet: 26 × 20 in. (66 × 50.8 cm); image: 16 × 16 in. (40.6 × 40.6 cm)

Plate 17
Rugged Trail 2, 2005
Blown glass
19 × 18½ × 18½ in. (48.3 × 47 × 47 cm)

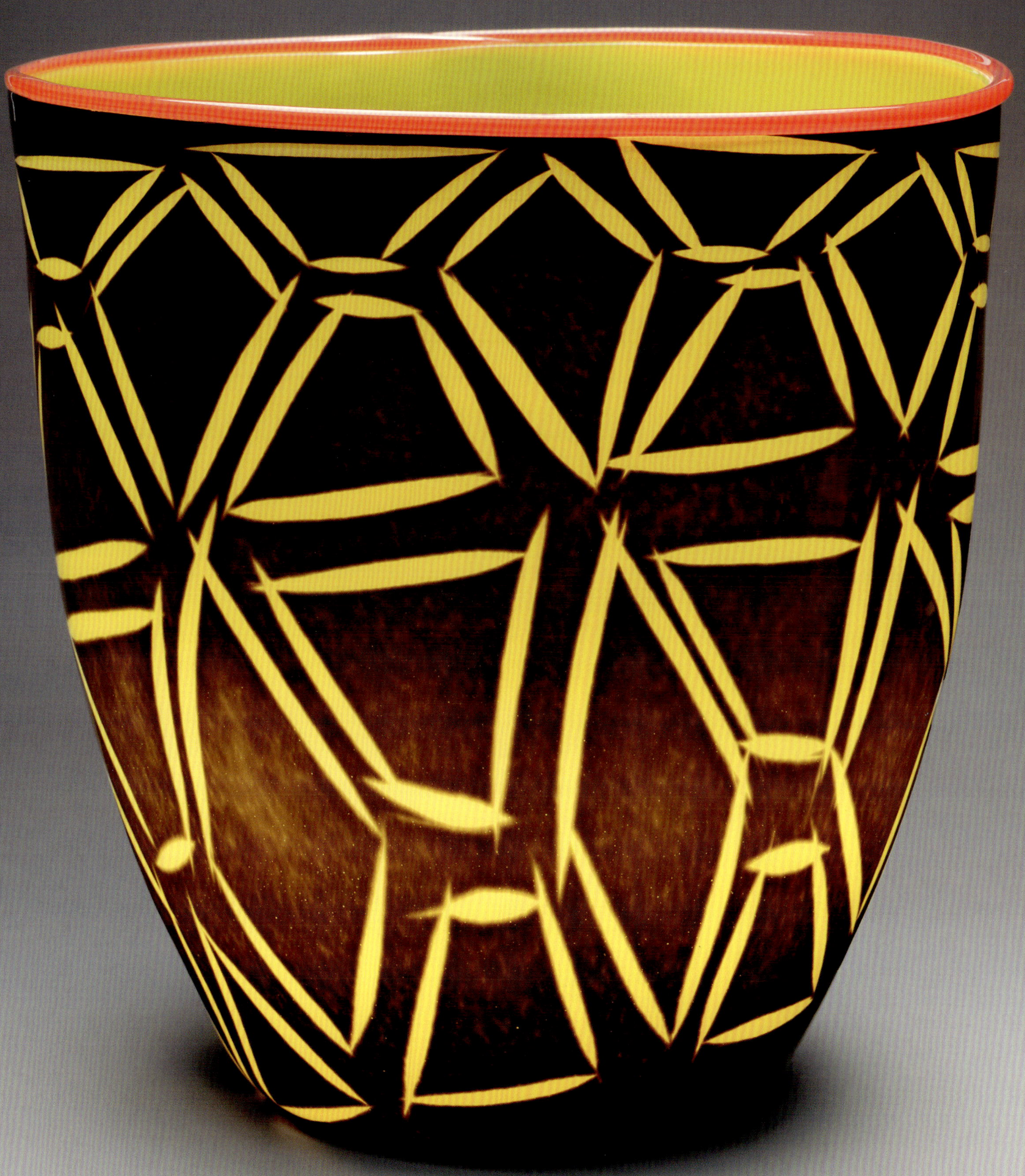

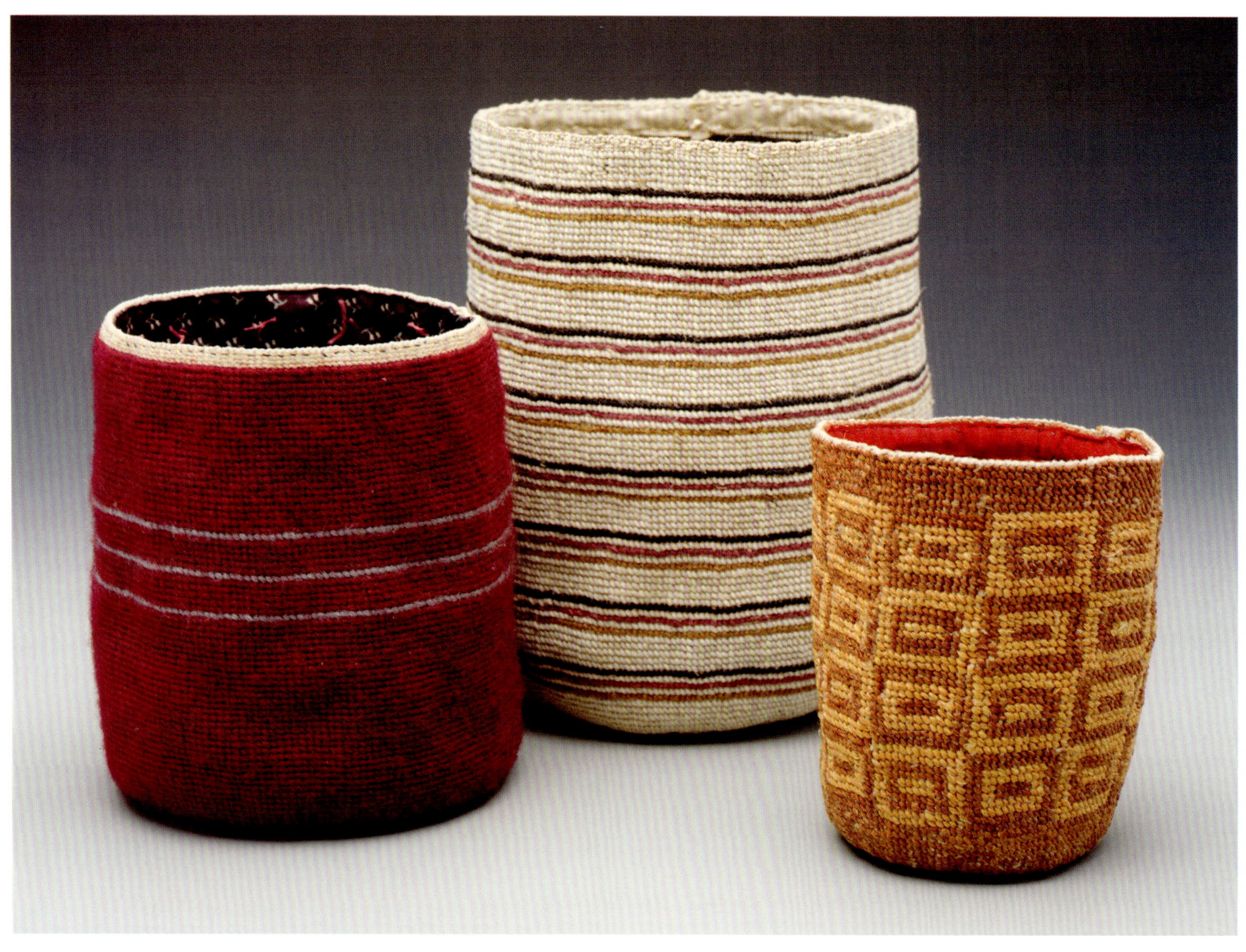

Plate 18 (left to right)
Red Basket, 1993
Waxed linen, wool, fabric, and thread
6 × 4½ × 4½ in.
(15.2 × 11.4 × 11.4 cm)

Tracks, 2012
Waxed linen, bias tape, and thread
8 × 5½ × 5½ in.
(20.3 × 14 × 14 cm)

Target, 1999
Waxed linen, bias tape, and thread
4½ × 3½ × 3½ in.
(11.4 × 8.9 × 8.9 cm)

Plate 19
Firehawk, 2005
Sandblasted blown glass
21½ × 9½ × 9½ in.
(54.6 × 24.1 × 24.1 cm)

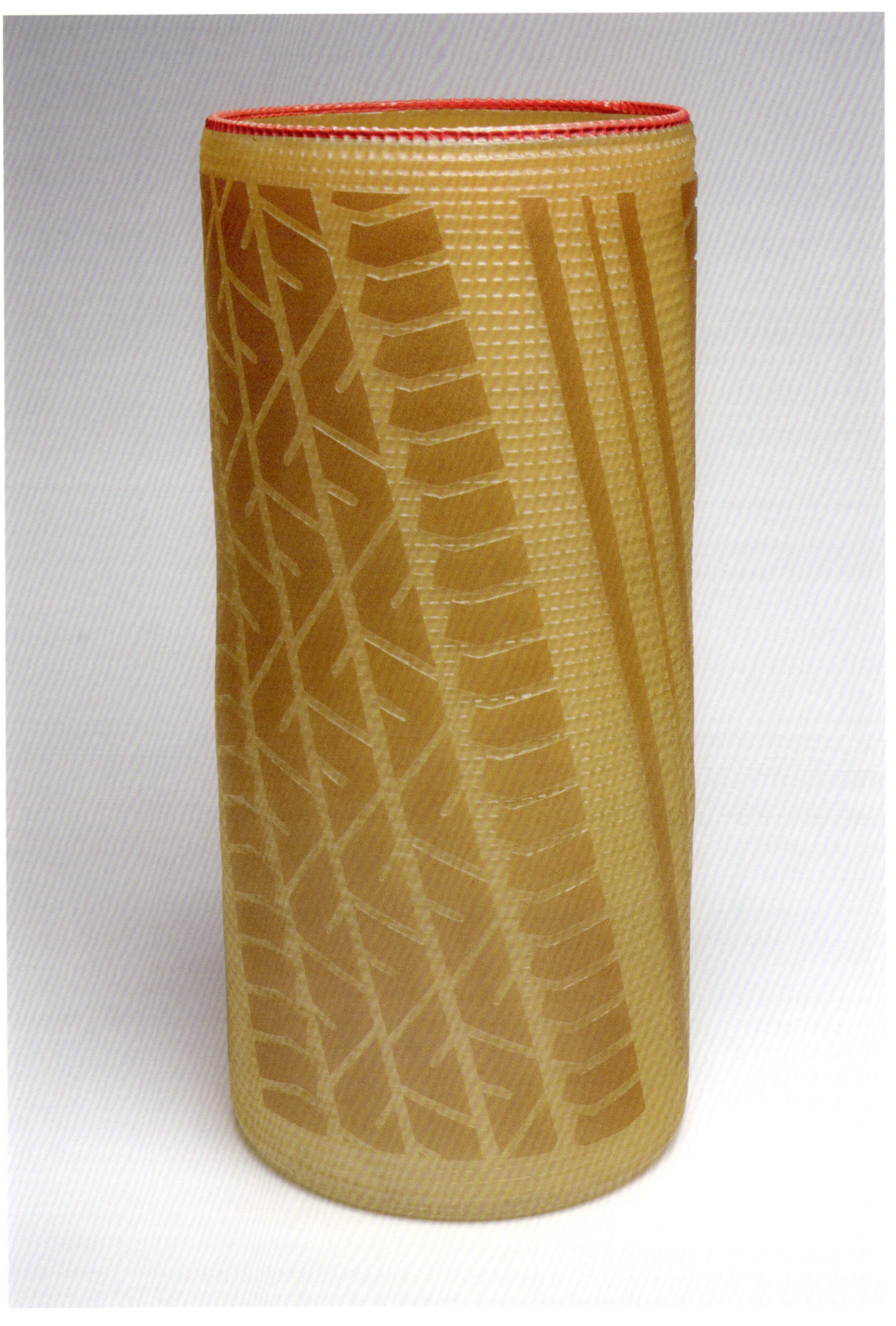

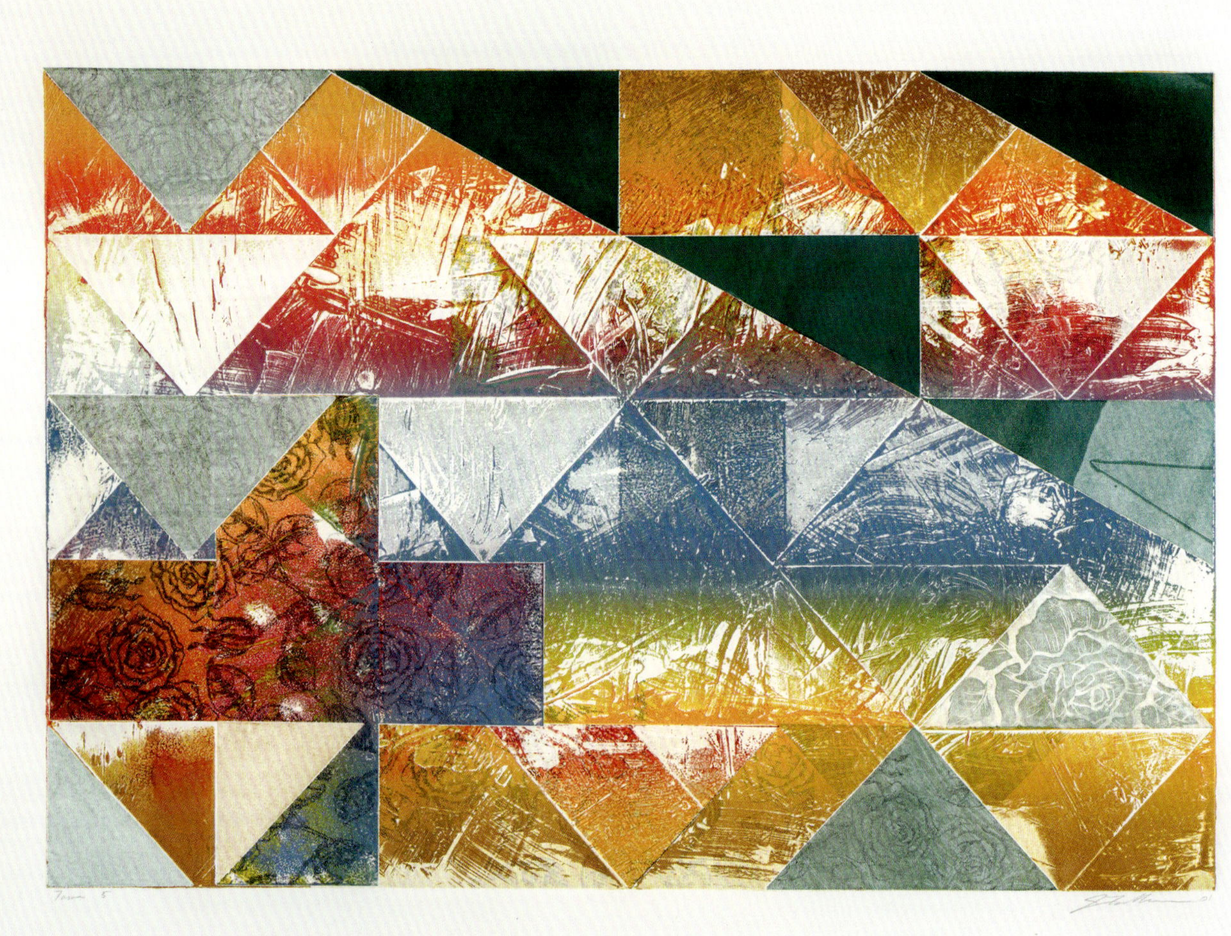

Plate 20
Tama 5, 2001
Collagraph, relief, stencil, aquatint, and drypoint monoprint
Sheet: 22½ × 30 in. (57.2 × 76.2 cm); image: 18¼ × 26 in. (46.4 × 66 cm)

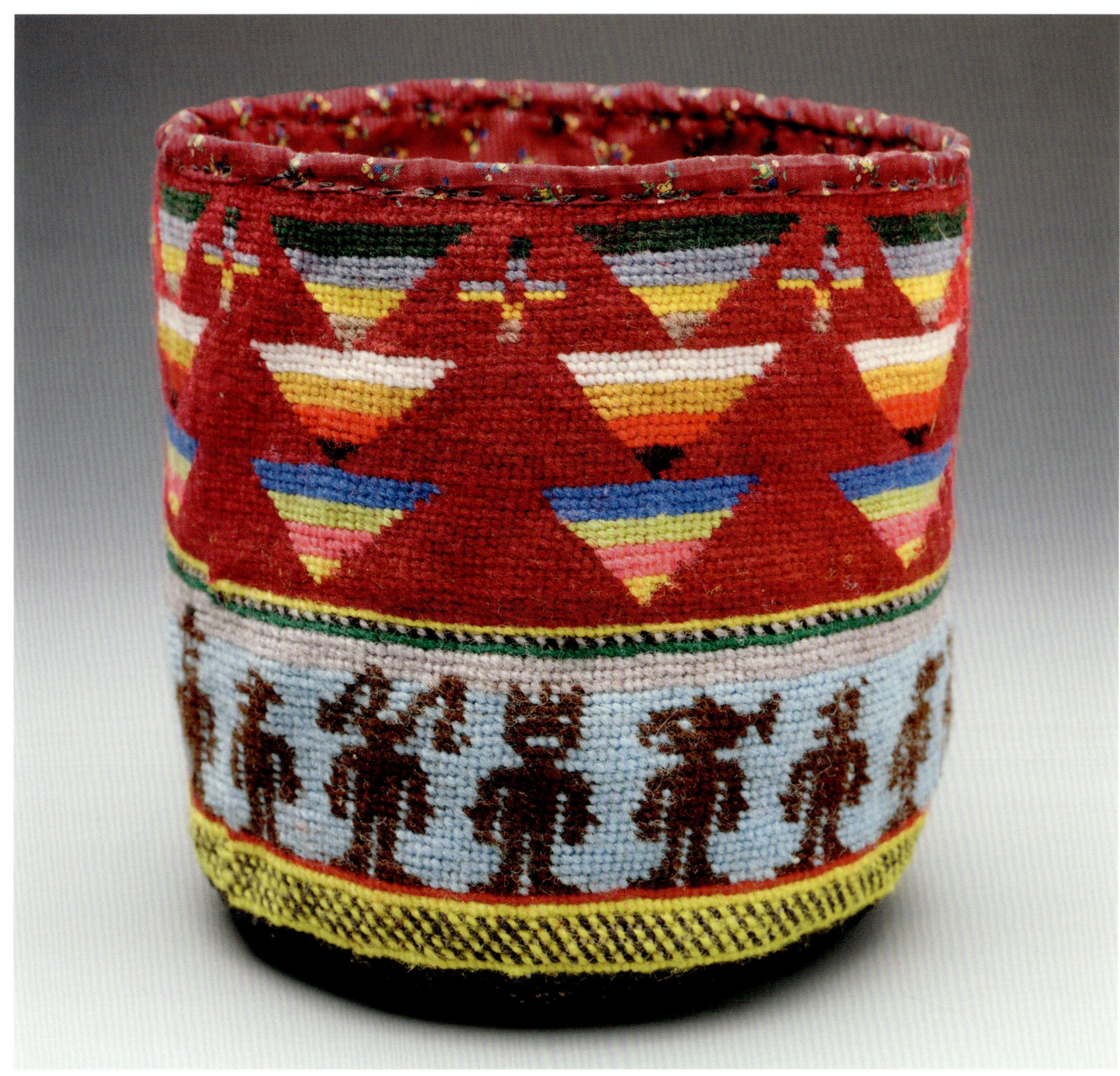

Plate 21
Gathering Under the Stars, 2010
Waxed linen, wool, fabric, and thread
8½ × 7½ × 7½ in.
(21.6 × 19.1 × 19.1 cm)

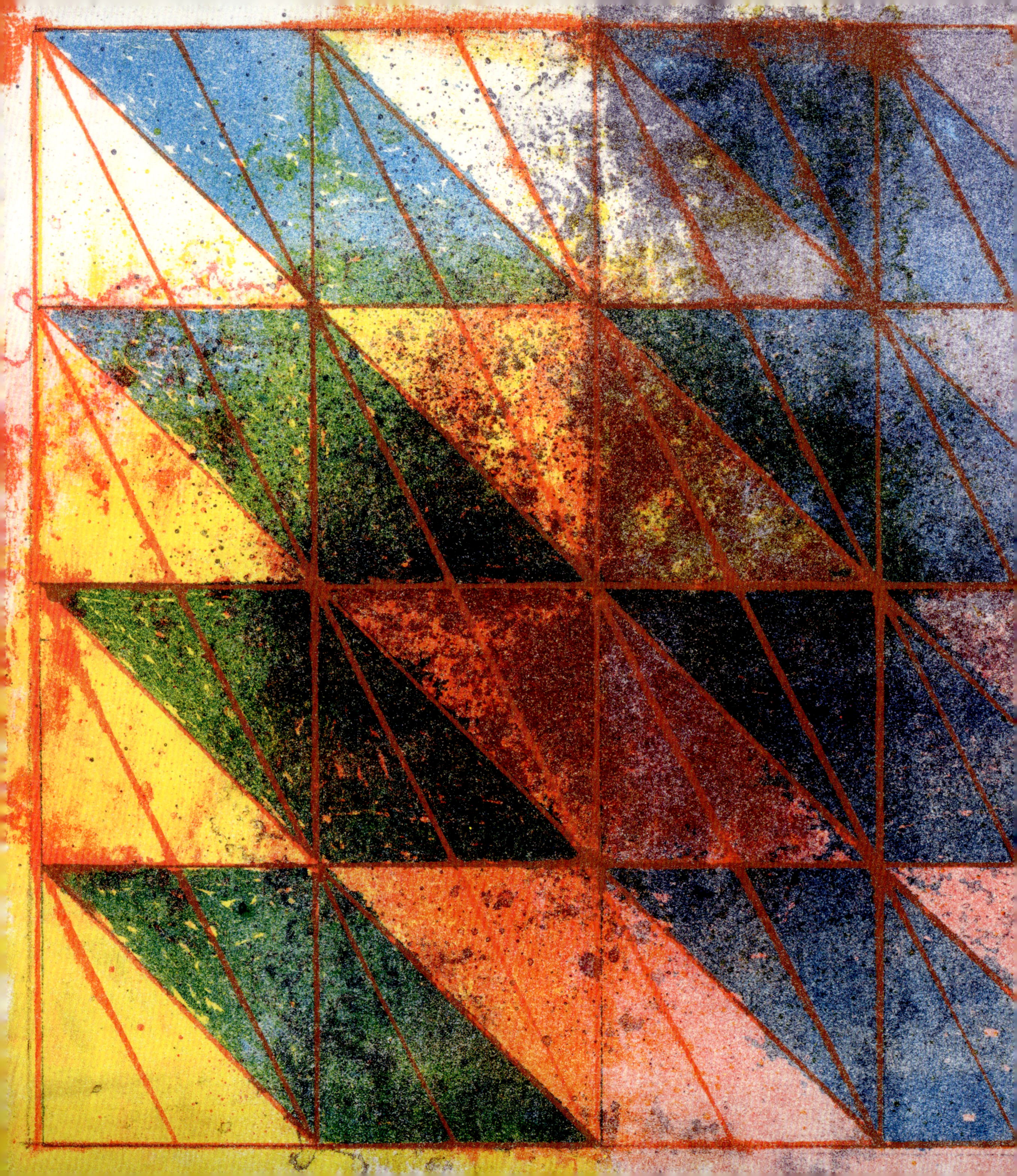

Joe Feddersen, American Landscape Artist

heather ahtone

INDIGENOUS LANDSCAPES

Every discussion of Joe Feddersen's work begins with placing him in Omak, Washington, an Okanagan citizen of the Confederated Tribes of the Colville Reservation, as part of the extended Plateau community (fig. 1). Like Thomas Hart Benton's relationship to Kansas and the Midwest, the sites of Feddersen's personal experience serve as the foundation for all of his work, a form of bedrock upon which all the layers of his work rest. The distinctive relationship between an artist and their work is rooted in a particular experience, a particular knowledge of the land, and a particular place. Each printed layer, each body of work, builds upon the former, contributing to the concretion of the collective to form a lush landscape that speaks to place, culture, and a distinctively American experience. This is the nature of American landscape art.

Feddersen's relationship to the Plateau region and his Interior Salish culture are intertwined inextricably through the body of his work. Within the printed images are visible the marks he finds on the land and the complex layers, like sedimentary rock deposited over time, bound together, forming rich textures and colorful combinations. Within the baskets, formed from waxed linen and wool, the repetition of texture reminds us of looking from a plane high above and seeing the repeated treetops so carefully organized to form a canopy informed by access to light and water below. The glass works become the repositories of the petroglyphic reminders that we, as humans, are part of a continuum of life inhabiting the land since human memory and ever evolving with our presence. What we see in Joe Feddersen's work is the embodiment of our human relationships to the landscape, connected by the force of water and ordered by the stars above.

Positioning Joe Feddersen as a landscape artist may work against the common Western definitions of landscape art, the perspectival view oriented to a horizon line bisecting earth from sky. The American landscape tradition is often presented as being birthed by the high horizon line of mountainscapes so beautifully painted by Albert Bierstadt and Thomas Cole (fig. 2) or the low shoreline in Peter Moran's lake and river portraits. The views these artists give us are of the grandeur and the expanse of the relationship between land and sky. In their works, the landscape was often celebrated for its raw power in a manner that expressed the strength of an early national identity. To understand Feddersen's imagery as landscape art, one has to reach deeper into the long history of the Americas and examine landscape art from an Indigenous perspective.

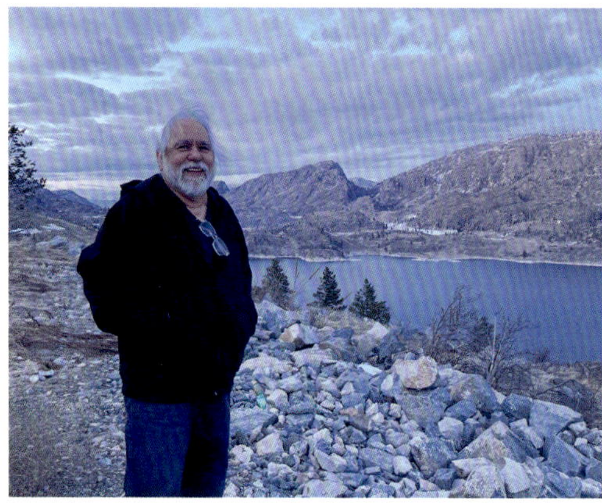

Fig. 1 Joe Feddersen at Omak Lake, January 19, 2023

The people who have lived on this continent for millennia share a love for the land, the views, and the relationships that exist between earth and sky and water. In fact, this love is often couched within familial terms representing the Indigenous philosophies established through creation stories that set our cultural worldviews in order.[1] For the Salish people, the land was a gift from the Creator, who rested a woman down and from her curves formed the mountains, from her hairs emerged the trees and flora, and, as the earth, she continues nurturing the people as her children. The grass that is used to weave is provided by her body. By harvesting the grasses and weaving the signs and symbols into the cultural materials that support human survival, Okanagan makers reciprocate the attendant care to the earth. Each act of making is an act of love and an act of breathing as a cultural person. Each act of weaving the natural materials of grass and bark weaves Okanagan culture to the landscape as a continuum of culture through this worldview.

Natural weaving elements, the grasses and cedar bark, have been woven into forms as carrying bags and gathering baskets and adorned with dyed and painted geometric designs that serve as references for the people's memory and knowledge—serving as mnemonic and semiotic devices for stories about the mountains (geology), fish scales (biology), and migrations (geography), stories that convey knowledge held in trust by each generation carried across centuries. The use of abstraction has become a time-honored form of humility, not to mimic the Creator's gifts but as an expression of humanity's recognition that these stylized designs allow for interpretation beyond any singularly evident coded reference. The geometric designs are conduits for intergenerational instruction and knowledge sharing. As each generation borrows designs from the hands of previous generations, they invigorate the knowledge (science, literature, and

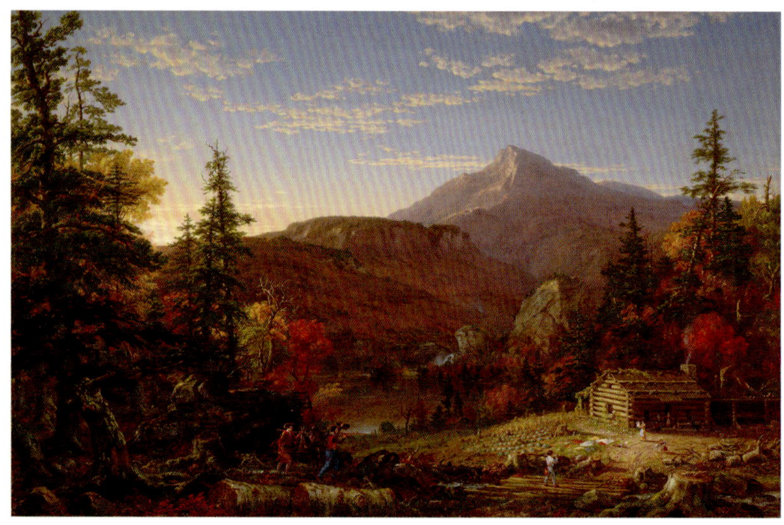

Fig. 2 Thomas Cole (1801–1848), *The Hunter's Return*, 1845. Oil on canvas, 40⅛ × 60½ in. (101.9 × 153.7 cm). Amon Carter Museum of American Art, Fort Worth, TX, 1983.156

philosophies), adapting it to encompass new lessons learned while holding precious the knowledge made available through the diligent care of ancestors. Through this process and the mechanisms of abstraction, whole bodies of knowledge are passed down that can flexibly expand/contract and encompass new experiences without sacrificing earlier lessons. For this reason, Indigenous knowledge is often tied to abstraction, both geometric and biomorphic. Each generation of each Indigenous cultural community is thereby presented with a set of visual tools that can be adopted and adapted to reflect their contemporary experiences while inheriting cultural philosophies gifted at the time of creation.[2]

In the twenty-first century, Indigenous artists remain culturally distinct within their own communities, bound through aesthetics and language, while continuing to participate in regional cultural exchanges and the global fine arts community. The intercultural network for exchange in the Plateau region, connected through rivers with the Northwest Coast and through mountain passes with the Northern Plains, is well documented and has an extended history predating the establishment of the United States.[3] Exchange within this region has continued uninterrupted for millennia for both American commodities and Indigenous cultures. The strength of that exchange and the intercultural environment remain part of what makes the area around the modern cities of Spokane, Portland, and Seattle culturally distinct. The definitions of *intercultural* intentionally extend beyond simply Indigenous and American, recognizing the multiplicity of Indigenous nations represented within the exchange and the relevancy of this region to ongoing exchanges with Polynesian, Asian, and, later, Russian networks. Connecting the expanse of the Plateau cultures between the Cascades and the Rockies (breaching national boundaries in the process), within which the Interior Salish community of Okanagan people is located, with the broader Plains cultural communities and the vast connections of the Northwest Coast people, facilitated by historic trade sites, most properly provides the backdrop for a discussion of Joe Feddersen's work. And this is the basic nature of American landscape art. Every site, each mountain and prairie, is part of a connection that extends across the continent and the globe. These sites are connected physically and metaphorically through the geometric designs passed between generations and shared through cultural exchanges. They remain connected, importantly, for all of us.

Think of the regularity with which you park your car within the bounding lines of a parking lot or drive on a grid of roads that organize and order our transit routes through cities and across interstate highways. The geometric systems we all read and are trained to follow and that bring order to our society are extensions of what we see on the landscape. For many, these signs and symbols are mediated by concrete

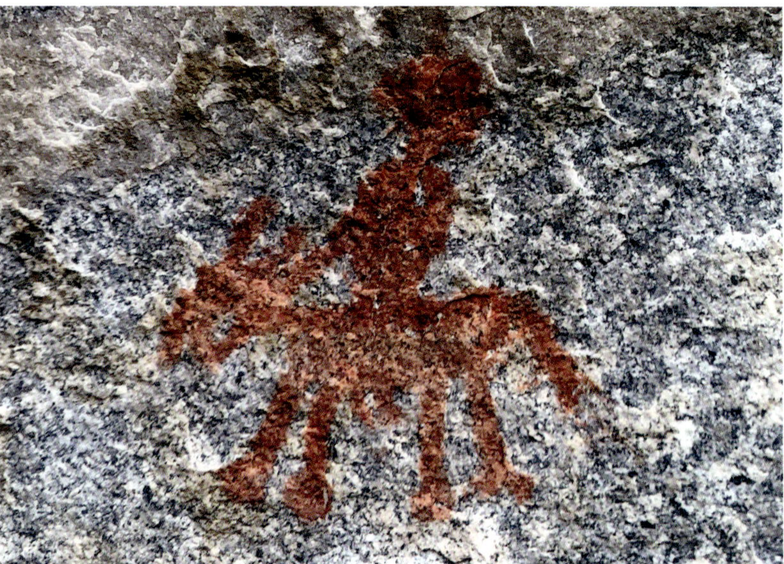

Fig. 3 Pictograph visited by Joe Feddersen in British Columbia, Canada

and steel but remain seemingly insignificant to our experience on the land, the earth. Yet that woman in the creation story remains the earth upon which we drive and build our cities. That woman is the source of our extractive petroleum industries and the sites where we bury our dead and our garbage. We mark her with our prayers as much as tire tracks, parking lots, and suburban cul-de-sacs.

It is this foundation from which Joe Feddersen works. Borrowing ancestral systems of marks and designs, combined with his own observations, he explores our relationship to the landscape, invigorating the system with the new symbols of our contemporary experience—power line towers and traffic diagrams—while allowing Coyote and petroglyph ancestors to enjoy our perceptions of "progress" and "improvements" (fig. 3). Like his ancestors, Feddersen makes art as a matter of breathing, not self-consciously wrestling with how to make something that presents itself as Okanagan, but simply making. In this process of prolific making, he expresses his love for the land, water, and sky.

LAND + PLACE

A maker his entire life, passively encouraged by parents who fostered looking closely and provided free access to tools and materials, Feddersen has cultivated his creativity since childhood. While he was always a maker and participated in art circles as early as 1982, it took a stint working in public service at the Grand Coulee Dam before Feddersen decided to pursue art as a potential career.[4] As a student at the University of Washington, under the mentorship of Robert Graves, then later Glen Alps, Joe Feddersen responded to an assignment by Michael Spafford to create a body of work within a series.[5] From this assignment, *Rainscapes* was initiated and would become the first major series by the artist (pls. 4, 5, 6). Feddersen chose the subject of rain and, to cultivate the body of the series, took the assignment as a point of material experimentation expanding from the prints he had been making in Alps's studio. Within the series, Feddersen used the varied diagonals so inherent in the arc of falling water and explored perspective through rain, shifting the picture plane so that the viewer is simultaneously seeing the printed lines that depict the long sweeping lines of falling rain while looking through a surface picture plane saturated with fallen raindrops; thus vertical and ground planes are conflated. Breaching the constraints of working with printmaking processes, primarily collagraphy and reliefs, where he focused on a surface built from ink and paper, Feddersen further interrogated applied texture, adding staples, brads, and pushpins. Effectively, he invigorated the surfaces, allowing color to glow from beneath the printed low-hanging clouds and for light to penetrate the raindrops, both as color and as a reflection off the metal of the mixed-media additions. This would become the first body of work to gain him a broad audience and following. But it was only a starting point. The response to the work, by collectors and printmakers alike, encouraged Feddersen to continue making.

Feddersen is forever an "aesthetic scientist," as he was accurately described by W. Jackson Rushing, fostering a practice of experimentation and playful rejection of material restrictions.[6] This is evident in the transition that occurred for him after he left the University of Washington to pursue a graduate degree at the University of Wisconsin-Madison. One of the most respected printmaking programs in the country, Madison also afforded Feddersen mentoring by Truman Lowe (Ho-Chunk), the acclaimed sculptor whose own curiosity about materials and process was a vibrant example to invigorate the younger artist's work. Feddersen went to Madison because he wanted to move away from the success of the *Rainscapes*, finding the market appetite for these works to be a form of creative constriction. As a student during the late 1980s, Feddersen shifted to exploring self-portraits as a subject that allowed him to continue investigating materials such as photography, painting, encaustic, glass, and emerging digital imagery.

What emerged as the *Self Portrait* series were printed images that repeatedly used the form of his torso, a silhouette of his broad shoulders and head, as a point of interrogation (pls. 2, 3). He played with the potential of mixing materials and processes using the same silhouetted torso format over and over again. Sometimes the torso was a photograph, sometimes a form constructed by dot-matrix marks. The interpretive play between self and landmark worked well with the shape. The incorporation of the dot-matrix printer effectively generated patterns that were interesting to Feddersen in the form of repeated horizontal lines and mechanically organized pinpoints of color. As Gail Tremblay described, "The rigid geometric grid, created by the computer, functions like threads in a tapestry in which color is blended with sophistication to create an emotional landscape of great complexity."[7] The format of a centralized torso on a horizontal composition became a playground for the interplay of mechanical and human-made marks, black-and-white photography, variations in scale, and layers of applied color. While the human torso is a common reference form in the history of art, one cannot help but also consider how Feddersen is reaching back to that moment of creation, using his own body, upon which he can experiment and cultivate new visual life-forms. Within this series, he relies on the placement of marks, artistic impulses for aesthetic purposes, and those borrowed from historical materials, like chevrons that wrap as bands across the shoulders, transforming his body into a stand-in for the earth in the process (pl. 27).

His intentional interrogation of the form through materials and marks produced a series of images that echoed the contemporaneous dialogue brewing about contemporary Indigenous art and identity. Lucy Lippard used Feddersen's *Self Portrait* from 1984 in the seminal publication *Mixed Blessings* to illustrate how the image, constructed through layers of materials, served as a metaphor for humanity's relationship to the environment.[8] She wrote, "The environment is also abstracted into ambiguous space. Sometimes the artist's head and shoulder become a mountain form and sometimes figure and ground merge entirely into a web of patterned color: culture and nature become one."[9] This reading of the work is grounded in Lippard's larger discussion, one that Feddersen would likely not reject.

However, it is important to note that while Feddersen may not reject the interpretation, what Lippard describes may not be a product of his specific intentions. In previous interviews with the artist, he has described to me the importance of allowing the viewer to bring their own perspectives to the work.

> *You know that when you tell the stories it helps bring things out in people. And there are a hundred different interpretations. And they're all right. It's that thing that stimulates them and brings out that idea within. That's more important to me. If I can create that much ambiguity to kind of transcend . . . it's not meant to be didactic or anything. It's meant to make you think of something or to think in a different way. A lot of times it has what you're thinking about seeped into your interpretation.*[10]

It is not Feddersen's intention to codify the interpretive potential of the work; rather, he intends to make work that is open to what others bring to the viewing. Perhaps he resists the need to control the interpretation because it would require him to work more restrictively and with less freedom. Feddersen has been adamant in our conversations that the making is a matter of breathing normally, an important lesson he learned from Glen Alps, whose instructional process was akin to philosopher-as-technician. Feddersen described that within his creative process, the act of making has to be part of the regular course of the lived experience, not something that emerges from a heightened awareness or intention.

This manifests as much in Feddersen's process for making as the act of working in diverse materials. Fearless, he has gained skills in a variety of media, in addition to those with which he prints: glass, linen and wool, and ceramics. Each provides a unique physicalness to the broader body, though they are inherently related to the landscape: glass from silica and other minerals, linen from flax, ceramic from clay. The freedom to explore and maintain a material flexibility is integral to his process. Prolific, he swims between objects using his visual vocabulary of signs and symbols, exploring how each manifests differently with each iteration.

LAND + RELATIONSHIPS

Indigenous design aesthetics from the Plateau region are characterized by geometric repetition that holistically moves across the entirety of the surface. The designs are rarely held to a vertical grid but are often organized in a manner that animates the surface on the diagonal. The formation of angles and triangles, visual devices that cause the eye to read the surface as in motion, deny the eye from becoming stagnant or focused on a single point as it moves across the visual plane. These motifs, symbols that have remained in continued use across time, are often locally codified but resist absolute interpretations because of differences between local systems, allowing for a vitality that evokes the cultural continuum. Feddersen described the importance of local context and how important it is to resist assigning designs with singular interpretations, as he learned from renowned weaver Elaine Emerson (Colville Confederated Tribes):

> *She went through and we spent an afternoon and she said this is this design and that is that design. And then she finished. As I was writing down the designs, she would describe them, and at the end, she said, "This is this design, but in the next valley it means something totally different." It gives you a basis that things aren't the same for all over the Plateau area or anything. But your different bands have different*

[interpretations] and they have different relationships to them. The context is really important.[11]

Feddersen's facility with materials is matched by his fluidity with motifs that emerge from his personal experiences. This practice may have developed out of necessity.

Upon graduation from Madison, Feddersen joined the faculty at The Evergreen State College, a school renowned for its interdisciplinary instructional program, which fostered intellectual exploration. Teaching printmaking allowed him to develop a methodical process to work through cultural motifs and color, mixing layers to explore the potential for printmaking as an expression of his artistic concepts.[12] In Feddersen's first retrospective publication, *Vital Signs*, Rebecca J. Dobkins writes:

> *During those early years of teaching, Feddersen was seeking direction for his art. He needed to find a way of working that was compatible with his nine-month teaching schedule, an inquiry that could be sustained over time until term breaks permitted more concentrated work.*[13]

The extended period in Madison, followed by the move to Olympia, had left Feddersen thinking about concepts of home, both the people and the landscape. He would spend his entire teaching career at The Evergreen State College (1989–2009), where he established deep friendships with his colleagues and cultivated a close circle of friends from among members of the Native arts community in the expanse between Portland and Seattle. The Sacred Circle Gallery opened in 1978 at the Daybreak Star Indian Cultural Center in Seattle and served as a critical hub where relationships were seeded that remain important to Feddersen today.[14] The site served as an ongoing introduction to contemporary Native art and hosted exhibitions that featured many nationally and regionally important artists. Feddersen's transition from Madison to Olympia fostered a period in which he drew upon his personal knowledge and experiences to generate images that would establish him within the community of artists with whom he was associating at the gallery and the college. Perhaps because of the distance from his Plateau homelands, he was initially drawn to use the textile motifs familiar from his cultural upbringing, as evident in several small series that relied on designs found on blankets and baskets, including *Journal*, *Pendleton Blankets*, and *Broken Baskets* (pls. 7, 9).

Once established at Evergreen, Feddersen initiated the *Plateau Geometrics* series in 1995, using multiple prepared plates etched with complementary designs, which he worked and reworked, generating the most extensive series of his career, with over 195 unique works

Fig. 4 Joe Feddersen, details from the *Plateau Geometrics* series, pls. 50–55, 58–59

(pls. 50–55, 58–59). Each print in this series is related to the others through the repetition of an extended set of etched plates. The images were built from multiple printed layers through which Feddersen explored combinations of color and textures, possibilities generated from shifting the orientation of the plates, printing the plates as relief and intaglio, or adding siligraphy (also called waterless lithography or vitreography), all the while learning about the materials and expanding his knowledge of the motifs. Each printed layer contributed colors built up as layers of light and shadow while relying on colors that resonated with the natural environment. Blues emerged at the edge of the warm browns, activated by a peek of red buried within the intaglio printed surface. These printed layers built up like the exposed stratification of the Plateau's basaltic lava flows softened by millennia of flood erosion.

Plateau Geometrics was a lightning rod for Feddersen's creativity. Relying on those early lessons from his parents to look closely, his active repetition—akin to a compulsion—with the series produced a deep love for complex surfaces flooded with rich colors. By the use of designs known as lightning, butterfly or vertebrae, mountain, ladder, and snake (fig. 4), Feddersen borrowed motifs tied to the landscape of his homelands. He interrogated the possibilities, fully exploring the combinations and relationships of each motif referential to natural phenomena, animals, or erosion that remained as marks on the land. While working on this series, Feddersen began thinking how contemporary humans leave marks on the land—societal flows that are as destructive as volcanic lava.

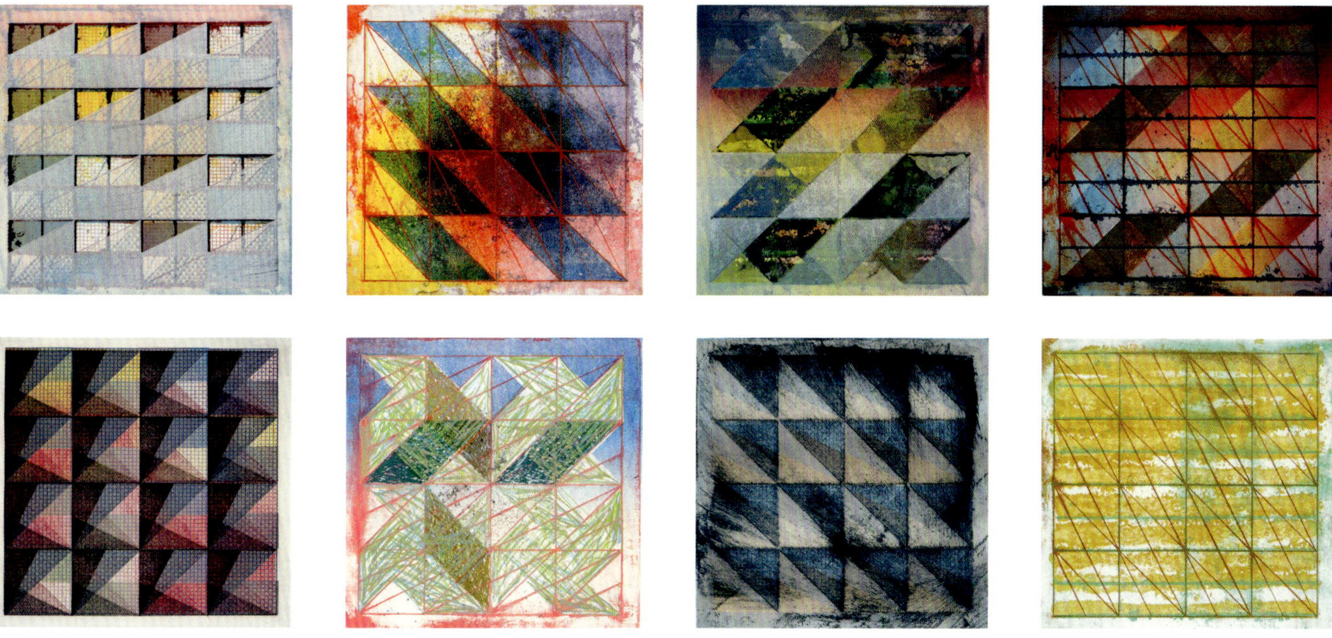

Our human impacts leave a residue on the earth, marks left on the land that are less likely to be the product of the gentle movement of deer across the earth's surface. Feddersen recognized how generations before him simply documented their own observations of land impacts, those from natural forces as described, and, later, recorded the movement of trains and roads across the landscape. He began chronicling his own traffic observations in the same materials that Okanagan artists had for centuries—he began weaving baskets. Early weaving lessons from his dear friend Elizabeth A. Woody (Navajo Nation/Yakama Nation/Confederated Tribes of Warm Springs artist, author, and educator) fostered what was a natural inclination for the act of weaving. Early baskets were twined with high-voltage towers (fig. 5) and traffic control diagrams, like parking lots and HOV lanes (pls. 48–49). The baskets were a breakthrough for Feddersen, not because the symbols were so powerful in and of themselves but because the artist was establishing his own visual vernacular in the process. The powerful relationship between these motifs, generally rendered in simplistic linear form, became an important ongoing practice of Feddersen's. As a Plateau community artist, he was generating an addition to the visual language of Colville cultural practices; this was important for his relationship to the landscape and his definitions of home.

By using motifs rooted in the landscape around Omak, Feddersen was generating an extension to the aesthetic language of his cultural communities, both Okanagan and Plateau. The linear constructions became a language that was his to define, or not, according to his practice, especially as they were visual motifs to which every viewer brought their own experiences. They were familiar and new simultaneously. The application of them following the aesthetic practices of the region, wrapped around the circumference of baskets, immediately made them feel customary. Those who know Feddersen personally recognize the easy humor with which the artist actively lives.

Fig. 5 Voltage towers connected to the Grand Coulee Dam, Columbia River, WA, March 30, 2024

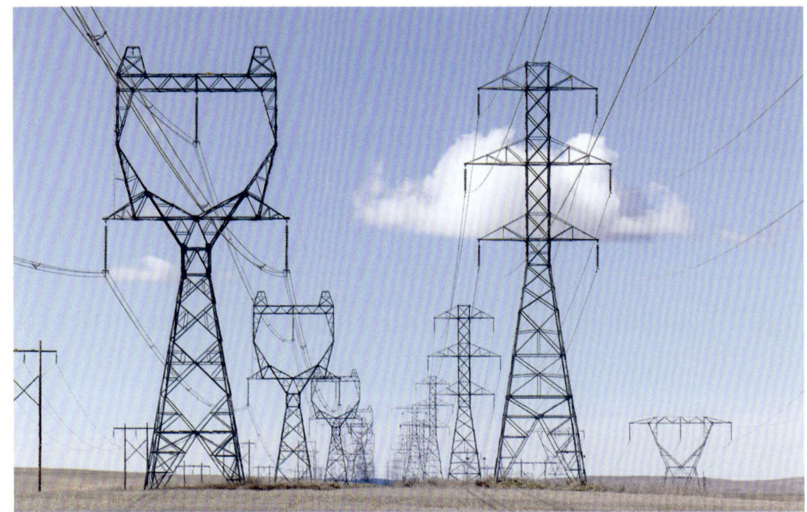

These symbols and motifs became the fodder from which Feddersen built the body of work included in his exhibition as a 2001 Eiteljorg Contemporary Art Fellow, an award in its second iteration, which required each of the six fellows to participate in a large exhibition at the Eiteljorg Museum of American Indians and Western Art in Indianapolis.[15] The extensive artworks needed for this exhibition created an opportunity for Feddersen to share a large range of the *Plateau Geometrics* and his early experimentation with baskets that integrated his playful attitude toward design motifs and color.

This body of work was named the *Urban Indian* and *Urban Vernacular* series, generated as bold commentaries on the overlay of designs that govern our human traffic patterns (pls. 45, 48). These expressive works, in prints and woven baskets, were negotiating a visual relationship to the Cascade Range of his homelands and the marks made to organize humans on the surface. Feddersen adopted the symbols and diagrams used for human migrations, including parking lot diagrams, HOV lane symbols, and tire tracks, which were presented very simplistically as linear designs. In his adaptation, they remain familiar but become appreciated as modernist art. Gail Tremblay noted:

> *As viewers reflect on the sources for this suite of designs, they come to appreciate not only the series title* Urban Indian *but also the ironies that shape urban Indian life, in which patterns of land use and landownership make a traditional lifestyle difficult.*[16]

Feddersen's baskets were initially woven from non-customary cultural materials, like waxed linen or wax-coated paper, with the designs applied to the surface. Relying on the clean repetition of the traffic motifs, he focused on exploring materials and symbols playfully, developing his skills and confidence, easily shifting between two- and three-dimensional applications of the motifs.

This preparation would become timely. When Feddersen was invited to participate in the National Museum of the American Indian's *Continuum 12* series, he was challenged by his friend Nora Naranjo Morse (Santa Clara Pueblo ceramicist) to think about opportunities to explore scale and responded with a new body of large-scale printed works. *Okanagan* was born as a series of massive print installations, several of which were over ten feet wide, composed of individually printed images that, when hung together, formed an extraordinary commentary on landscapes through geometric design combined with monumental scale (pl. 60).

With a growing confidence in his own capacity to work through designs, color, textures, and scale, Feddersen saw the addition of his small hand-built baskets for the *Continuum 12* exhibition (2004) risked being grotesquely overshadowed by the scale of the print installation. So he sought a creative partner with whom he could construct larger baskets formed from glass, a material with which he had experimented in Madison. Through a series of introductions, Feddersen became acquainted with accomplished glass artist Preston Singletary (Tlingit). Feddersen envisioned integrating the potential scale of glass with the forms of his handwoven baskets, which were often four to six inches tall; he hoped the resulting forms could hold the gallery space in balance with the print installation. The glass baskets created from the collaboration between Feddersen and Singletary were between ten and fourteen inches in diameter and as much as fourteen inches in height. The cloudy white glass forms were etched to mimic the surface of woven baskets and finished with the traffic diagrams emerging from Feddersen's woven baskets and prints.[17] Importantly, these initial glass baskets would introduce Feddersen to new audiences.

One of the glass baskets exhibited in the *Continuum 12* exhibition, *Parking Lot* (2003), was selected to be included in *Changing Hands: Art Without Reservation II*, the second of a trio of nationally touring exhibitions organized by the Museum of Arts and Design, New York (fig. 6). A landmark project, each of the three iterations of *Changing Hands* introduced contemporary Native art to broad audiences through the eponymous publication series and as the exhibitions navigated through nationally significant contemporary art museums, sites not inherently designated for Indigenous art collections.[18] *Parking Lot* traveled the continent and engaged viewers as a product of glass—perceptively a material not generally associated with customary Indigenous art—that read as a highly modernist work. Many viewers read the highly geometricized design as Indigenous until they read the title. Feddersen's usurpation of the traffic diagram as a customary Indigenous design was, in fact, a highly Okanagan thing to do.

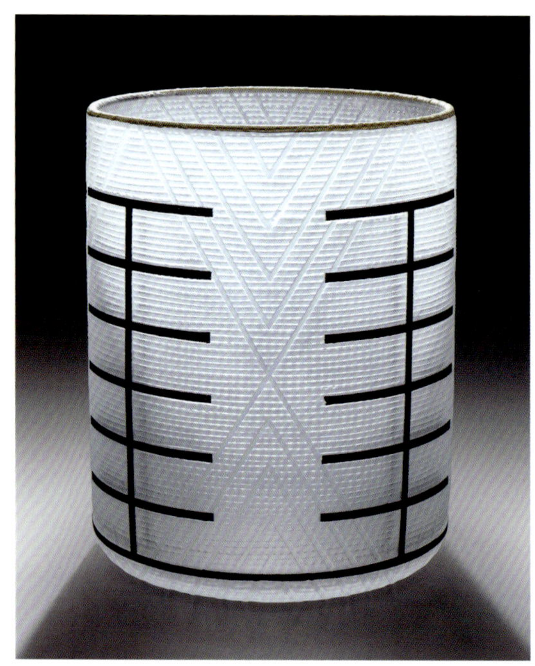

Fig. 6 Joe Feddersen, *Parking Lot*, 2003. Sandblasted blown glass, 14 × 10¾ in. (35.6 × 27.3 cm). Nerman Museum of Contemporary Art, Johnson County Community College, Overland Park, Kansas

LAND + MARKERS

Okanagan people, as part of the broader Colville Confederated Tribes, have traveled in the highlands of their valley forever, as long as they can remember, which, as described earlier, goes back to creation. Their close relationship to the land has fostered a familiarity with the marks on the hillsides etched under the hooves of generations of migratory deer or the gentle displacement of sand from a slithering snake. These signs have been translated into customary cultural designs that continue to be used, a creative act by community members affirming relationships between the culture and the landscape. Feddersen's intentional placement of a parking lot diagram on a glass basket was a product of this customary practice with his artistic practice of relying on his observations, which are then expressed through the casual, albeit ongoing, exploration of artmaking. The diagram, a product of the emergence of American car culture in the early twentieth century, is familiar to every member of society, young and old, as we organize our transitions between commercial and residential spaces across the earth's surface. The parking lot design's ubiquitous presence as a marker on the landscape suited Feddersen's aesthetic concerns and translated well into Okanagan and Plateau aesthetic practices for circuitous balance, holding the placement in harmony with the etched design of the basket texture and pattern.

While the *Changing Hands II* exhibition traveled, Feddersen continued exploring the parking lot design in woven baskets and on prints, ever playing with scale. Likewise, he experimented with HOV designs, tire track profiles, and the grids of chain-link fences; each was appreciatively handled to retain the aesthetic sensibilities of customary cultural practices, including an emphasis on balance, application on the entirety of the surface, and care for placement so that the object can be seen from any side and enjoyed uninterrupted. His playfulness with using the designs is in response to a natural curiosity as much as his resistance against creating images too contrite, which he feared would happen if he controlled the placements too tightly.

Feddersen's interest in retaining creative freedom within his work is also expressed in his animated portraits that emerged in 2001. The first figures in the series known as *Role Call* (a play on the homophones of *role* and *roll*) appeared on the rims of woven baskets (fig. 7), an army of figures that have permeated across multiple bodies of work since (pls. 21, 36, 38, 39). Feddersen was contemplating the importance of what we see each day, characters within our daily dramas. He recalls thinking about how the eagle, absent from the landscape in his childhood due to the use of dichlorodiphenyltrichloroethane (DDT) as an agricultural insecticide, had returned to the region and became a familiar neighbor of sorts, commonly seen on a daily basis.[19] Drawing upon the way that high school yearbooks depict familiar faces, Feddersen began animating what he saw as he moved about. He described the portraits as resulting from "looking around, like a winter

Fig. 7 Joe Feddersen, detail of *Gathering Under the Stars*, 2010. Waxed linen, wool, fabric, and thread, 8½ × 7½ × 7½ in. (21.6 × 19.1 × 19.1 cm). Collection of the artist

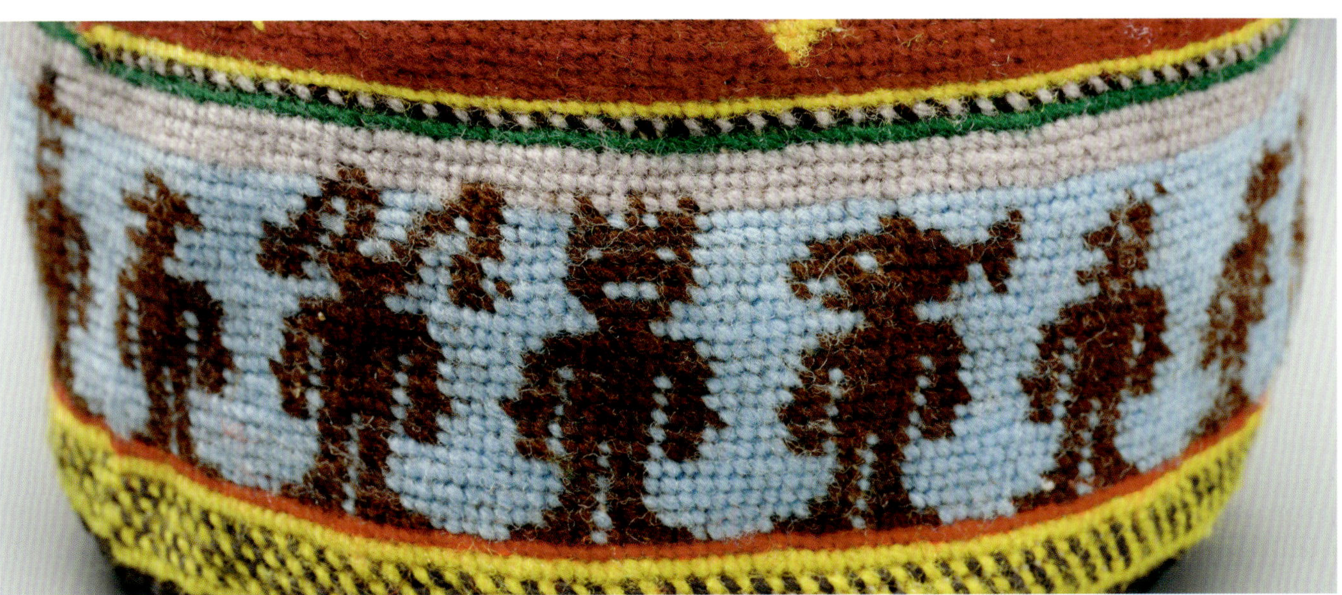

calendar marking a time and place, looking around and seeing what is around. Who survived? What are they doing?"[20]

Within this documentary approach to what is seen in one's environment, Feddersen created an animated series of portraits of televisions, cable antennae, deer, fir trees, bighorn sheep, coyote, and bear—each animated with arms and legs, often lined up like the grid of students waiting for their senior portraits to be taken. Each figure has a personality that vibrates through the bold use of color and facial expressions. They are repeatedly shown in conversation as they form a line around the rim of a basket, engaging with the viewer as they stand alone in the grid of an installation. The *Role Call* series figures remain a long-term presence within Feddersen's work, later traveling together in the *Canoe Journeys* series of ceramic works that emerged in 2015 (pls. 82–95). The playful exploration of the designs through the range of materials within his wheelhouse led to experimentation with fused glass.

Feddersen has appreciated the potential of glass as a material since Madison, valuing its dense and fragile qualities, which allows it to be read as multivalent signifiers, including as commentary on society's relationship with the environment. His continued experimentation with glass would fortuitously generate a new series in 2011. When invited to exhibit at the Sun Valley Arts Center (now Sun Valley Museum of Art), Feddersen devised three concept proposals: a petroglyph wall, a large wind chime, or a charm bracelet. Once the list was composed, Feddersen saw the opportunity to create all three in a single body. The resulting installation would become the first in a series that he titled *Charmed* (pl. 22). Using a home kiln and glass pieces, he began making "charms," clear glass pendants formed into recognizable designs ranging in size from four to ten inches in height. The charms are tied individually into position on a filament, spaced out so that each string holds multiple symbols, collectively suspended from the ceiling along a single horizontal plane in multiple vertical rows against a wall. The glass figures are hung adjacent enough to generate a high ring as the air is moved by a viewer's passage through the gallery. The clear glass forms are barely visible, mostly when light casts a highlight along a side, but the shadows on the wall behind are larger and more densely visible, especially when multiple points of light cast layers of shadows (fig. 8).

The *Charmed* series evocatively incorporates landscape in a powerful tour de force that draws upon all of Feddersen's previous conceptual work. In *Charmed*, he references the petroglyphs abundantly located in the Cascade Range, marks made upon the land by previous generations, inscribing a human presence that documents relationships and lifeways that remain cogent for the local Indigenous communities through stories and songs. He draws upon the symbols

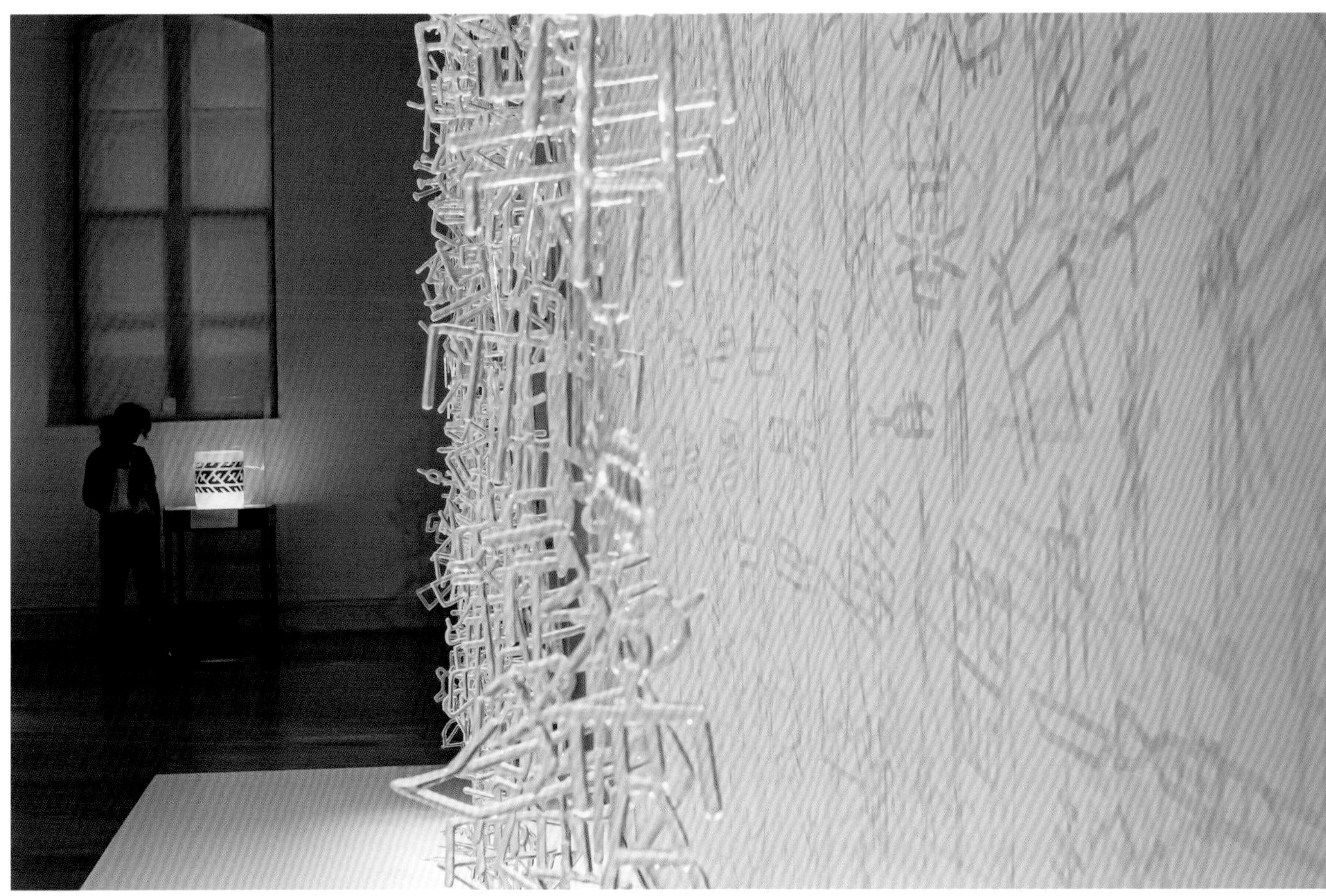

Fig. 8 Installation photography of *Sharing Honors and Burdens: Renwick Invitational 2023*. Renwick Gallery of the Smithsonian American Art Museum, 2023, courtesy of Smithsonian American Art Museum

that orient contemporary society to the land, such as map triangles that identify mountains or stop sign octagons. He draws upon his *Role Call* figures as they are part of the landscape. He draws upon the high-voltage towers, the flowers, spiders, and butterflies that dance at the edge between the earth and sky. He draws upon the use of glass as a material, formed from earthen silica fused by exposure to extreme heat (just under 1500°F) that renders it impermeable to liquids yet delicately brittle to impacts. He draws upon light, intentionally casting shadows upon the wall to reference petroglyphs and time simultaneously. And, because of their nuanced role within his other work, the glass installations facilitate commentary on time through the temporal placement and the shadows casting visual whispers that comment on the impermanence within our human experience.

Subversively, time is the invisible actor throughout Feddersen's oeuvre. As a maker of works that are intentionally cultivated as contemporary artworks, not mimicking customary practices or pejoratively rejecting cultural materials, Feddersen celebrates the continuum of his culture across time rooted in the Okanagan Valley. With each installation of *Charmed*, the very movement of the air serves as a visual reminder that our presence on the landscape is temporary. With each addition to the series, Feddersen has revisited previously treated subjects: *Omak Mountain*, *Spotted Lake*, and the *Bestiary* (a series of prints and woven and glass baskets depicting the range of life-forms familiar to the Plateau region). The evolution of these images as clear glass and light evokes the one constant in the landscape: change. Like the best philosophies found globally, the simplest of ideas is often the most difficult to understand.

Feddersen, committed to close observation and the natural practice of artmaking, can be seen to have fully embodied the teachings of his mentor, Glen Alps, within his long career: the importance of breathing and making as a natural act rather than holding one's breath as precious oxygen. Feddersen teaches the viewer to look closely, as he was taught by his parents, to see the designs and landscape markers as evidence of our own imprint upon the land. Effectively, the landscape can be seen as Feddersen's silent partner in the studio. Through the *Charmed* series and the related *Echo* series of photo prints of the charms, Feddersen has reached a summit within his artmaking (pls. 23–26). Though his works do not present a singular perspectival view of the landscape, through the expanded body of his oeuvre, one can see that the landscape is present throughout, depicted within the baskets or printed as traffic diagrams. While calling him a landscape artist may be perceived as an abstract statement, through this discussion of the relationship between Plateau and Okanagan art with Feddersen's ongoing practice, this essay exposes that there can be many interpretations of relationships to the land. When asked in an interview if he saw himself as a landscape artist, Feddersen stated:

> *I think I've always been a landscape artist. I've been always interested in the space, in the light, in the color. And, uh, there are figurative elements that come in. But I always think of it as, this is the world around me, and as a landscape kind of a thing.*[21]

Within contemporary art, the priority for Western cultural perspectives has restricted the interpretation that aligns the art of many Indigenous artists from North America, as well as from all other inhabited continents, as landscape art. It is the hope that, through this examination of Joe Feddersen's larger body of works and their related content, his personal interests in making, and the related importance of his cultural relationship to place and land, the reader may be able to see that understanding one's relationship to the earth through a non-Western cultural lens is generative of new forms of looking closely. If Joe Feddersen has taught us anything through his art, it is to breathe and look closely.

Notes

1. The author is an Indigenous American, as a citizen of the Chickasaw Nation and a descendant of a long line of strong Choctaw women.

2. For further discussion on Indigenous landscape art, see heather ahtone, "Sky as Place, Land as Body, and Landscape as Spiritual Compass," in *The Land Carries Our Ancestors: Contemporary Art by Native Americans* (Washington, DC: National Gallery of Art, 2023).

3. Early explorers and traders tapped into the already well-established trade network along the Columbia River, documenting the annual trade rendezvous at The Dalles and the Celilo Falls site as far back as 1811. As Western worldviews encountered Indigenous philosophies, they found a robust market where they could participate, extracting material resources to generate their own wealth. The environment fostered the establishment of an American city on the site, facilitating markets beyond the annual gatherings associated with the salmon cycles. See https://www.oregonhistoryproject.org/articles/historical-records/the-columbia-river-trade-network/ (accessed June 28, 2023).

4. Rebecca J. Dobkins, "Joe Feddersen: Pulses and Patterns," in *Joe Feddersen: Vital Signs*, ed. Dobkins (Salem, OR: Hallie Ford Museum of Art at Willamette University, 2008), 17–30.

5. Gail Tremblay, "Speaking in a Language of Vital Signs," in Dobkins, *Joe Feddersen: Vital Signs*, 37.

6. W. Jackson Rushing III, "Joe Feddersen: Sacred Geometry," in *After the Storm: The Eiteljorg Fellowship for Native American Fine Art*, ed. Rushing (Seattle: University of Washington Press, 2001).

7. Tremblay, "Speaking in a Language of Vital Signs," 39.

8. Lucy R. Lippard, *Mixed Blessings: New Art in a Multicultural America* (New York: The New Press, 1990), 29.

9. Lippard, *Mixed Blessings*, 29.

10. Joe Feddersen, interview with the author, Oct. 16, 2017, transcript, 22–23.

11. Joe Feddersen, interview, Oct. 16, 2017, 22.

12. The Evergreen State College uniquely fosters interdisciplinary study through collaborative learning programs. For more information, see www.evergreen.edu (accessed June 28, 2023).

13. Dobkins, "Joe Feddersen: Pulses and Patterns," 24.

14. Oral history interview with Joe Feddersen, Apr. 29 and May 6, 2021. Archives of American Art, Smithsonian Institution.

15. Rushing, "Joe Feddersen: Sacred Geometry," 33–40.

16. Tremblay, "Speaking in a Language of Vital Signs," 46.

17. For an in-depth discussion on one of these baskets, see heather ahtone, "Reading Beneath the Surface: Joe Feddersen's *Parking Lot*," *Wicazo Sa Review* 27, no. 1 (2012): 73–84.

18. The author became familiar with Feddersen's *Parking Lot* through the related exhibition catalogue. More information is available at the organizing museum's website: https://madmuseum.org/content/changing-hands (accessed July 23, 2023).

19. Joe Feddersen, phone conversation with the author, n.d. [2023].

20. Joe Feddersen, phone conversation with the author.

21. Oral history interview with Joe Feddersen.

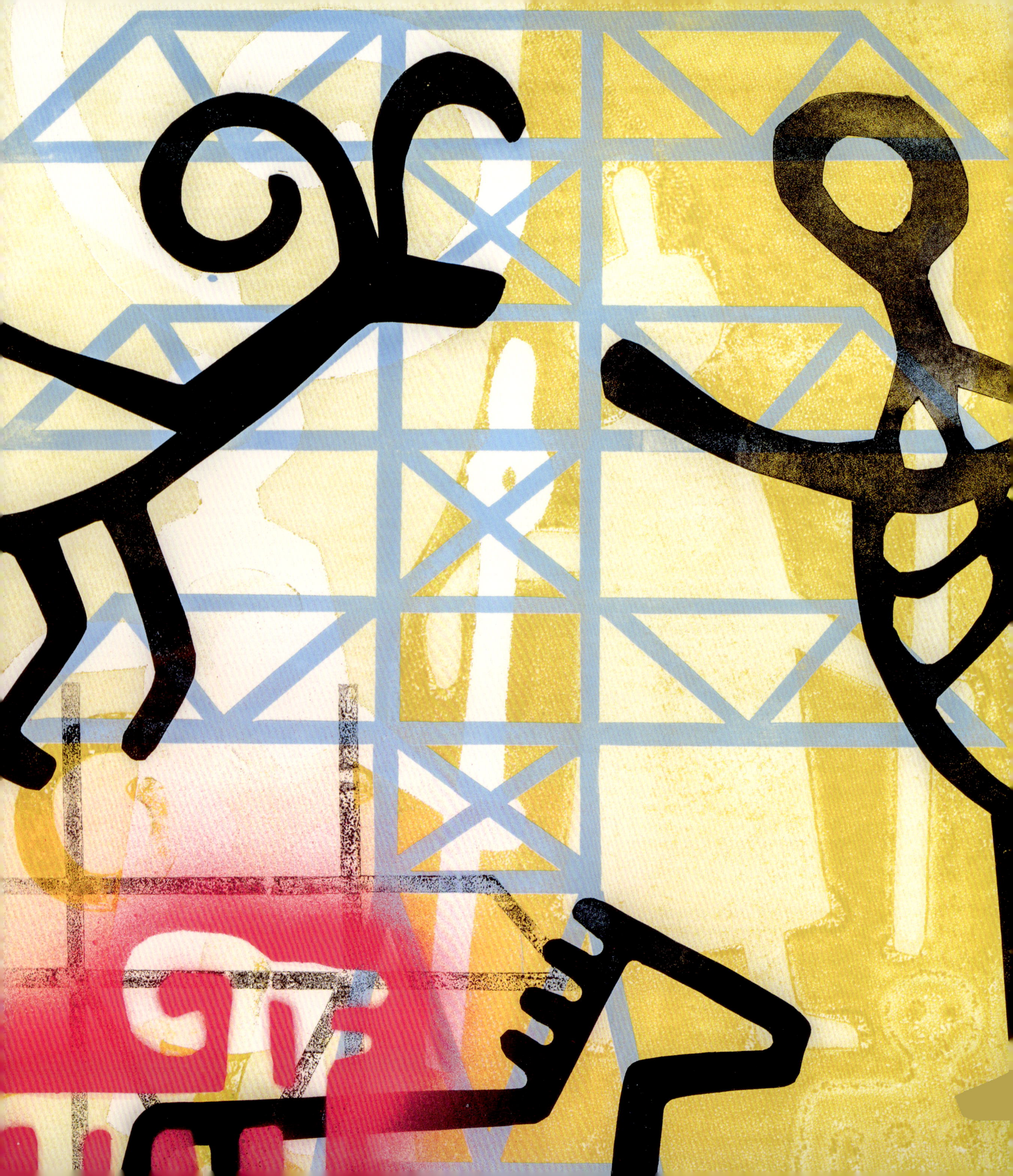

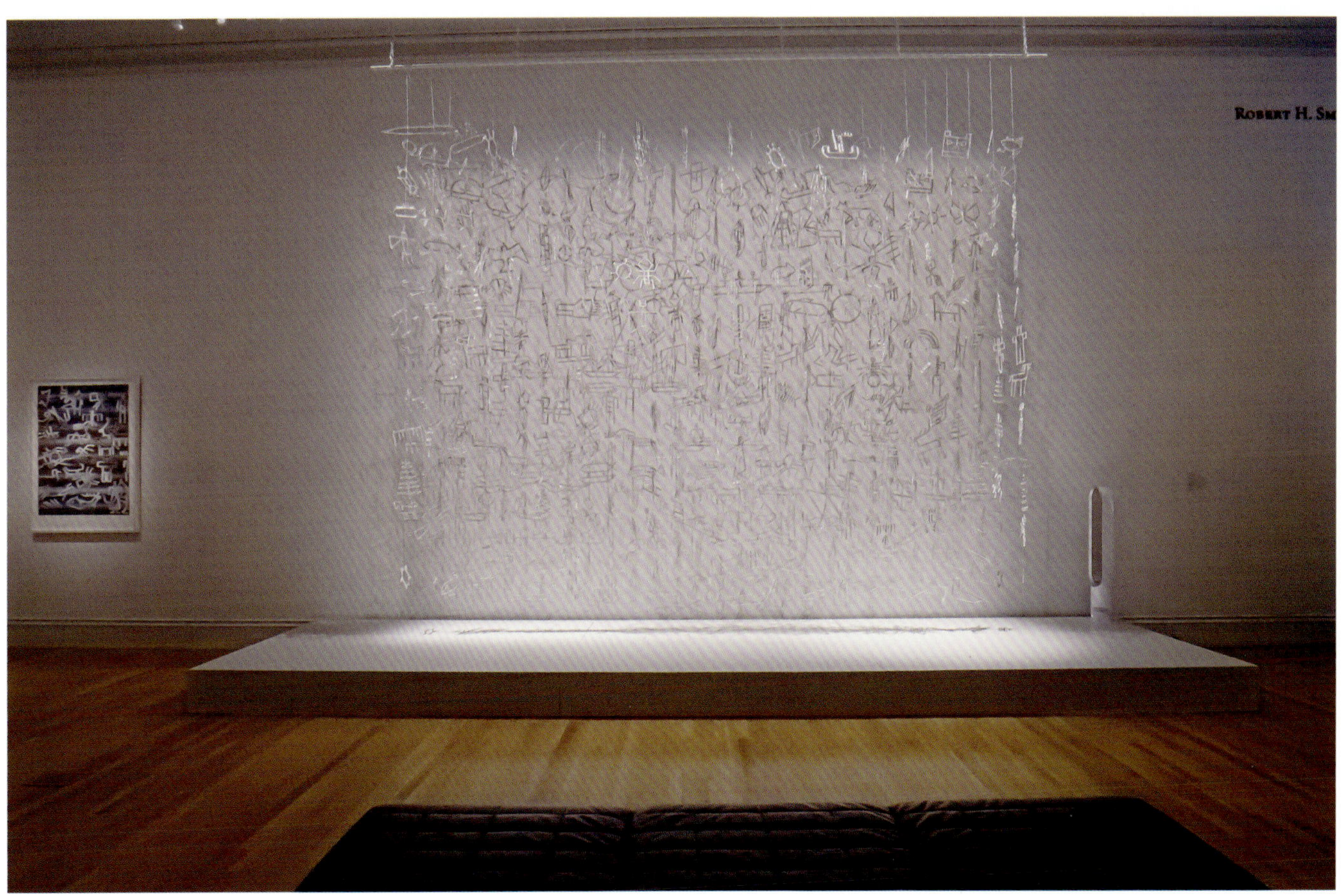

Plate 22
Charmed (Bestiary), 2023
Fused glass and filament
120 × 180 × 10 in.
(304.8 × 457.2 × 25.4 cm)

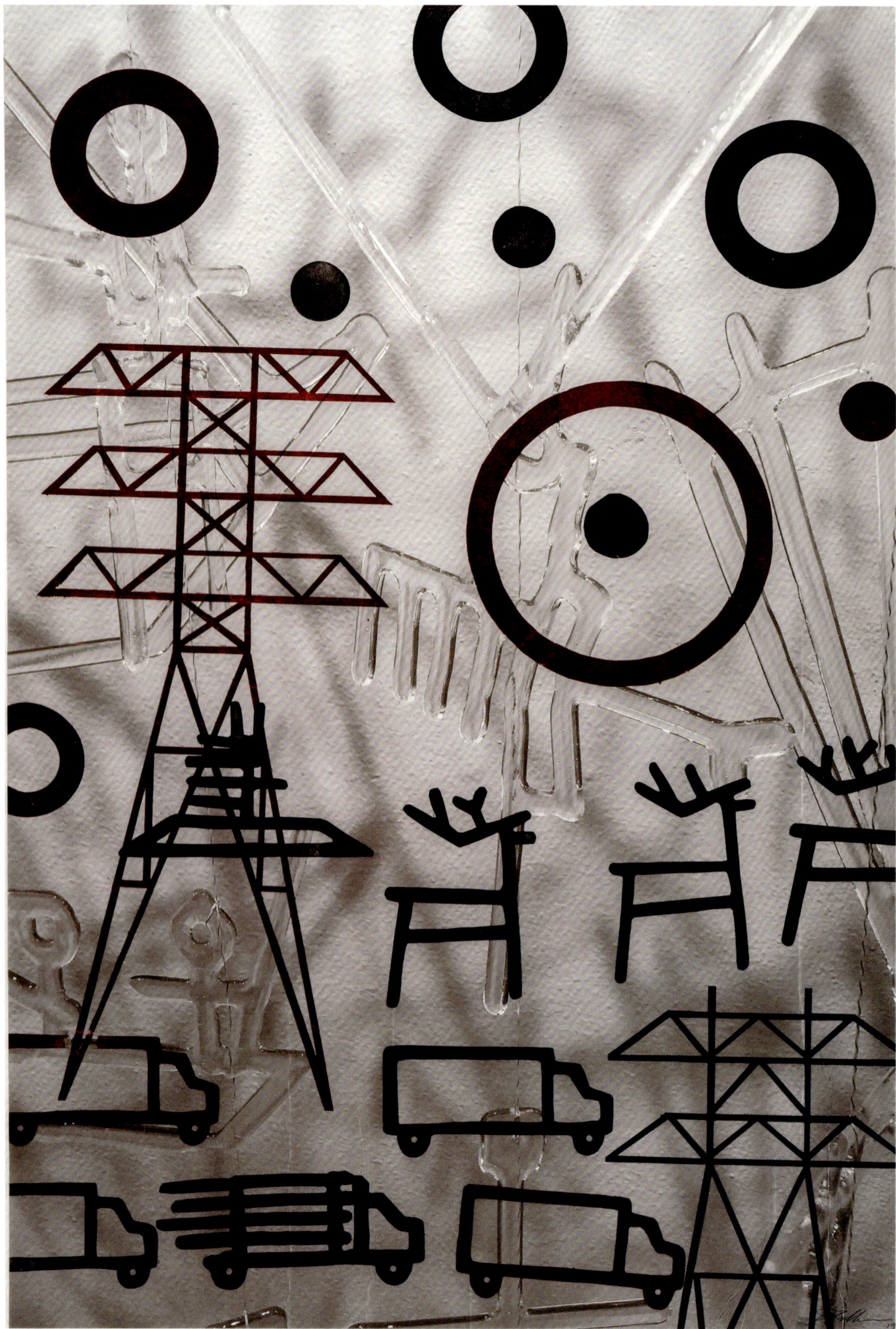

Plate 23
Echo 12, 2019
Pigment inkjet, relief, and stencil monoprint
52½ × 35 in.
(133.4 × 89 cm)

Plate 24
Echo 11, 2019
Pigment inkjet, relief, and stencil monoprint
52½ × 35 in.
(133.4 × 89 cm)

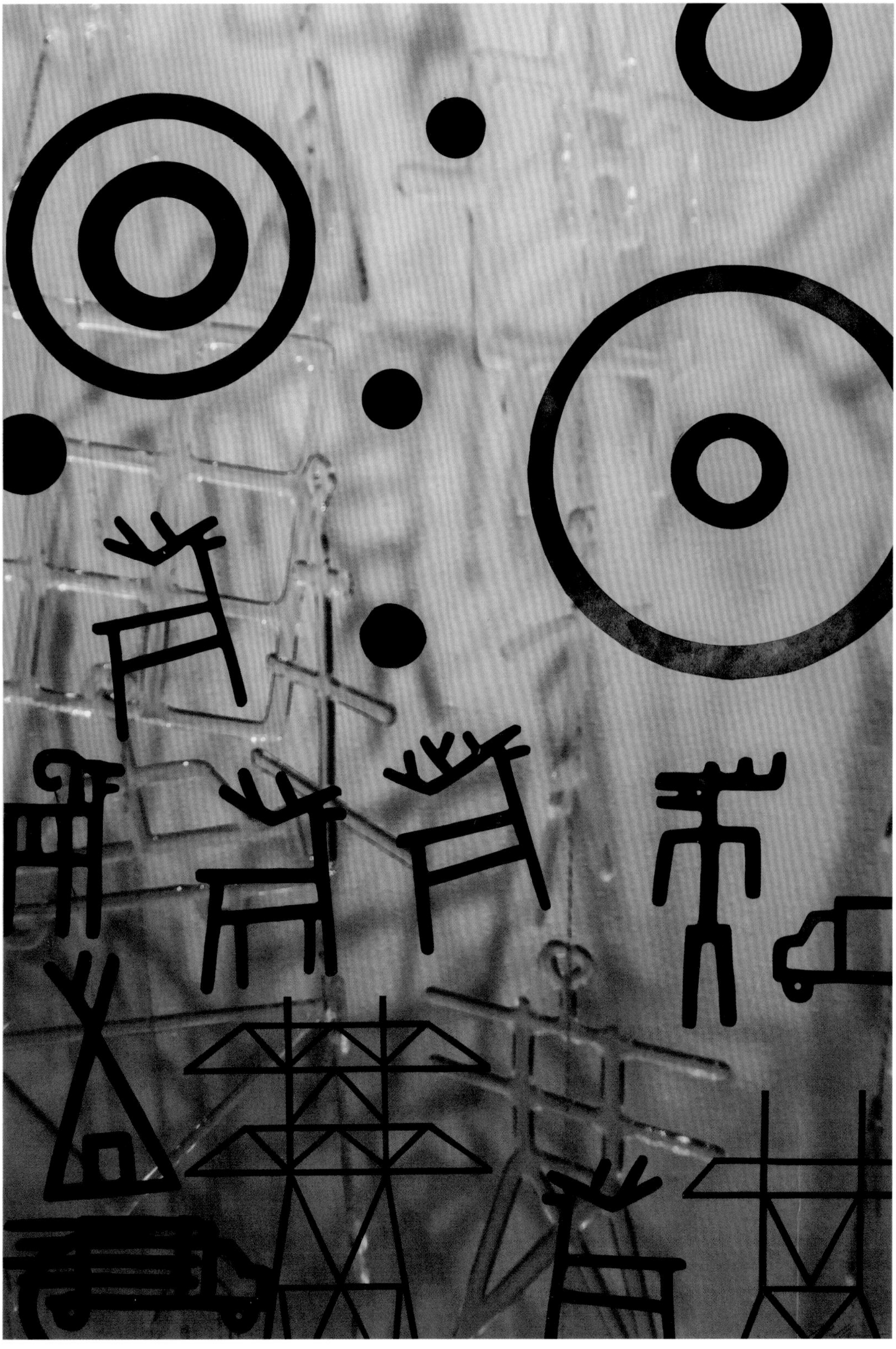

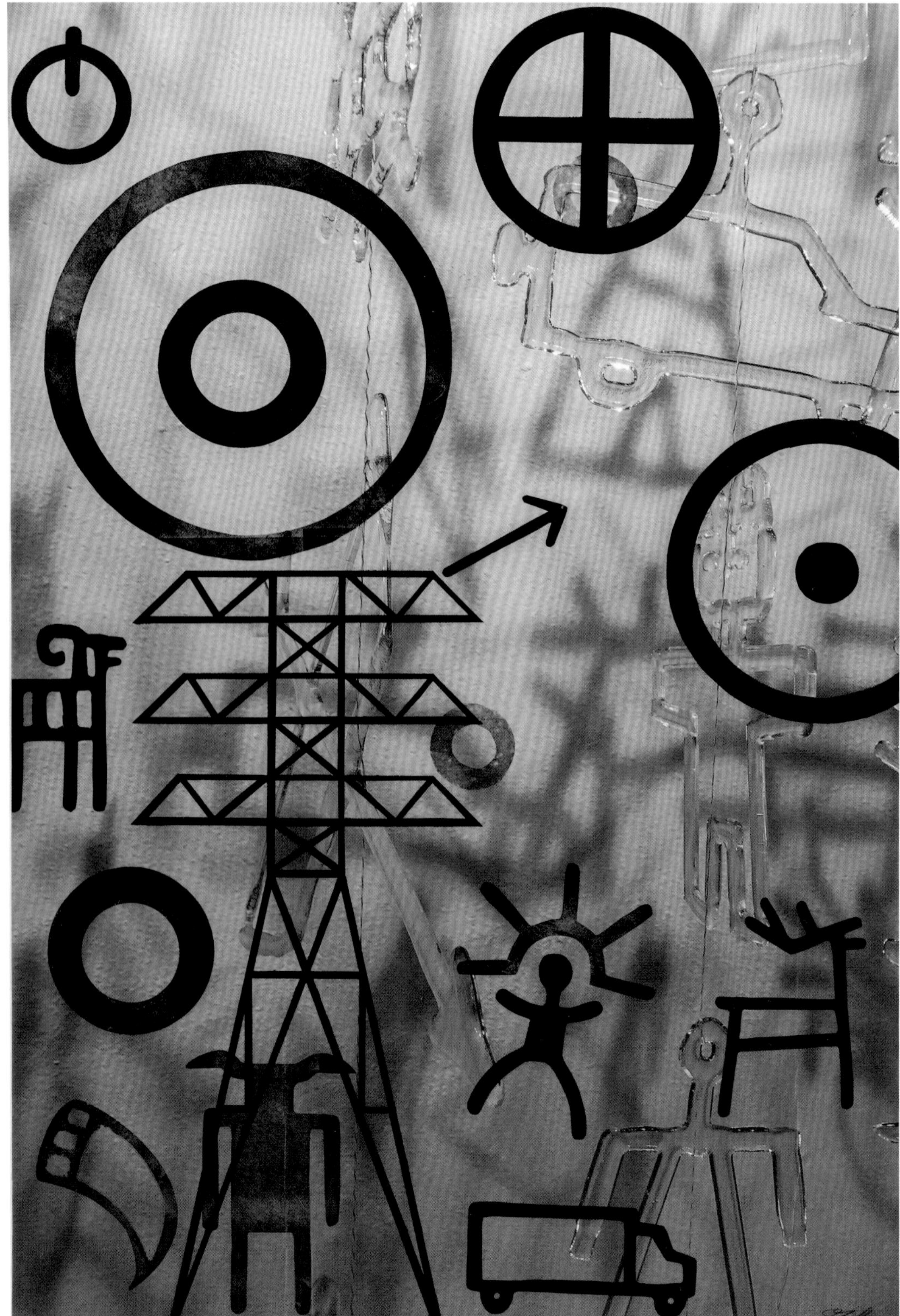

Plate 25
Echo 3, 2019
Pigment inkjet, relief, and stencil monoprint
52½ × 35 in.
(133.4 × 89 cm)

Plate 26
Echo 6, 2019
Pigment inkjet, relief,
and stencil monoprint
52½ × 35 in.
(133.4 × 89 cm)

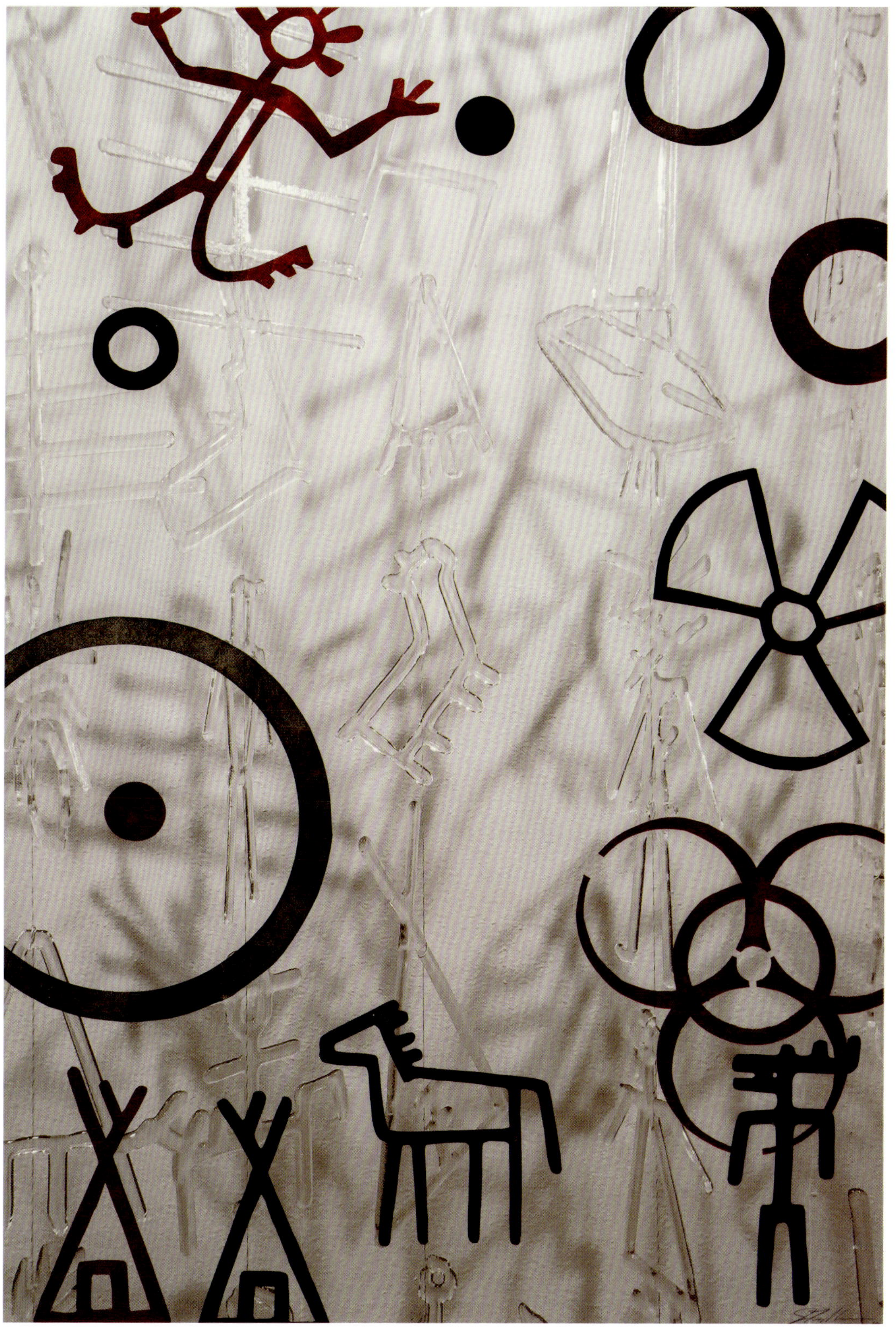

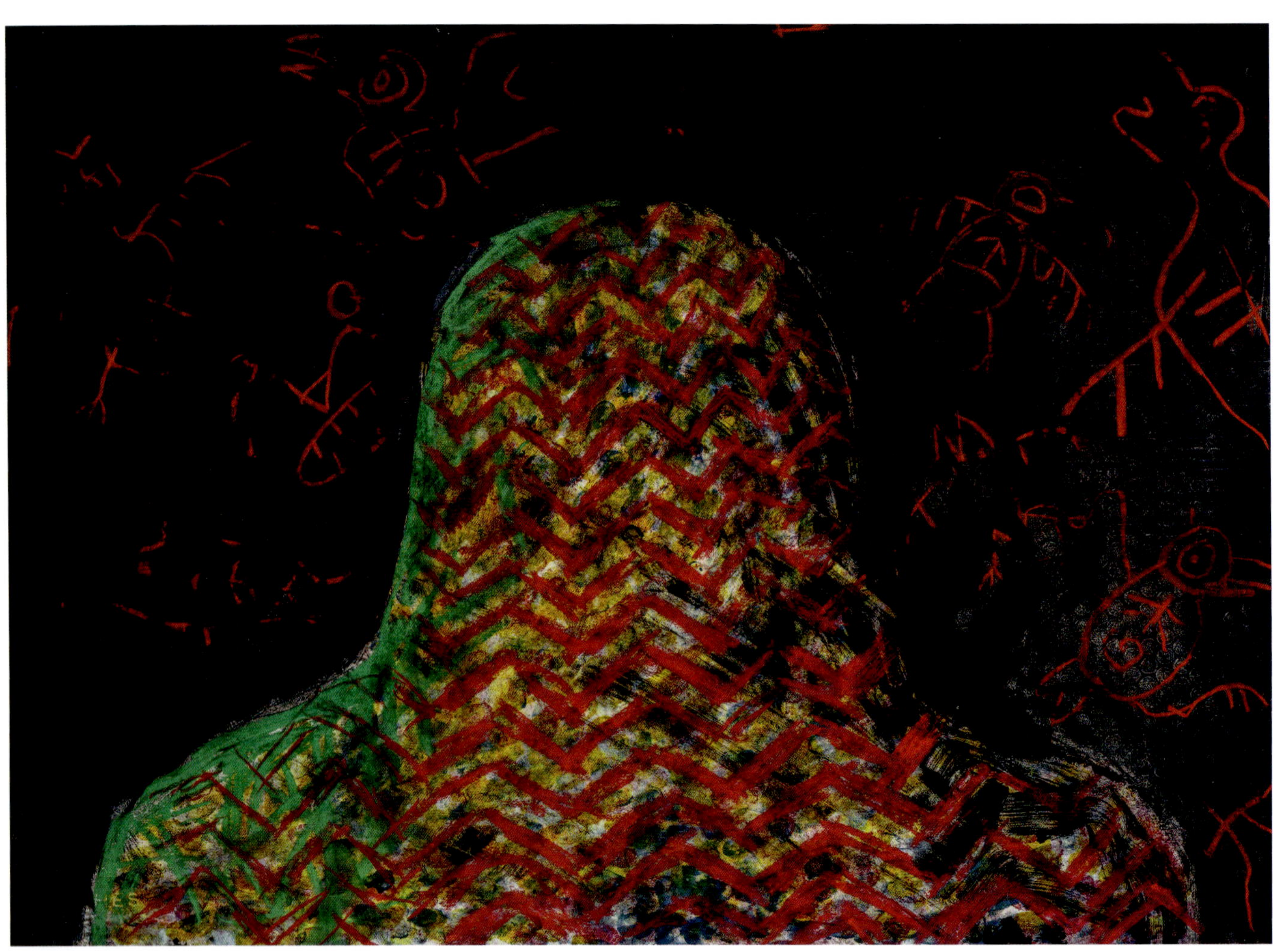

Plate 27
Inheritance Obscured by Neglect, 1989
Pastel, acrylic, and ink on paper
22 × 30 in. (55.9 × 76.2 cm)

Abalone Teardrops

He comes from there
    A secret prayerful society singing and dancing nourishing snow.

He comes from there
    That place carved with rattlesnake trails and eel tracks.

He comes from there
    Where Eagle slapped abalone teardrops from her iridescent face.

He comes from there
    A spot where people are born of the blood from the heart of a monster.

He comes from there
    Those that understand why seven giant wicked devils stand trapped.

Miles R. Miller - Yakama

Miles R. Miller, "Abalone Teardrops," in *Terrain: Plateau Native Art & Poetry*, ed. Joe Feddersen, 2014

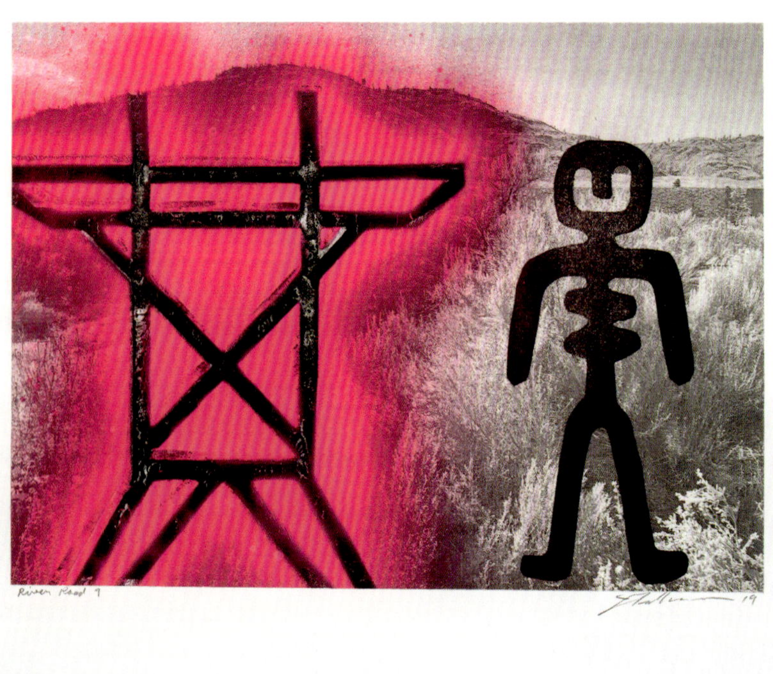

Plate 28
River Road 9, 2019
Relief, toner print, and stencil monoprint with spray paint
Sheet: 19 × 15 in. (48.3 × 38.1 cm); image: 8 × 11 in. (20.3 × 27.9 cm)

Plate 29
Omak Lake 2, 2019
Relief and stencil monoprint with spray paint
Sheet: 26 × 19½ in. (66 × 49.5 cm); image: 19 × 14½ in. (48.3 × 36.8 cm)

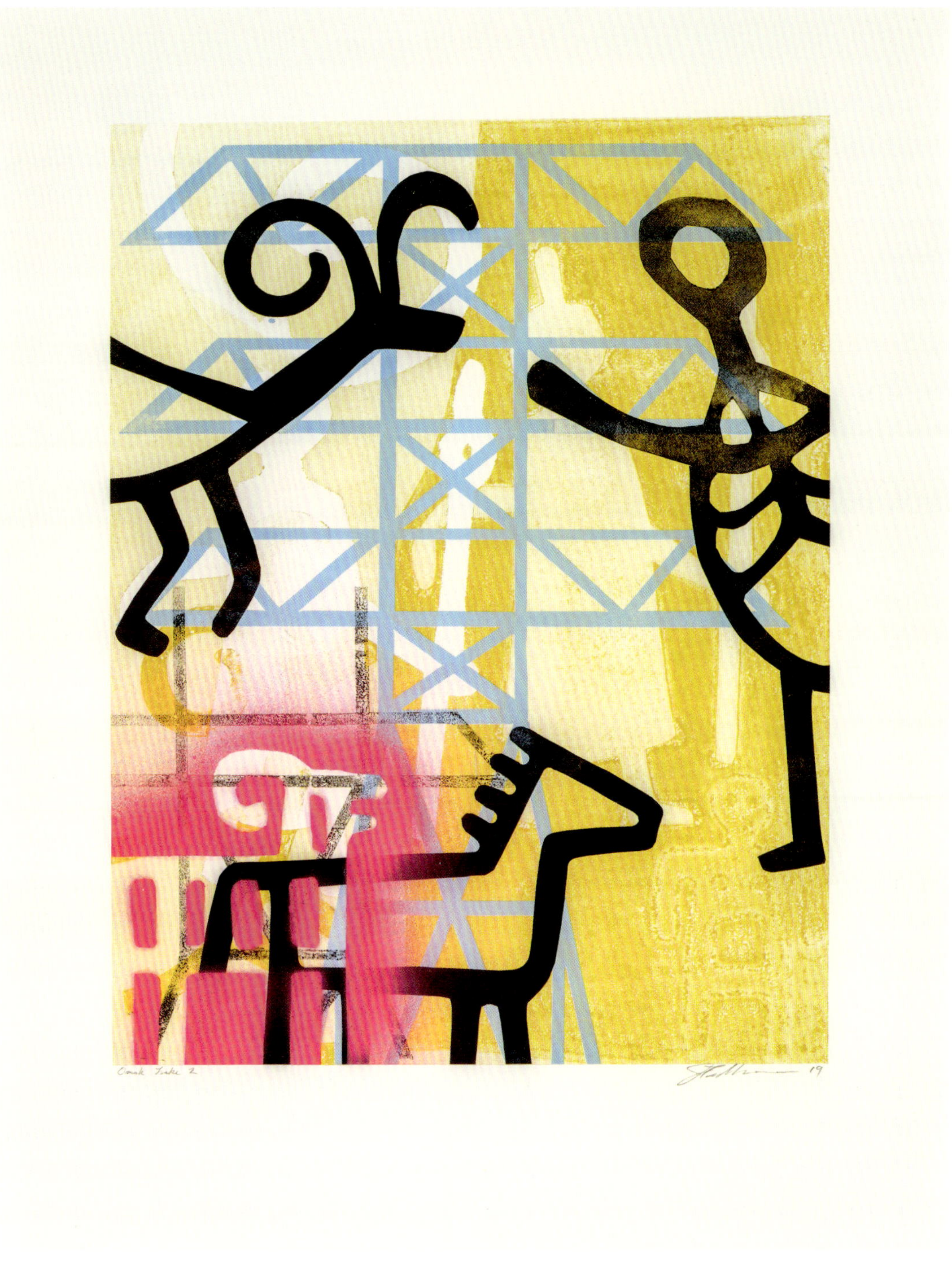

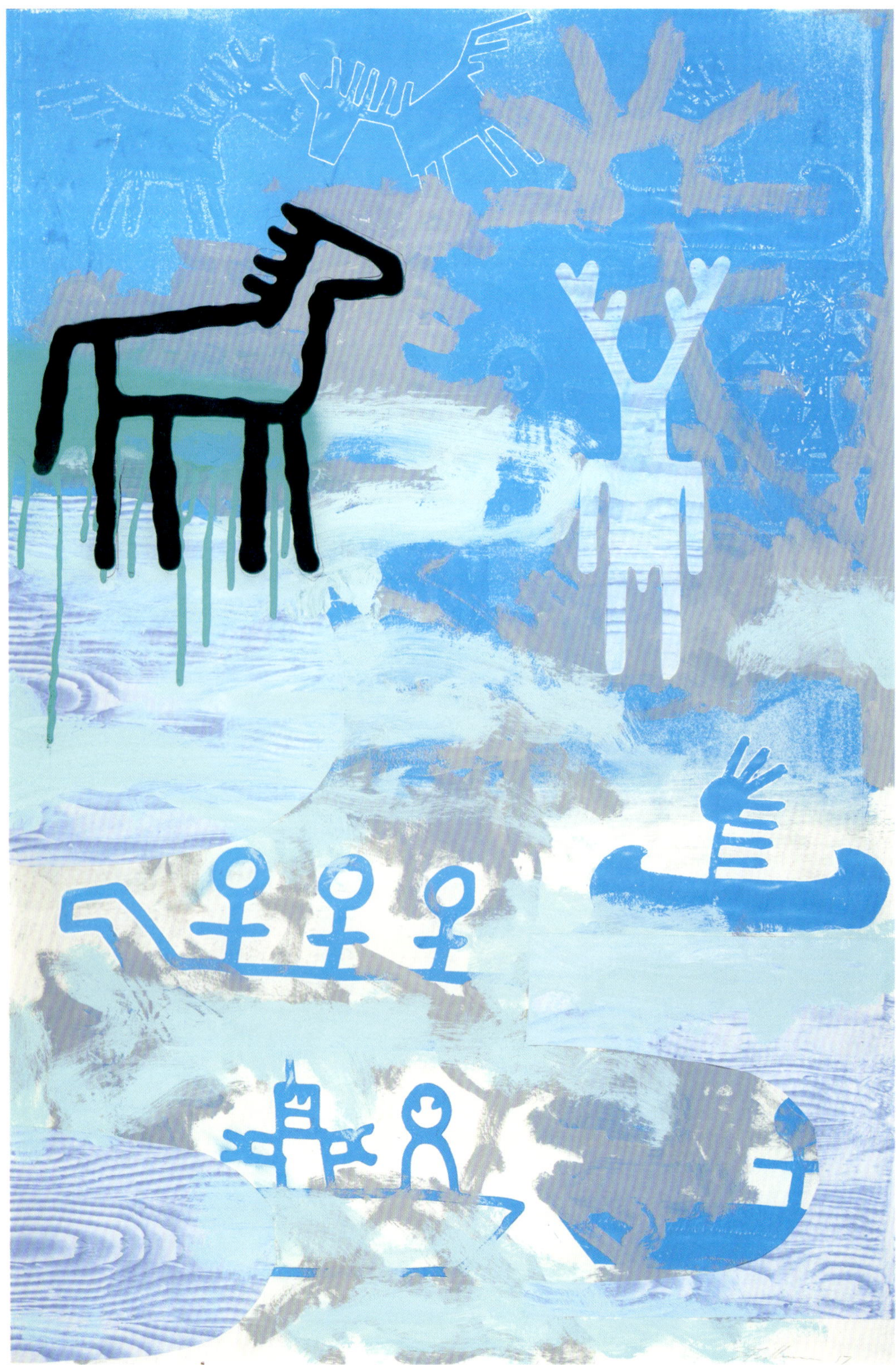

Plate 30
Vivid Day, 2017
Relief and stencil monoprint
with acrylic and collage
35½ × 23 in. (90.2 × 58.4 cm)

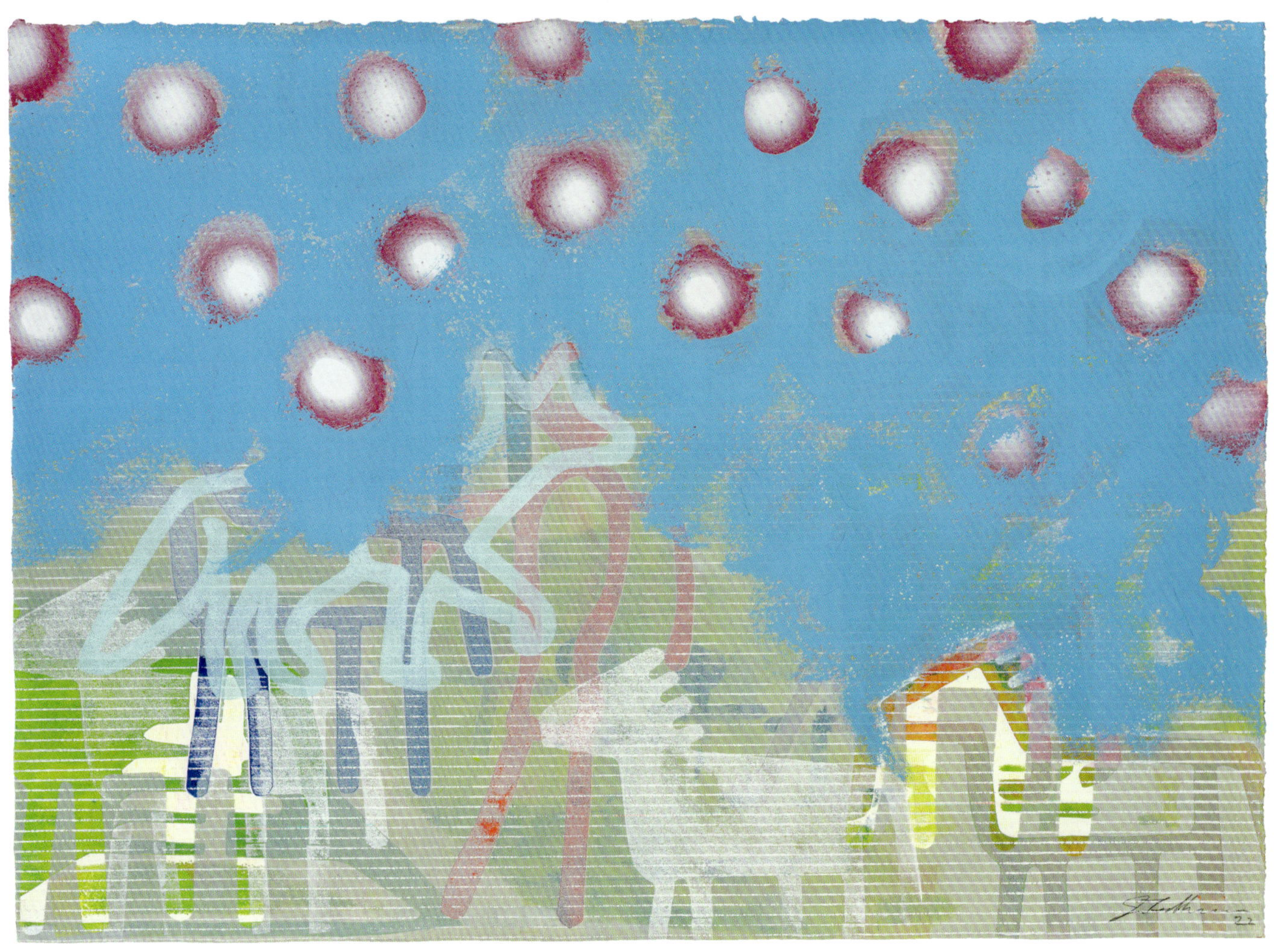

Plate 31
Snowing, 2022
Relief and stencil monoprint
with acrylic
22 × 29½ in. (55.9 × 74.9 cm)

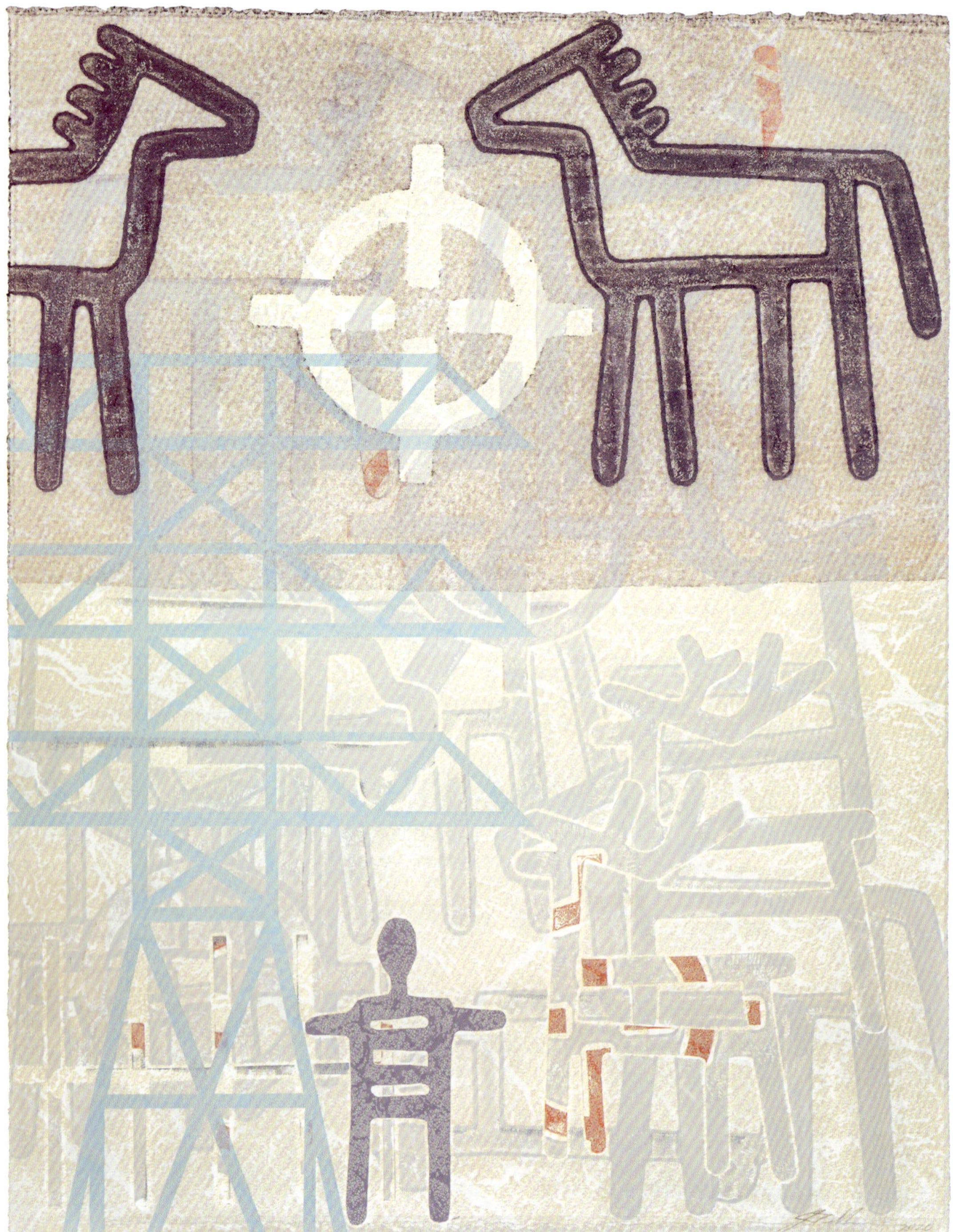

Plate 32
Inhabited Landscapes 2, 2020
Collagraph, relief, and stencil monoprint
26 × 20 in.
(66 × 50.8 cm)

Plate 33
Inhabited Landscapes 10, 2020
Collagraph, relief, and stencil monoprint
26 × 20 in.
(66 × 50.8 cm)

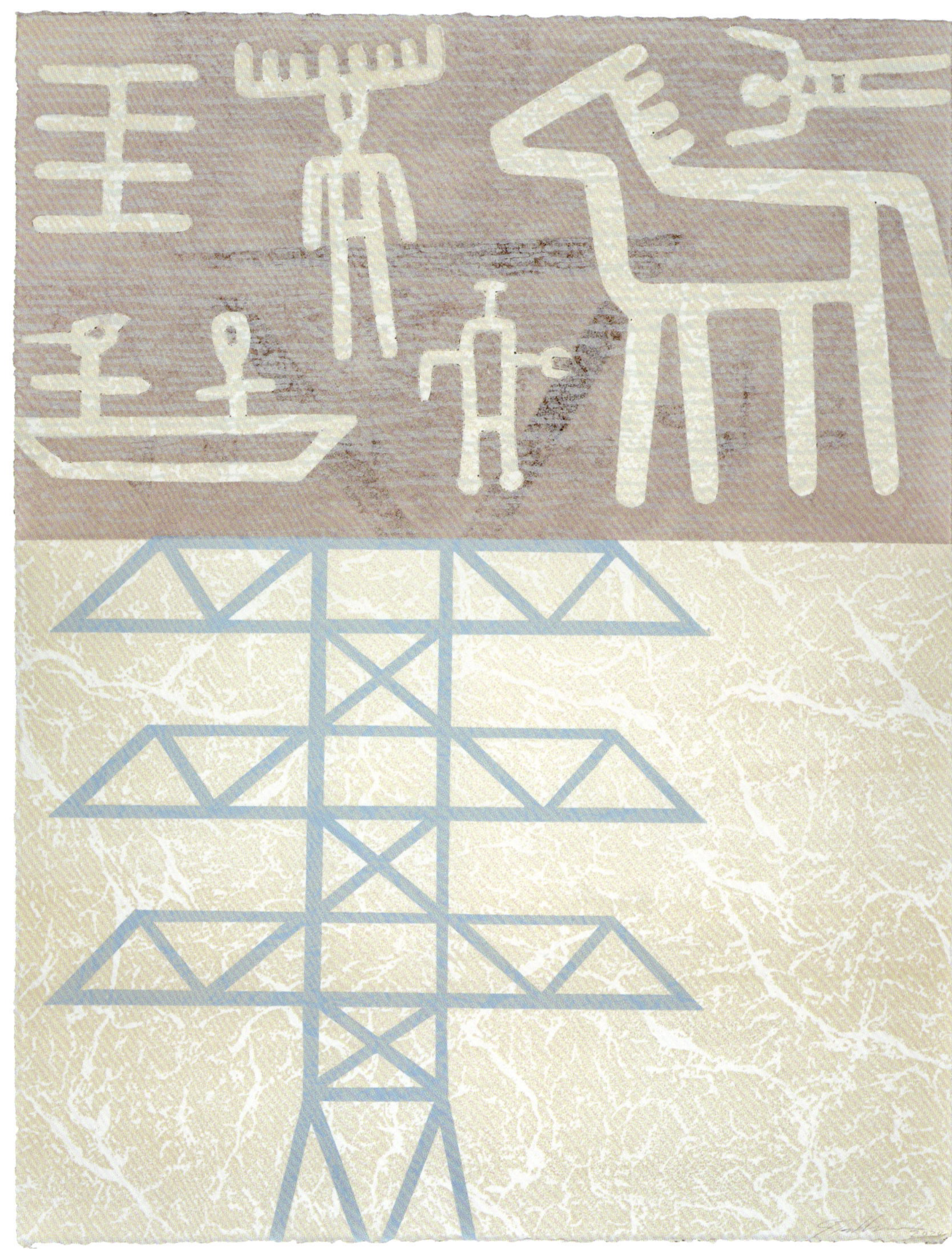

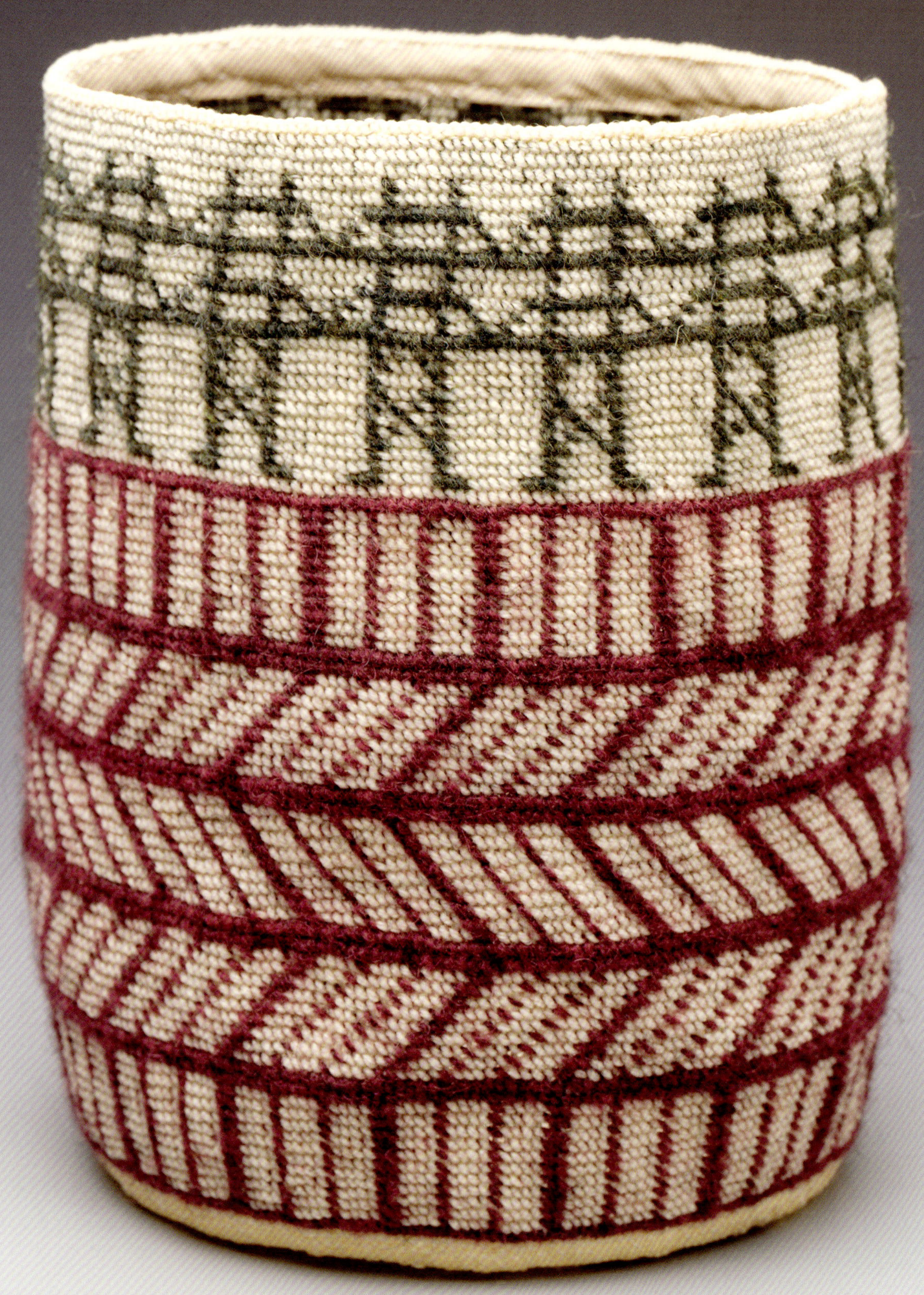

Plate 34
Eagle with High Voltage Towers, 2018
Waxed linen, wool, bias tape, and thread
6½ × 4 × 4 in.
(16.5 × 10.2 × 10.2 cm)

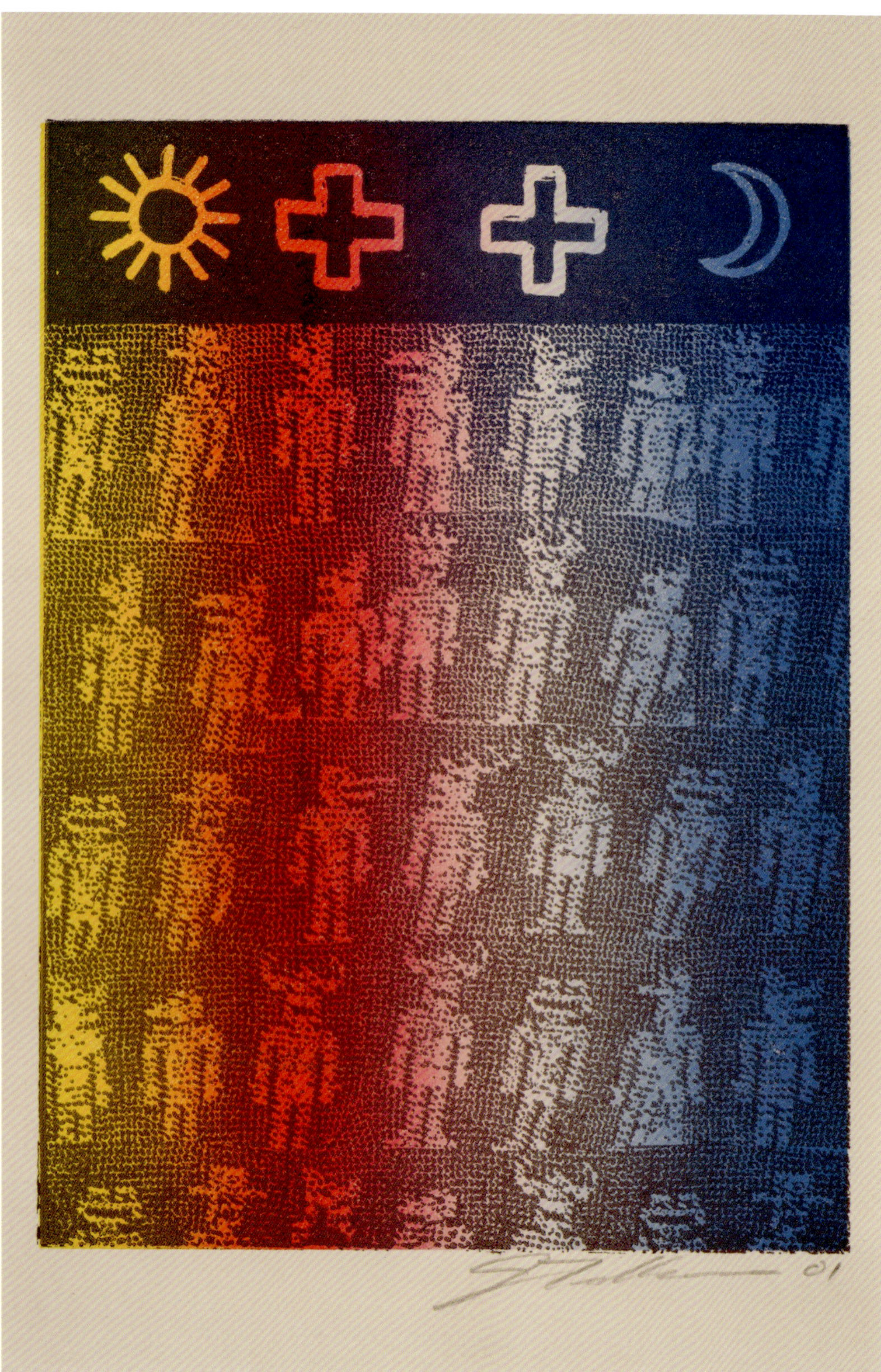

Plate 35
Untitled, 2001
Relief print
Sheet: 9 × 5½ in.
(22.9 × 14 cm);
image: 7 × 5 in.
(17.8 × 12.7 cm)

Plate 36
Okanogan Bestiary, 2023
Waxed linen, bias tape,
thread, and wool yarn
8 × 8½ × 8½ in.
(20.3 × 21.6 × 21.6 cm)

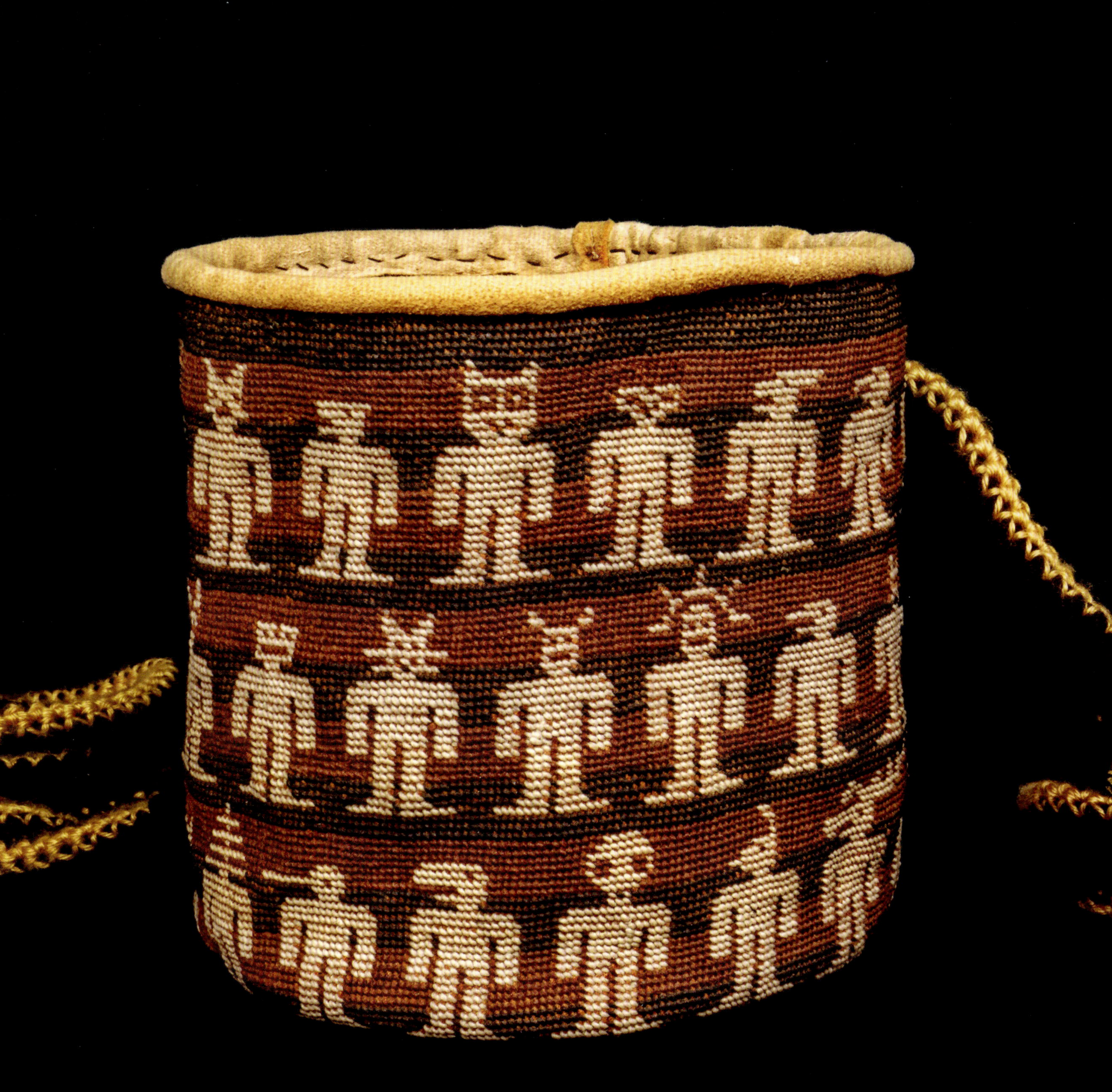

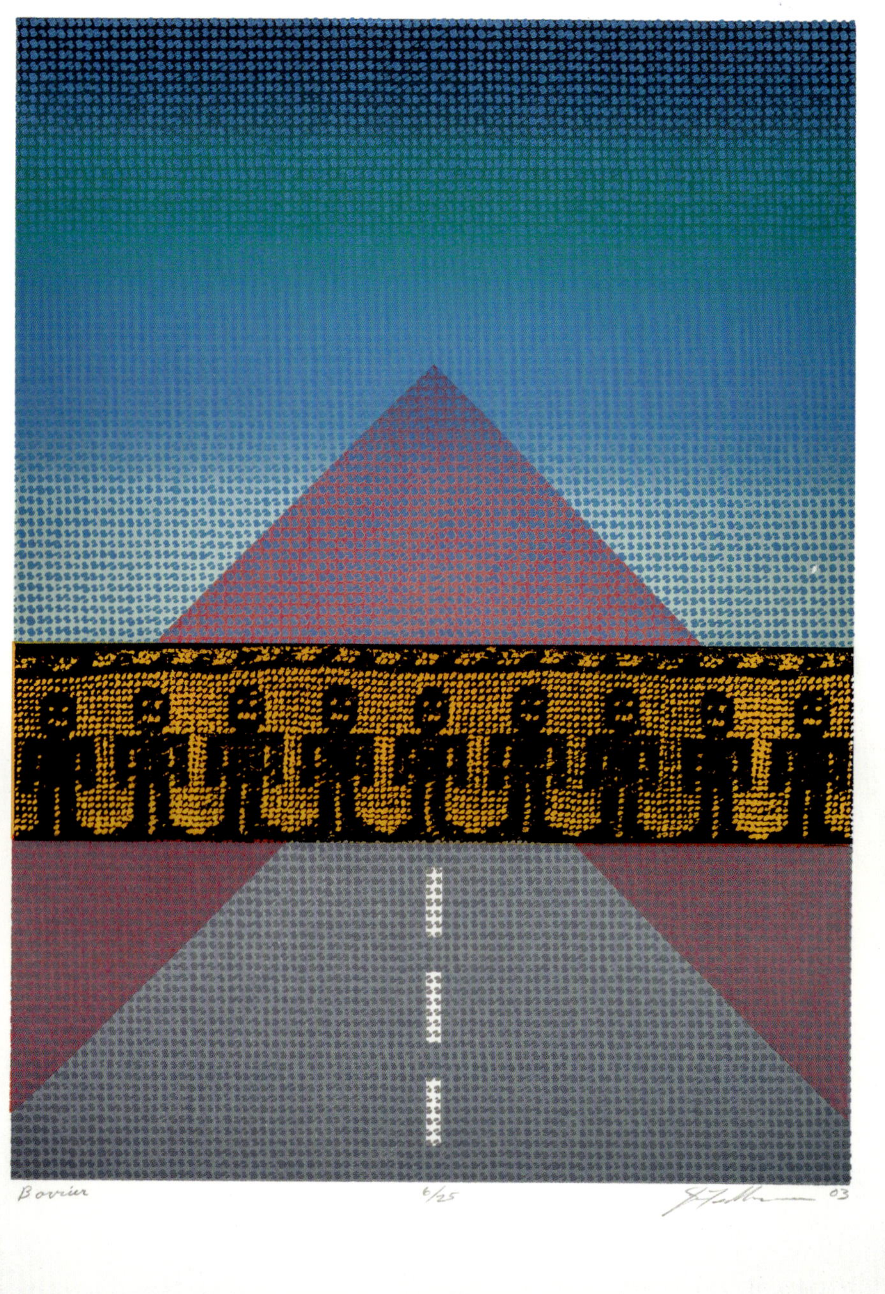

Plate 37
Barrier, 2003
Screenprint
Sheet: 20 × 15 in.
(50.8 × 38.1 cm);
image: 16½ × 12 in.
(41.9 × 30.5 cm)

Plate 38
Canoe Journey, 2021
Waxed linen, bias tape,
and thread
7 × 5 × 5 in.
(17.8 × 12.7 × 12.7 cm)

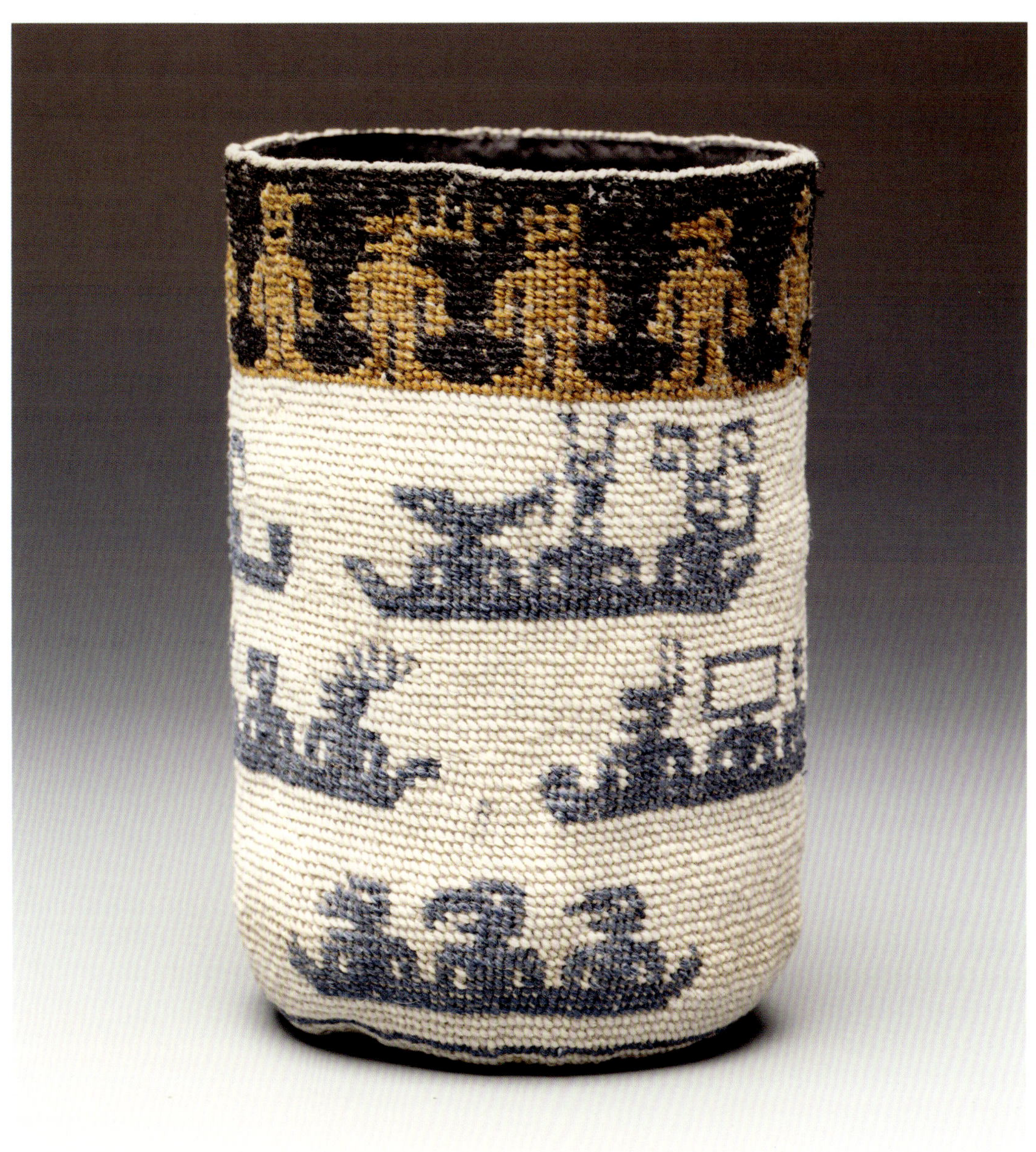

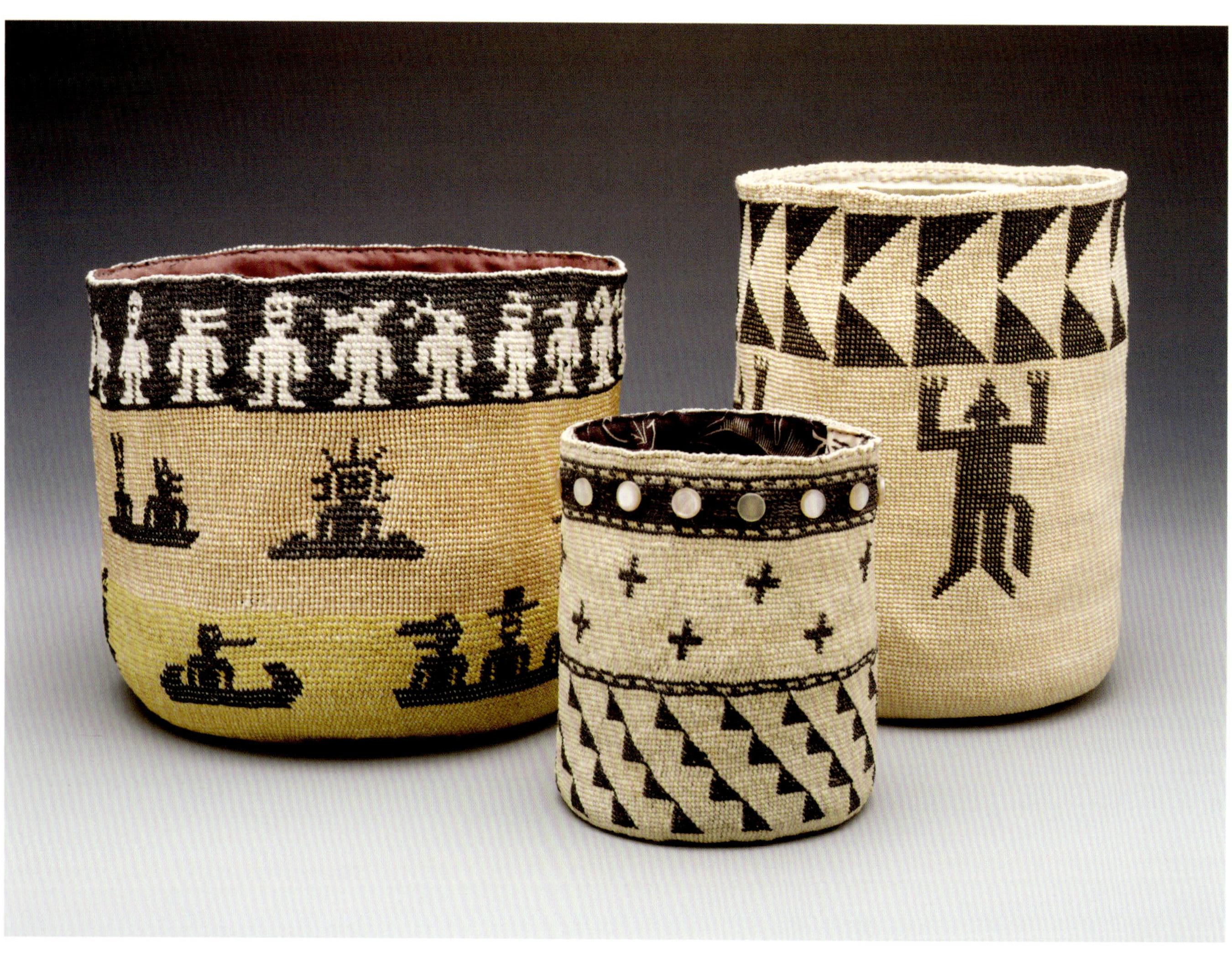

Plate 39 (left to right)

Canoe Journey, 2018
Waxed linen, bias tape, and thread
7 × 10 × 10 in.
(17.8 × 25.4 × 25.4 cm)

Stairs and Stars, about 1995
Waxed linen, fabric, mother-of-pearl buttons, and thread
6 × 4½ × 4½ in.
(15.2 × 11.4 × 11.4 cm)

Coyote and Flying Geese, 2014
Waxed linen, bias tape, and thread
9½ × 7 × 7 in.
(24.1 × 17.8 × 17.8 cm)

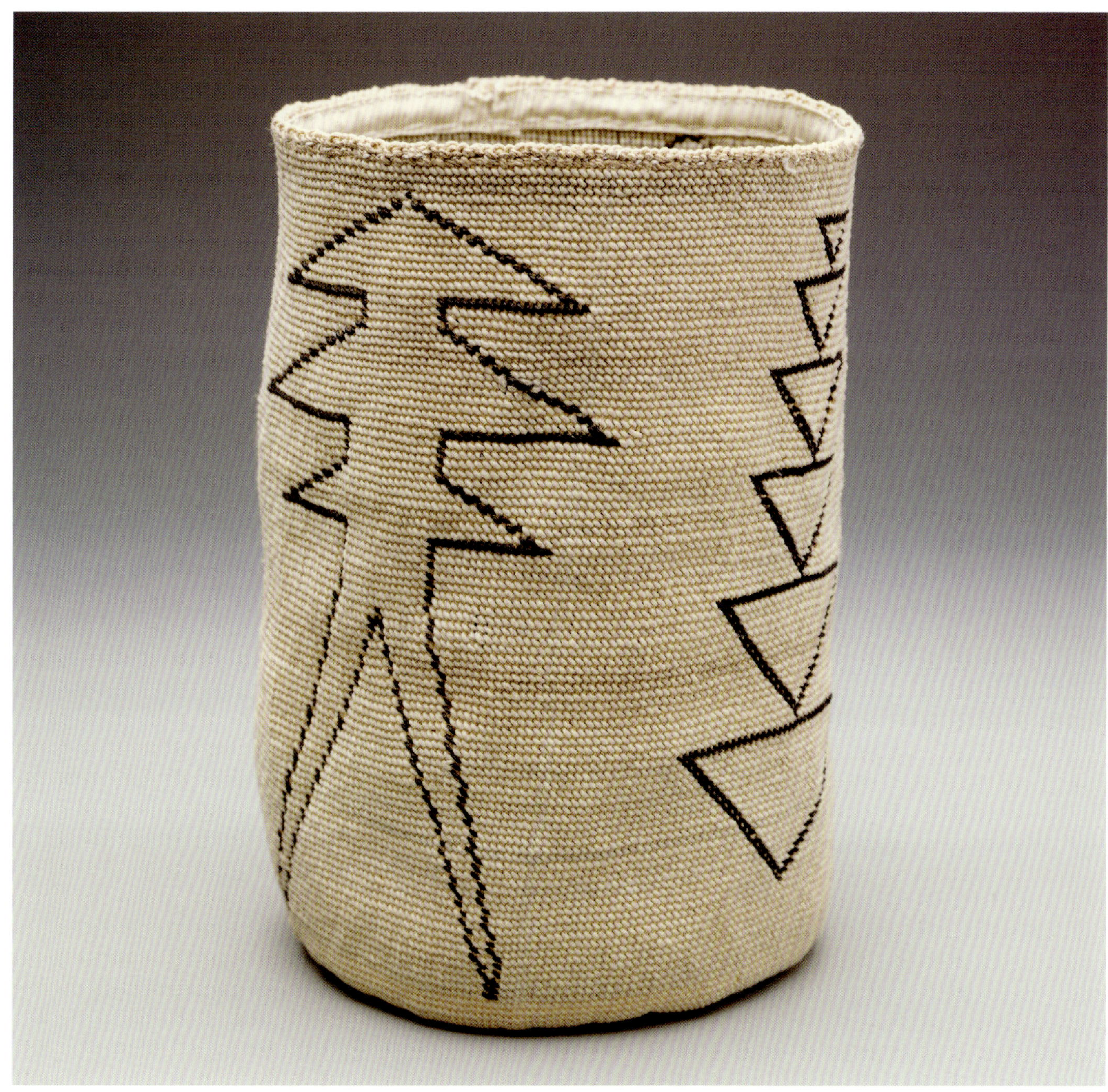

Plate 40
Omak, 2012
Waxed linen, bias tape,
and thread
9 × 6 × 6 in.
(22.9 × 15.2 × 15.2 cm)

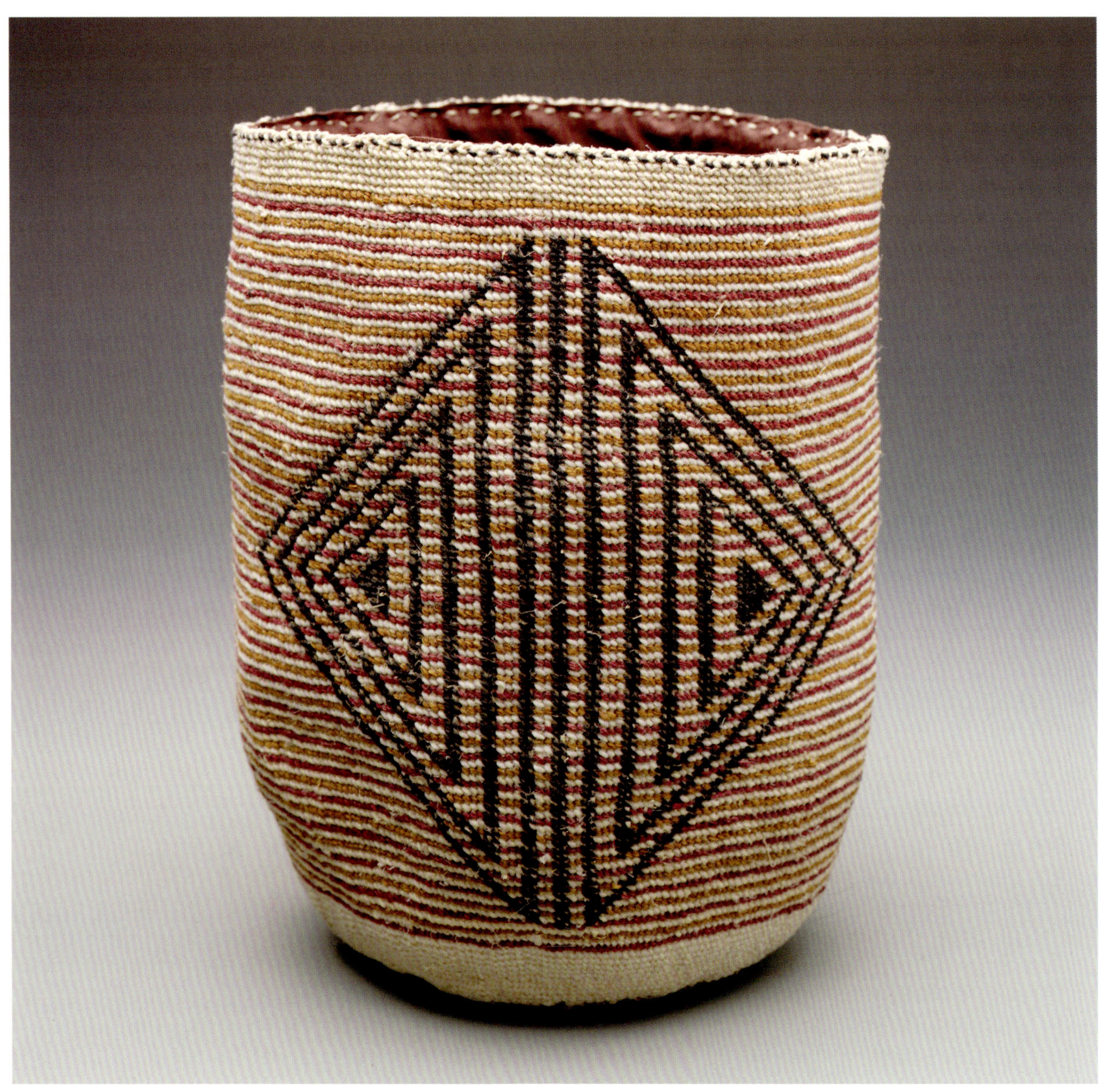

Plate 41
Elevator, 2022
Waxed linen, bias tape, and thread
9½ × 6 × 6 in.
(24.1 × 15.2 × 15.2 cm)

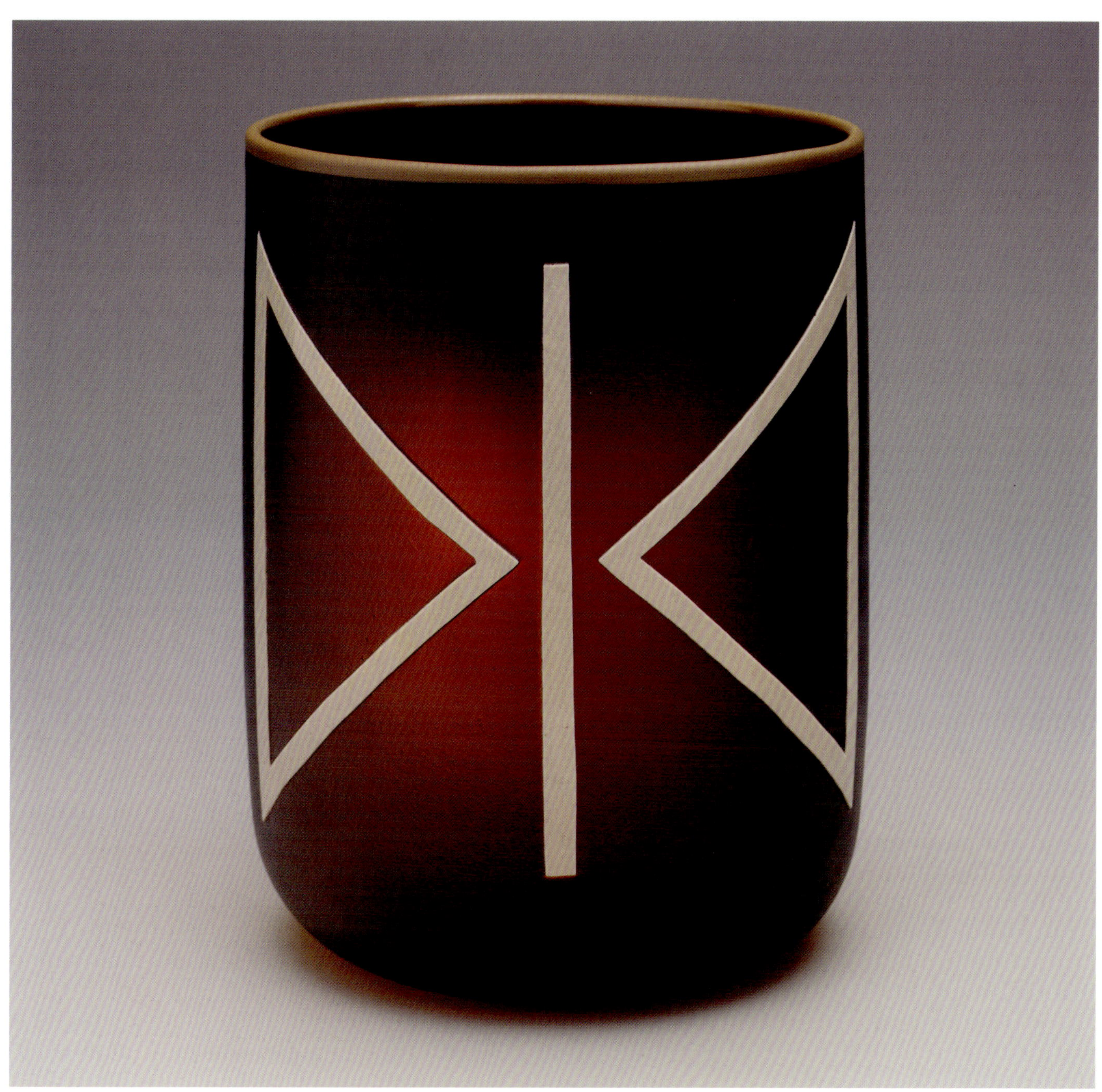

Plate 42
Elevator, 2022
Sandblasted blown glass
9 × 6½ × 6½ in.
(22.9 × 16.5 × 16.5 cm)

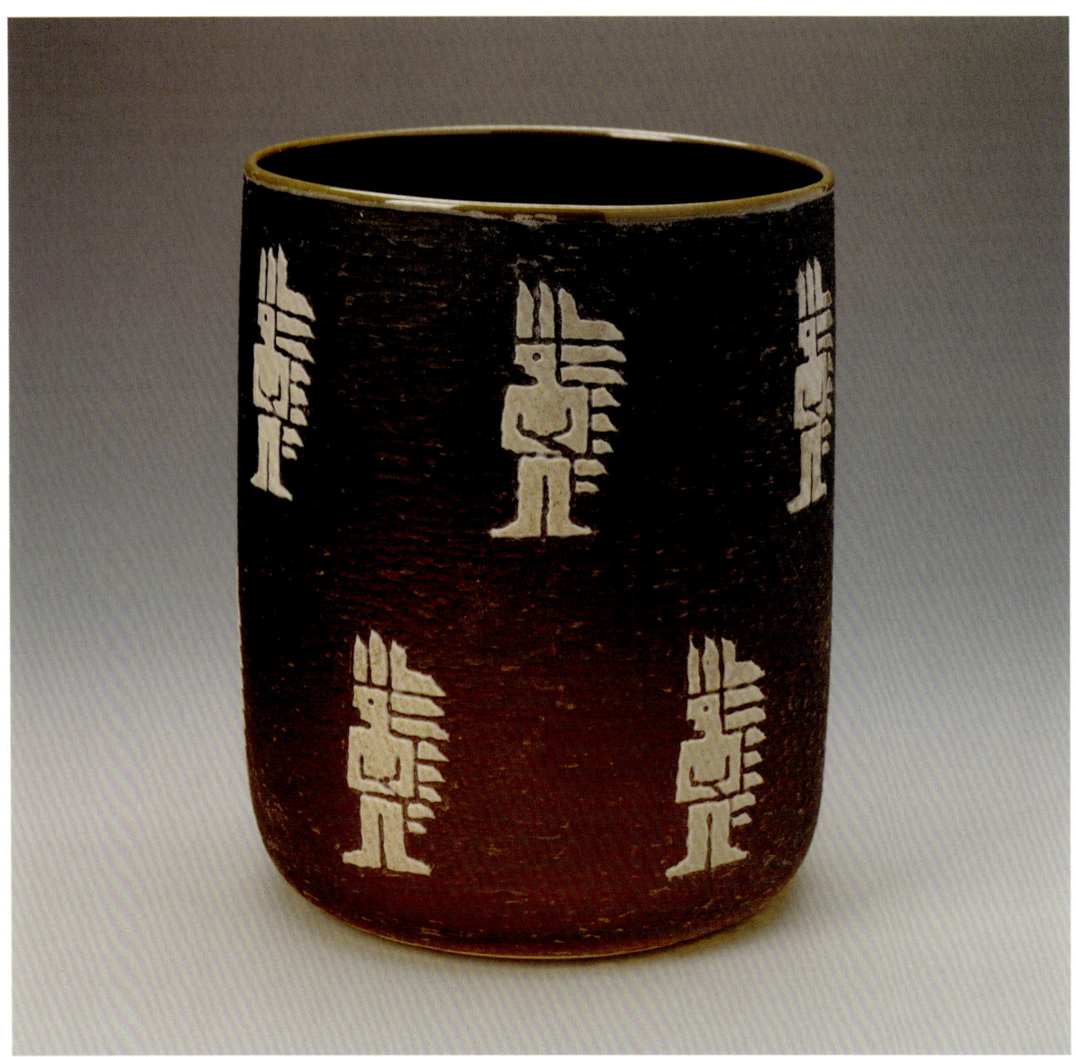

Plate 43
All Chiefs, 2014
Hand-engraved blown glass
9 × 7 × 7 in.
(22.9 × 17.8 × 17.8 cm)

Plate 44
Clear-cut II, 2009
Sandblasted blown glass
19½ × 8 × 8 in.
(49.5 × 20.3 × 20.3 cm)

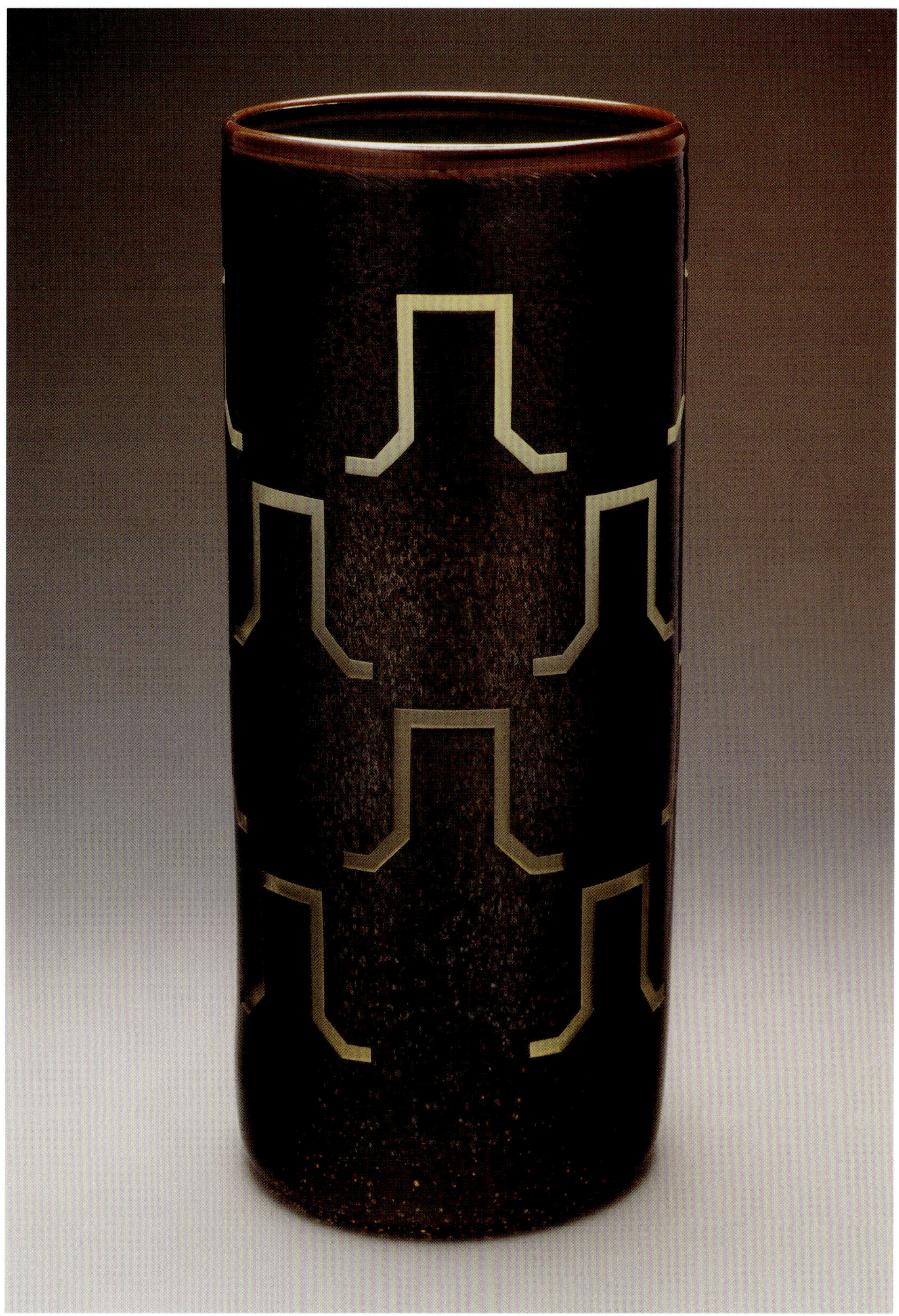

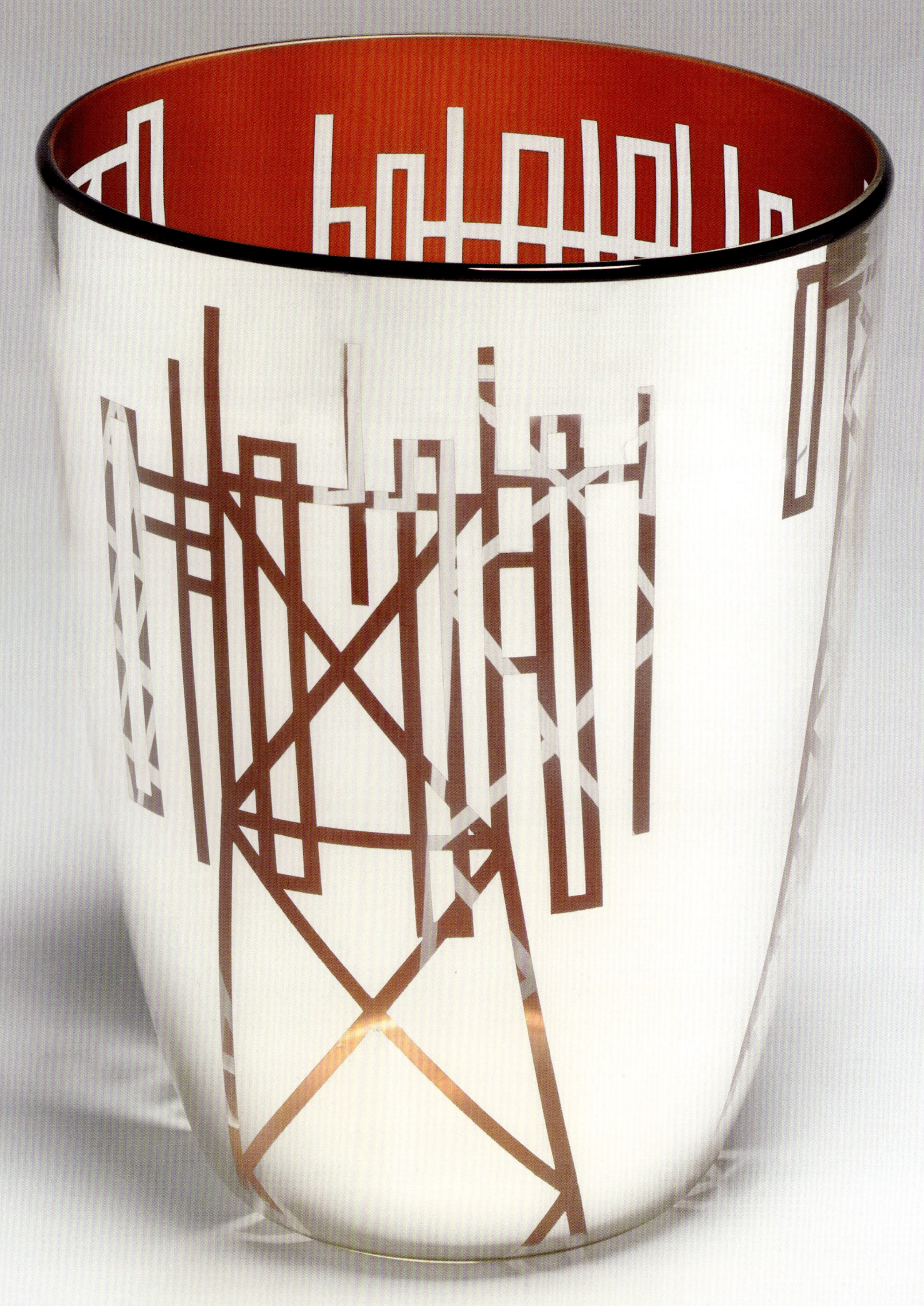

Plate 45
Urban Vernacular: Communication Towers, 2008
Blown glass with silver mirroring and copper enamel
18½ × 14 × 14 in.
(47 × 35.6 × 35.6 cm)

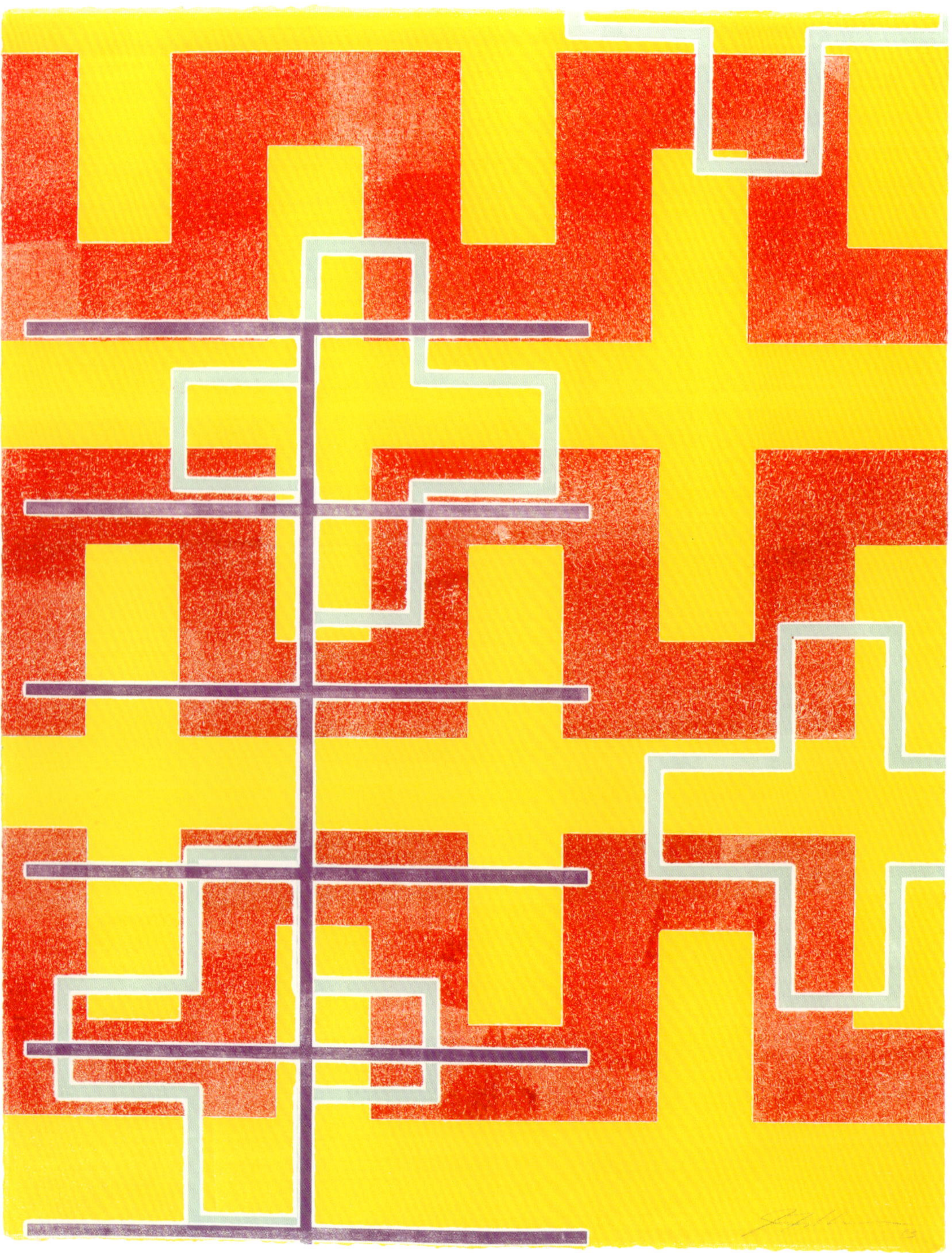

Plate 46
Palouse Series, 2003
Relief and stencil
monoprint
26 × 20 in. (66 × 51 cm)

Plate 47
Chain Link, 2003
Sandblasted blown glass
16½ × 12½ × 12½ in.
(41.9 × 31.8 × 31.8 cm)

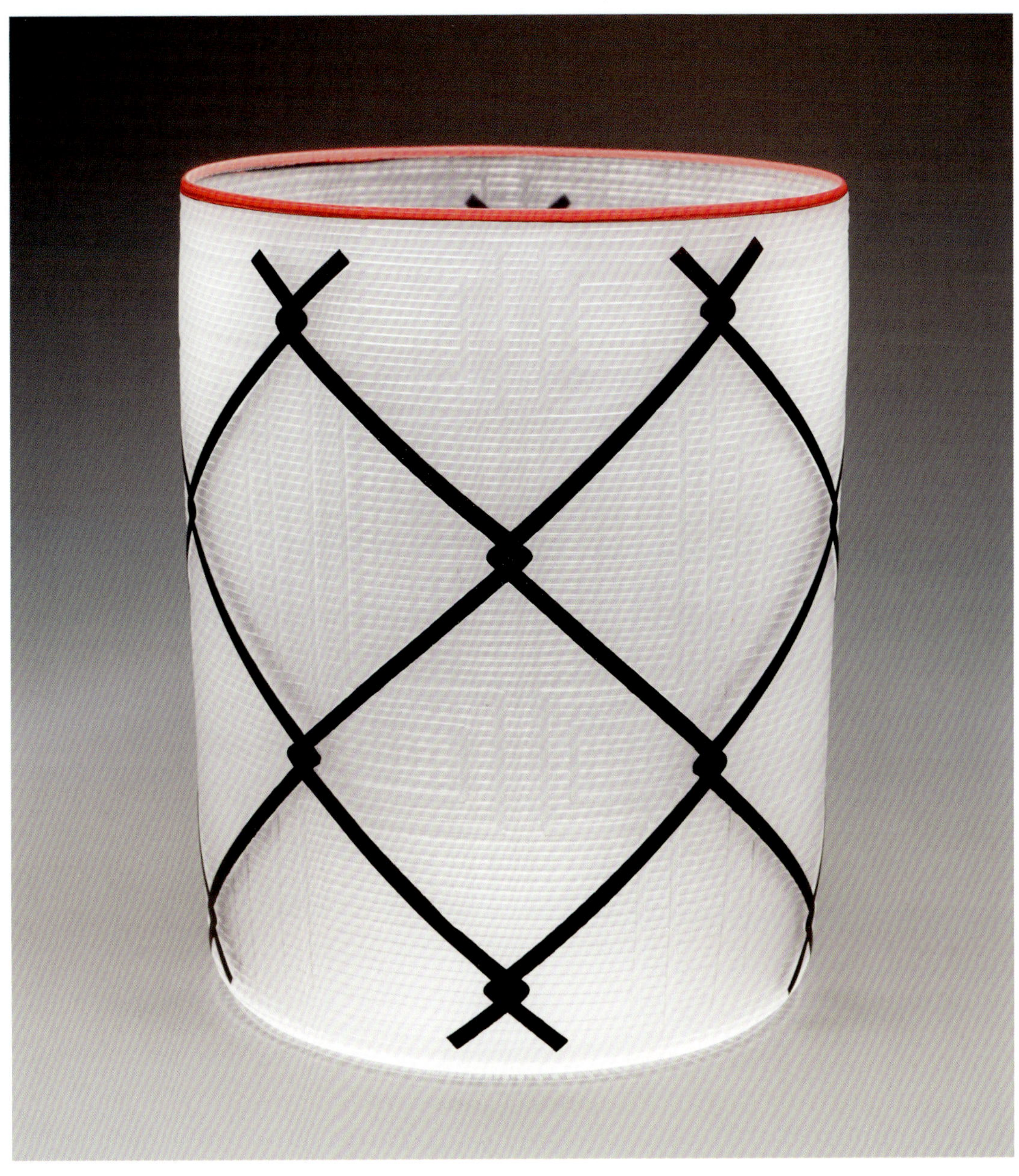

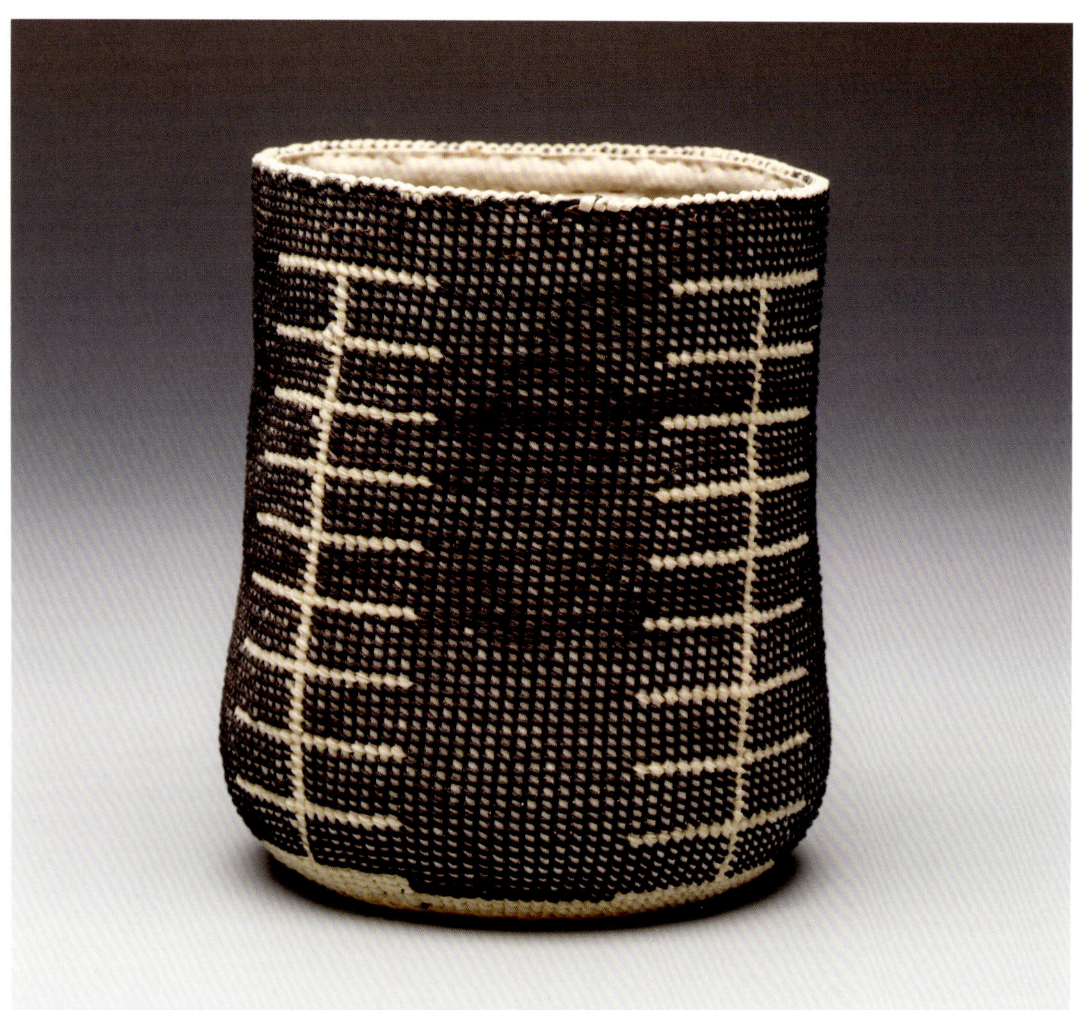

Plate 48
Parking Lot, from the *Urban Indian* series, 2002
Waxed linen, bias tape, and thread
6 × 4½ × 4½ in.
(15.2 × 11.4 × 11.4 cm)

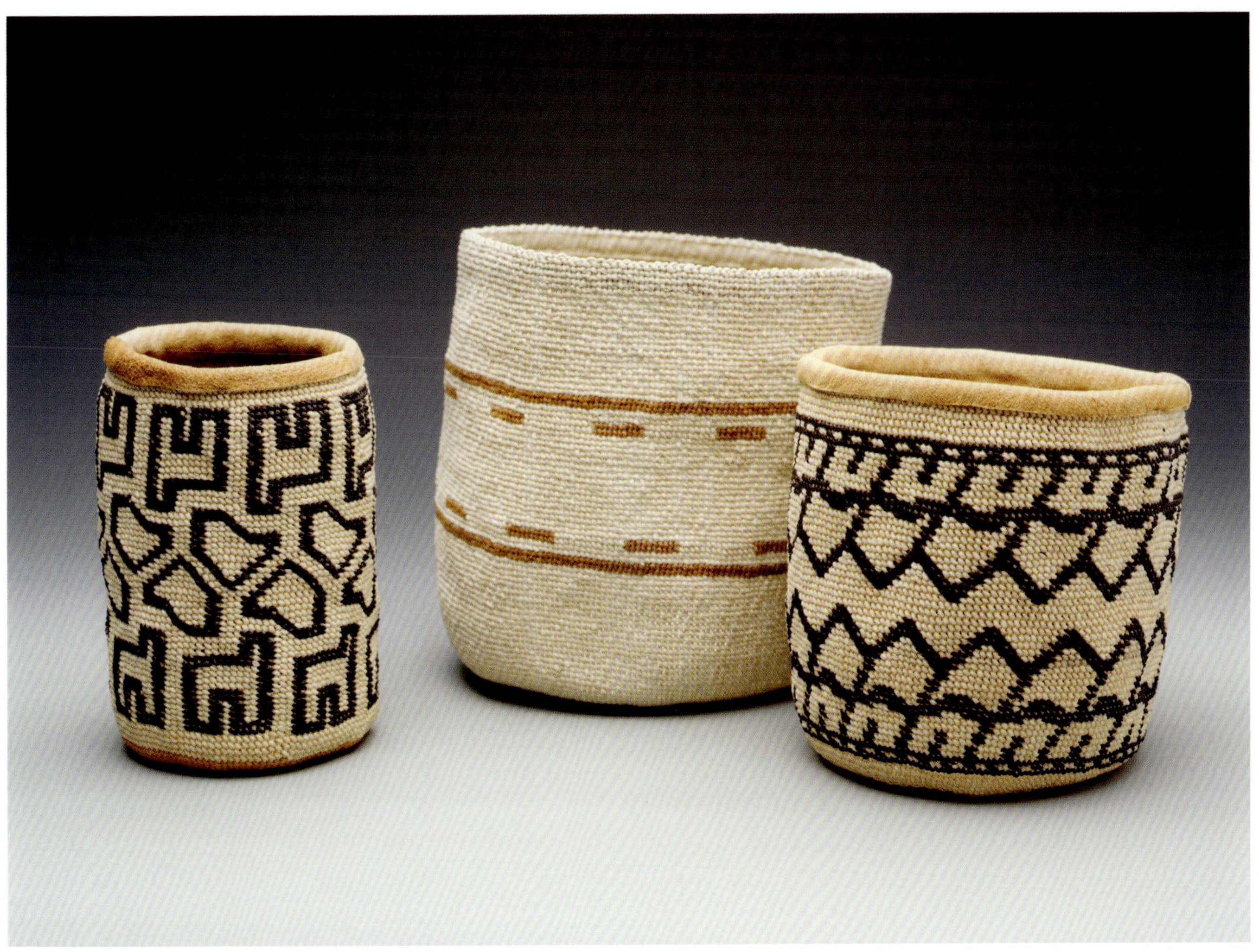

Plate 49 (left to right)
Wild Cat, 2009
Waxed linen and brain-tanned deer hide
6½ × 4 × 4 in.
(16.5 × 10.2 × 10.2 cm)

Turn Lane, 2018
Waxed linen, bias tape, and thread
8 × 7 × 7 in.
(20.3 × 17.8 × 17.8 cm)

Wintermaster Plus, 2012
Waxed linen and brain-tanned deer hide
6 × 6 × 6 in.
(15.2 × 15.2 × 15.2 cm)

Twanat

Blue Moonlight in swooped clouds thin to dark expanses as gliding eagles mate at crosses of upward elliptical loops. Beating pulses synchronize heartbeats among the tule reed longhouses.

An old wound in the land healed over years of corruption and charging horse soldiers. The children ran over the embankment. No alarm more frantic than pounding hooves and the silence on the lifting of spirits and cracking bones. The valley courses with Nee Mee Poo souls.

At times one hears music in the leaves. It's light as in illumination. Light as rapture. Run off torrents with moonlight. Exhale. Breathe deep, organ pipes moan under the ribs from church. The ancestors sing despite conversion.

This is not one voice but the beginning of all voices in unison. Yes, crescendo waves of spiral utterances of the Plateau canyons. The river returns pervasive with silver and red nusoox.

Elizabeth Woody – Warm Springs, Navajo

Elizabeth A. Woody, "Twanat," in *Terrain: Plateau Native Art & Poetry*, ed. Joe Feddersen, 2014

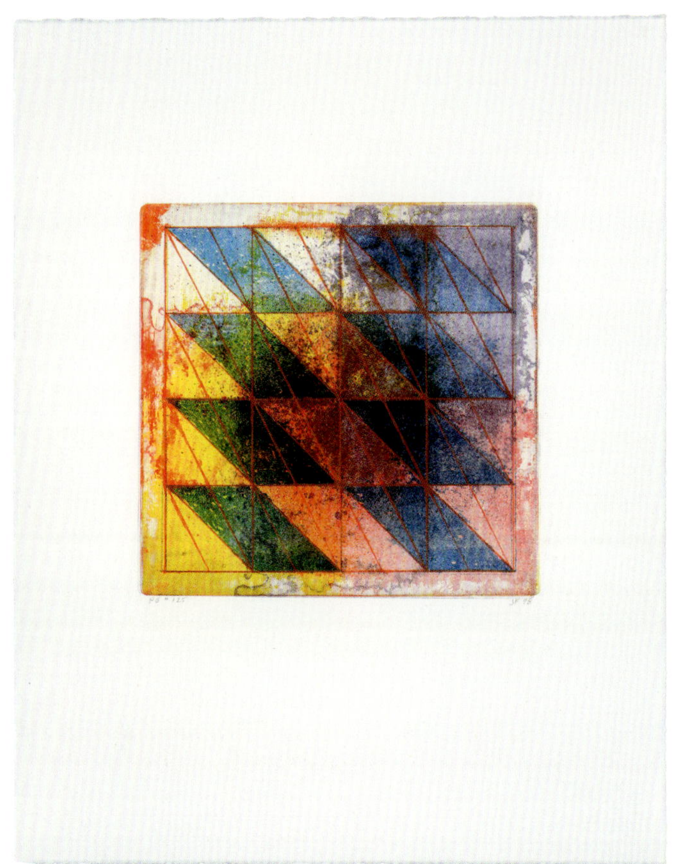

Plate 50
Plateau Geometrics #125, 1998
Siligraphy and drypoint monoprint
Sheet: 26 × 20 in. (66 × 50.8 cm);
image: 12 × 12 in. (30.5 × 30.5 cm)

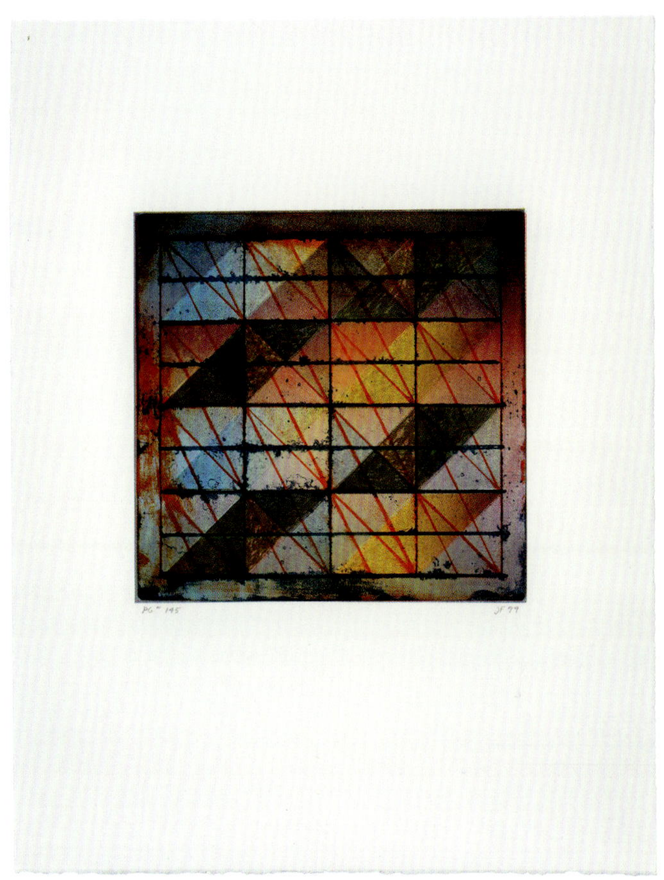

Plate 51
Plateau Geometrics #145, 1999
Siligraphy and relief monoprint
Sheet: 26 × 20 in. (66 × 50.8 cm);
image: 12 × 12 in. (30.5 × 30.5 cm)

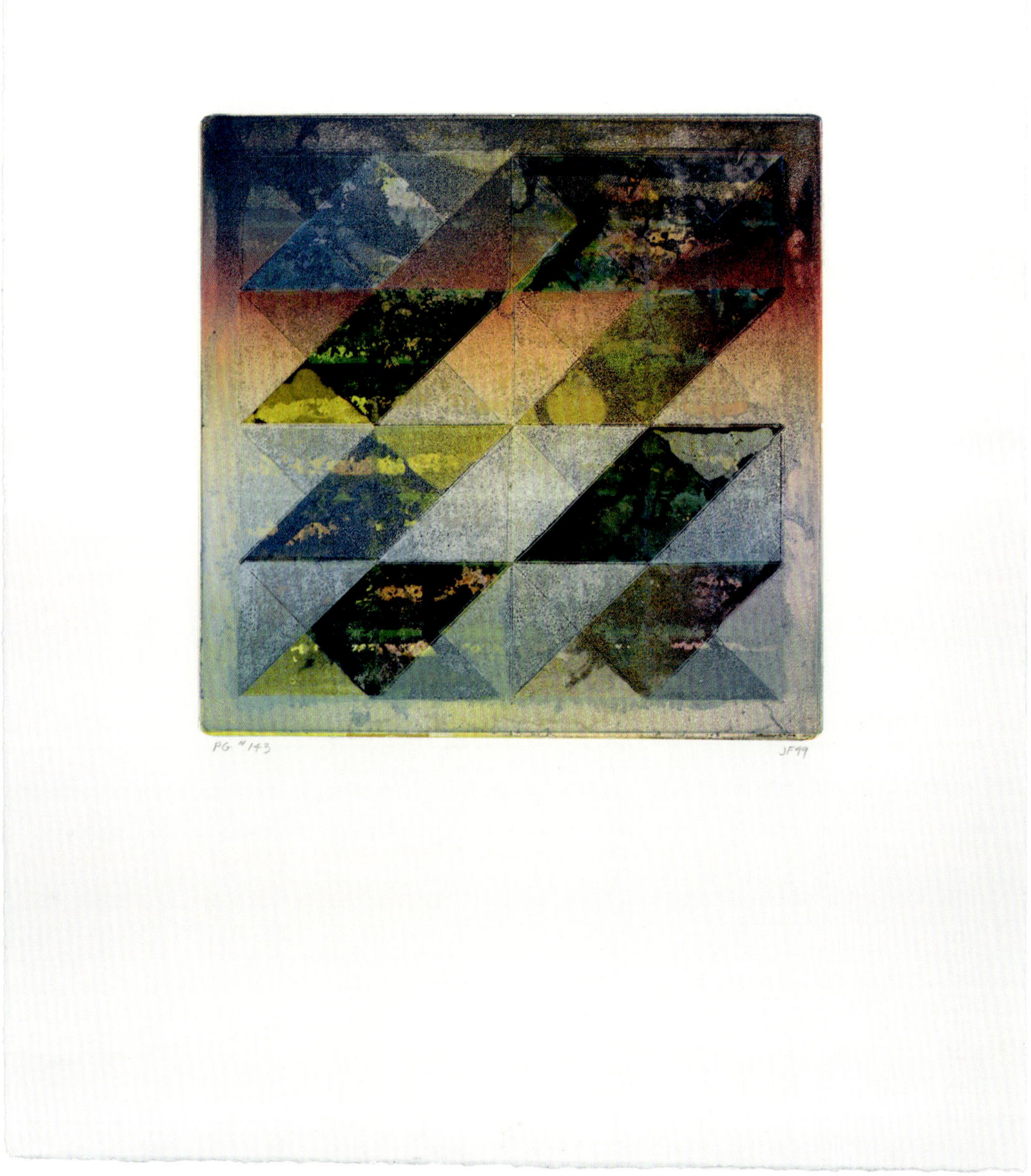

Plate 52
Plateau Geometrics #143, 1999
Siligraphy and relief monoprint
Sheet: 26 × 20 in. (66 × 50.8 cm); image: 12 × 12 in. (30.5 × 30.5 cm)

Plate 53
Plateau Geometrics #16, 1995
Aquatint and relief monoprint
Sheet: 26 × 20 in. (66 × 50.8 cm);
image: 12 × 12 in. (30.5 × 30.5 cm)

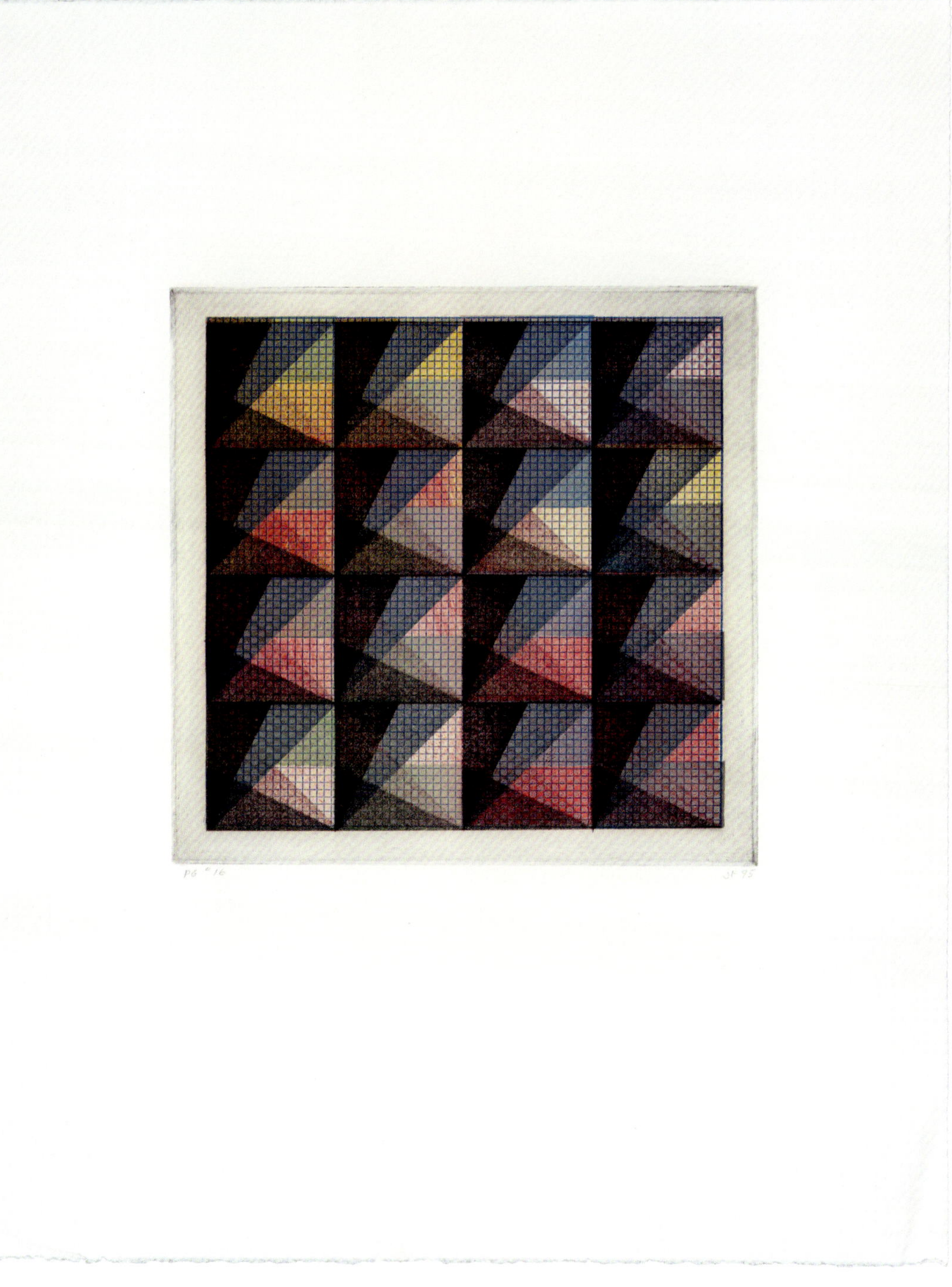

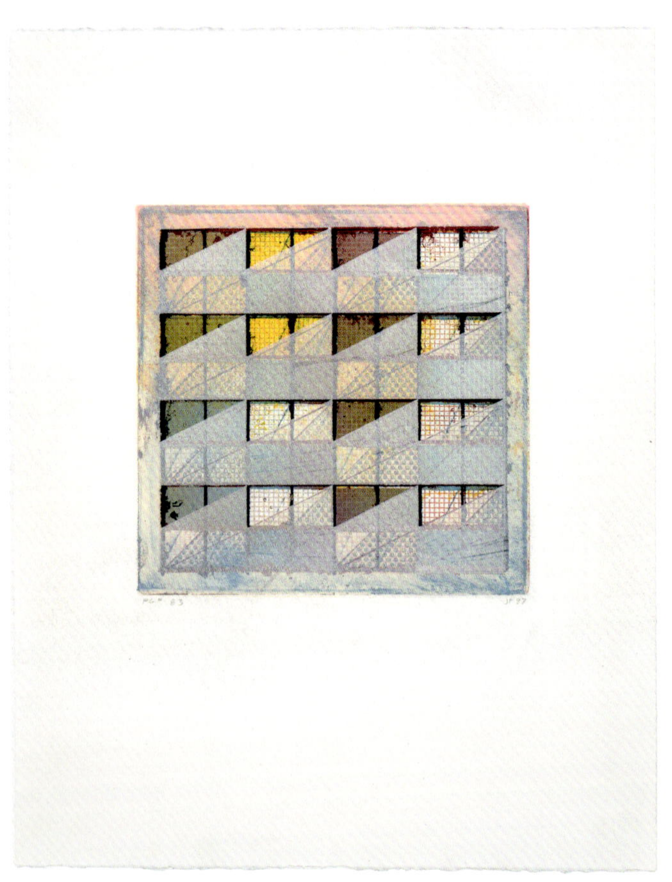

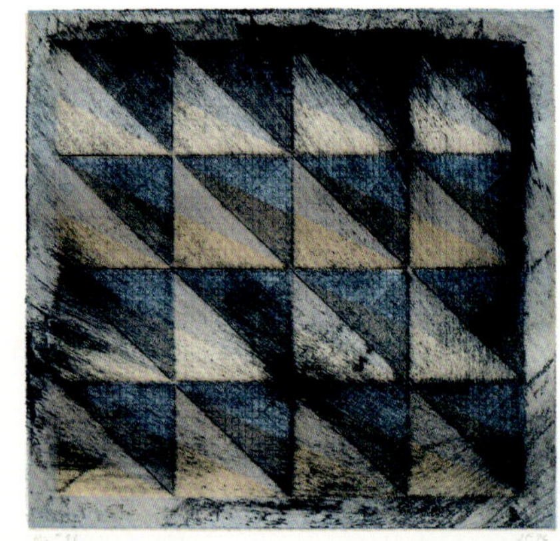

Plate 54
Plateau Geometrics #83, 1997
Siligraphy, drypoint, and relief monoprint with pearlescent powder
Sheet: 26 × 20 in. (66 × 50.8 cm); image: 12 × 12 in. (30.5 × 30.5 cm)

Plate 55
Plateau Geometrics #48, 1996
Intaglio and relief monoprint
Sheet: 26 × 20 in. (66 × 50.8 cm); image: 12 × 12 in. (30.5 × 30.5 cm)

Plate 56
Pin Wheel, 1998
Relief print
Sheet: 26 × 20 in.
(66 × 50.8 cm);
image: 12 × 12 in.
(30.5 × 30.5 cm)

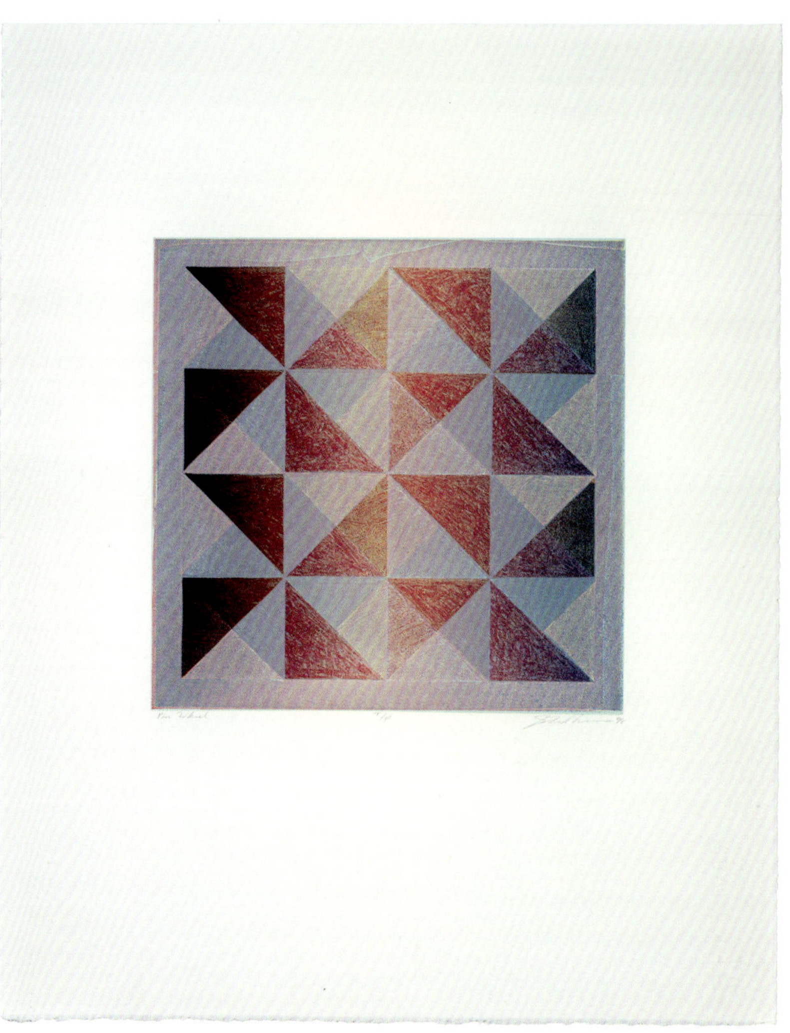

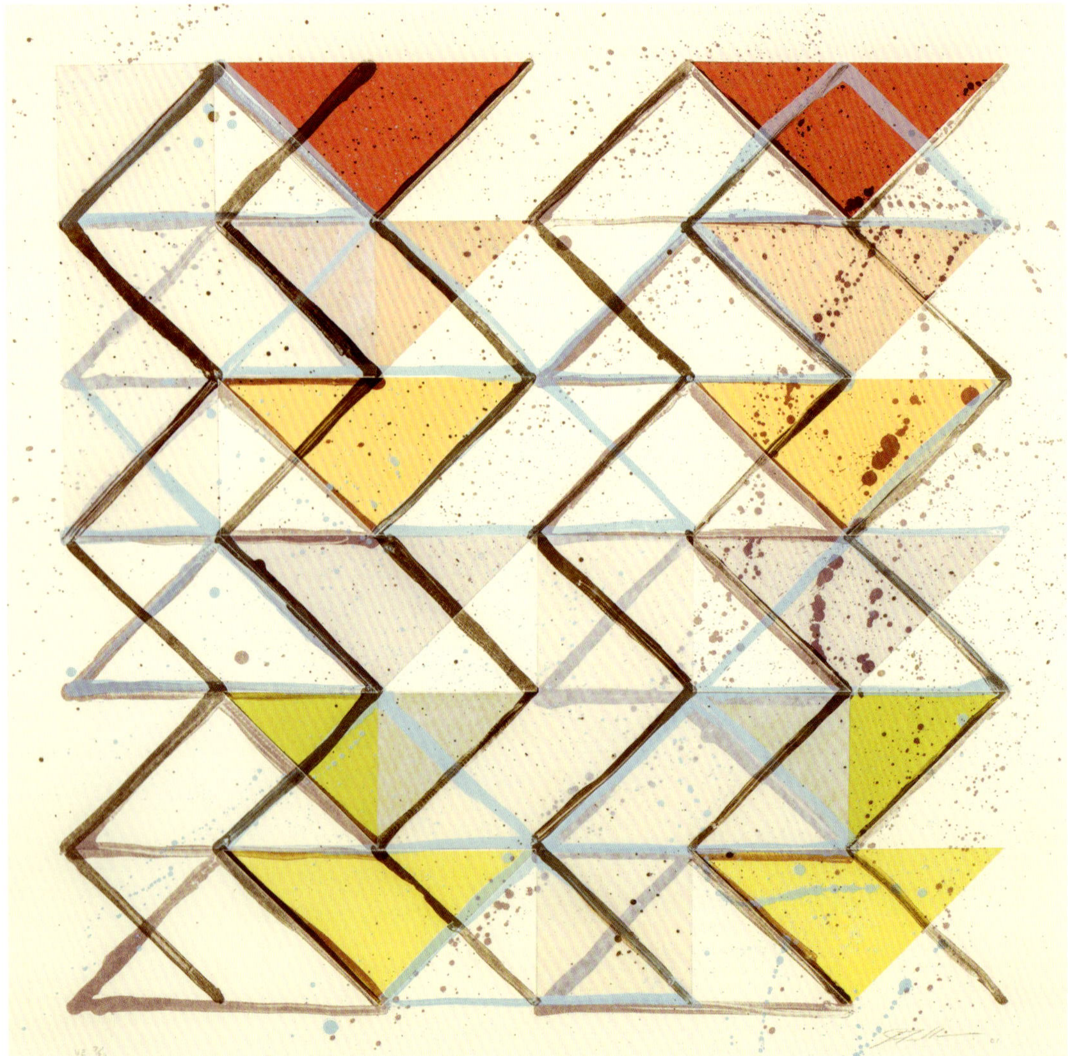

Plate 57
Interwoven Sign, 2001
Lithograph with chine collé
30 × 30 in. (76.2 × 76.2 cm)

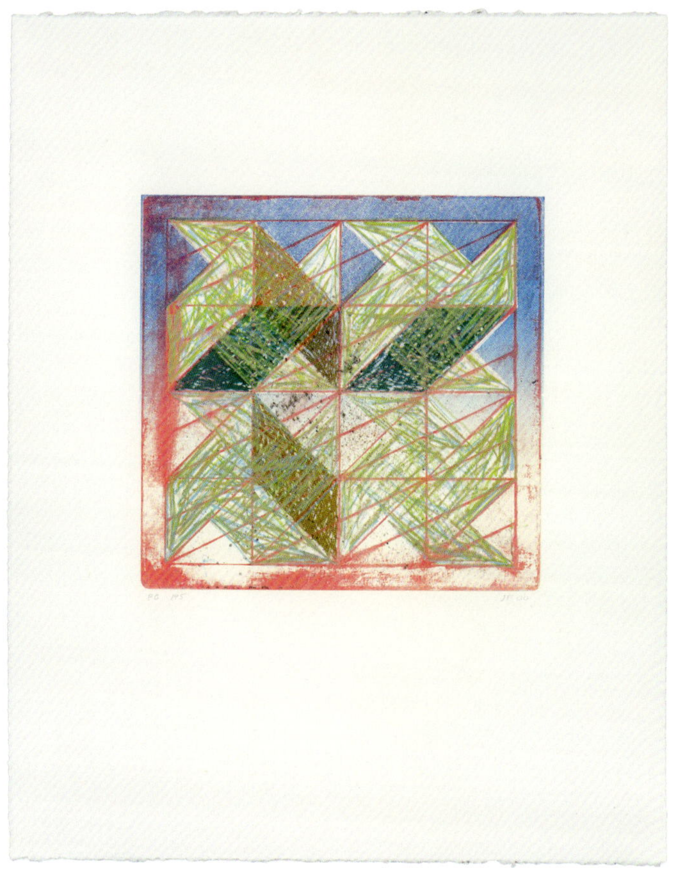

Plate 58
Plateau Geometrics #195, 2000
Siligraphy and relief monoprint
Sheet: 26 × 20 in. (66 × 50.8 cm);
image: 12 × 12 in. (30.5 × 30.5 cm)

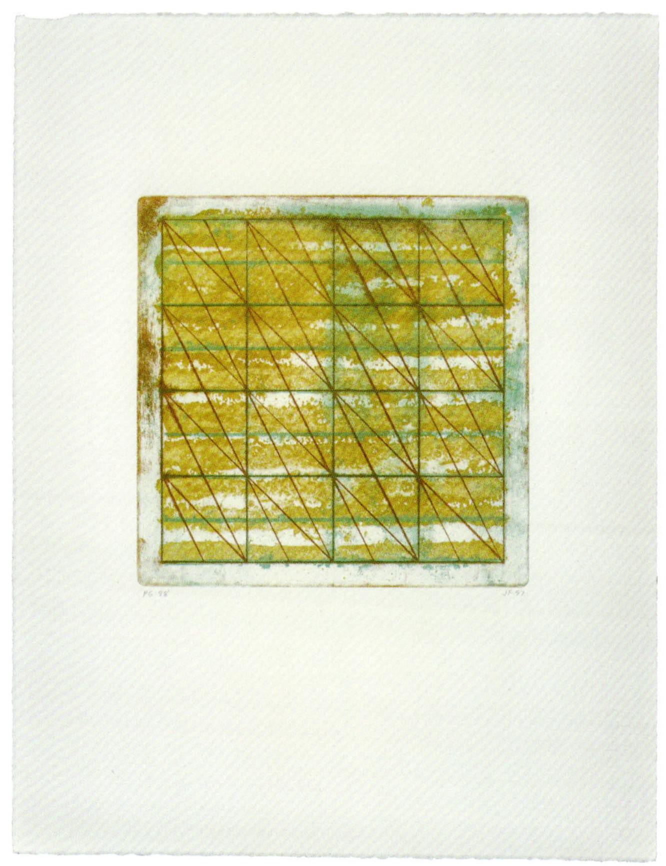

Plate 59
Plateau Geometrics #98, 1997
Siligraphy monoprint
Sheet: 26 × 20 in. (66 × 50.8 cm);
image: 12 × 12 in. (30.5 × 30.5 cm)

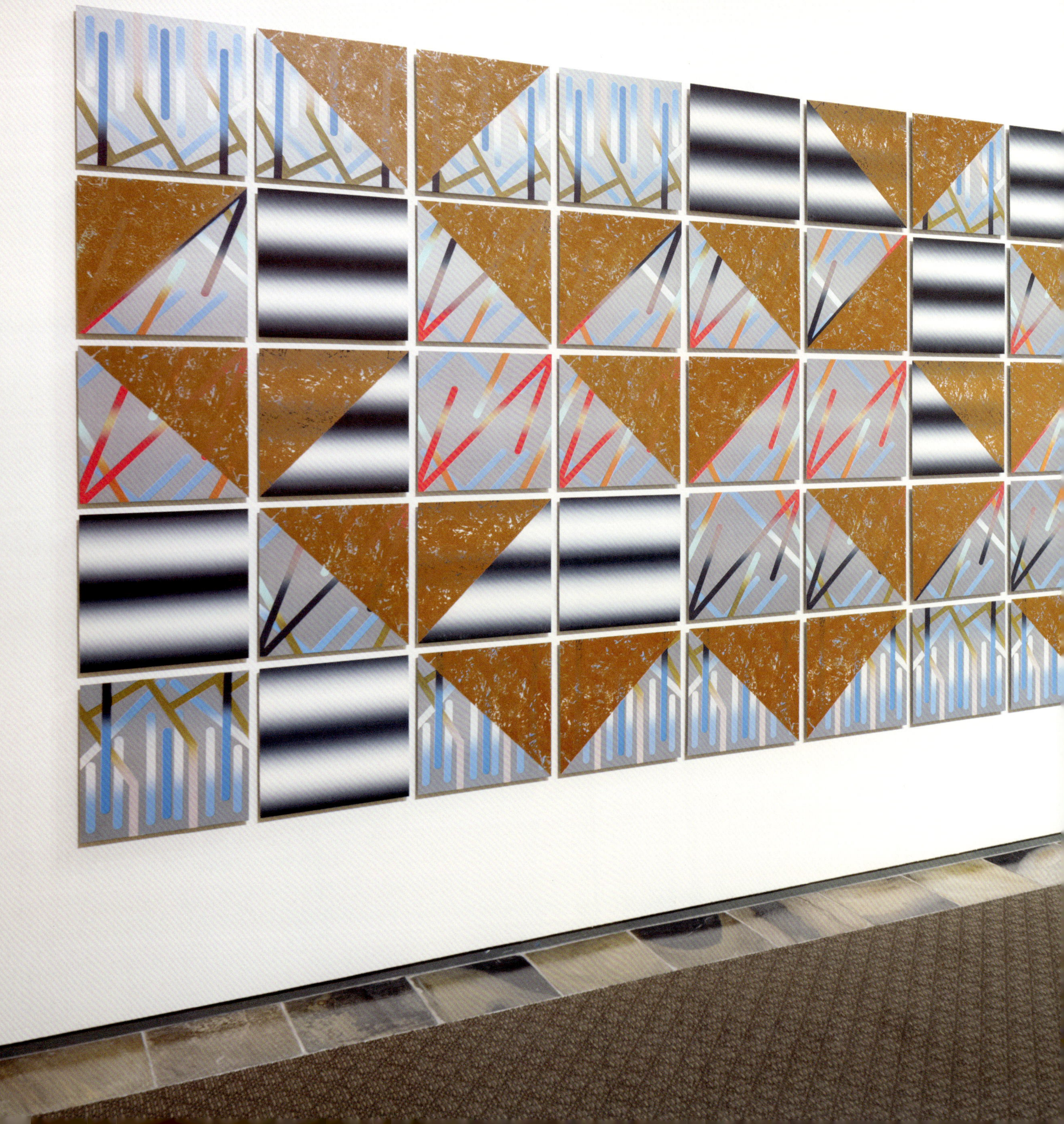

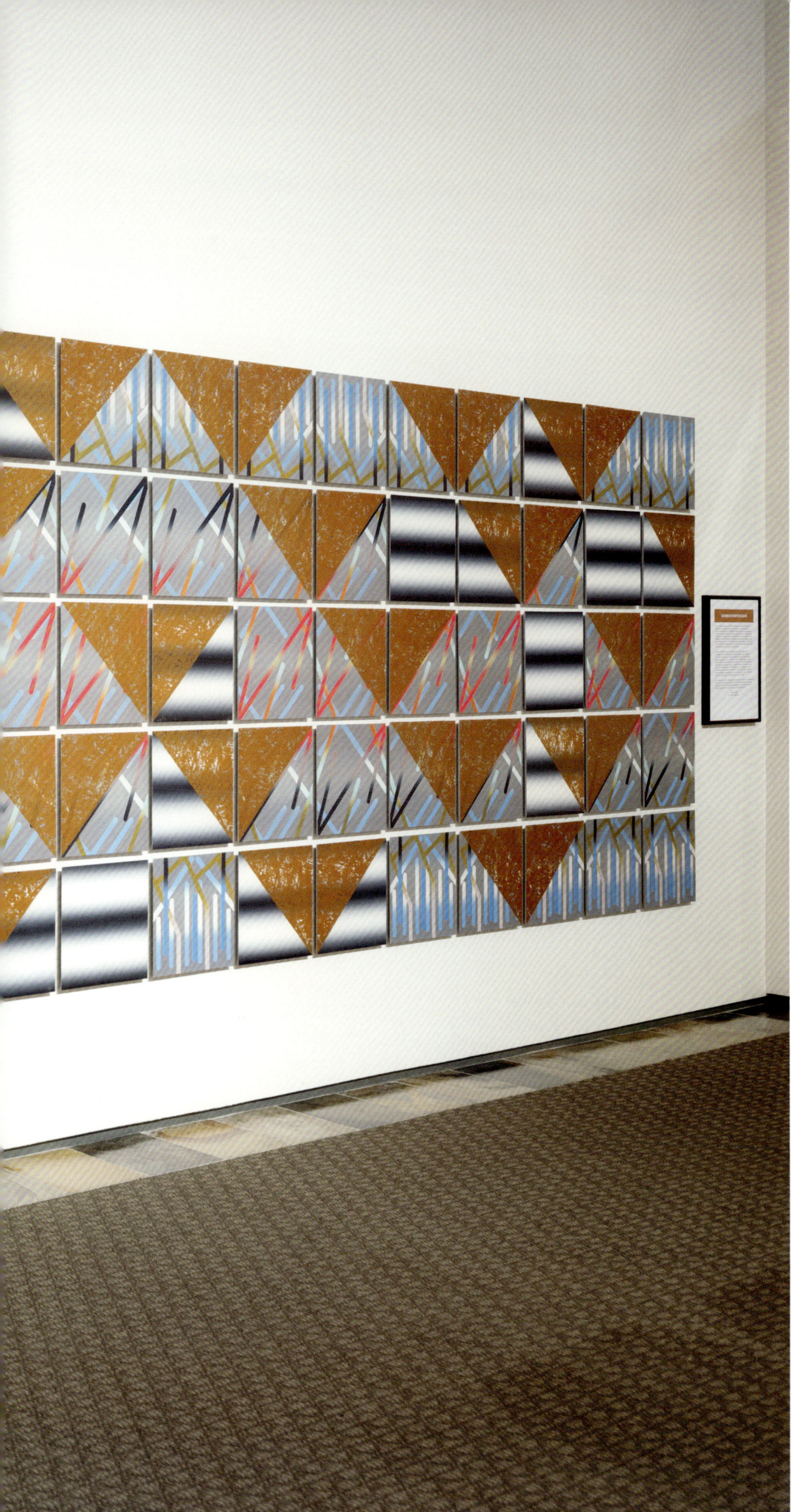

Plate 60
Okanagan V, 2006
Relief on paper mounted
on panels
Overall: 70 × 252 in.
(177.8 × 640.1 cm);
each panel: 14 × 14 in.
(35.6 × 35.6 cm)

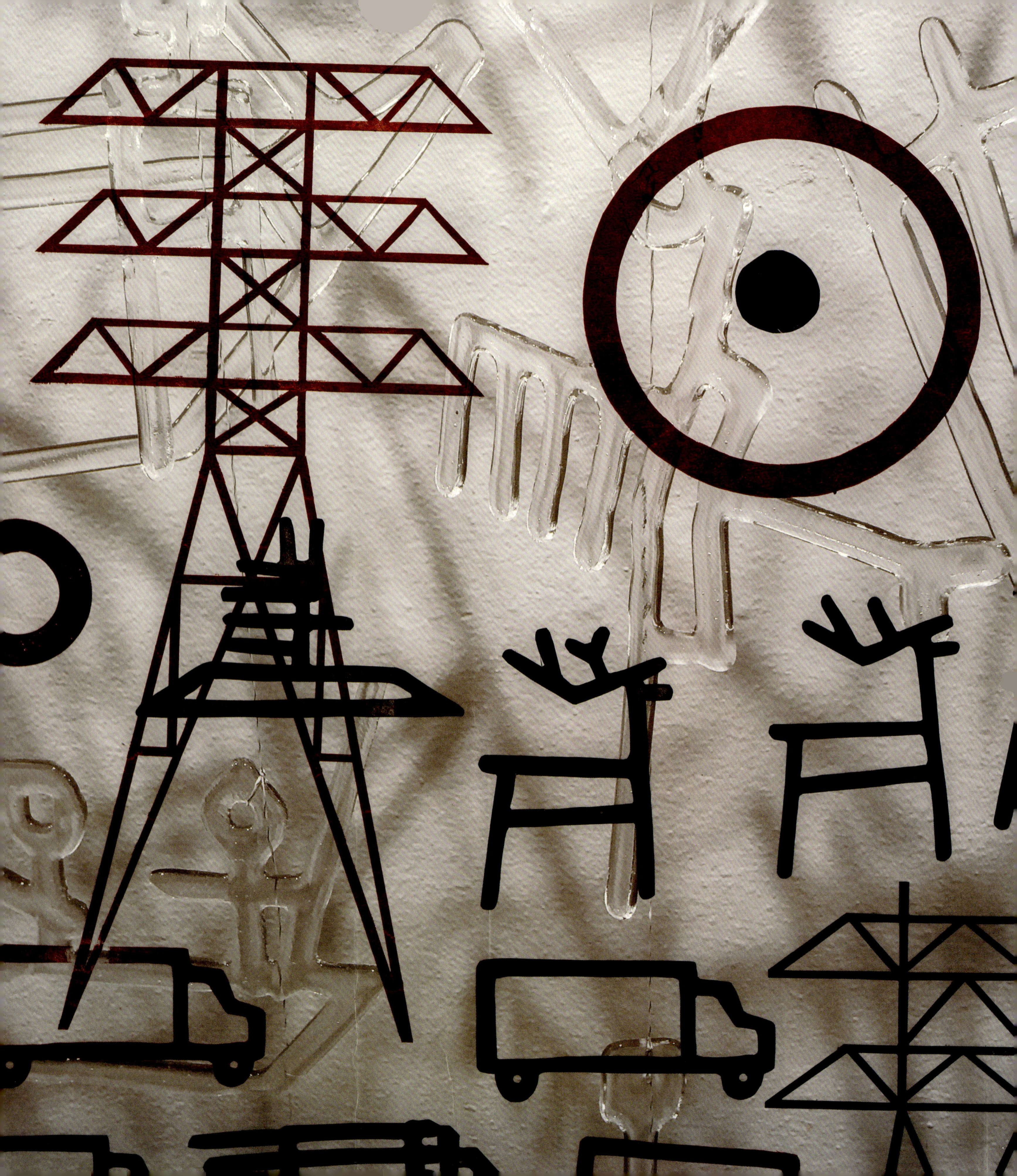

Joe Feddersen: I Am Home

Rachel Allen

Everything around you becomes part of your artwork. Just let it come in and be part of it.[1]

—Joe Feddersen

EARTH RECORDS/RECORDS

When Joe Feddersen recalls his childhood and the specifics of the land, he remembers digging tunnels, climbing cliffs, sliding down hills, building forts, swimming in the river, and running through thickets. His playful memories describe an intimate relationship with the Okanagan, a region east of the Cascade Range stretching from British Columbia into Washington State. There he engaged all levels of the environment, experiencing the view not only from high ground but also from underground, from underwater, and in thick foliage. This is key to what Feddersen offers as a landscape artist. Less concerned with the grand vistas traditional to American landscape painting, he prefers the dense layering of a thicket. This is truer to his experience of the land, as he seldom sees everything at once. Deeply personal, this closer perspective indicates a familial relationship instead of seeing a stranger from a distance. Like generations before, Feddersen still travels among the mountains, lakes, and rivers of his ancestral territory, generously sharing keen observations through his art.

Seeing the world in layers is perhaps what makes Feddersen such a natural and accomplished printmaker. His virtuosic prints can contain numerous overlaid colors and textures. His tendency to look *through* rather than *at* the landscapes has characterized this practice since his breakout print series, *Rainscapes* (1983–94) (pls. 4–6). Rather than the conventional view of far-off rainstorms in the paintings of Thomas Cole or John Steuart Curry, each *Rainscape* print positions the viewer inside a phenomenal downpour. After *Rainscapes*, the artist sought to incorporate the abstract visual language of Plateau Native art history (figs. 1, 3). In his considerable *Plateau Geometrics* print series (1994–2001), richly discussed by heather ahtone in this volume (pp. 66–67), Feddersen uses his artistic inheritance as a point of departure, following Plateau practices of iteration and innovation (fig. 2). At this pivotal moment, he celebrates diverse print processes while grounding

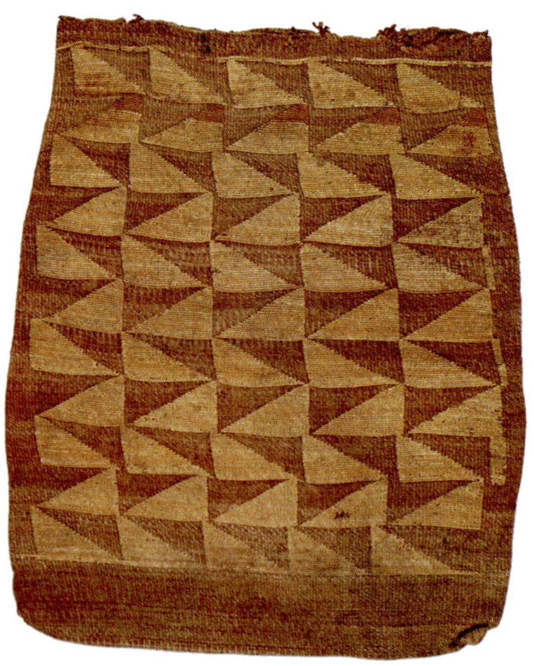

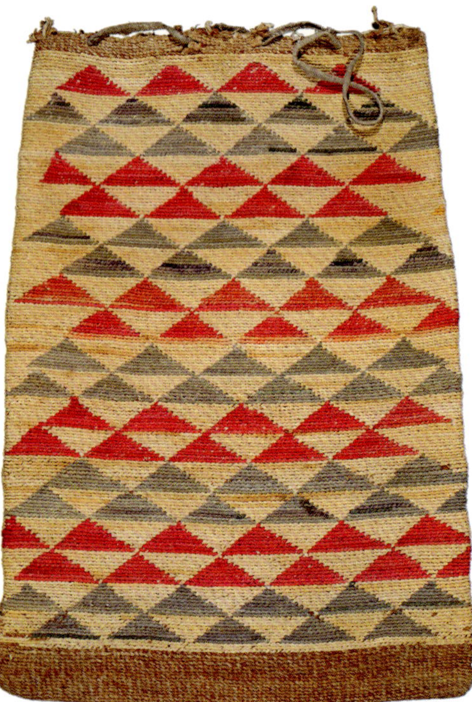

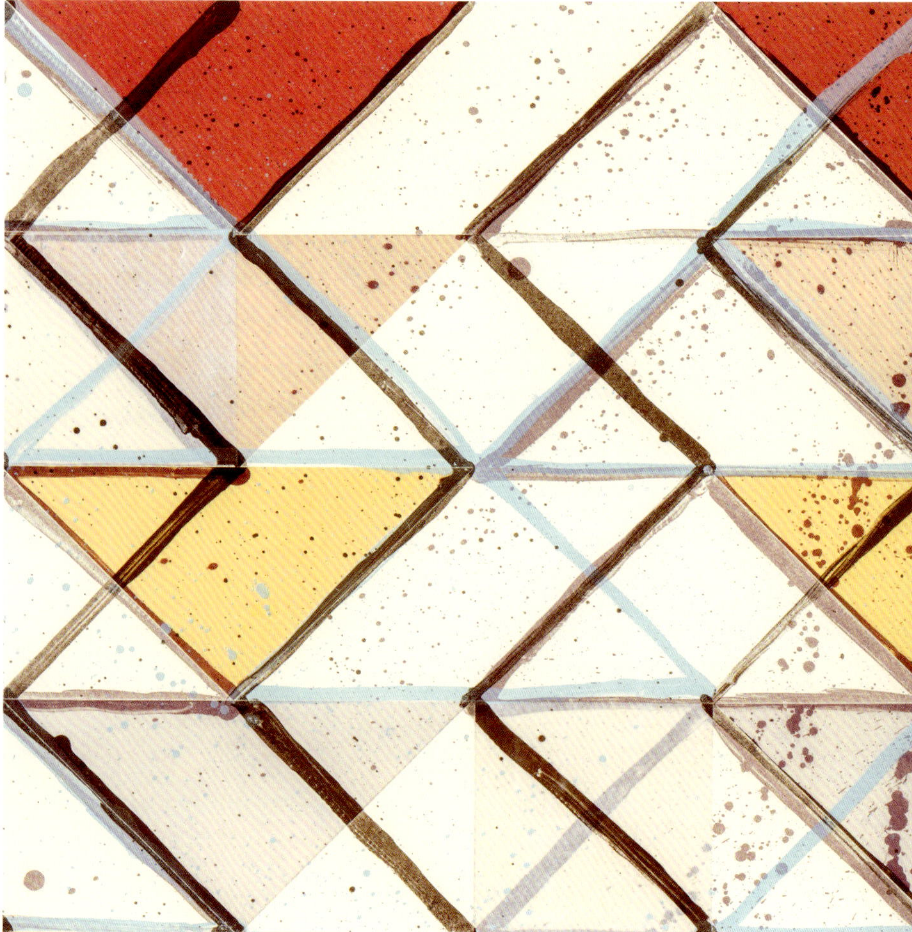

Clockwise from top left
Fig. 1 Unidentified Plateau maker, false embroidery flat twined bag, 19th c. Hemp and cornhusk, 24⅜ × 16¾ in. (61.9 × 42.5 cm). Northwest Museum of Arts and Culture, Spokane, WA, The Chap C. Dunning Memorial Collection, gift of Chap C. Dunning, 1962, 1780.641

Fig. 2 Joe Feddersen, detail of *Interwoven Sign*, 2001. Lithograph with chine collé, 30 × 30 in. (76.2 × 76.2 cm). Northwest Museum of Arts and Culture, Spokane, Washington; gift of Dr. and Mrs. Luis Vela 2021, 4458.1

Fig. 3 Unidentified Colville maker, false embroidery flat twined bag, late 19th to early 20th c. Hemp, cornhusk, cotton, smoked tanned hide, aniline dye, 20¼ × 14⅝ in. (51.4 × 37.1 cm). Northwest Museum of Arts and Culture, Spokane, WA, museum purchase, 1938, 970.1

the practice in his home culture.[2] Like the structure of Plateau weaving, Feddersen's prints contain an interior architecture, as if situated in an environment instead of viewing it from a distance. Artistic investigations demonstrate his persistent view *through* material, landscape, and history.

In *Interwoven Sign* (2001), pieces of diaphanous paper sit between printed layers of diagonal lines, triangles, and drips (pl. 57).[3] These layers of chine collé (glued thin paper) partially obscure the imagery behind, imbuing the work with a sense of physical distance and depth. As abstractions of the landscape, the geometry appears to come forward and recede, as if viewed through layers of trees, mountains, water, or fog. These graphic illustrations of distance connect the print to the woven bags that inspired it (figs. 1–3). These twined bags, low profile or "flat" when empty, are typically woven by twisting paired wefts around each warp. With dyed strands, the colorful design is incorporated at the time of construction.[4] Overlapping zigs and zags in *Interwoven Sign* echo the twists and turns of twining. Like those fibers, the print's geometries weave new arrangements while maintaining their integrity as lightning or butterfly motifs. Though the motifs are made of ink rather than the dyed strands of twining, they bond to paper, another fibrous substrate that supports Plateau abstraction. Together as a landscape view, woven X-ray, and set of imbricated symbols, *Interwoven Sign* demonstrates Feddersen's deep commitment to the environment, weaving practices, and symbology.

Feddersen scales up this creative inquiry in his mural-sized print installation series, *Okanagan* (2002–6). *Okanagan* refers to Feddersen's cultural community as well as geography in its Northwest Plateau territory.[5] From the Okanogan Highlands to the North Cascades, tectonic, volcanic, and glacial activity sculpted geologically complex mountains flanked by deep valleys. This land, which has been uplifted, scraped, smashed, folded, buried, and shifted over millions of years, constitutes the artist's ancestral home.[6] Breathtakingly complex, Feddersen's expansive installations move through Earth's record, from ancient geological formations to contemporary marks on the land.

This geological reformation becomes evident in Feddersen's *Okanagan V* (2006), a set of ninety square panels arranged in a grid over twenty-one feet long (pl. 60). The design's recurrent triangles recite the mountain motifs of the flat twined bags. However, Feddersen's mosaic structure visually assembles individual right triangles into increasingly larger and overlapping triangles. The geometry coalesces and fragments across the plane as if continually remaking and reconfiguring itself, just as the land has done for millions of years. Strong diagonal lines of the accumulated forms slice the gridded format, reaching dramatic peaks and equally low vales. Filtering through the ink layers, a base of metallic grays might correspond to the rich

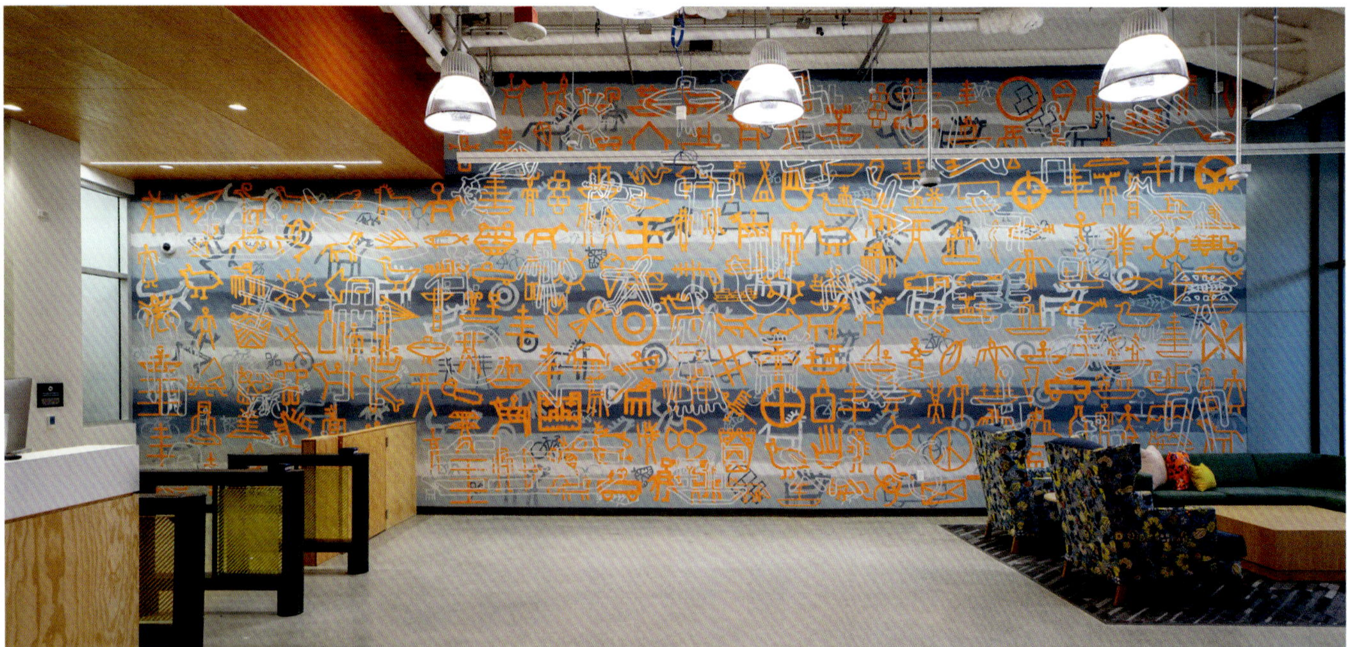

Fig. 4 Joe Feddersen, *Occupied Terrain*, 2021. Vinyl stencil, acrylic paint

mineral deposits in the Okanagan, subject to copper, zinc, silver, and gold extraction since the nineteenth century.[7] Luminous color bands dart across the work's silvery finish with the energy of an atom's electrons. A russet texture overlays this lively movement while allowing undersurfaces to peek through. Just as the various terranes (pieces of Earth's crust) fold and overlap the Okanagan, these topmost earthen segments pepper the surface of *Okanagan V*, revealing interlaced histories of movement and change.

Earth's sublime power can inspire fear, but for Feddersen, it supports life. Instead of questioning whether nature or humans have the control, his work views land as providing people with a maternal relationship of reciprocal care. Deploying the languages of abstraction, the artist presents the complexity of this historic bond. When viewing *Okanagan V*, it can be difficult to decide which shape is in front of the other, as they seem to switch positions. Background and foreground take turns, like the geological movements of the land or our mutual caregiving with her. Geometric abstraction movements in Europe and the US sought to empty pictures of external meaning or reality in search of pure form. Far from expunging content, the Plateau abstraction that predates these movements is replete with meaning specific to person and place. Scholar Jackson Rushing writes of Feddersen's abstraction as "both open and closed." Though accessible for its formal qualities, personal and cultural knowledge remains private.[8] From this perspective, the work can be appreciated but not always interpreted.

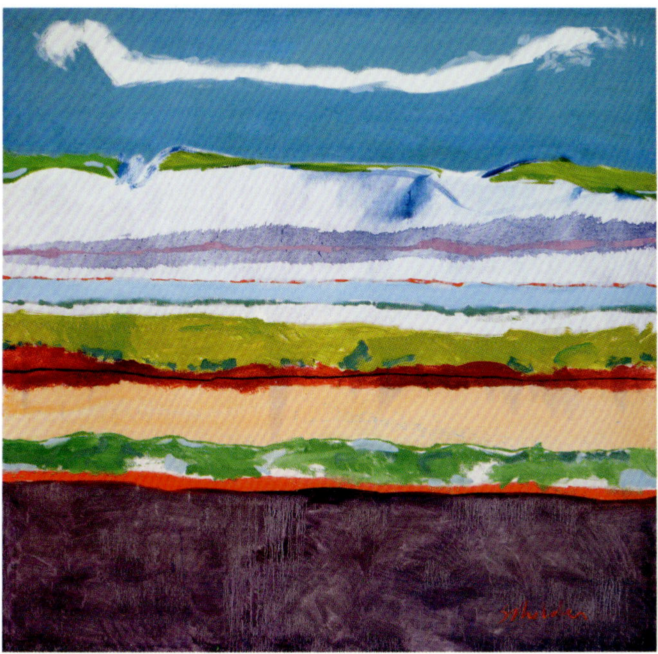

Fig. 5 Fritz Scholder (1937–2005, Payómkawichum [Luiseño]), *New Mexico No. 5*, 1965. Oil on canvas, 60 × 60 in. (152.4 × 152.4 cm). Northwest Museum of Arts and Culture, Spokane, WA, transfer from Museum of Native American Cultures, Spokane, 1992, F. Scholder, SCHOLDER.1967.1

For some, *okanagan* means a "site of rendezvous" or "place of gathering."[9] Feddersen adds that others say it means "looking up to the mountain tops." He explains that Okanagan people would spend summertime in the mountains for access to lush resources such as huckleberries.[10] To gather such provisions, people on the Plateau use another type of basket. Termed "sally bags" by collectors and anthropologists, these cylindrical twined bags make effective containers for carrying or storing foods, medicines, and household items. A deft weaver, Feddersen advances the practice of weaving baskets and stories. In Okanagan history, Coyote's hubristic antics leave him without a new name, as all others were taken by the time he arrived (very late) at the naming ceremony. But in Feddersen's *Coyote Receives His Name* (2012), the trickster sports the heads of the names he could have had, such as Frog, Snake, or Salmon (pl. 97). Additionally, newer names join the pageant: Parking Lot and Television.[11] Since it was Coyote's job to prepare for the arrival of humans, perhaps it is fitting for him to go by "Flat-Screen TV" on occasion. With this move, we see not only the artist's humor but also his understanding of the landscape. No separation exists between mountains, the parking lots carved into them, and our histories of each. Everything is part of the environment, and stories can help us to reconcile more recent changes.

Feddersen continues to weave humor and wisdom into baskets that reference urban aspects of the landscape.[12] Woven patterns might first appear as time-honored designs of the Plateau. But in a cross-cultural play of abstraction, they form schematics of elevator buttons, parking lots, cul-de-sacs, turning lanes, and automotive tire treads (pls. 11, 17, 19, 34, 41–42, 47–49). At first blush, this humorous trick on the expectations of Native design deserves a chuckle. Upon reflection, Feddersen's incorporation of this "urban vernacular," such as the tire treads, generates sophisticated landscape expression. Now part of the environment, tread patterns become an iteration of the artist's visual language, holding as much personal and place-based meaning as older symbols. Additionally, many automotive tire products deliberately reference the romanticized West to entice customers with the nostalgia of a wide-open frontier with trailblazing opportunities: Open Country, Wilderness, and Rugged Trail. Fixed in the American imagination, this myth of an unpopulated wilderness ripe for exploration erases millennia of Indigenous history. For Feddersen, his sleight of hand in pattern and name rests on the surface of a deeper consideration, as tire tracks comprise one of many layers of Earth's strata that bear human imprints. In *Okanagan V*, for instance, the multicolored pinballing lines trace the patterns of Eagle, Timberline, and Wilderness tire treads.[13] As seen in Feddersen's woven and inked surfaces, contemporary activities imprint the land already layered with his ancestral history.

Equally skilled in glasswork as in printmaking and weaving, Feddersen fabricates his cylindrical baskets in blown glass. Vibrant color and refracted light heighten the drama in one of the artist's largest glass baskets, *Rugged Trail 2* (2005), named after the tire tread pattern on the outside (pl. 17). Brilliant yellow emanates from the vessel's interior through slits in the brown glass, reminiscent of molten rock bursting through cracks of a cooler surface. Like in his prints, layers of glass create a record from ancient geology to recent tire tracks. However, viewing this three-dimensional record requires moving around the vessel to see all sides. Traversing around this glass basket, just like the environment, requires time. While this glass basket is more fragile than its woven counterparts, it is still a useful container. It holds the environment's history and the artist's story, just as Plateau baskets have always done.

Feddersen's work also records the events between geological shifts and yesterday's drive. Throughout the Okanagan, beautiful striations, which hold particular importance for the artist, sweep across exposed rock faces. He explains:

> *You look across and you see the horizontal lines that go across the landscape.... It was caused by just people and animals walking on the landscape over 20,000 years. Repetition creates form. So every step reinforces the lines that are already there. And it's kind of like a land acknowledgment. We were here for 20,000 years, it's our place. When I look at it, I see a reminder of our place here. So when you look at my work and the horizontal lines going across, it's referencing the land and the place and our occupation.*[14]

From large-scale murals to handle-held baskets, horizontal lines undergird much of Feddersen's work (pls. 9, 18, 36, 41). In *Occupied Terrain* (2021), blue hues stack floor to ceiling beneath hundreds of outlined forms and symbols (fig. 4). Together, all are present in the landscape: petroglyphs, animals, insects, baskets, plants, viruses, kites, bicycles, canoes, hashtags, arrows, envelopes, voltage towers, trucks, airplanes, and radioactivity. Despite their density, they do not hide Earth's strata. Contemporary movement follows the innumerable horizontal paths previously laid across the land.

Not only reconstructing the lines of the land, Feddersen's Earth records build on marks made by preceding artists. Coming of age in the 1970s, Feddersen entered a scene where artists were reevaluating relations between personal identity and the land itself. Many Native American artists had broken out of expected styles, engaging multiple art histories. Prominent twentieth-century painter Fritz Scholder (1937–2005, Payómkawichum [Luiseño]) mixed the Californian trend of bringing subjects back into abstraction with the impulse to forge new visual modes for Native expression.[15] In his early landscapes, such as *New Mexico No. 5*, Scholder paints the stratification of the earth near where he taught in Santa Fe (fig. 5). Here, Scholder primarily concerns himself with brilliant passages of color textured with subtle variations in viscosity. In the 1960s, Feddersen saw Scholder's paintings reproduced in magazines that came to his home in Omak.[16] He would reinterpret Earth's striations fifty years later. As a trained printmaker, Feddersen approached his *Occupied Terrain* mural in serial applications. Covering large areas of the wall with stenciled imagery, he prioritized each step with different colors, rendering strikingly different impressions. In its final state, figures peek out from previous layers. Feddersen's Earth record collapses and merges a cross section of the land's strata with aerial and elevation views.

Feddersen decisively states, "Repetition creates form." Rhythmic repetition characterizes many Plateau designs as well as Feddersen's recurring figures and patterns. In his *Palouse Series* (2003) (pl. 46), the artist reanimates the vivid color and terrestrial repetition of the region southeast of his home. The picturesque hills and fertile soil of the Palouse result from Pleistocene wind amassing a deep layer of fine-grained sediment, or loess.[17] Plateau peoples tended the rolling grasslands of the Palouse until the expansion of settler farming converted it to wheat country. By the late 1930s, artists in the region followed their Midwest counterparts in representing narrative scenes of rural or small-town life. Spokane-born artist Jane Dunning Baldwin (1908–1991) depicts the Palouse in *Wheat Barony,* a woodblock print featuring an agricultural estate (fig. 6).[18] A haunting picture in black ink with barren trees grieves low wheat prices that will not recover until World War II. In striking contrast, a nourishing yellow vitalizes the overlapping rectilinear patterns traversing the paper in Feddersen's *Palouse Series*. As seen in much of his work, the artist internalized the teaching of his undergraduate printmaking mentor, Glen Alps, who emphasized the catalytic power of yellow to give everything an energy.[19] For the *Palouse Series*, a splendid gold stands in for the life-giving loess and its gilded harvest. In Feddersen fashion, this Palouse record mixes viewpoints, arranging an aerial view of the Palouse with the Native knowledge and care encoded in repeated basket designs.

With a translucent yellow, Feddersen engages repetition in a series of twenty-four glass baskets titled *Codex* (2009) (pl. 61). Repetition is considered a basic principle of design, as well as a central characteristic of minimalism, the extreme abstraction typically composed of

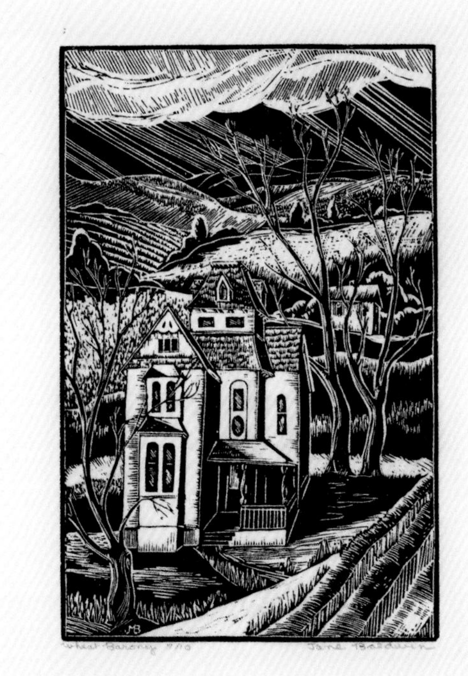

Fig. 6 Jane Dunning Baldwin (1908–1991), *Wheat Barony*, 1937. Woodblock on paper, sheet: 11 × 8 in. (27.9 × 20.3 cm); image: 8 × 5 in. (20.3 × 12.7 cm). Northwest Museum of Arts and Culture, Spokane, WA, museum purchase from the artist, 1987, 3230.8

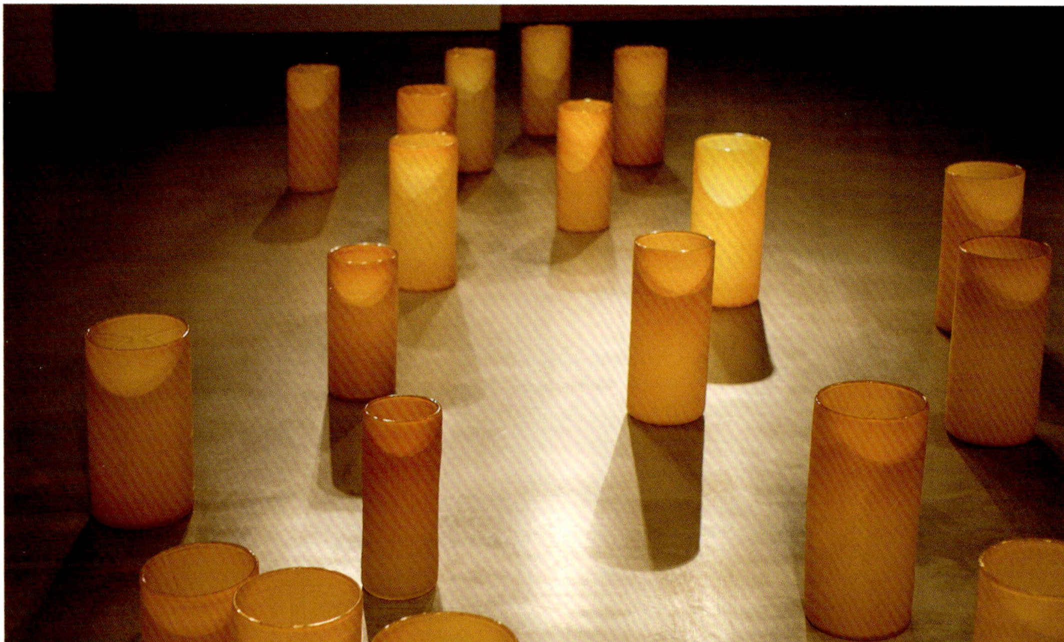

Fig. 7 Joe Feddersen, *Codex*, 2009. Blown and sandblasted glass, dimensions variable. Installation view, Evergreen Gallery, The Evergreen State College, Olympia, WA

geometric shapes void of organic materials or evidence of the artist's hand. Feddersen acknowledges his early exposure to this style and his fascination with the "coldness" of Donald Judd's (1928–1994) sculptures.[20] Perhaps this accounts for the mirrored finishes on some of his *Urban Vernacular* glass baskets (pl. 45). *Codex*, however, references Eva Hesse's (1936–1970) *Repetition Nineteen III* (1968), an installation of nineteen fiberglass and polyester resin containers on the floor. When she first created the installation, the vessels were clear. Fiberglass deteriorates over time, discoloring the objects to their current pale ocher. In *Codex*, Feddersen's color match to *Repetition Nineteen III* is nearly perfect. Homage to Hesse seems natural for Feddersen. As a leader in revising minimalism, Hesse engaged with repetition but not uniformity. Further, her forms hold a striking resemblance to cylindrical Plateau baskets. *Codex* glass baskets vary in size with slight bends that nod to Hesse's slumping shapes while bearing motifs of Feddersen's visual language. The artist displayed them in his 2009 exhibition, *Joe Feddersen: Pattern Recognition*, at the gallery of The Evergreen State College upon his retirement (fig. 7). Here, Feddersen strays from Hesse's tight grouping and spreads the twenty-four vessels across the floor. Light washes over the glass, revealing subtle basket patterns unique to each one. Feddersen's Earth records contain multiple art histories.

For Feddersen, it is about not just what was but what is happening now. Looking through the landscape and her art histories, he sees the records of past events and accounts for the present. In works such as *Occupied Terrain*, he iterates petroglyphs from his ancestors.

Petroglyphs stand as truth-tellers for Indigenous history often erased by historic landscape paintings. Like his ancestors, Feddersen draws his own forms in a distilled linework that renders sophisticated representations of the world around him. His *Bestiary* series of prints and fused glass installation focuses on the animals and insects of his home environment (pls. 22, 99–103). For him, this work "is about celebrating all of the life that lives here."[21] The Earth record Feddersen leaves is one of finding joy in his home on the Okanagan.

WATER RETURNS/RETURNS

A cache of salmon line the exterior of *Snipe Woman Steals Salmon* (2014), one of Feddersen's woven baskets (pl. 77). "There's one story about the Snipe Woman damming the river and not letting the salmon come up and Coyote has to go down there and let the salmon free," the artist remembers.[22] In Okanagan history, Coyote engineers a scheme to take down a large dam when no one is looking, bringing salmon to famished people. The story unfurls like a map, detailing the terrain and foodstuffs around waterfalls within the Columbia River Basin. In time, Coyote assembles the roaring Kettle Falls to accommodate his rescued fish, giving rise to an epicenter of salmon harvest and trade.[23]

Thousands of years later, the giant dam reappeared. At the height of the Great Depression, construction began on what remains the largest hydroelectric producer in the United States, the Grand Coulee. The dam attracted a flurry of outsiders and activities, including artists. Painter Clyfford Still (1904–1980) served as one of the first instructors of an art colony less than twenty miles north of the dam, for "at Nespelem and nearby Coulee Dam, landscape material is second to none."[24] Following the same impulse, Z. Vanessa Helder's (1904–1968) most significant work depicts the Grand Coulee fabrication in lively color and empathetic detail through a series of twenty-two watercolor paintings (fig. 8).[25] However, the dam had catastrophic results for those upriver.

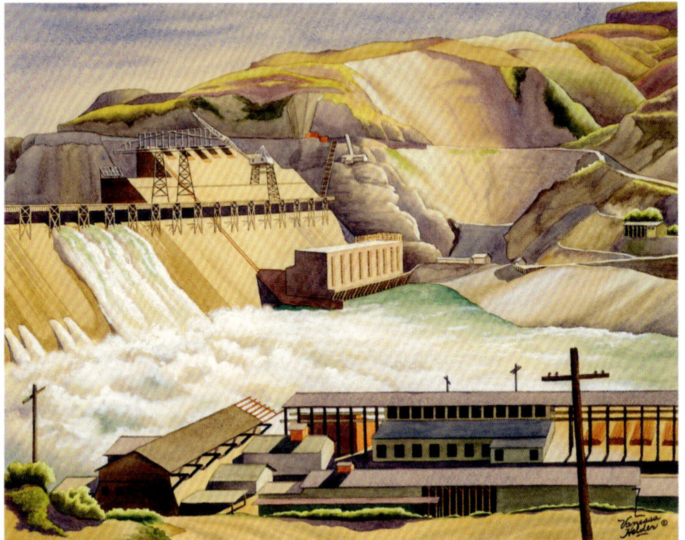

Fig. 8 Z. Vanessa Helder (1904–1968), *Coulee Dam, Looking West*, 1939–41. Watercolor on paper, 18 × 21⅞ in. (45.7 × 55.6 cm). Northwest Museum of Arts and Culture, Spokane, WA, museum purchase from the artist, 1954, 2585.3

In 1940, Kettle Falls fell silent, completely submerged in reservoir waters stilled by the Grand Coulee Dam. The concrete blockade ceased salmon runs, devastating the economy of the Colville Confederated Tribes that had relied on them since Coyote introduced the first stock. No fish ladder was built. US and state officials took some steps to preserve migrations early on, though the efforts proved ineffective.[26] Additionally, Colville citizens did not receive what was promised to them: compensation for the use of their land, free electricity, and revenue percentage.[27] Many had to seek employment at the dam or its supporting infrastructures. Even three decades later, Feddersen could not turn down a good job with the public utility district. For seven years, he worked at two dams while earning his associate's degree.[28]

With hydroelectric power dominating the Columbia River watershed, it is common to see lines of voltage towers carrying electricity away from the dams in all directions. Slightly anthropomorphic, Feddersen previously viewed the towers as thieves stealing from his community to supply the cities. Since then, settlements have been reached with the Confederated Tribes of the Colville Reservation for the Grand Coulee and Wells Dams.[29] "So now we are compensated for them. It kind of changes the meaning of these towers that were once like thieves taking our resources. . . . There's not a lot of wealthy people around here. . . . So it really helps our community," Feddersen explains.[30] Silent giants in the landscape, the voltage towers appear in the artist's prints and baskets, records that they are here now (pls. 23–25, 28, 29, 32–34, 72–74, 85, 89). They are part of the environment. Feddersen's interest in them extends to their form, a vertical pattern of triangles that integrate seamlessly into his visual vocabulary. In his signature move, Feddersen stacks, layers, and reconfigures tower geometry into constructions as varied as the ecology on which they are based.

Feddersen's concern for rivers naturally includes canoe travel. Like their coastal relations, inland nations participate in Canoe Journeys, voyages on the river with celebratory gatherings at the landings. In 2016, the Colville, Coeur d'Alene, Spokane, Kootenai, and Kalispel tribes journeyed to Kettle Falls by dugout canoe for the first time in over eighty years.[31] Tribal members united as paddlers on the historic waterway while carrying hope and spiritual responsibility for salmon return in the upper Columbia. Amid preparations the year before, Feddersen embarked on his own artistic *Canoe Journeys* series (2015–16) (pls. 82–95). His readiness involved hand-built, low-fired ceramic figures in various canoes, catamarans, rafts, and inner tubes. Feddersen explains that his work often takes note of important community events and celebrates them. In his characteristically joyful manner, he desired a freshness and spontaneity for each ceramic, seeing them as three-dimensional gesture drawings.[32] And like his prints, every surface bears the imprint of pattern or texture. The whimsical characters include his friends, Coyote, animal people, and personifications of landscape motifs developed over his career. Though traveling the river together, the pieces seem episodic, reinterpreting historical, legendary, and personal events. In one, Coyote replaces George Washington in a comical remake of Emanuel Leutze's famous painting, *Washington Crossing the Delaware* (1851). Another memorializes his friend's lost basket in a humorous capsizing of their canoe (pl. 83). This mashup of time and place suits Feddersen's layering of landscape histories and Indigenous storytelling. Canoe Journeys resume on the Columbia River and paddle through Feddersen's work.

Feddersen relies on his relationships (or fellow paddlers) as much as he supports them. There is no doubt that beloved artist and curator Truman Lowe (1944–2019, Ho-Chunk) influenced Feddersen's understanding of water and canoe travel. Lowe's delicate sculptures and installations evidence his deep love for moving water. After studying with him in graduate school, Feddersen formed a brotherly bond with Lowe that included trips out on the river. Lowe remarked, "Canoeing gave me the feeling of being on the earth while being suspended above it."[33] Similarly, Feddersen's canoes suspend in layers of ink, cooled glass, and woven rows (pls. 69, 80, 96). The negative space around them might denote the river but could also signify an equally spiritual place.

Emulating his mentors, Feddersen seems most proud of the ways he supports other artists by bringing them together and facilitating community. With experience participating in and facilitating numerous print folios, books, and exchanges throughout his career, he organized *Terrain: Plateau Native Art & Poetry* (2014) (pl. 107). For this folio, Feddersen invited thirty-three Plateau Native artists and poets from all career stages to contribute. Artists provided block prints, and authors submitted single-sheet poems. Corwin Clairmont (b. 1946, Confederated Salish and Kootenai Tribes), participating artist and close friend of Feddersen, printed the design on the outside of the folios. Folded from one large sheet of paper, they follow printmaking conventions while resembling folded rawhide carrying bags. In total, ninety-two sets were printed, fifteen of which were donated to museums. In so doing, Feddersen and the other established artists helped all participants gain the accolade of having work in public collection holdings.

One *Terrain* contributor, artist and author Lawney L. Reyes (1931–2022, Sinixt [Lakes]), is known for his many publications, largely memoir and biography. In his books Reyes details the history of the Grand Coulee Dam, his brother's activism, and the Pacific Northwest Fish Wars. Despite advances and affirmations since that time, Native fishing rights are still under siege. Recently vandalized fishing nets on the Okanogan River spurred Feddersen's basket pair, *Fishing* (2023) (pl. 81).[34] On the bottom two-thirds of the baskets, Feddersen weaves a restored net pattern. Completely intact, they are ready to be used again. Above, circling paddlers keep watch over the nets.

Like nets, Feddersen celebrates the traps of the Plateau. Hollow conical vessels with thin color bands honor the ingenuity and architectural beauty of ancestral fish traps (pls. 75–76). As glass, Feddersen's traps are unfit to capture fish but rather stay ashore as reminders of the critical river migrators. As the Canoe Journeys summon the salmon, these fish traps hold space for them to return. This invitation, or perhaps prayer, has seen answers in recent years. Aided by Colville Tribal biologists, Chinook salmon have spawned in the upper Columbia River system for the first time since the Grand Coulee Dam construction.[35] In 2023, the United States came to an agreement with the Confederated Tribes of the Colville Reservation, the Coeur d'Alene Tribe, and the Spokane Tribe of Indians "to support Tribally led efforts to restore healthy and abundant salmon populations in the Upper Columbia River Basin."[36]

It is telling that Reyes, who experienced the flooding caused by the Grand Coulee Dam firsthand, chose to illustrate Coyote in his power (fig. 9). We know that Coyote received power instead of a new name and often uses that power to help people. Some say he will come back to smash the dams, freeing the salmon.[37] After all, he has done it before. Until then, Feddersen's art reminds us that water returns hope, and the salmon will follow.

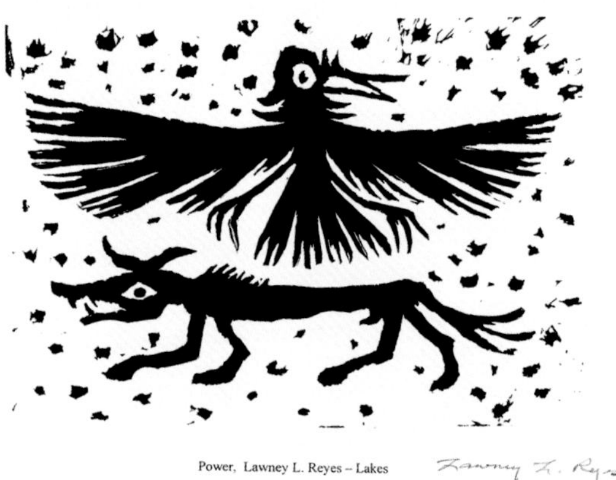

Fig. 9 Lawney L. Reyes (1931–2022, Sinixt [Lakes]), *Power*, from the *Terrain* folio, 2014. Linocut on paper, 8 × 10½ in. (20.3 × 26.7 cm). Northwest Museum of Arts and Culture, Spokane, WA, gift of the Longhouse Education & Cultural Center, The Evergreen State College, and Joe Feddersen, 4316.1

SKY REPAIR/RE-PRAYER

Whittled into the coastline, merged ocean and river waters constitute the Salish Sea's complex estuary, the Puget Sound. Vi taqʷšəblu Hilbert (1918–2008, Upper Skagit), a respected elder who played a considerable role in revitalizing the language and culture of the Pacific Northwest, mentored Feddersen during his time on the sound, becoming a close friend.[38] Hilbert encouraged Feddersen to include legends in his work, which he recounts:[39]

> *The legend goes something like this: The Creator came to the Puget Sound and he gave all the people different languages. All of them were beautiful languages. And the world was different back then. The sky was lower and the people kept going up into the upper world and it was causing chaos in the world below. So the people, even though they had different languages, came together and devised a way to push the sky up. They decided that they would use poles, they would push up the sky. And so in unison they would push up. On the fourth try, the sky let go and it went up to where it is today. And the people that were in the upper world that didn't participate became the constellations that we see today. What I like about the legend is that it talks about how people can come together even though they are*

really different. They can make change in the world and make it a better place to live.[40]

Feddersen illustrates this history in several glass baskets from his *Changer* series (pls. 64–65). On each, terrestrial figures encircle the lower portion of the basket as they utilize poles to raise the starlit upper registers. The artist skillfully evokes this strong upward movement through a gradient that mimics the appearance of a clear sky turning a deeper blue as it extends upward from the horizon. Lower figures stand in black on light blue, and those above shift to white on a dark blue background. No individual loses detail or contrast. This equal treatment does not position the viewer at a single point looking onto a landscape but provides access to the cross section of celestial events. As people hoist up the sky, the animals, hunters, and canoes that did not join in the lift become trapped in the upper world. In *Changer 4* (pl. 64), stars envelop the newcomers as they transition to constellations.

This climactic moment of the sky breaking free, resetting the location of the firmament, offers a sense of dynamic space. In the *Changer* baskets, the cosmos is populated and saturated with color. It is not an empty void but a skyworld of transformation with consequences for those who wander too close. Feddersen reminds us that the sky and atmosphere persist as active space. Literary scholar Steven Connor notes the variability of our atmosphere, stating, "What we know as 'open air' is in fact no such thing. It is heterogenous, spasmodic, tremulous, given to crisis. . . . The outside air is never uniform, but hysterically zoned and striated."[41] Even still, it is easy to take the encompassing life-sustainer for granted. Bidding us to remember the air, art theorist Monika Bakke traces artistic shifts in aerial thinking from Yves Klein's iconic *Leap into the Void* (1960) photomontage to Tomás Saraceno's *On Air* (2004) and *Flying Garden/Air-Port-City* (2005) multimedia installations. For Bakke, the artists express a turn from empty air (or void) to an atmosphere "saturated with data flows."[42]

Ever observant, Feddersen contends with this information-soaked reality in works such as *Cell Phone Tower* (2009), a white glass basket with the black outlines of cell towers (pl. 63). Cell towers, or cell sites, are raised structures that support antennae and electronic communications equipment. Many of us have learned to "unsee" the ubiquitous structures hiding in plain sight that wirelessly connect our mobile phones to wired infrastructure.[43] Cell towers with latticework, like those on Feddersen's basket, bring past signal towers to mind. However, unlike the iconic Eiffel Tower (1889) or Nikola Tesla's Wardenclyffe Tower (1901–17), today's mundane structures no longer signify the future. They are designed to disappear.[44] These cell towers that recede into the background of our daily lives operate by tapping into something actually invisible: the electromagnetic spectrum that constantly surrounds us.[45]

Yet Feddersen noticed the cell towers sprouting up around him and recorded their presence as additions to the landscape. In *Cell Phone Tower*, the artist employs his elegant geometry to describe the forms in two dimensions on a curved surface. The towers ring the vessel, just as cell towers likewise cluster in particular zones.[46] Behind Feddersen's towers, the subtle woven texture etched into the glass suggests the atmosphere of radiofrequency that surrounds them. Prominent horizontal lines in the finish point to a striated atmosphere where various signals share bandwidth and airspace is regulated. Moreover, the narrow bands mimic the horizontal strata in Feddersen's larger body of work. However, in *Cell Phone Tower*, the lines overlay an airspace. But the sky contains more than data. Feddersen addresses the weather in *Rainscapes*, historic wind on the Palouse, and even unsettles the air with fans in his *Charmed* installations (pls. 4, 22, 46). Like the land and waters, the sky supports layers of history and activity.

In the skyworld legend of the Puget Sound, Feddersen retells this history for his own audience. For him, storytelling is the "primary source" for artmaking, where tradition is "embedded in personal history."[47] Hilbert stressed the importance of the ambiguity in legends, which are told for the sake of contemporary audiences, and that all interpretations were acceptable.[48] Feddersen takes this position in his work, stating, "A lot of my work does have a certain ambiguity in them. I'm hoping that it will transcend the personal and gain more meaning for other people."[49]

For the legend behind the *Changer* series, Feddersen offers his analysis in his conclusion: "What I like about the legend is that it talks about how people can come together even though they are really different. They can make change in the world and make it a better place to live." Revisiting the legend in light of Feddersen's evaluation tempts further consideration of possible interpretations. For the ancient people of the Salish Sea, the sky posed an inconvenience, if not a crisis. Several recent airborne crises come to mind, from chemical warfare to the COVID-19 pandemic (figs. 10, 11). However, one contemporary emergency seems to parallel the ancient quandary of a low, perilous sky.

As wildfires rage in the Northwest, the sky again feels as if it is sinking back down, smothering those below with billowing smoke. The western United States and Canada have suffered from fires and smoke for decades, and these dangers have grown increasingly common across the continent. In 2023, Canada reached its worst fire season on record, causing more than a third of the US population to be placed under air quality alerts.[50] Since wildfire smoke contains fine particles

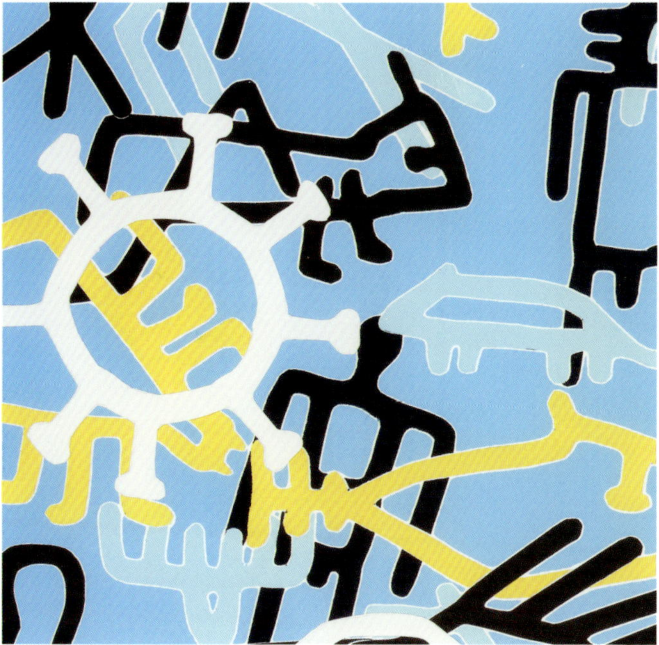

Fig. 10 Joe Feddersen, detail of COVID-19 virus in *Bestiary 1*, 2021. Relief and stencil monoprint, sheet: 44 × 30 in. (111.8 × 76.2 cm), image: 41 × 30 in. (104.1 × 76.2 cm). Collection of Jordan D. Schnitzer

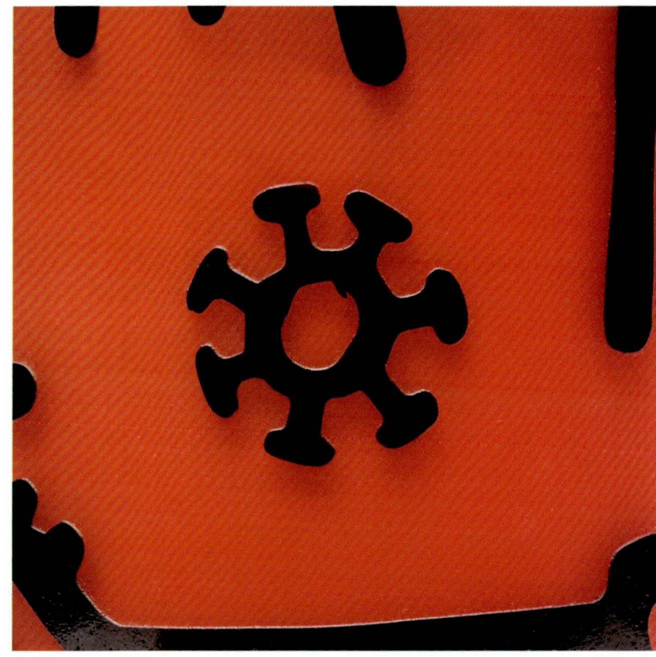

Fig. 11 Joe Feddersen, detail of COVID-19 virus in *Bestiary Basket 1*, 2021. Sandblasted blown glass, 15 × 8 × 8 in. (38 × 20.3 × 20.3 cm). Collection of Jordan D. Schnitzer

and hazardous gases, it can irritate the eyes and respiratory system, as well as worsen chronic heart and lung diseases.[51] As people collide with the sky now, they risk serious health consequences.[52]

Yet just as peoples of the Salish Sea tended the sky, so do Native peoples cultivate the land with fire and smoke. Cultural burning or prescribed burning refers to the practice of lighting small, low-intensity controlled fires for a desired purpose. These fires often creep along the ground under the trees without burning them completely. Cleared undergrowth allows root systems to retain the water that supplies rivers and streams. This sophisticated Indigenous environmental management in the Pacific Northwest rendered beautiful landscapes that early Europeans admired as "well-stocked parks," "luxuriant lawns," and "a perfect 'Eden.'"[53]

However, the pervasive American myth of an untouched, pristine wilderness prior to European arrival reinforced the assumption that fire was a destructive force only to be extinguished.[54] Suppression guided US conservation policy by the twentieth century, resulting in forests vulnerable to catastrophic fires from the accumulation of fuels in the lower layers.[55] Simultaneously, US policy toward Native nations evolved from nineteenth-century removal to mid-twentieth-century termination, separating Native people from lands they had managed for millennia.[56] These destructive policies worked in tandem, penalizing Native people for scientific practices and environmental management. Still, a 2016 official assessment of one fire that affected the Colville Reservation proved that regions managed by controlled burns produced smaller fires that were safely suppressed by firefighters.[57]

Wildfire smoke is the largest source of particle pollution in Washington State, yet cultural burning brings renewal: smoke can be a toxin or a prayer.[58] For Plateau people, fire nurtures the plants that make and fill baskets. Likewise, carefully tended fire in a hot shop prepares blown glass to be inflated by the artist's breath. In this way, Feddersen's woven and glass baskets originate from controlled flames. For many Indigenous peoples, fire is medicine. In the right dose, fire nurses a healthy ecosystem and cultivates crucial resources.

Feddersen's art is enriched with history and environmental knowledge to help us imagine what is possible.[59] In response to the *Changer* series, we might ask, How do we lift the sky (or change the world) to make a more hospitable environment for all? We must find our word for *push*—our shared understanding and agreements with each other—so that *together* we can lift the sky.

Notes

1. Joe Feddersen, conversation with heather ahtone and the author, Feb. 18, 2023.

2. Phone conversation with Joe Feddersen, Feb. 26, 2024.

3. From a variable edition of twenty lithographs created at the Rutgers Center for Innovative Print and Paper. In 2006, it was renamed the Brodsky Center for Print and Paper, and in 2018, it moved from Rutgers University, New Jersey, to the Pennsylvania Academy of the Fine Arts in Philadelphia.

4. This type of decoration is termed "false embroidery" or "external weft wrap." For flat twined bag construction and decoration, see Mary Dodds Schlick, *Columbia River Basketry: Gift of the Ancestors, Gift of the Earth* (Seattle: University of Washington Press, 1994), 152–54.

5. Politically, many members residing in the US are citizens of the Confederated Tribes of the Colville Reservation, a sovereign Native nation. Both spellings, Okanogan and Okanagan, have also come to specify geography in the region.

6. "North Cascades," Geologic Provinces, Washington State Department of Natural Resources, https://www.dnr.wa.gov/programs-and-services/geology/explore-popular-geology/geologic-provinces-washington/north-cascades (accessed Jan. 19, 2024).

7. While participating in the Pacific Railroad surveys in 1853, General (then Captain) George B. McClellan found gold in the Cascades. Activity proceeded around Fort Colville and then productively at Mount Chopaka in 1871. Regional zinc mining began around 1883, and silver mining around 1885. Wayne S. Moen, "The Mineral Industry of Washington—Highlights of Its Development—1853–1980," *Washington Geologic Survey Information Circular* 15, no. 74 (1982): 4–5.

8. W. Jackson Rushing III, "Joe Feddersen: Sacred Geometry," in *After the Storm: The Eiteljorg Fellowship for Native American Fine Art, 2001*, ed. Rushing (Seattle: University of Washington Press, 2001), 39.

9. Gail Tremblay, "Speaking in a Language of Vital Signs," in *Joe Feddersen: Vital Signs*, ed. Rebecca J. Dobkins (Salem, OR: Hallie Ford Museum of Art at Willamette University, 2008), 48.

10. Joe Feddersen, conversation, Feb. 18, 2023.

11. See heather ahtone on the related *Role Call* series in this volume, pp. 71–73.

12. For more on the *Urban Indian* and *Urban Vernacular* series, see ahtone, pp. 69–70 of this volume.

13. Tremblay, "Speaking in a Language of Vital Signs," 51.

14. Joe Feddersen, conversation, Feb. 18, 2023.

15. Scholder was greatly influenced by Bay Area Figurative Movement artists such as Wayne Thiebaud and Nathan Oliveira. He was an instructor at the Institute of American Indian Arts in Santa Fe, New Mexico, from 1964 to 1969.

16. Rebecca J. Dobkins, "Joe Feddersen: Pulses and Patterns," in *Joe Feddersen: Vital Signs*, ed. Dobkins (Salem, OR: Hallie Ford Museum of Art at Willamette University, 2008), 19.

17. "Columbia Basin," Geologic Provinces, Washington State Department of Natural Resources, https://www.dnr.wa.gov/programs-and-services/geology/explore-popular-geology/geologic-provinces-washington/columbia-basin#.4 (accessed Jan. 19, 2024).

18. For more on Jane Dunning Baldwin and the Pacific Northwest Regionalists, see J. J. Creighton, *Indian Summers: Washington State College and the Nespelem Art Colony, 1937–41* (Pullman: Washington State University Press, 2000), 5; Liz Miller, *Memorabilia: The Regional Prints of Jane Dunning Baldwin* (Spokane, WA: Eastern Washington State Historical Society, 1989).

19. Joe Feddersen, conversation, Feb. 18, 2023; Dobkins, "Joe Feddersen: Pulses and Patterns," 21.

20. Oral history interview with Joe Feddersen, Apr. 29 and May 6, 2021. Archives of American Art, Smithsonian Institution.

21. Joe Feddersen, conversation, Feb. 18, 2023.

22. Joe Feddersen, conversation, Feb. 18, 2023.

23. "How Coyote Broke the Salmon Dam," in *Confederated Tribes of the Colville Reservation Upper Columbia River Book of Legends*, comp. Jennifer K. Ferguson (Nespelem: Confederated Tribes of the Colville Reservation, 2011), 95–100.

24. Patricia Failing, *Clyfford Still: The Colville Reservation and Beyond, 1934–1939* (Denver: Clyfford Still Museum, 2015), 17.

25. For more on Helder, see Margaret E. Bullock and David F. Martin, *Austere Beauty: The Art of Z. Vanessa Helder* (Tacoma, WA: Tacoma Art Museum, 2013).

26. Lawney L. Reyes, *B Street* (Seattle: University of Washington Press, 2008), 144–45.

27. Laurie Arnold, *Bartering with the Bones of Their Dead: The Colville Confederated Tribes and Termination* (Seattle: University of Washington Press, 2012), 155n57.

28. Dobkins, "Joe Feddersen: Pulses and Patterns," 20.

29. Confederated Tribes of the Colville Reservation Grand Coulee Dam Settlement Act, Pub. L. No. 103–436, 108 Stat. 4577 (1994).

30. Joe Feddersen, conversation, Feb. 18, 2023.

31. Becky Kramer, "Tribes End Canoe Journey at Kettle Falls, Celebrate Hope of Salmon's Return," *Spokesman-Review* (Spokane), June 18, 2016, https://www.spokesman.com/stories/2016/jun/18/tribes-canoe-journey-ends-at-kettle-falls/.

32. Joe Feddersen, phone conversation, Feb. 24, 2024.

33. Jo Ortel, *Woodland Reflections: The Art of Truman Lowe* (Madison: University of Wisconsin Press, 2003), 88.

34. Joe Feddersen, conversation with the author, Nov. 11, 2023.

35. Eli Francovich, "For the First Time in More than 80 Years, Salmon Spawning in the Upper Columbia River," *Spokesman-Review* (Spokane), Dec. 17, 2020, https://www.spokesman.com/stories/2020/dec/17/for-the-first-time-in-more-than-80-years-salmon-sp/.

36. US Department of the Interior, "Biden-Harris Administration, Tribes Reach Historic Agreement Supporting Efforts to Restore Healthy and Abundant Salmon Populations to Upper Columbia River Basin." Press Release, Sept. 21, 2023, https://www.doi.gov/press releases/biden-harris-administration-tribes-reach-historic-agreement-supporting-efforts-restore.

37. Mourning Dove, *Mourning Dove: A Salishan Autobiography*, ed. Jay Miller (Lincoln: University of Nebraska Press, 1990), 227n21.

38. Feddersen attended the University of Washington in Seattle, where he learned Lushootseed language and culture from Hilbert. In Olympia, Feddersen taught at The Evergreen State College for twenty years, where Hilbert served as the Evans Chair Scholar during Feddersen's tenure.

39. Joe Feddersen notes the importance of the term "legend" for Hilbert, as it denoted real history as opposed to a "story." Joe Feddersen, conversation, Feb. 18, 2023.

40. Joe Feddersen, conversation, Feb. 18, 2023.

41. Steven Connor, "Building Breathing Space," in *Going Aerial: Air, Art, Architecture*, ed. Monika Bakke (Maastricht, The Netherlands: Jan van Eyck Academie, 2006), 127.

42. Monika Bakke builds on the work of media theorist Lev Manovich, in Bakke, "Air Is Information," in Bakke, *Going Aerial: Air, Art, Architecture*, 10–12.

43. Steven E. Jones, *Cell Tower (Object Lessons)* (New York: Bloomsbury Academic, 2020), 1–11.

44. Jones, *Cell Tower*, 1–20.

45. Jones, *Cell Tower*, 14.

46. Usually arranged in hexagonal formations to maximize the coverage area. See Jones, *Cell Tower*, 3.

47. Joe Feddersen and Elizabeth Woody, "The Story as Primary Source: Educating the Gaze," in *Native American Art in the Twentieth Century: Makers, Meanings, Histories*, ed. W. Jackson Rushing III (New York: Routledge, 1999), 182.

48. Joe Feddersen, conversation, Feb. 18, 2023.

49. Joe Feddersen, conversation, Feb. 18, 2023.

50. Joe Sutton, Taylor Ward, and Zoe Sottile, "Canadian Wildfire Smoke Reaches Europe as Canada Reports Its Worst Fire Season on Record," *CNN*, June 27, 2023, https://www.cnn.com/2023/06/26/americas/canada-wildfire-season-worst-2023/index.html; Nouran Salahieh, Joe Sutton, and Lauren Mascarenhas, "More than a Third of the US Population, from the Midwest to the East Coast, Under Air Quality Alerts from Canadian Wildfire Smoke," *CNN*, June 28, 2023, https://www.cnn.com/2023/06/27/us/canada-wildfire-smoke-great-lakes/index.html.

51. Centers for Disease Control and Prevention, "Protect Yourself from Wildfire Smoke," https://www.cdc.gov/air/wildfire-smoke/default.htm (last modified May 18, 2023).

52. Katelyn O'Dell et al., "Estimated Mortality and Morbidity Attributable to Smoke Plumes in the United States: Not Just a Western US Problem," *GeoHealth* 5, no. 9 (Sept. 2021): https://doi.org/10.1029/2021GH000457.

53. Robert T. Boyd, "Introduction," in *Indians, Fire, and the Land in the Pacific Northwest*, ed. Robert T. Boyd (Corvallis: Oregon State University Press, 2021), 1–2.

54. "Smokey Bear Syndrome," see Boyd, "Introduction," 19.

55. The 1911 Weeks Act to the Wilderness Act of 1964; John Alan Ross, "Proto-historical and Historical Spokan Prescribed Burning and Stewardship of Resource Areas," in Boyd, *Indians, Fire, and the Land in the Pacific Northwest*, 279–80.

56. For more on Termination Era policy and the Colville Confederated Tribes, see Arnold, *Bartering with the Bones of Their Dead: The Colville Confederated Tribes and Termination*.

57. USDA Forest Service, "FY 2015 Wildland Fire Management Annual Report," US Department of the Interior, Nov. 29, 2016, 46, https://www.doi.gov/sites/doi.gov/files/uploads/fy_2015_wfm_annual_report_11292016.pdf.

58. "Wildfire Smoke Information," Wildfire Smoke, State of Washington Department of Ecology, https://ecology.wa.gov/air-climate/air-quality/smoke-fire/wildfire-smoke (accessed Jan. 19, 2024).

59. bell hooks, *Outlaw Culture: Resisting Representations* (New York: Routledge, 2015), 281.

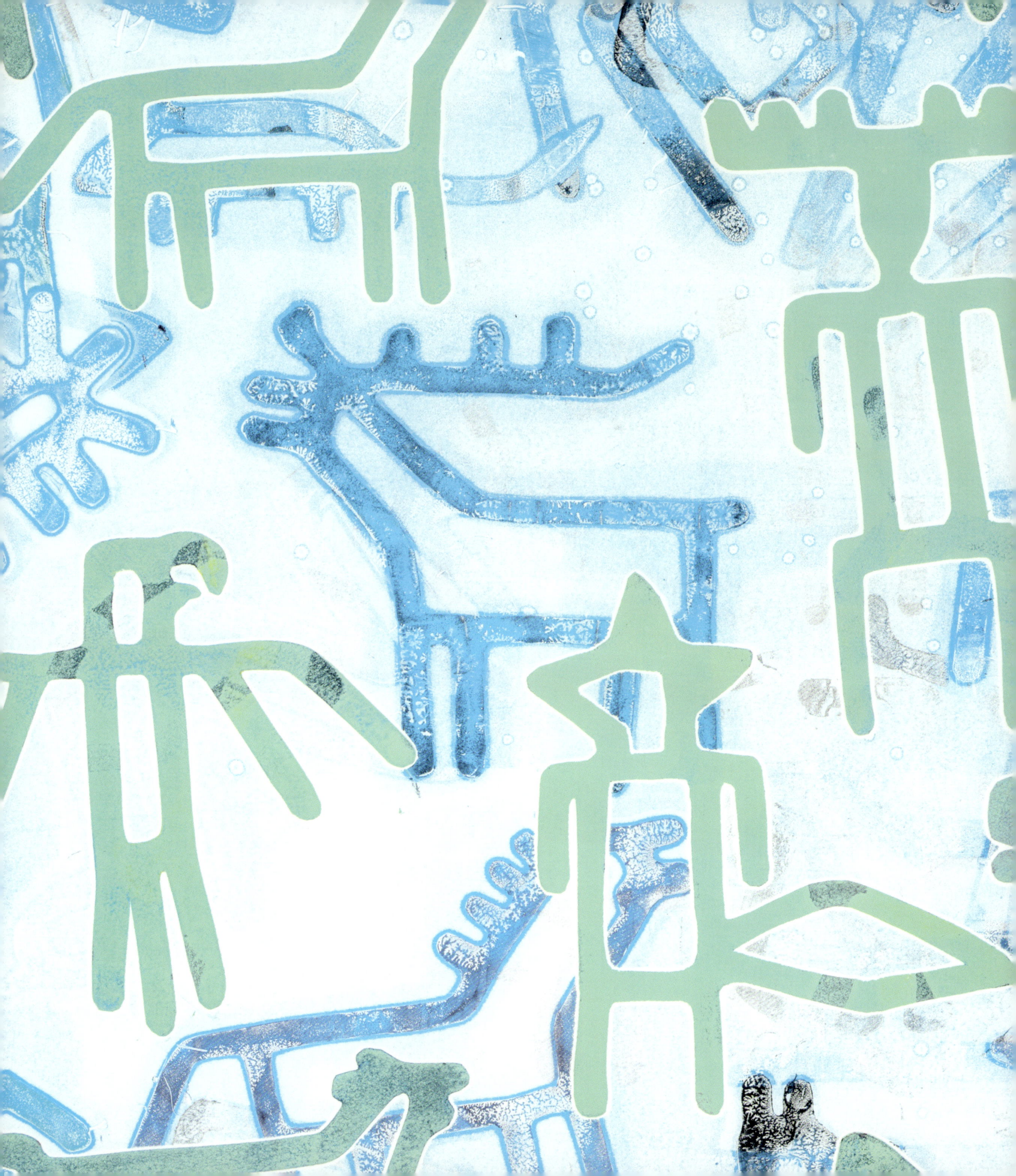

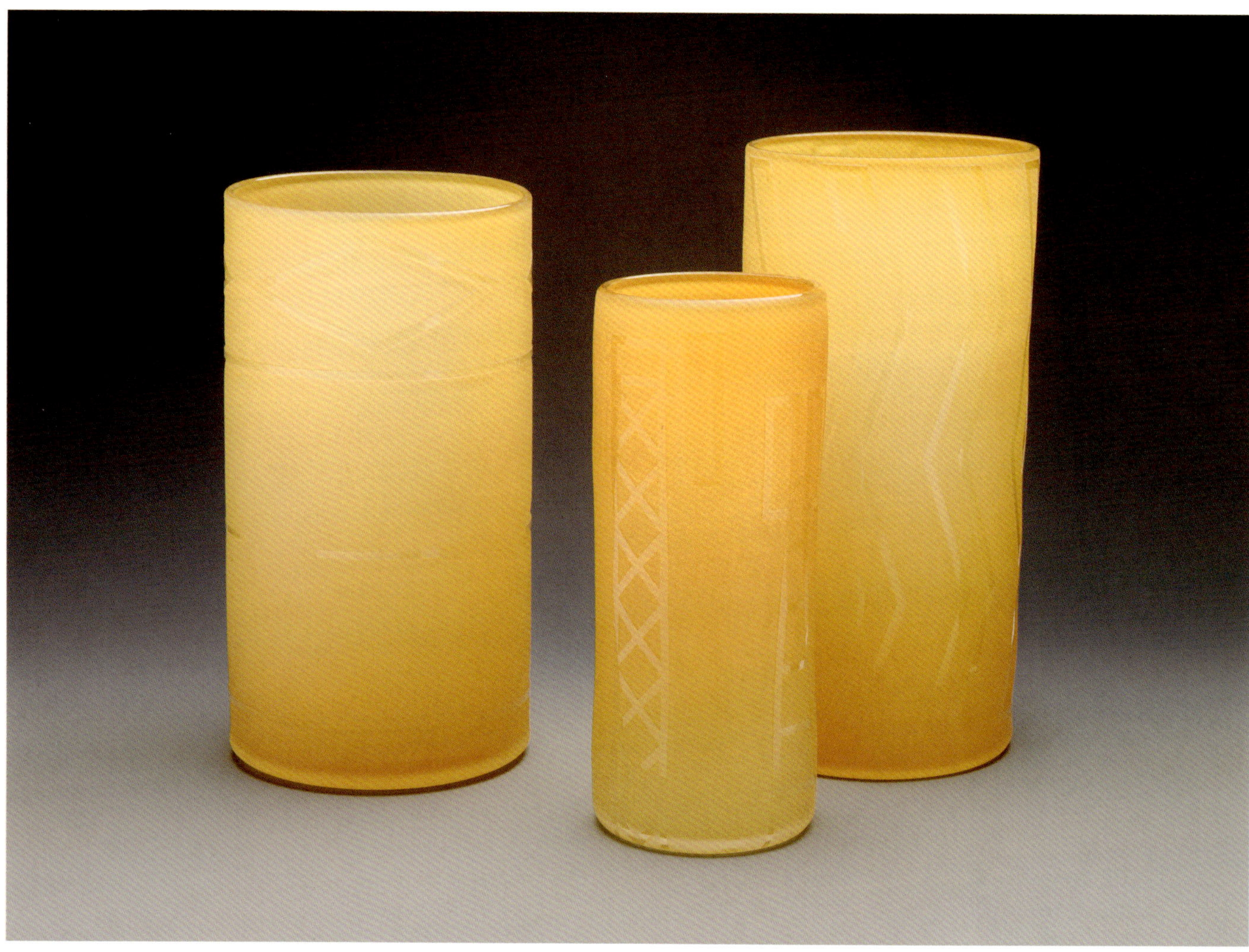

Plate 61 (left to right)
Codex: Freeway with HOV, 2009
Sandblasted blown glass
18 × 9½ × 9½ in.
(45.7 × 24.1 × 24.1 cm)

Codex: Cell Tower, 2009
Sandblasted blown glass
16½ × 7 × 7 in.
(41.9 × 17.8 × 17.8 cm)

Codex: Lightning, 2009
Sandblasted blown glass
19 × 9½ × 9½ in.
(48.3 × 24.1 × 24.1 cm)

Plate 62
Cell Tower, 2009
Waxed linen, wool, bias tape, and thread
5½ × 3 × 3 in.
(14 × 7.6 × 7.6 cm)

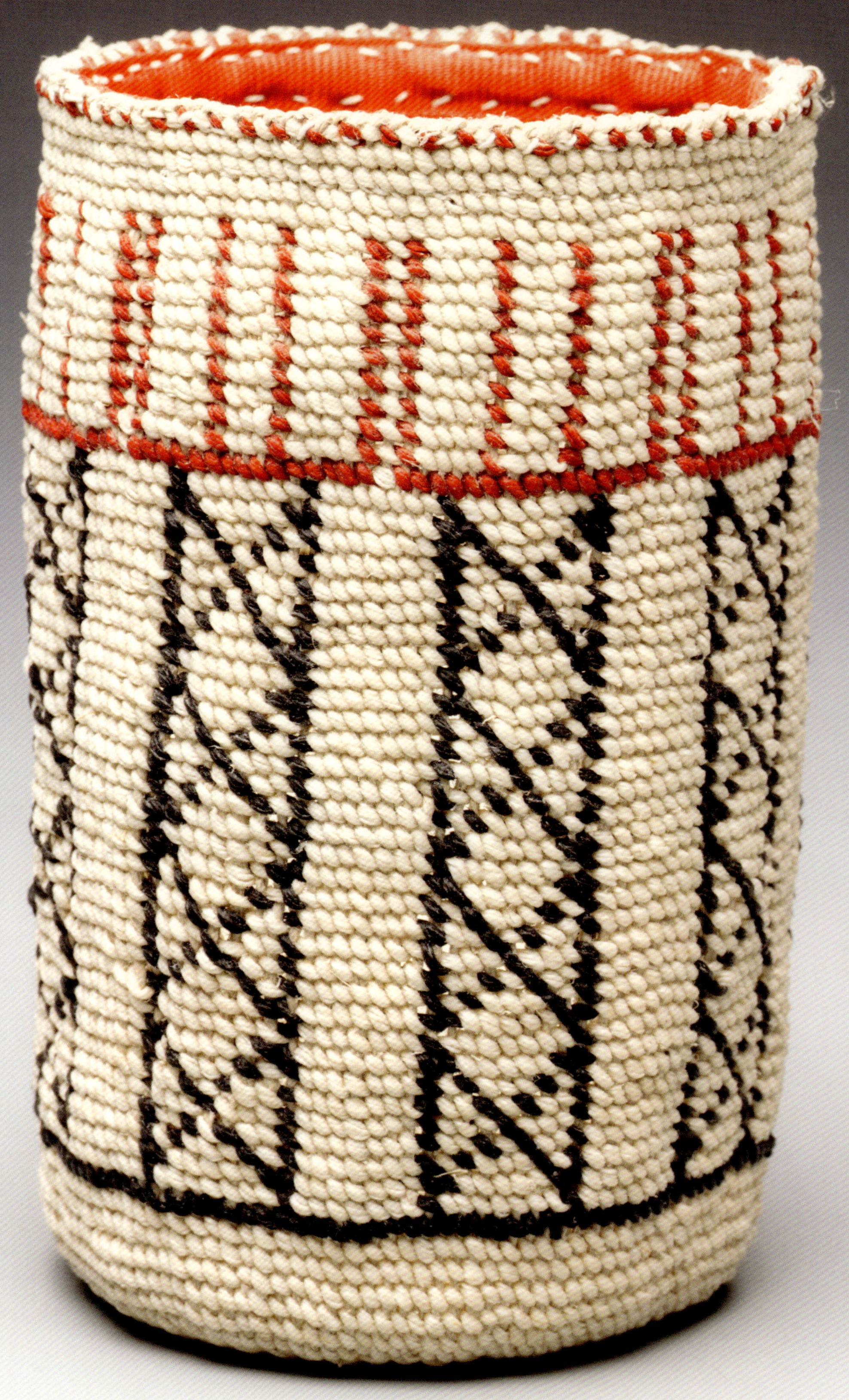

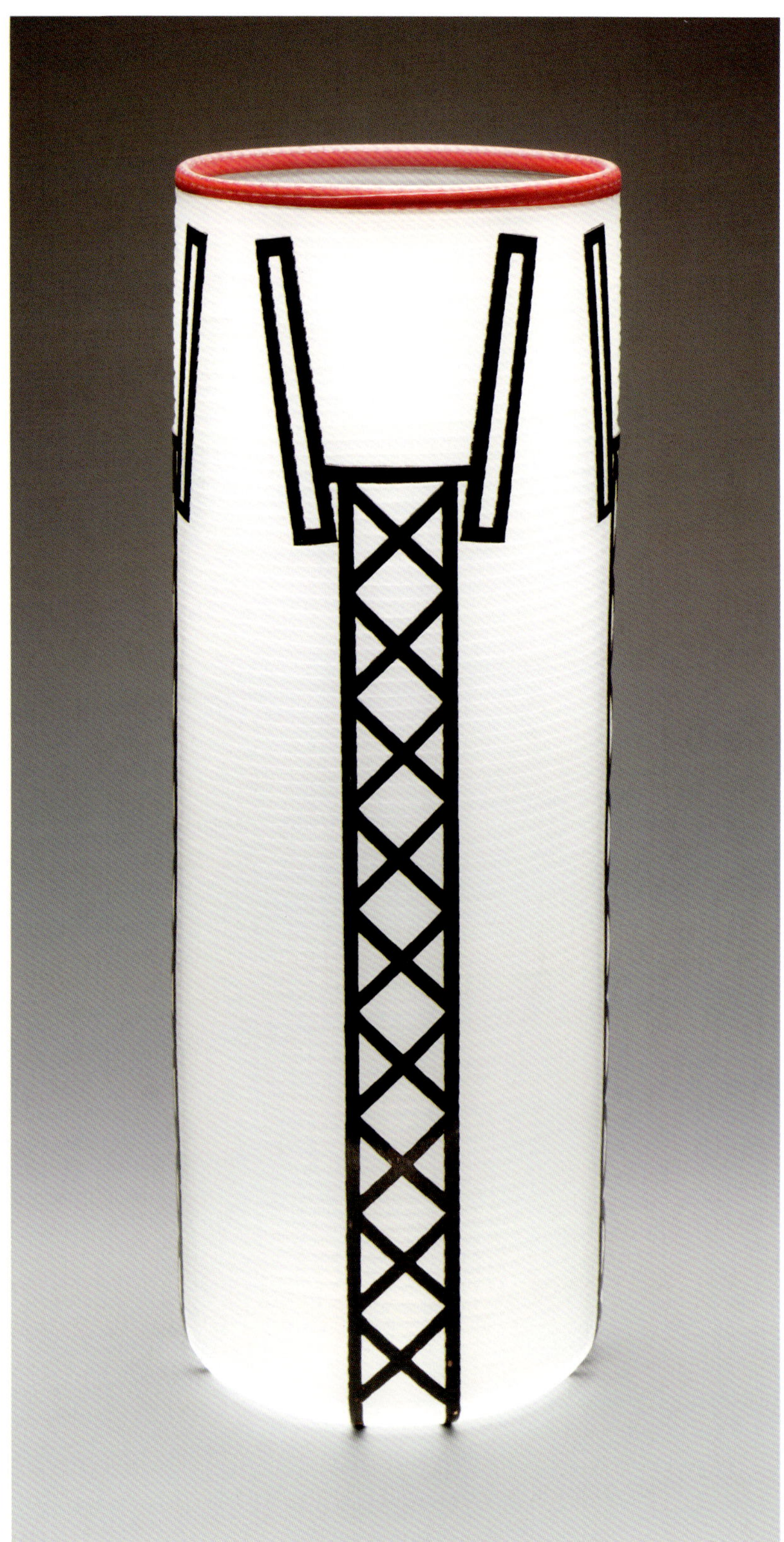

Plate 63
Cell Phone Tower, 2009
Sandblasted blown glass
22 × 8 × 8 in.
(55.9 × 20.3 × 20.3 cm)

Plate 64 (left)
Changer 4, 2012
Sandblasted blown glass
24½ × 10½ × 10½ in.
(62.2 × 26.7 × 26.7 cm)

Plate 65 (right)
Changer 3, 2012
Sandblasted blown glass
22 × 9 × 9 in.
(55.9 × 22.9 × 22.9 cm)

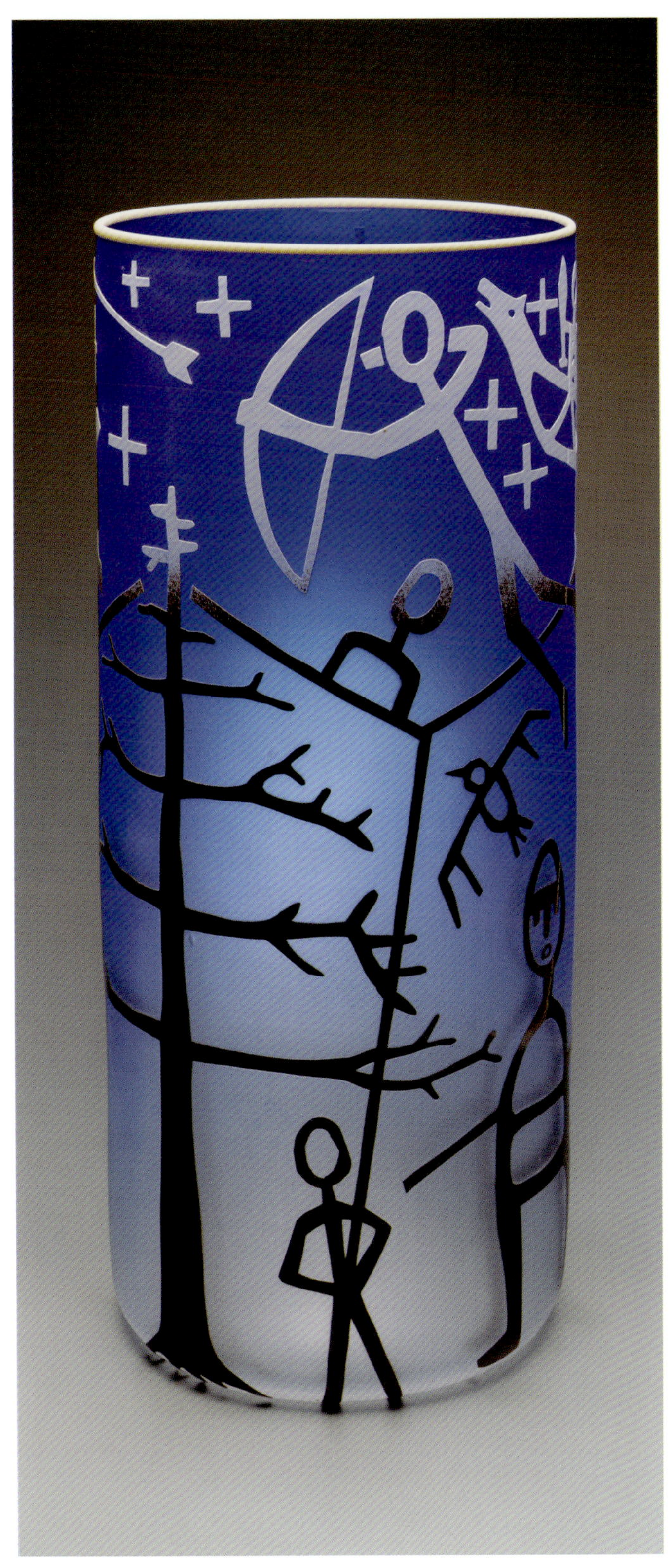

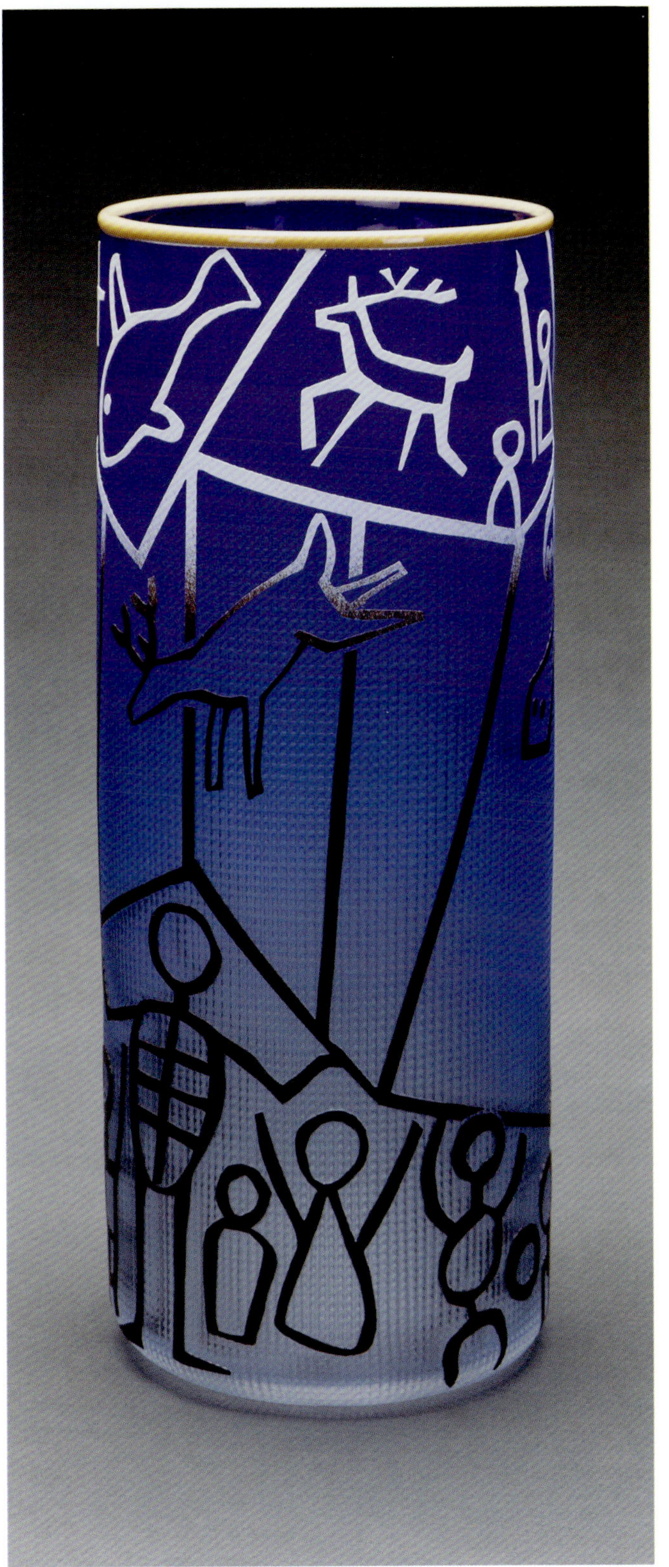

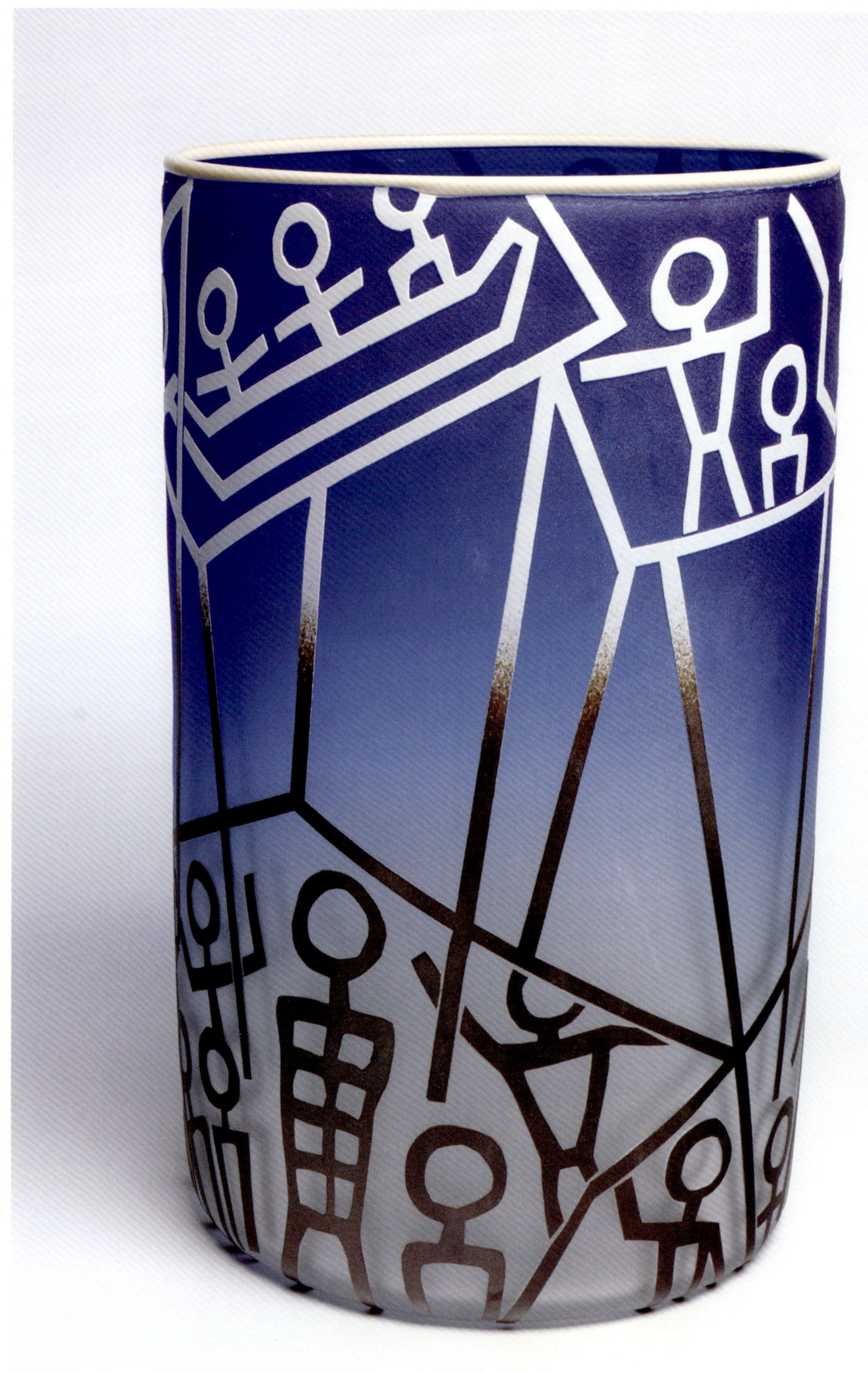

Plate 66
Raising the Sky, 2011
Sandblasted blown glass
19 × 11 × 11 in.
(48.3 × 27.9 × 27.9 cm)

Plate 67
Elk at Canoe Race, 2018
Relief monoprint with collage, spray paint, acrylic, and graphite
24 × 18 in. (61 × 45.7 cm)

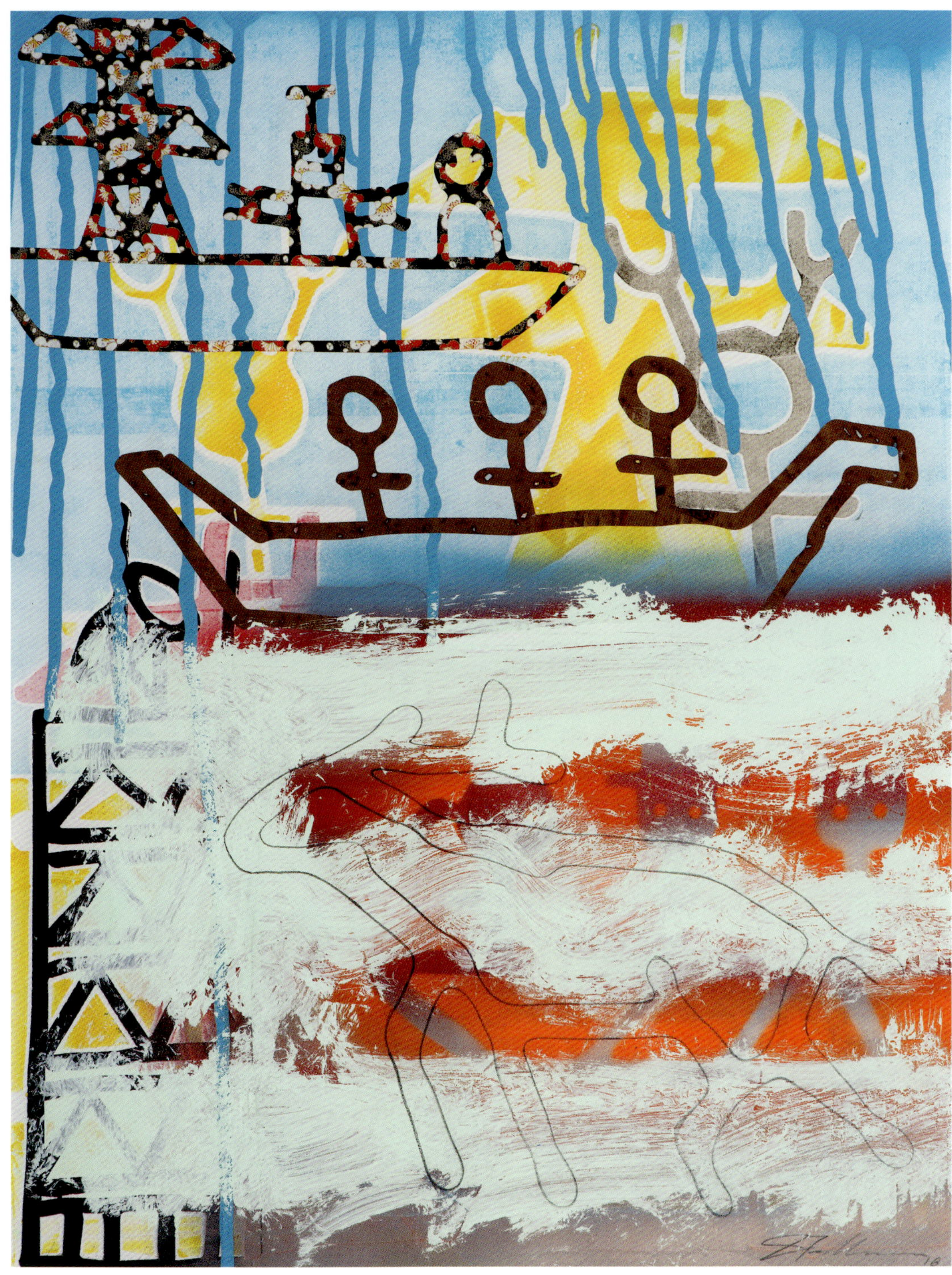

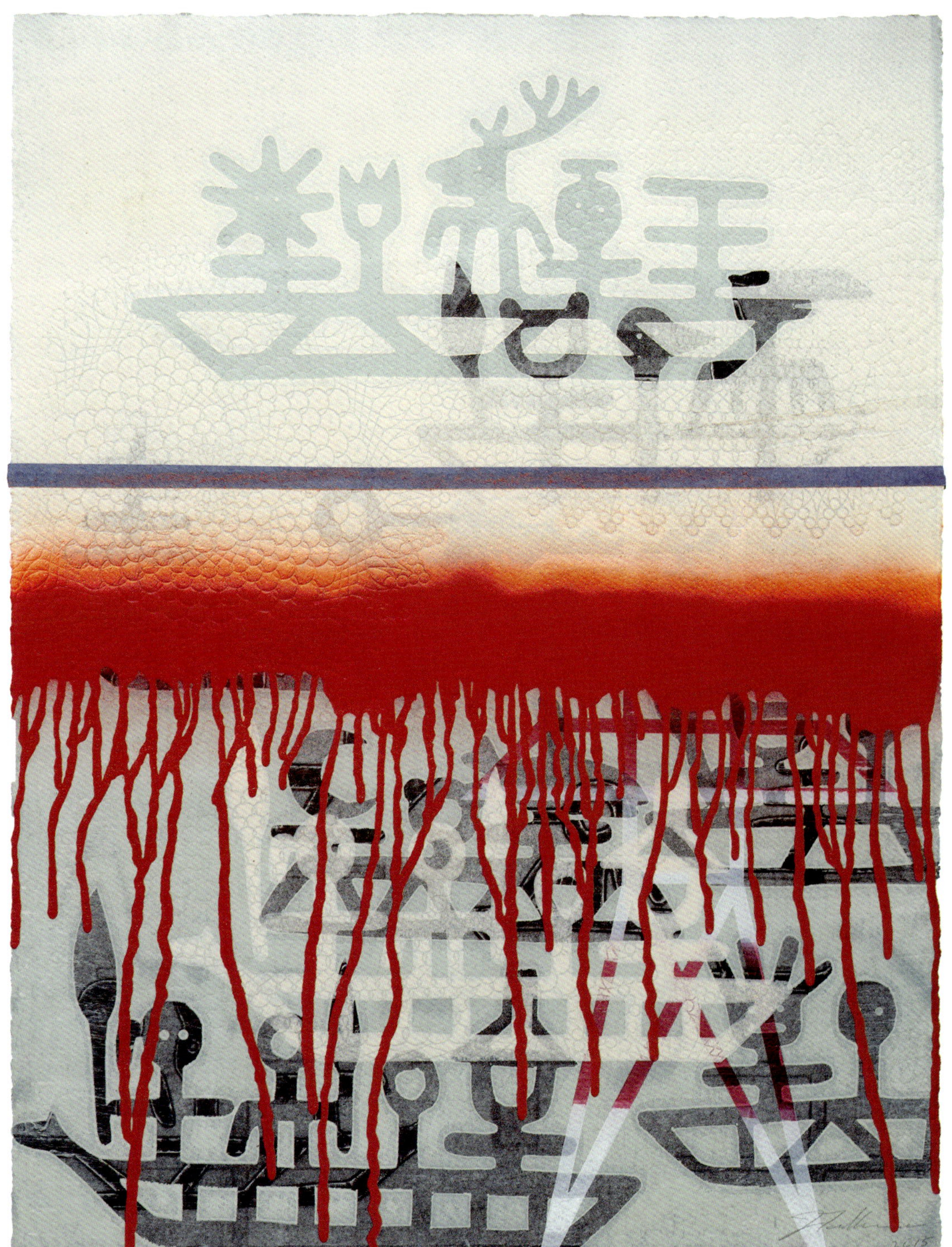

Plate 68
Black Ghost, 2015
Relief, collagraph, and stencil monoprint with spray paint
30 × 22 in.
(76.2 × 55.9 cm)

Plate 69
Geese Flying Over, 2015
Relief, collagraph, and
stencil monoprint
30 × 22 in.
(76.2 × 55.9 cm)

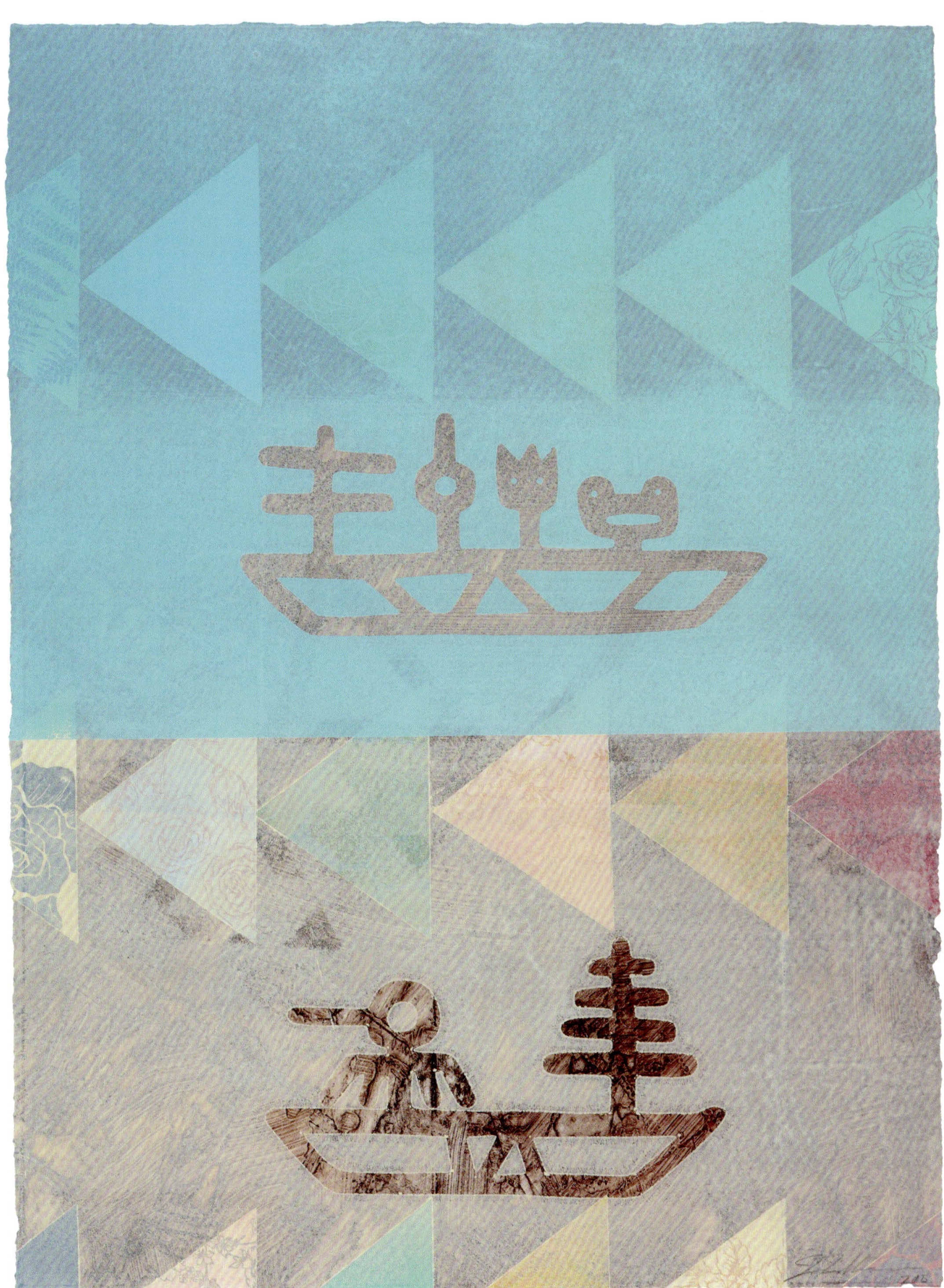

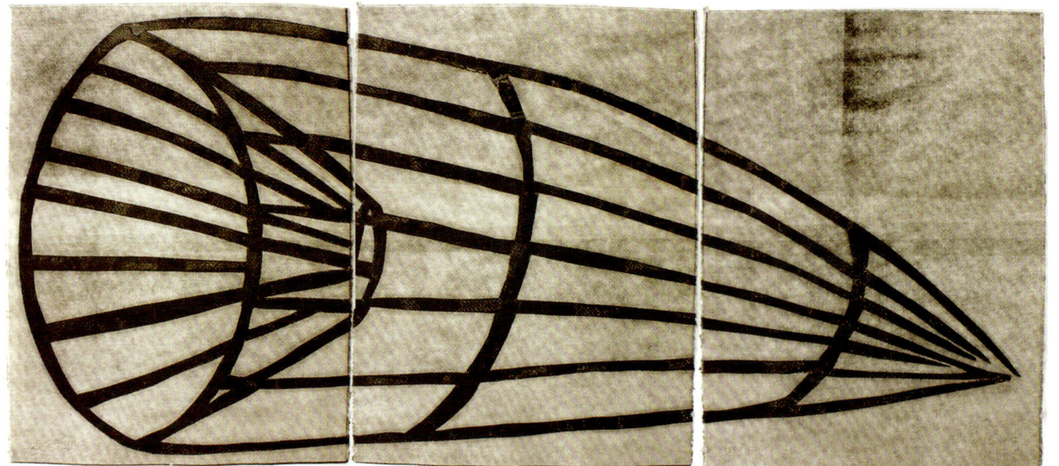

Plate 70
Fish Trap II, 2014
Monotype
Overall: 30 × 67 in.
(76.2 × 170.2 cm)

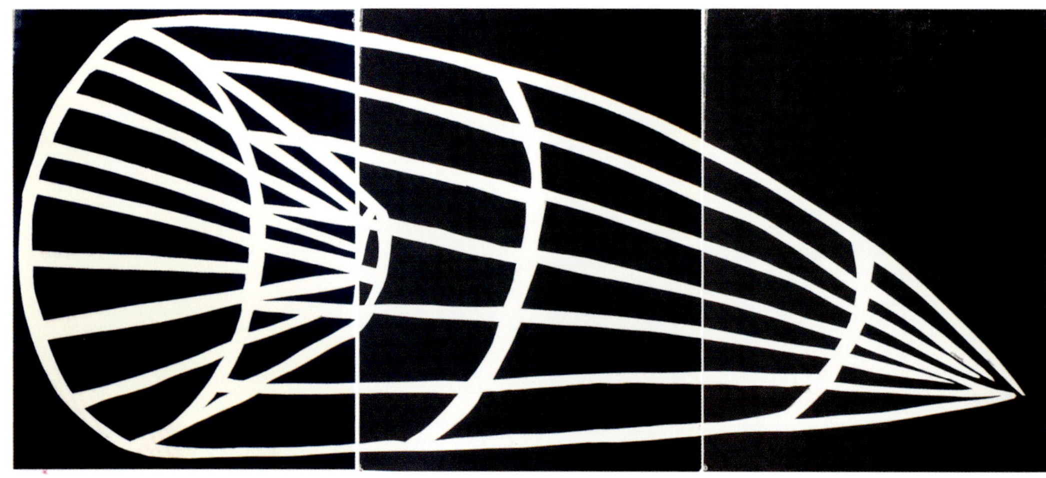

Plate 71
Fish Trap, 2014
Monotype
Overall: 30 × 67 in.
(76.2 × 170.2 cm)

Plate 72
Voltage Tower, 2014
Monotype
Overall: 90 × 66 in.
(228.6 × 167.6 cm)

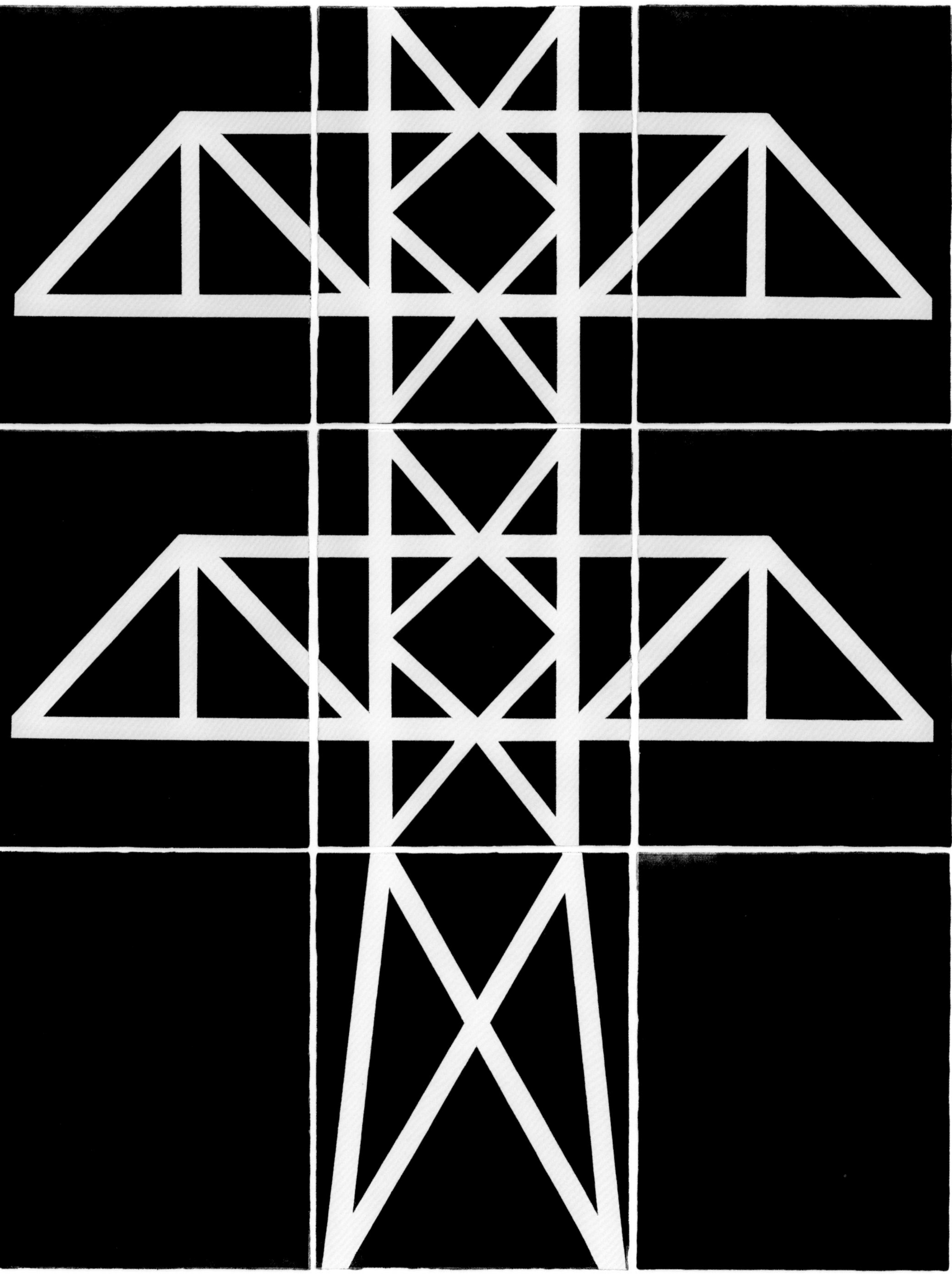

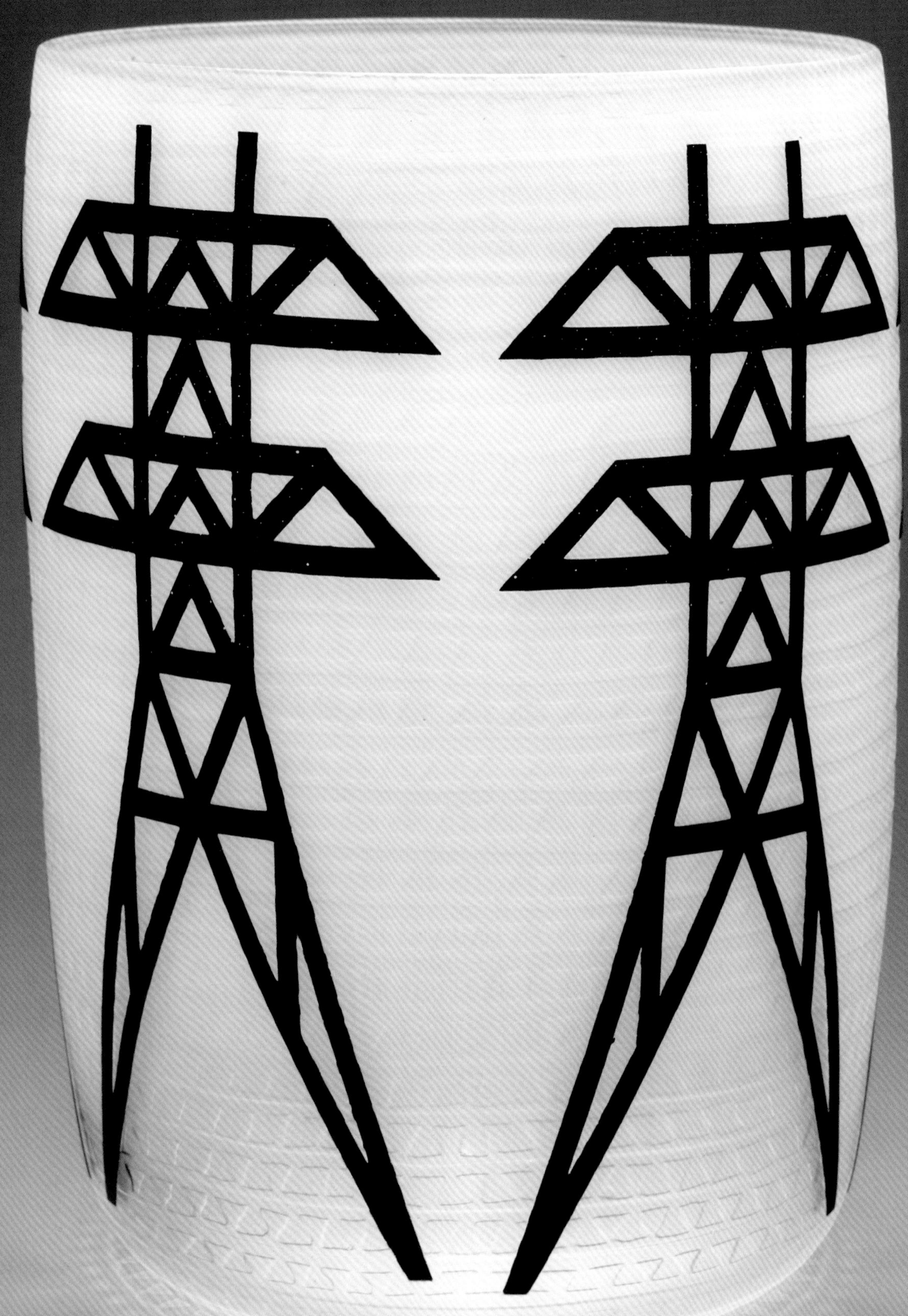

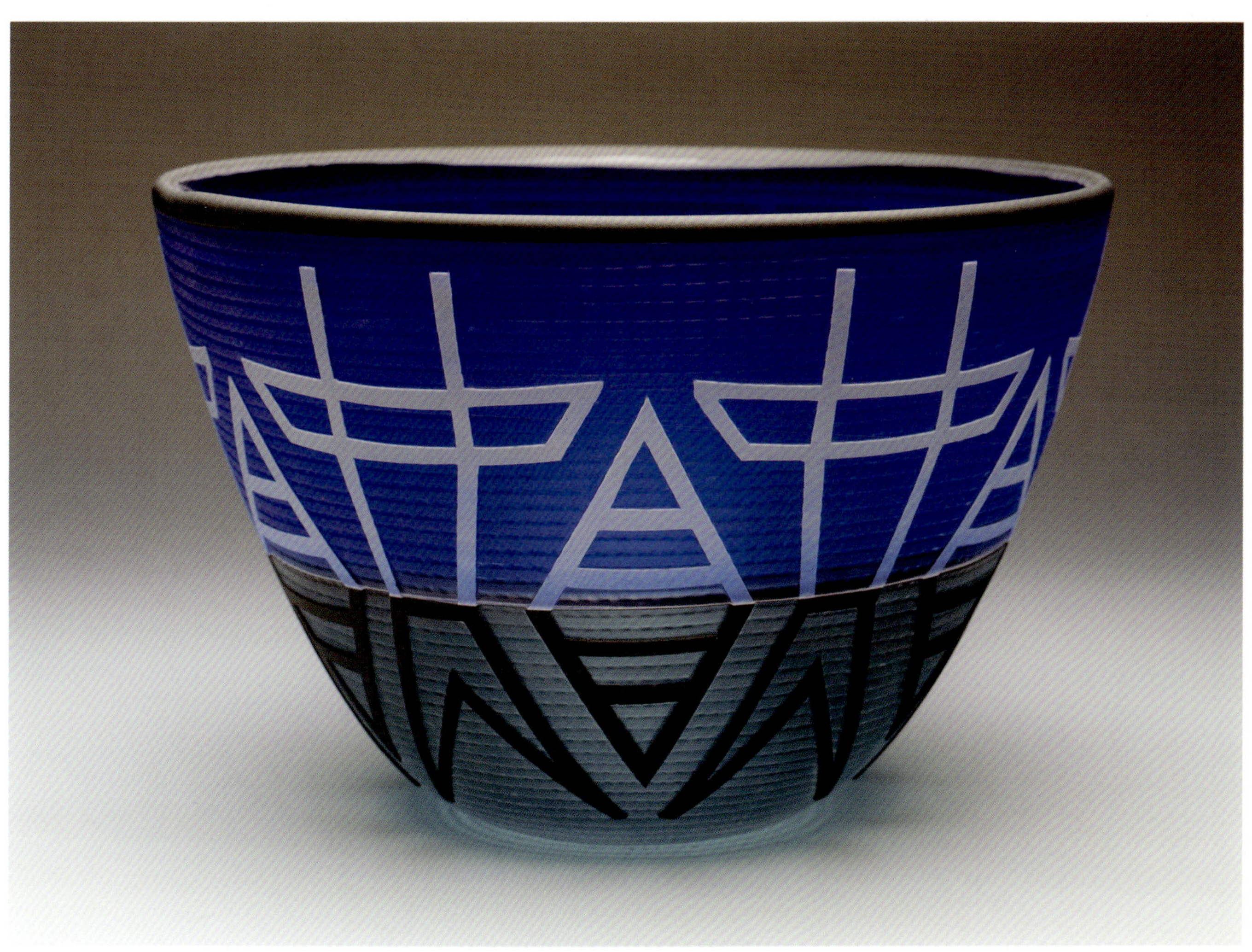

Plate 74
High Voltage Tower, 2004
Sandblasted blown glass
9 × 13 × 13 in.
(22.9 × 33 × 33 cm)

Plate 73
Black High Voltage Tower,
2023
Sandblasted blown glass
15 × 9 × 9 in.
(38.1 × 22.9 × 22.9 cm)

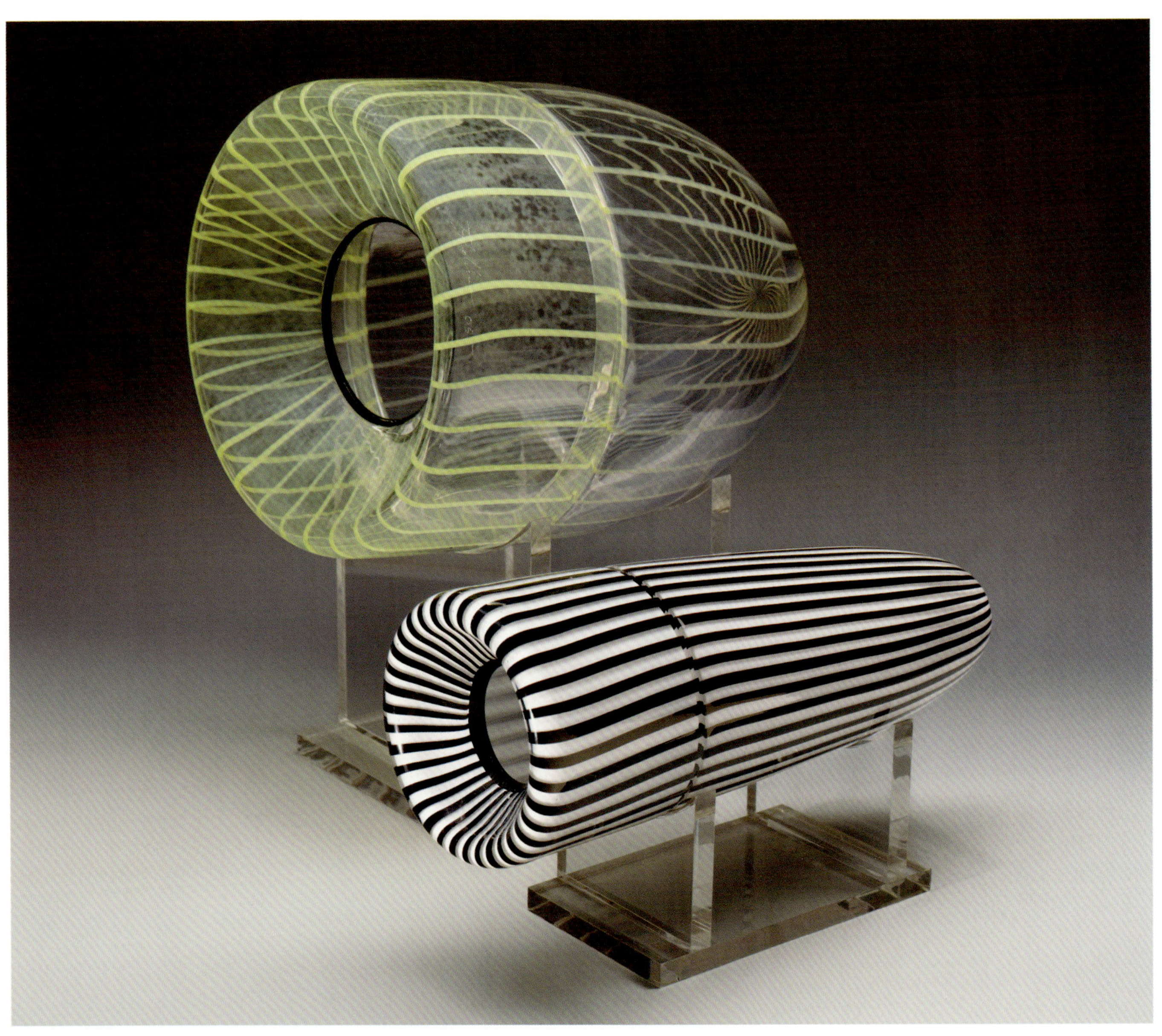

Plate 75
Fish Trap V, 2005
Blown glass
13 × 17 × 13 in.
(33 × 43.2 × 33 cm)

Fish Trap IV, 2005
Blown glass
7 × 18 × 7 in.
(17.8 × 45.7 × 17.8 cm)

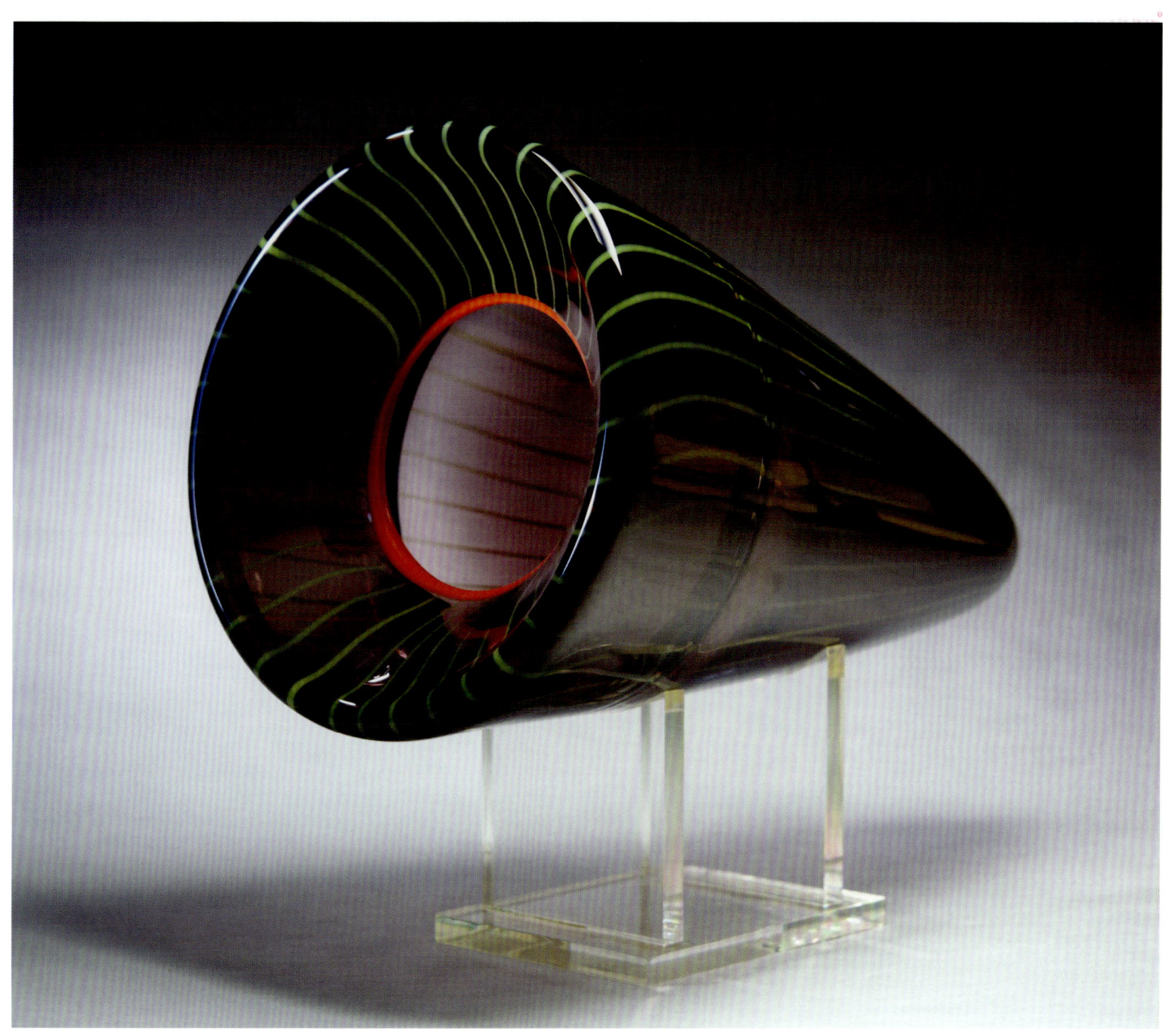

Plate 76
Fish Trap II, 2005
Blown glass
14 × 22½ × 14 in.
(35.6 × 57.2 × 35.6 cm)

Salmon

You are in the fine bones
of our babies, as you are in us
It is life we see
as you fight up the river.
In your memory at certain places
The water spills in a burst of light
Over great rocks, fast towards the Pacific.
The falls are gone now
 and our path of water
lies wide as the sea itself.
Salmon,
 we can only be grateful
that you come again.
We can promise
 we will fight for you,
 we will sing for you,
we are not separate,
you make the precious bones
 of our babies.

Ramona Wilson – Colville Confederated Tribes

Ramona Wilson, "Salmon," in *Terrain: Plateau Native Art & Poetry*, ed. Joe Feddersen, 2014

Plate 77
Snipe Woman Steals Salmon, 2014
Waxed linen, bias tape, and thread
9 × 5½ × 5½ in.
(22.9 × 14 × 14 cm)

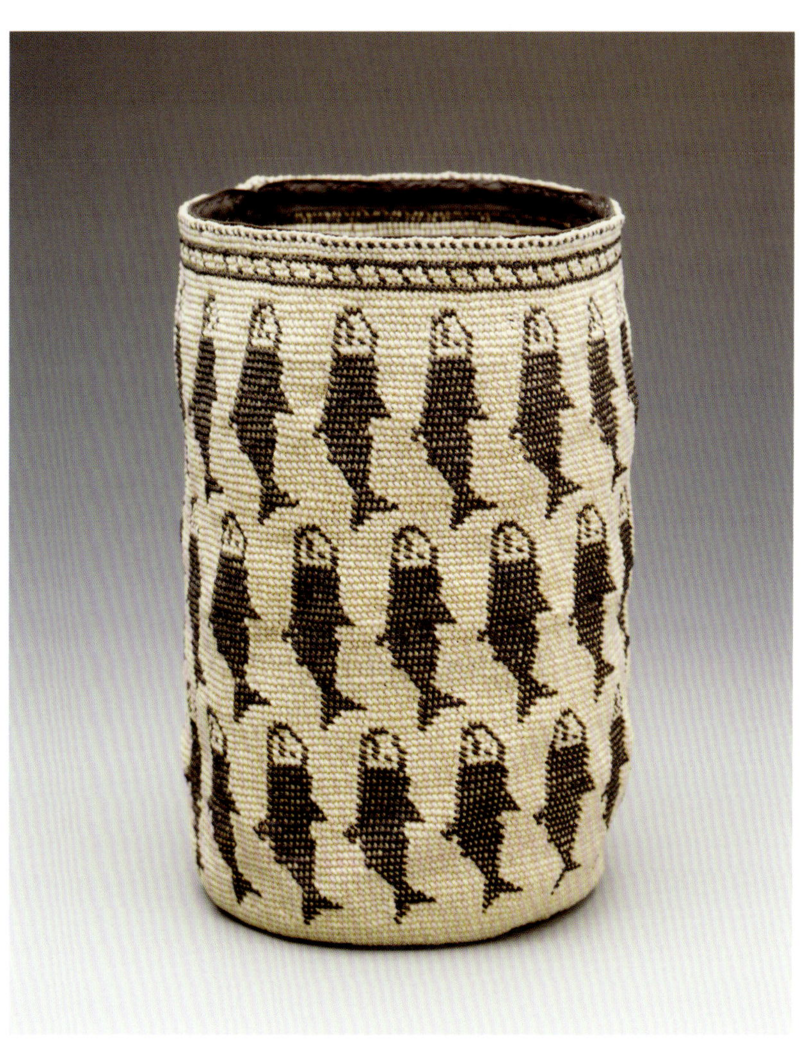

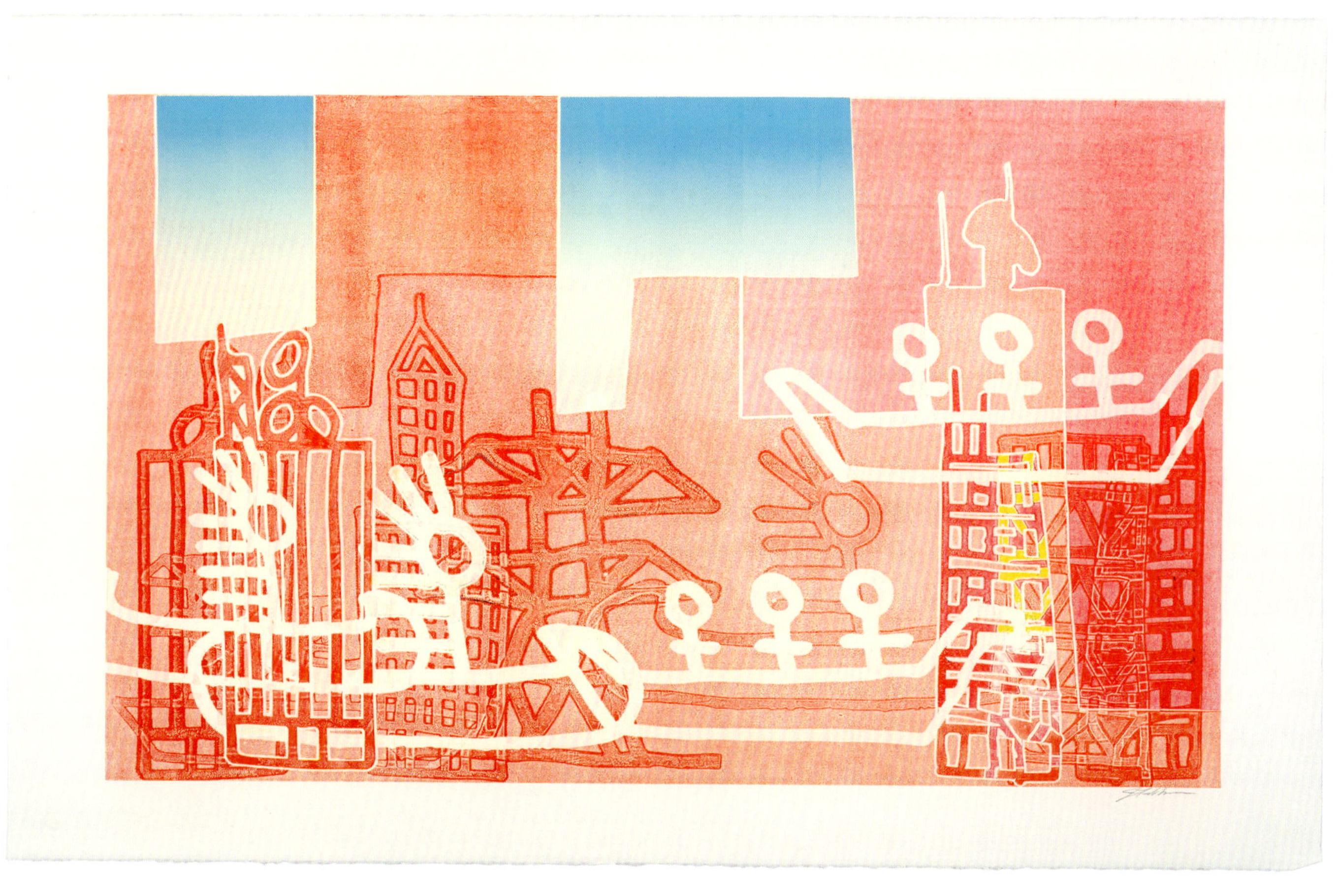

Plate 78
Red Urban Canoeing,
2017
Relief and stencil
monoprint
Sheet: 25 × 40 in.
(63.5 × 101.6 cm);
image: 14½ × 19 in.
(36.8 × 48.3 cm)

Plate 79
Yellow Urban Canoeing, 2017
Relief and stencil monoprint with collage
Sheet: 30 × 22½ in. (76.2 × 57.2 cm); image: 24 × 18 in. (61 × 45.7 cm)

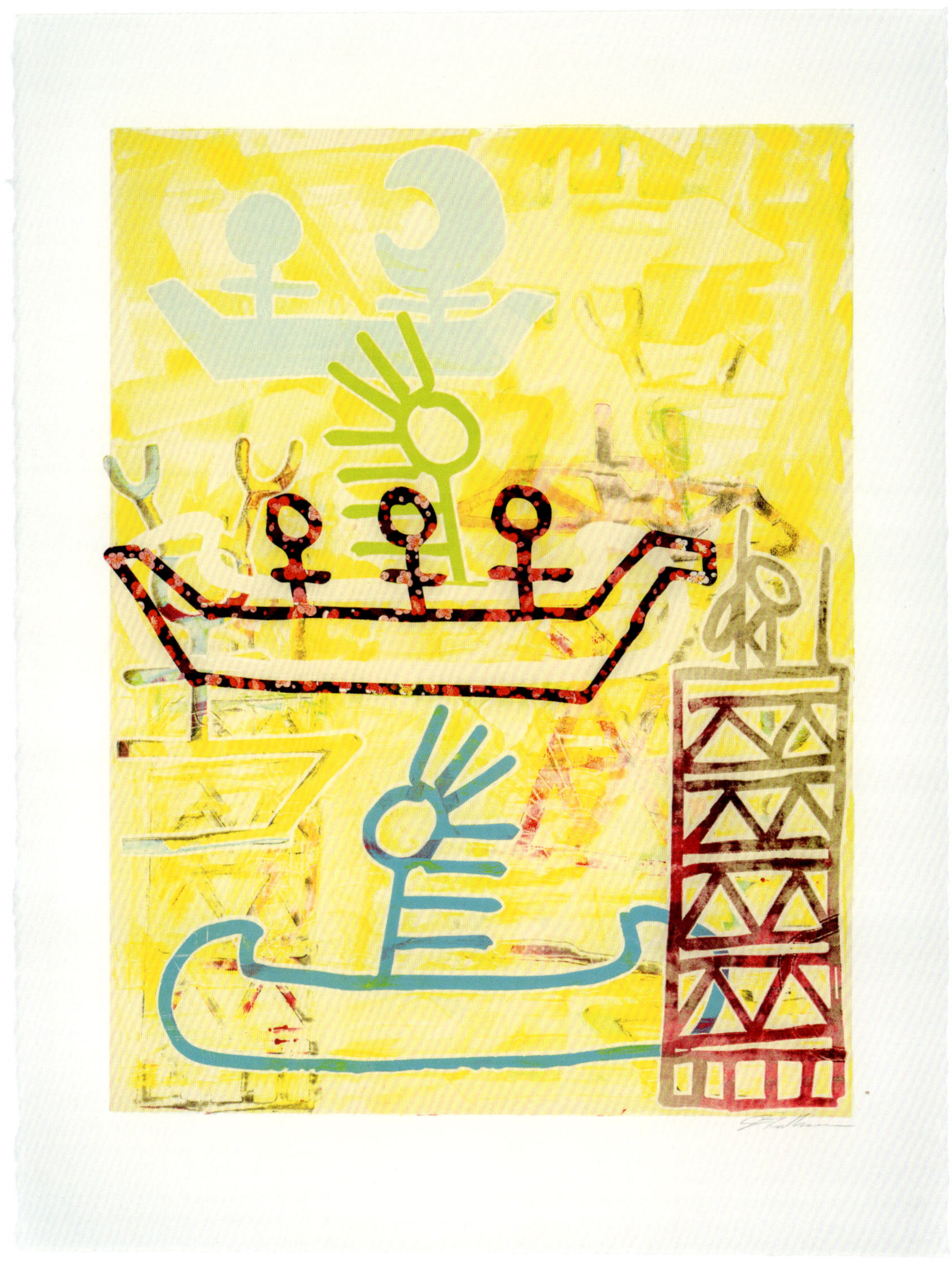

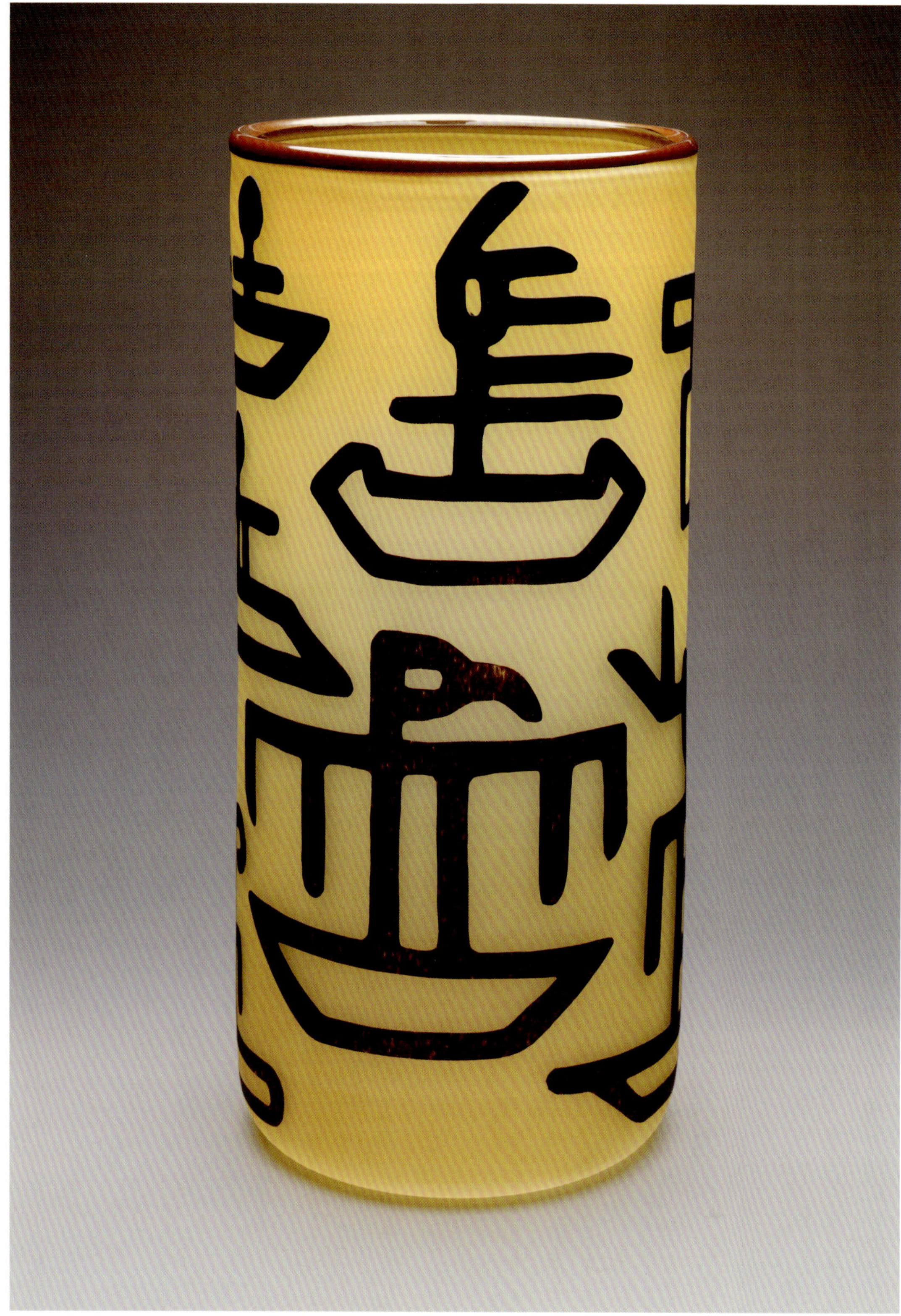

Plate 80
Canoe Journey, 2019
Sandblasted blown glass
22 × 9½ × 9½ in.
(55.9 × 24.1 × 24.1 cm)

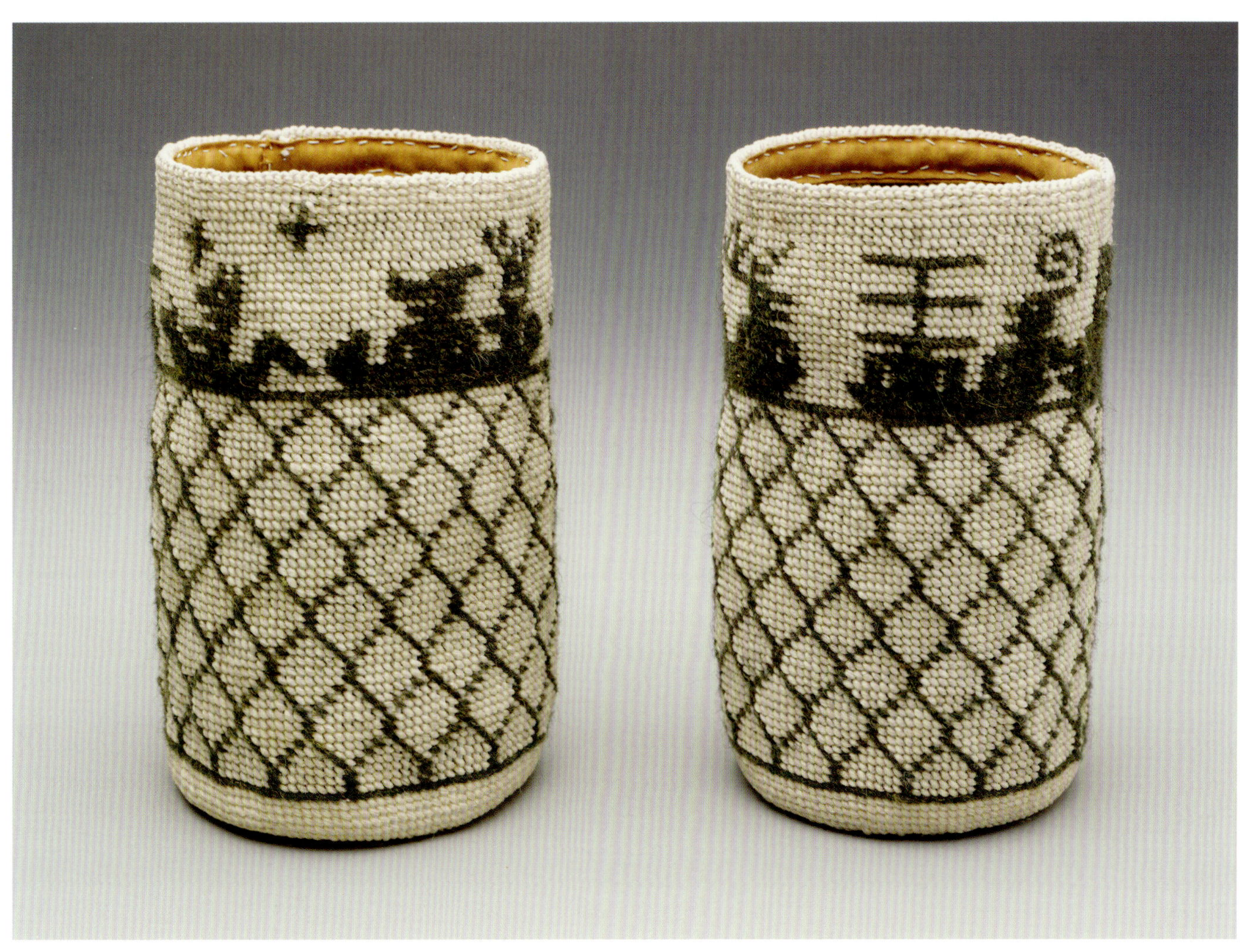

Plate 81
Fishing, 2023
Waxed linen, wool, bias tape, and thread
Each: 6½ × 3½ × 3½ in. (16.5 × 8.9 × 8.9 cm)

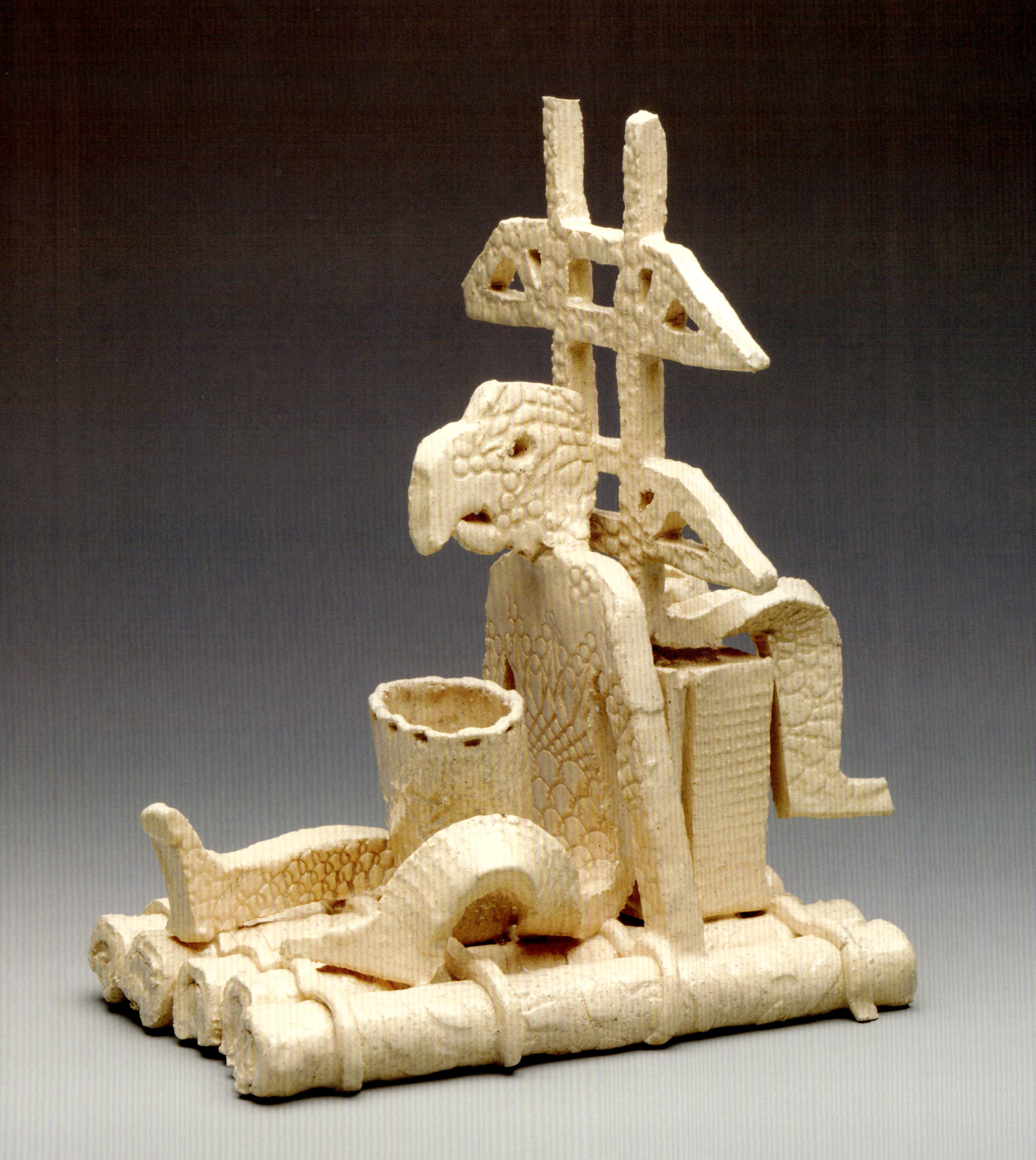

Plate 82
Canoe Journey: Crow in Sturgeon Nose Canoe, 2016
Low-fire ceramic
8½ × 17 × 13 in.
(21.6 × 43.2 × 33 cm)

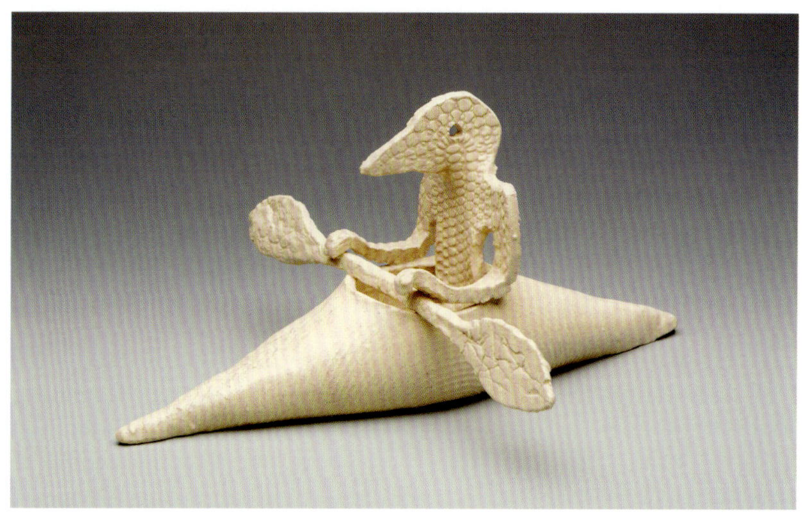

Plate 83
Canoe Journey: Capsized Canoe, 2016
Low-fire ceramic
8½ × 17 × 7½ in.
(21.6 × 43.2 × 19.1 cm)

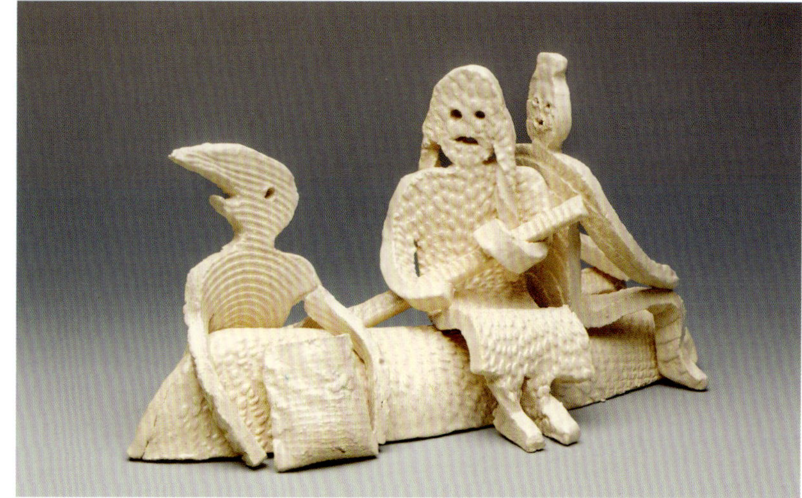

Plate 84
Canoe Journey: Person in Canoe, 2016
Low-fire ceramic
9 × 16 × 4 in.
(22.9 × 40.6 × 10.2 cm)

Canoe Journey: Wolf, 2016
Low-fire ceramic
8½ × 14 × 9 in.
(21.6 × 35.6 × 22.9 cm)

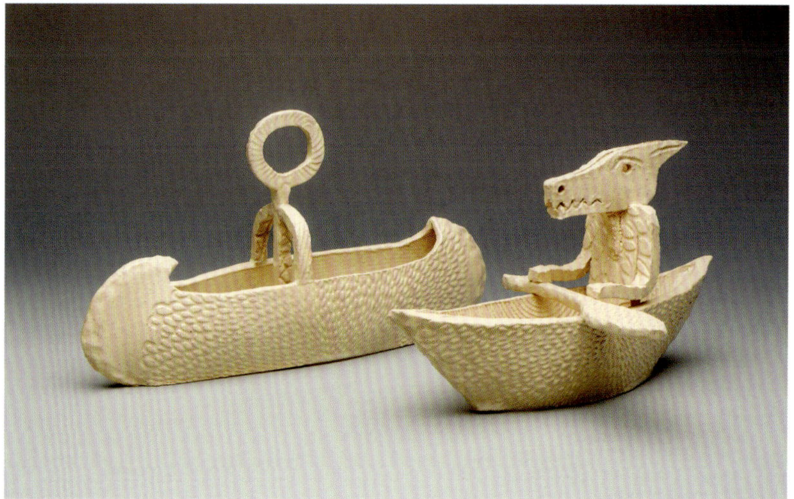

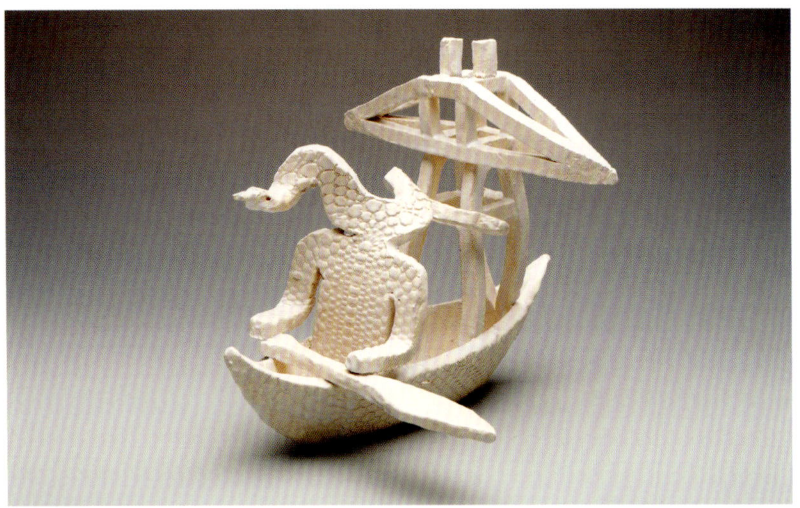

Plate 85
Canoe Journey: Snake and High Voltage Tower, 2016
Low-fire ceramic
11½ × 14 × 11½ in.
(29.2 × 35.6 × 29.2 cm)

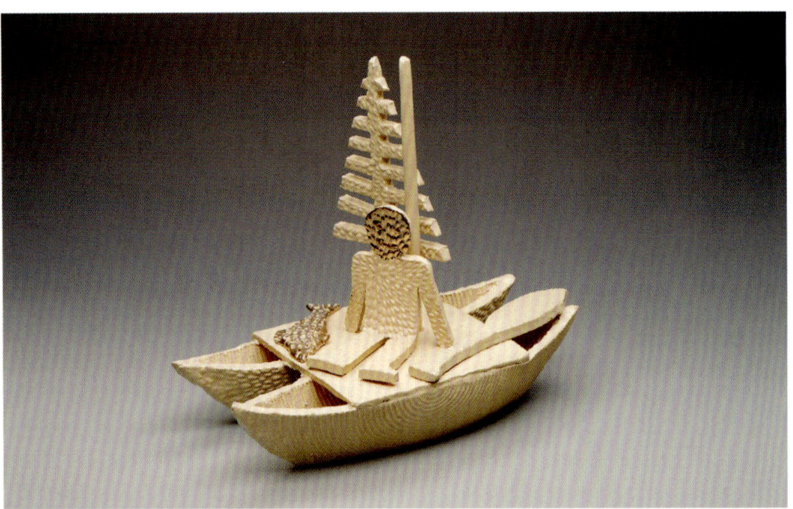

Plate 86
Canoe Journey: Catamaran, 2015
Low-fire ceramic with gold leaf
8 × 7 × 15 in.
(20.3 × 17.8 × 38.1 cm)

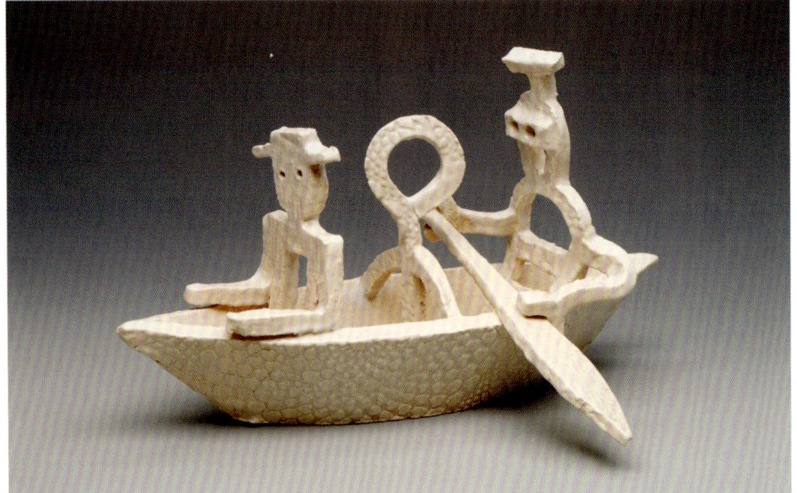

Plate 87
Canoe Journey: Robot Rowing, 2016
Low-fire ceramic
9½ × 16 × 9½ in.
(24.1 × 40.6 × 24.1 cm)

Plate 88
Canoe Journey: Tulip, Parking Lot, Alien, 2016
Low-fire ceramic
9½ × 20 × 12 in.
(24.1 × 50.8 × 30.5 cm)

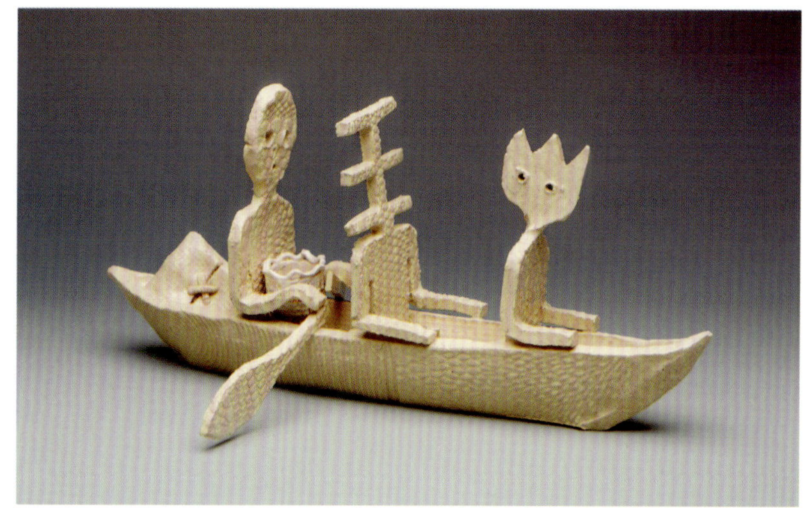

Plate 89
Canoe Journey: Raft, 2016
Low-fire ceramic
11½ × 7 × 10 in.
(29.2 × 17.8 × 25.4 cm)

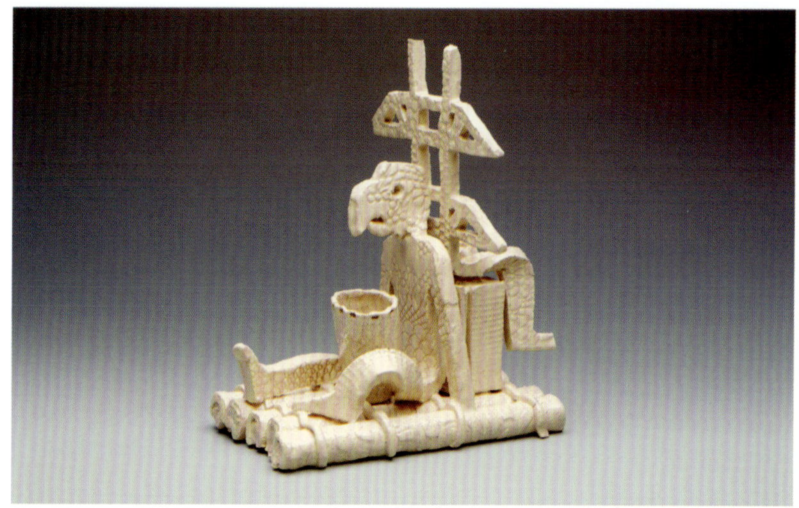

Plate 90
Canoe Journey: Flat Screen and Hatted Man, 2016
Low-fire ceramic
8½ × 16 × 7 in.
(21.6 × 40.6 × 17.8 cm)

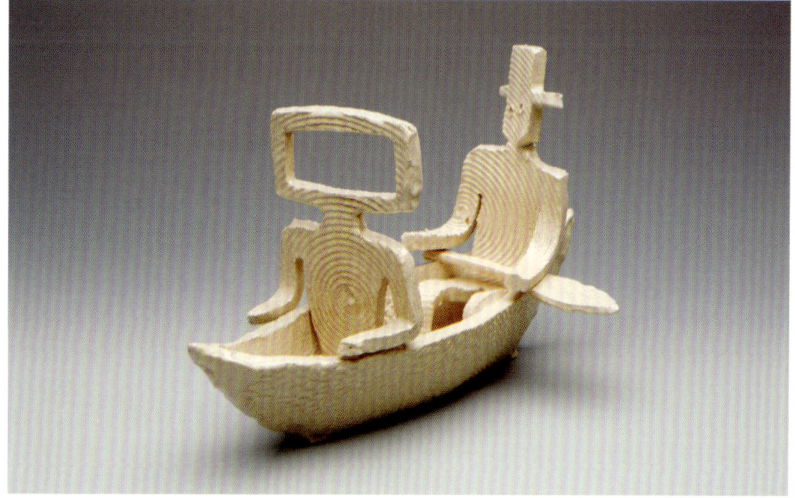

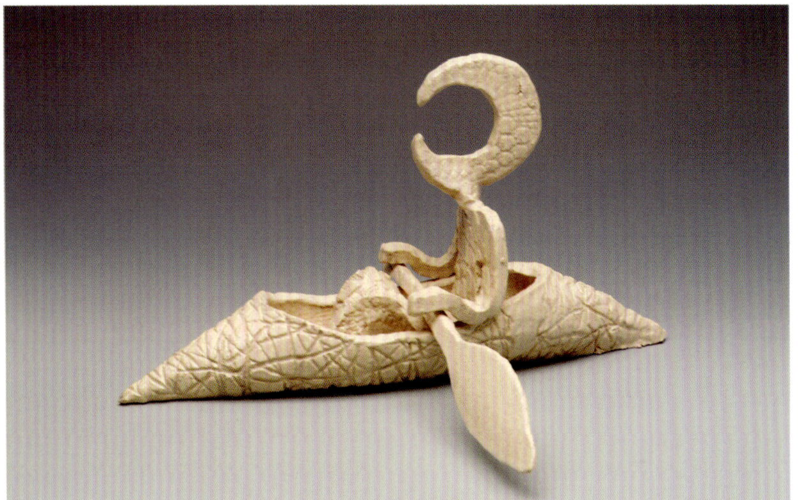

Plate 91
Canoe Journey: Moon, 2016
Low-fire ceramic
10 × 13 × 17 in.
(25.4 × 33 × 43.2 cm)

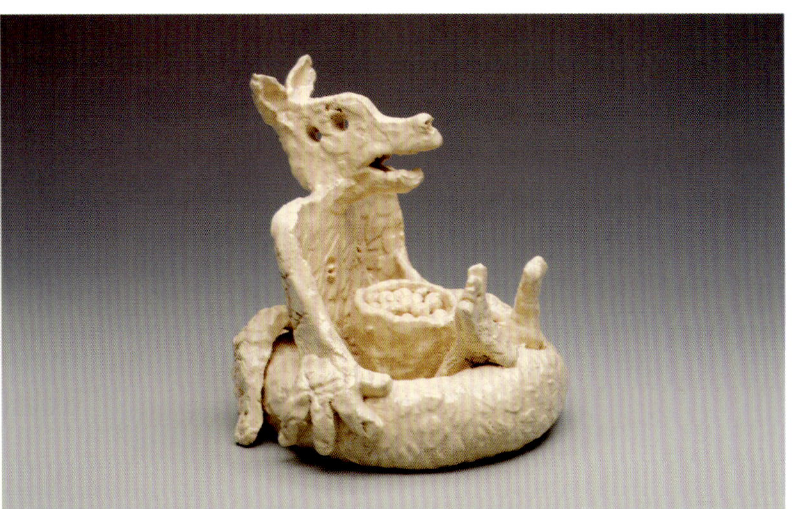

Plate 92
Canoe Journey: Coyote in Inner Tube, 2016
Low-fire ceramic
6½ × 7 × 7½ in.
(16.5 × 17.8 × 19.1 cm)

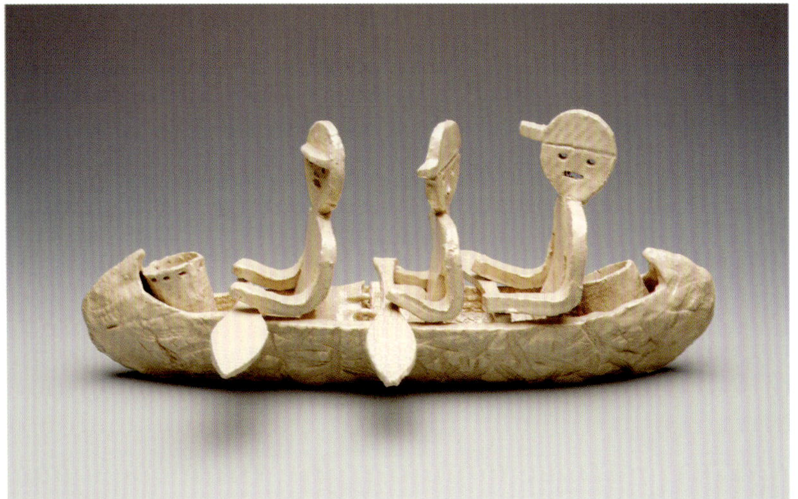

Plate 93
Canoe Journey: Troop, 2016
Low-fire ceramic
8 × 18 × 12 in.
(20.3 × 45.7 × 30.5 cm)

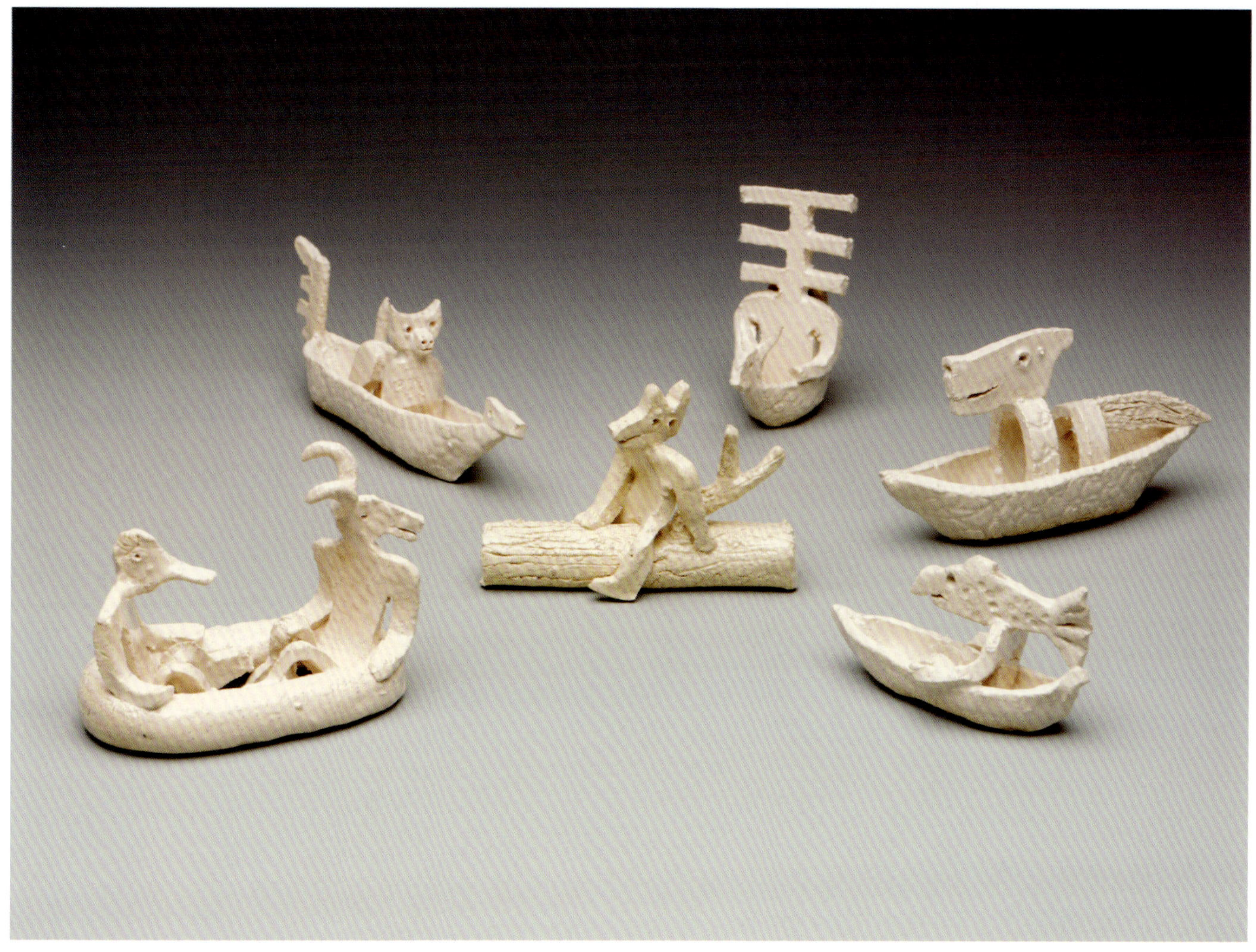

Plate 94
Small Canoe Journey,
2016
Low-fire ceramic
Dimensions variable

Plate 95 (following spread)
Canoe Journey 1, 2015
Low-fire ceramic
13 × 27 × 12 in.
(33 × 68.6 × 30.5 cm)

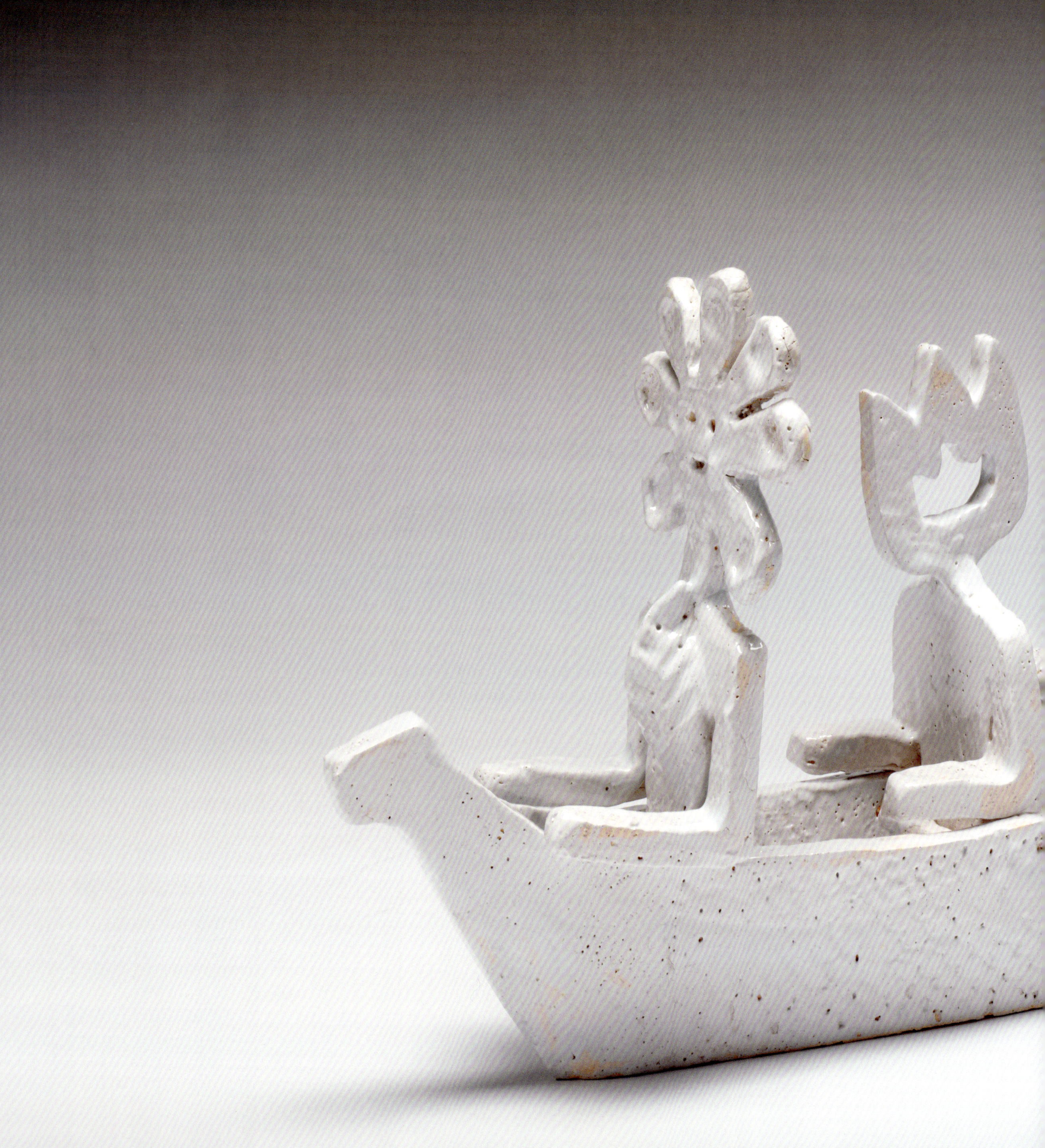

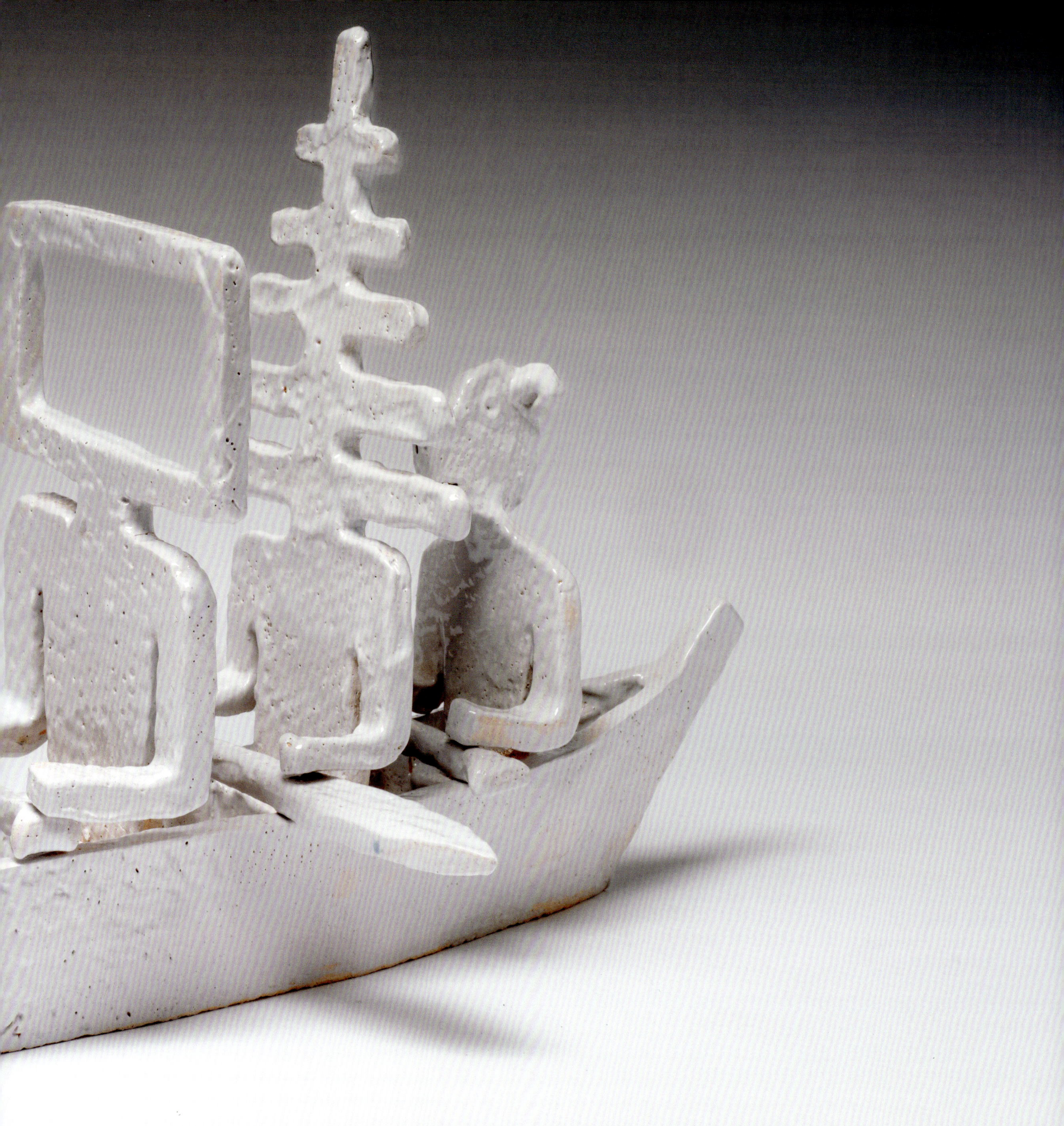

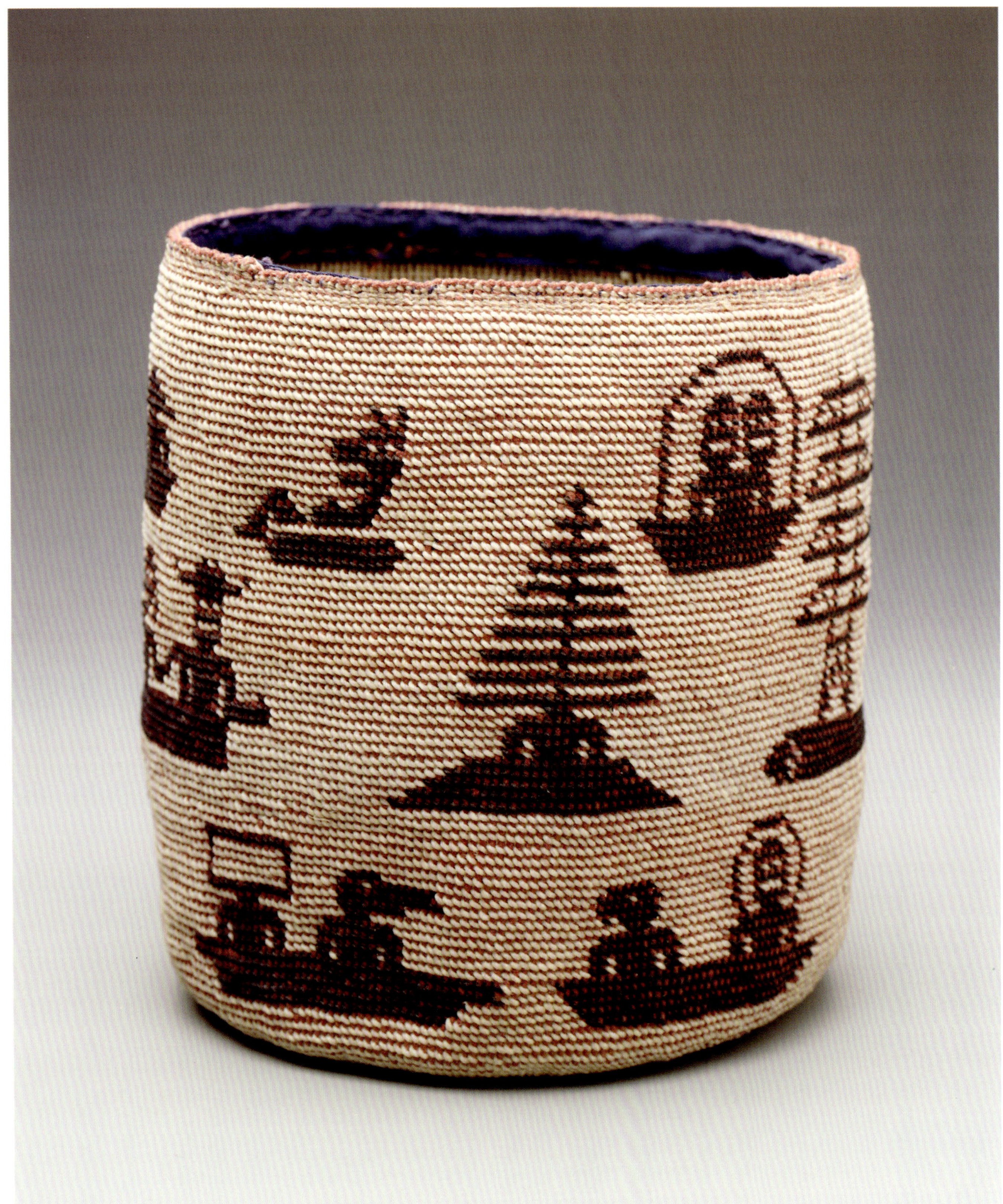

Plate 96
Canoe Journey, 2016
Waxed linen, bias tape, and thread
6½ × 6 × 6 in.
(16.5 × 15.2 × 15.2 cm)

Plate 97
Coyote Receives His Name, 2012
Waxed linen, bias tape, and thread
8½ × 7 × 7 in.
(21.6 × 17.8 × 17.8 cm)

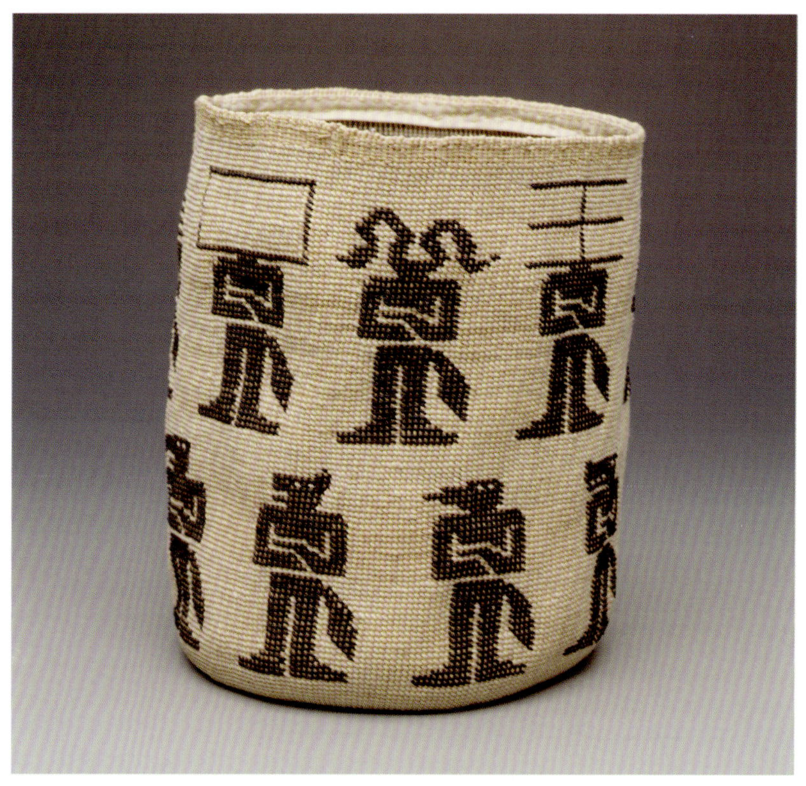

Plate 98
Coyote Receives His Name, 2013
Carved blown glass
9 × 6½ × 6½ in.
(22.9 × 16.5 × 16.5 cm)

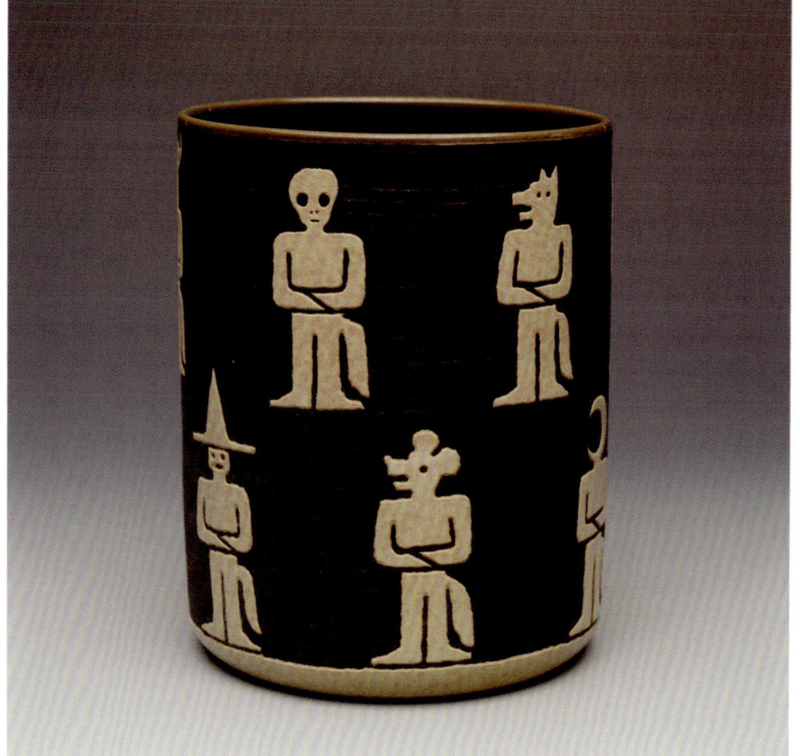

Plate 99
Bestiary Basket 1, 2021
Sandblasted blown glass
15 × 8 × 8 in.
(38.1 × 20.3 × 20.3 cm)

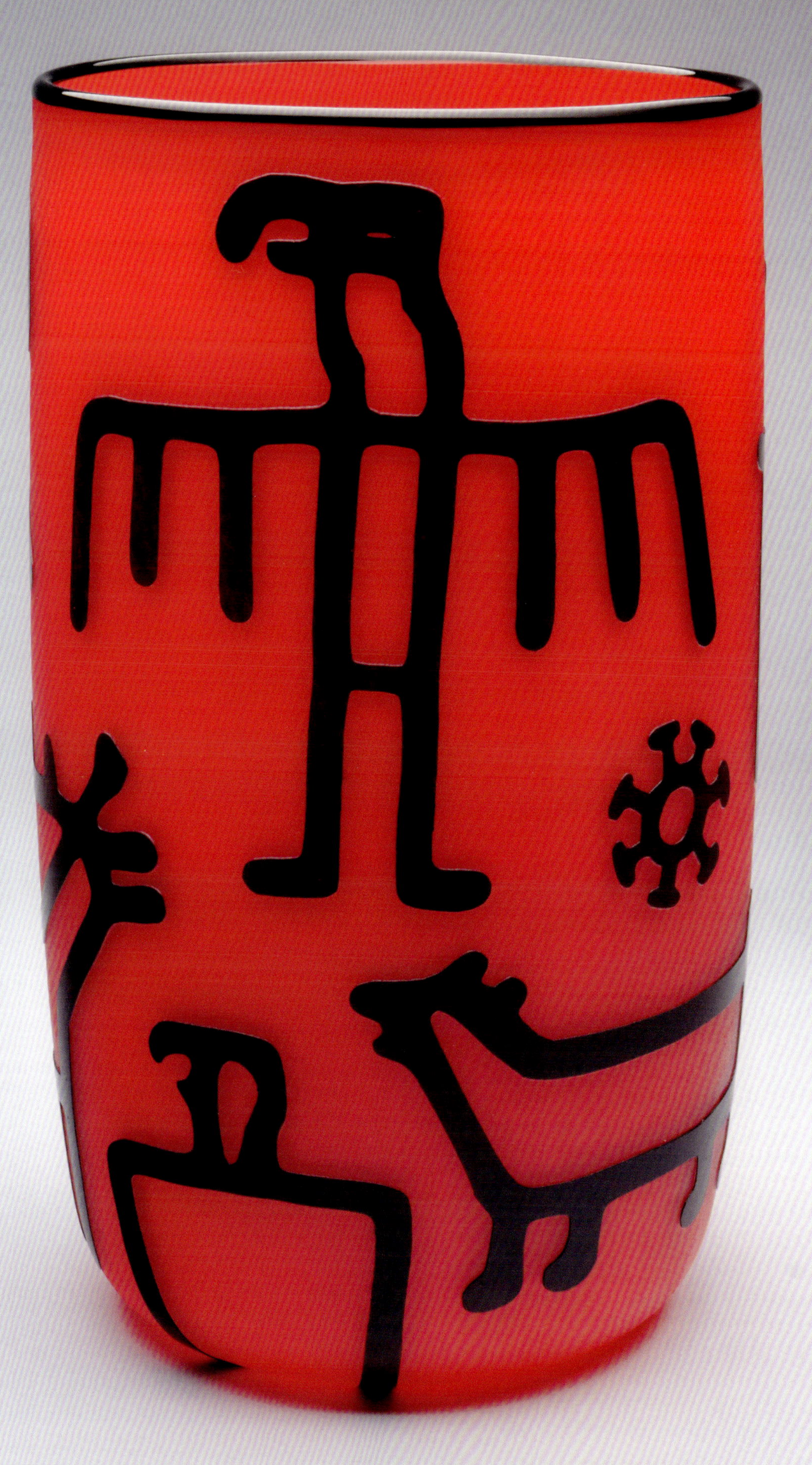

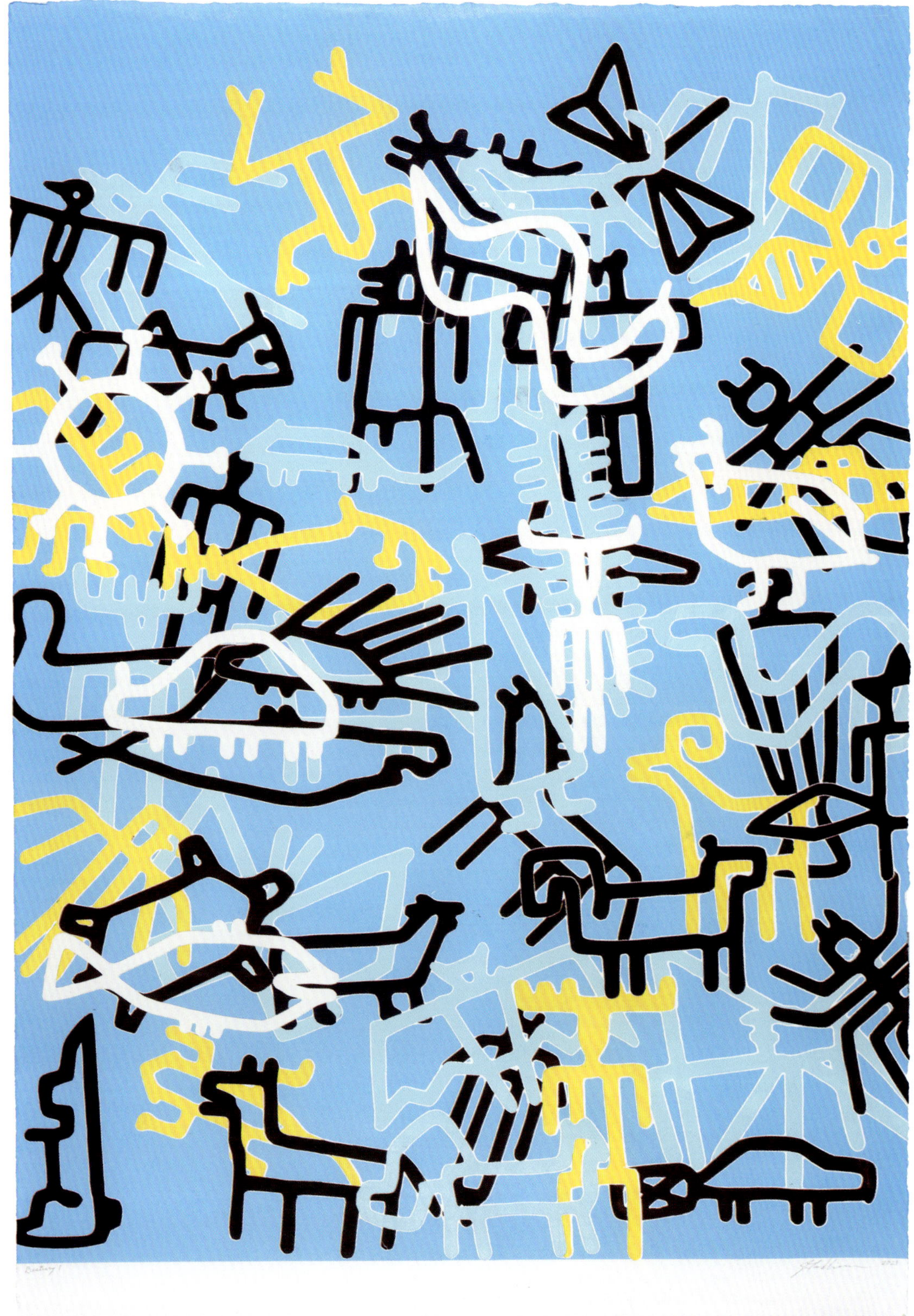

Plate 100
Bestiary 1, 2021
Relief and stencil monoprint
Sheet: 44 × 30 in. (111.8 × 76.2 cm); image: 41 × 30 in. (104.1 × 76.2 cm)

Plate 101
Bestiary 12, 2021
Relief and stencil monoprint with acrylic
Sheet: 44 × 30 in. (111.8 × 76.2 cm); image: 41 × 30 in. (104.1 × 76.2 cm)

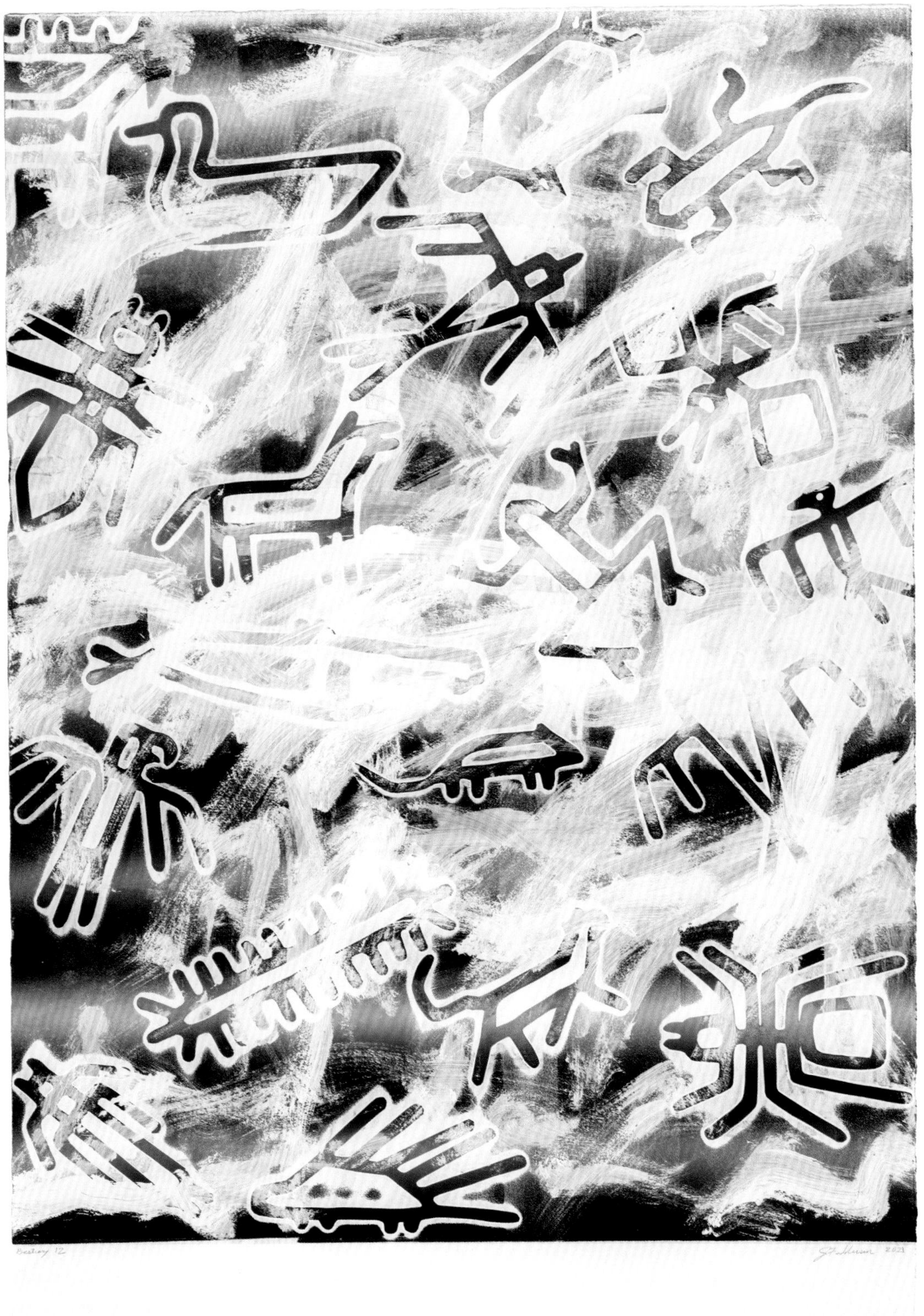

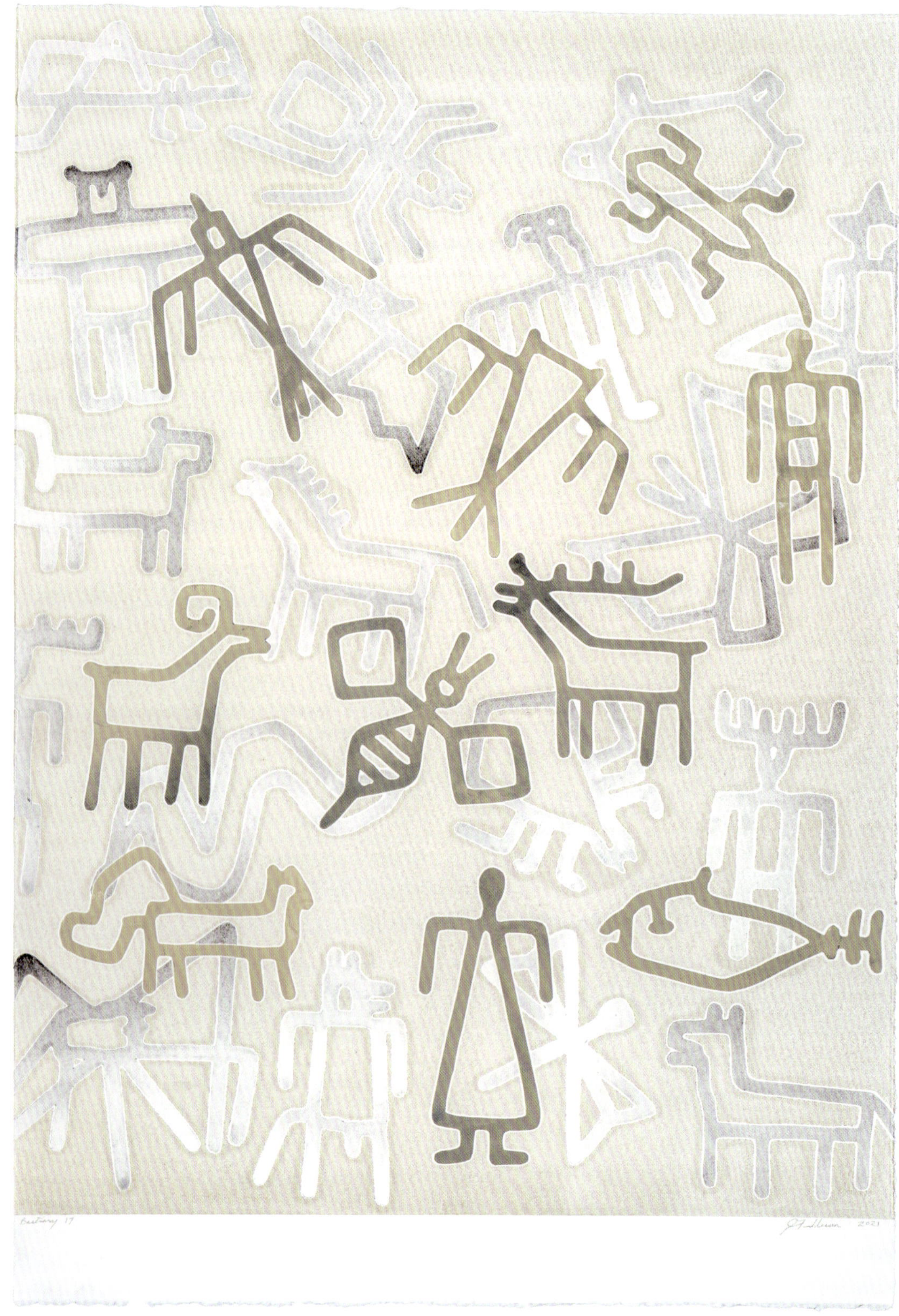

Plate 102
Bestiary 17, 2021
Relief and stencil monoprint
Sheet: 44 × 30 in. (111.8 × 76.2 cm); image: 41 × 30 in. (104.1 × 76.2 cm)

Plate 103
Bestiary 7, 2021
Relief and stencil monoprint
Sheet: 44 × 30 in. (111.8 × 76.2 cm); image: 41 × 30 in. (104.1 × 76.2 cm)

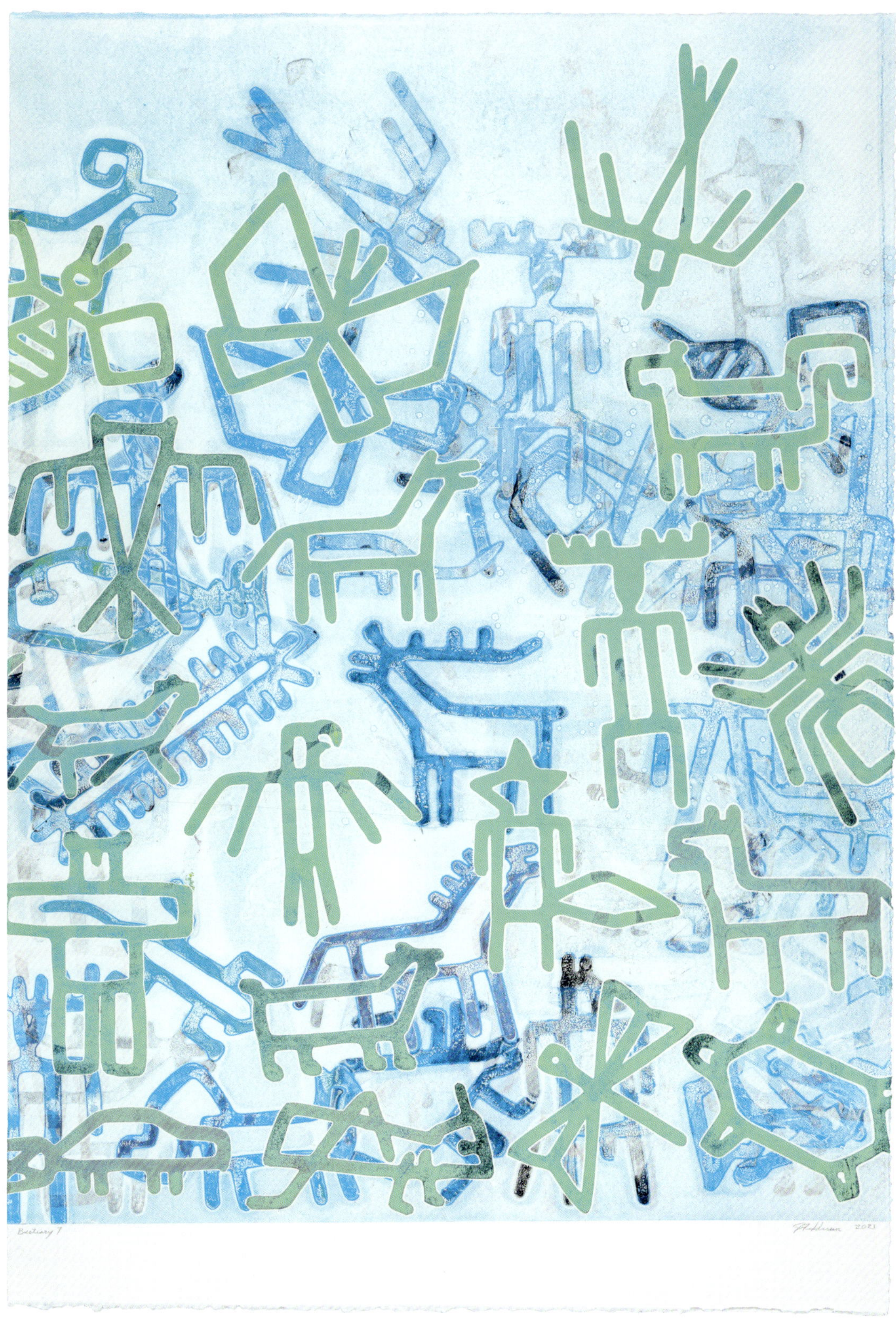

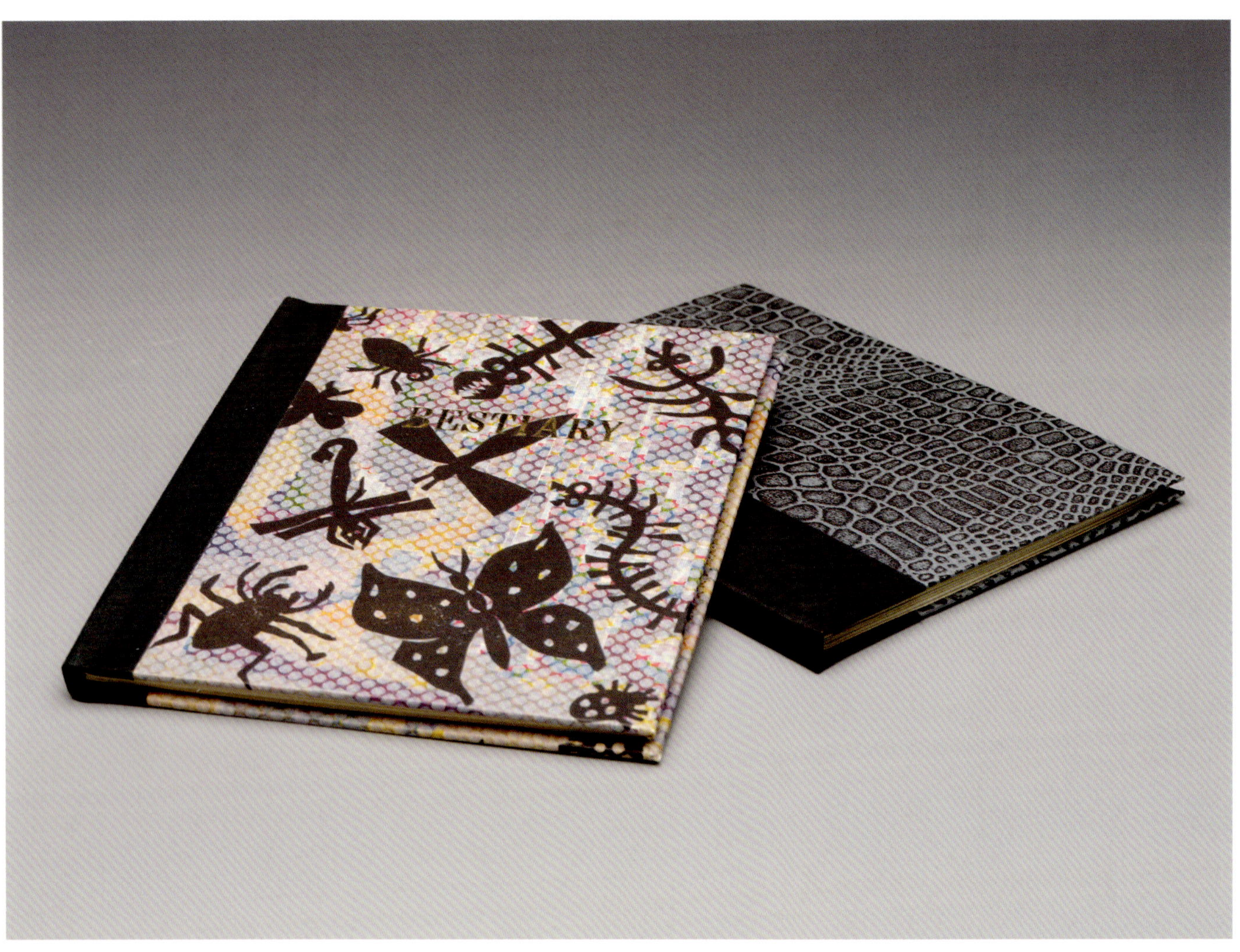

Plate 104

Bestiary, ed. Joe Feddersen and Bill Ransom, 2002
Handbound book
9 × 7 in. (22.9 × 17.8 cm)

Anthropomorphic Consciousness: Putting On the Skin of the Other, ed. Joe Feddersen and Bill Ransom, 2005
Handbound book
9 × 7 in. (22.9 × 17.8 cm)

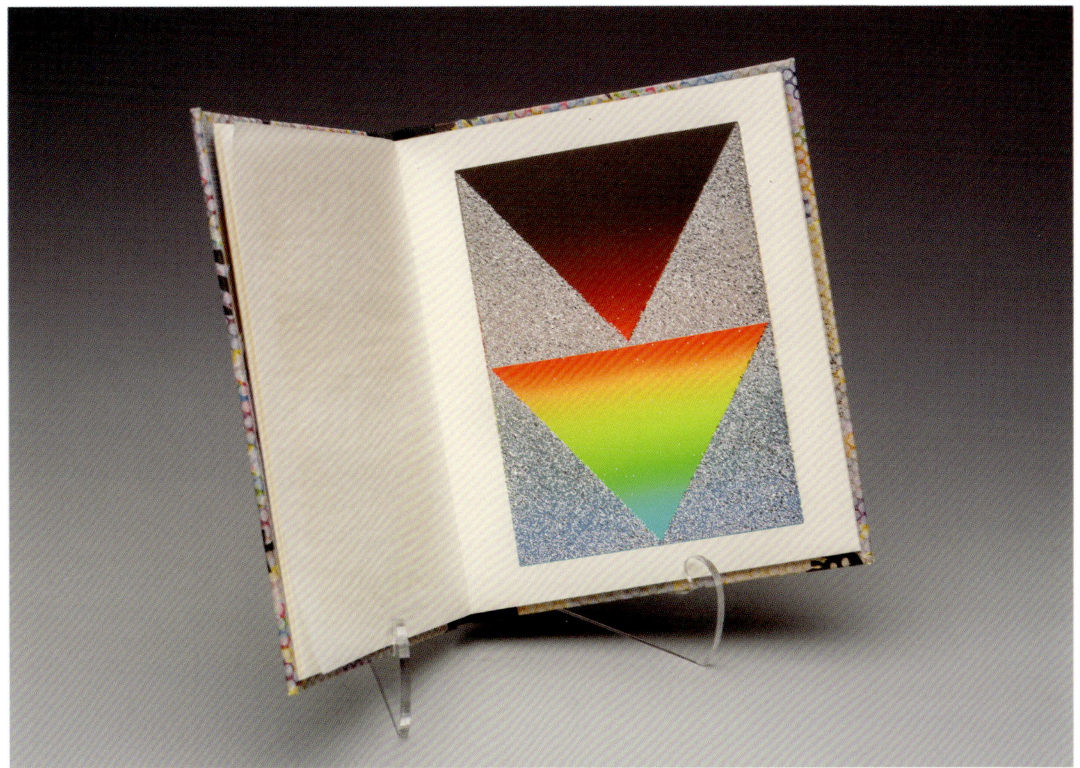

Plate 105
Joe Feddersen, *Butterfly*, in *Bestiary*, ed. Joe Feddersen and Bill Ransom, 2002
Linocut with glitter in handbound book
9 × 7 in. (22.9 × 17.8 cm)

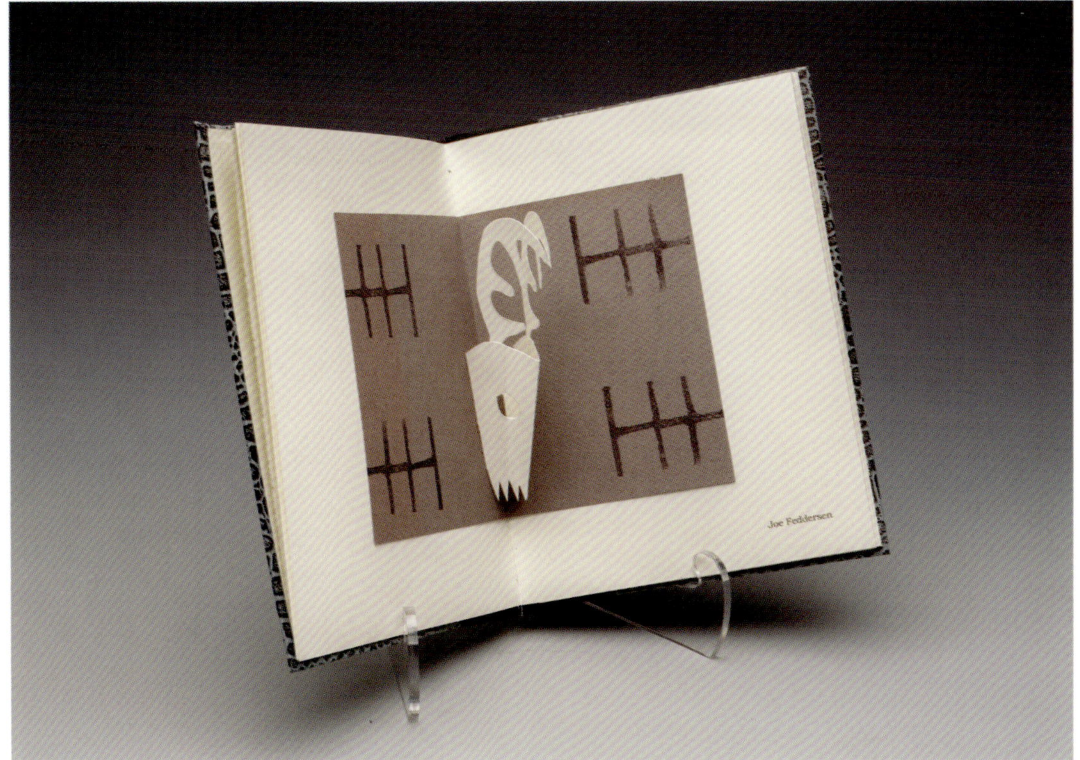

Plate 106
Joe Feddersen, Untitled, in *Anthropomorphic Consciousness: Putting On the Skin of the Other*, ed. Joe Feddersen and Bill Ransom, 2005
Relief print with collage in handbound book
9 × 7 in. (22.9 × 17.8 cm)

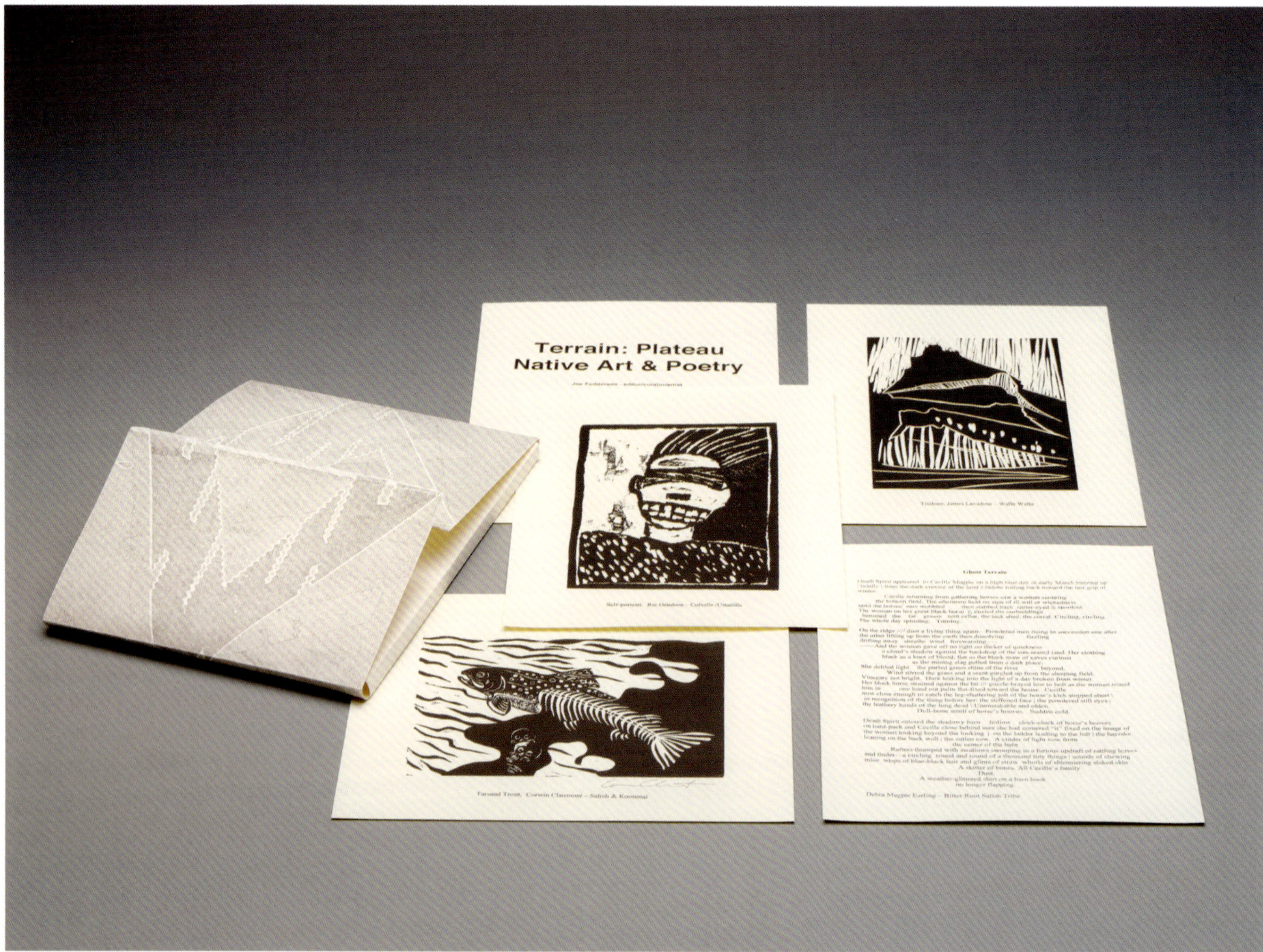

Plate 107
Terrain: Plateau Native Art & Poetry, ed. Joe Feddersen, 2014
Linocut, LaserJet, and monoprint on paper
10½ × 8 in. (26.7 × 20.3 cm)

Plate 108
Gauntlets, 1998
Toner print and glue on rice paper
Each: 13 × 10 × 3 in. (33 × 25.4 × 7.6 cm)

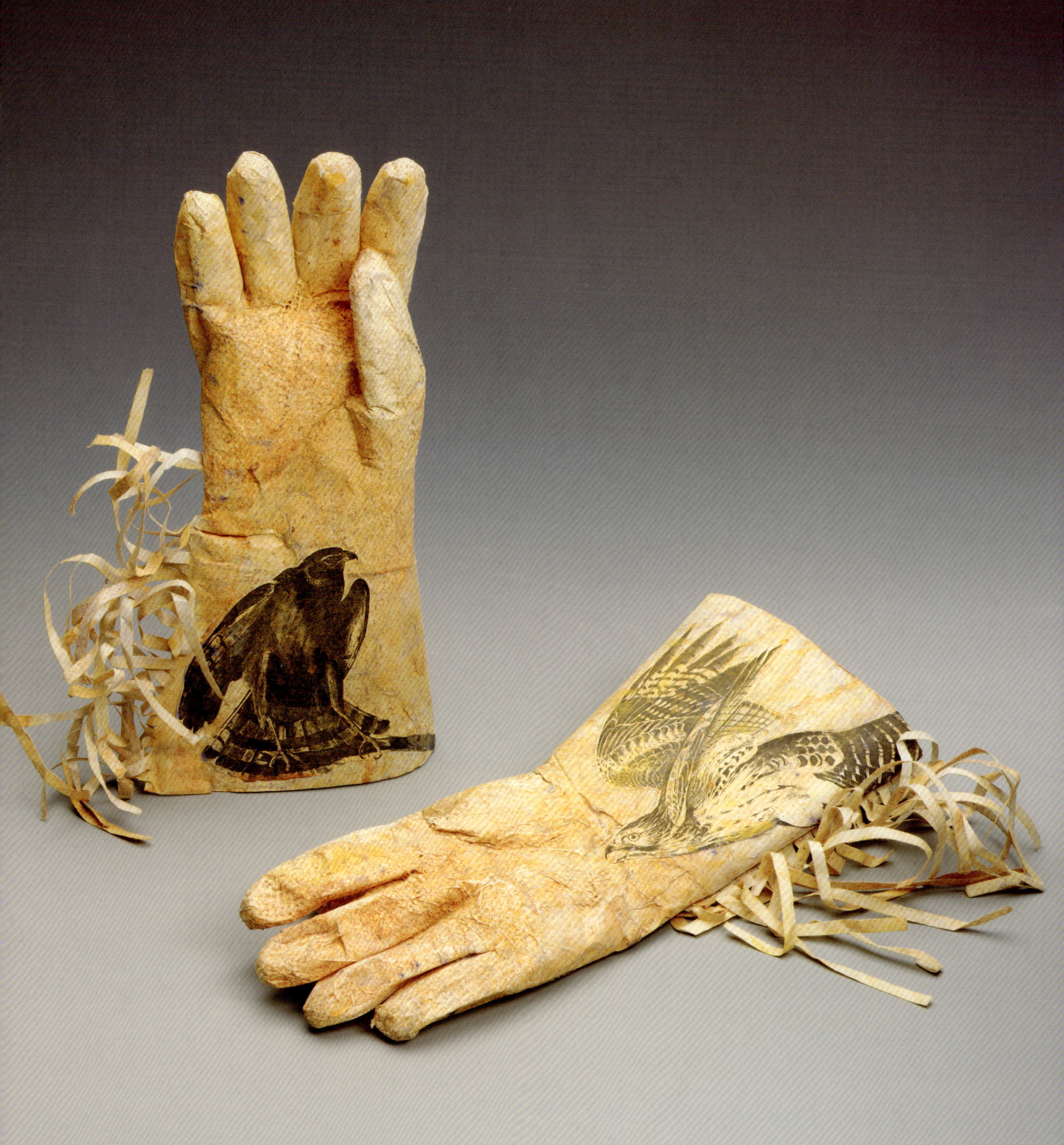

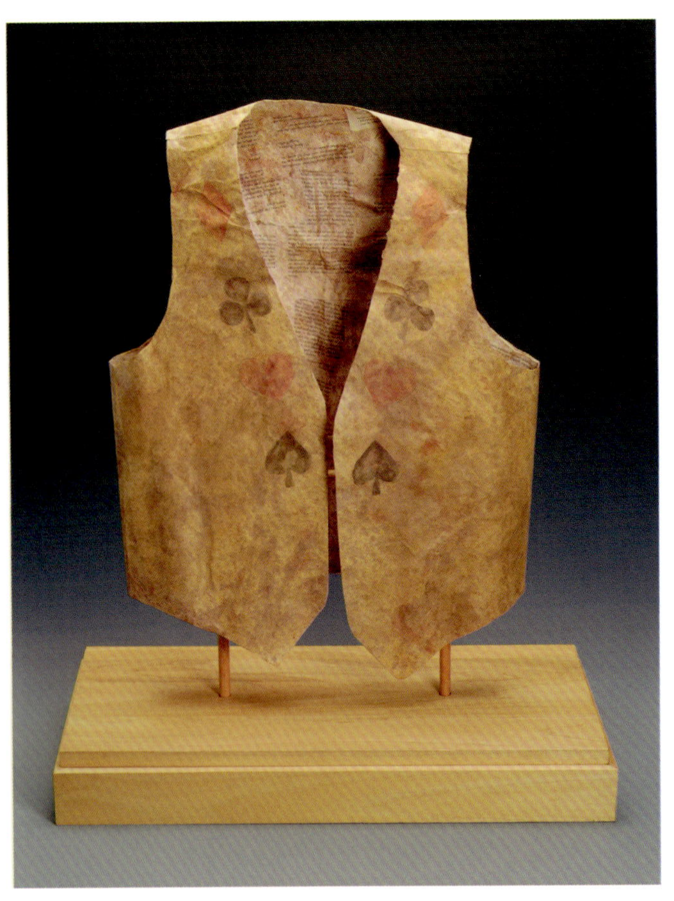

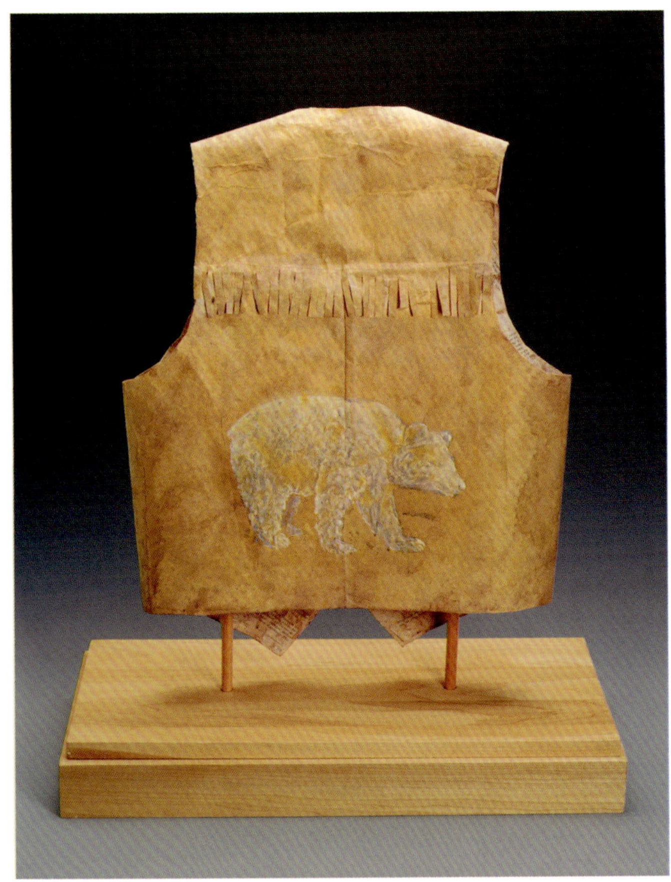

Plate 109
Grandfather's Vest, 1998
Egg tempera and glue on rice paper and book pages
25 × 18½ × 4 in.
(63.5 × 47 × 10.2 cm)

Plate 110
Small Bingo, 2017
Waxed linen, bias tape, and thread
6½ × 4 × 4 in.
(16.5 × 10.2 × 10.2 cm)

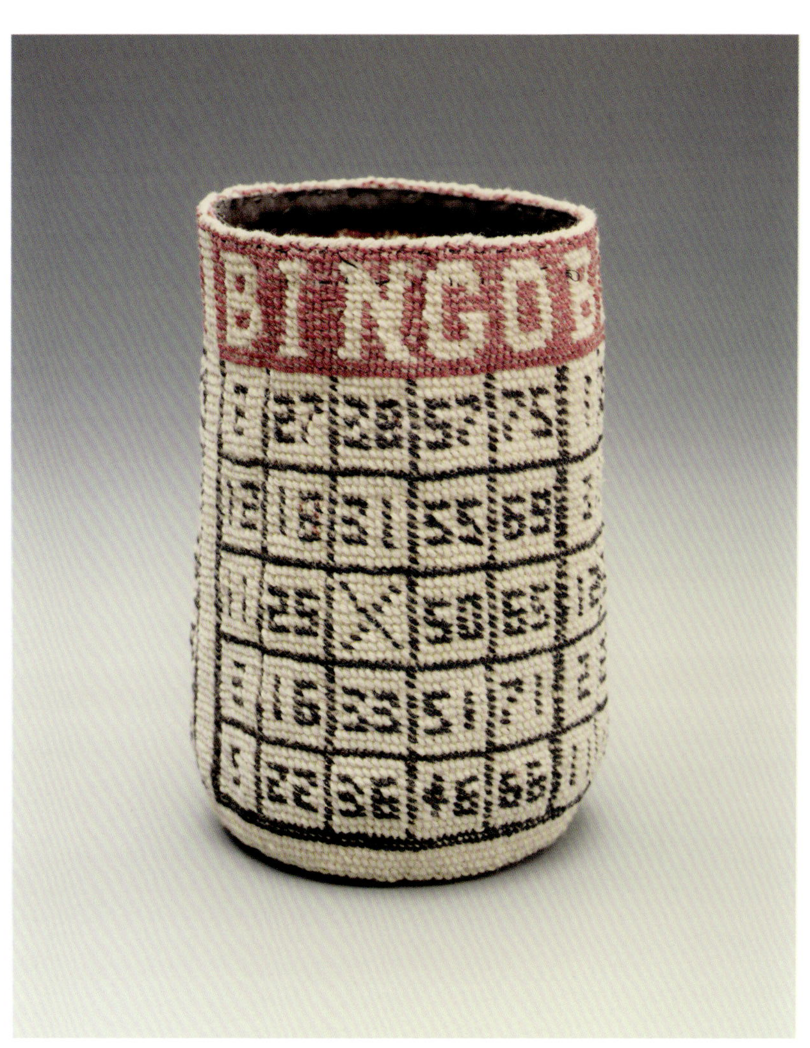

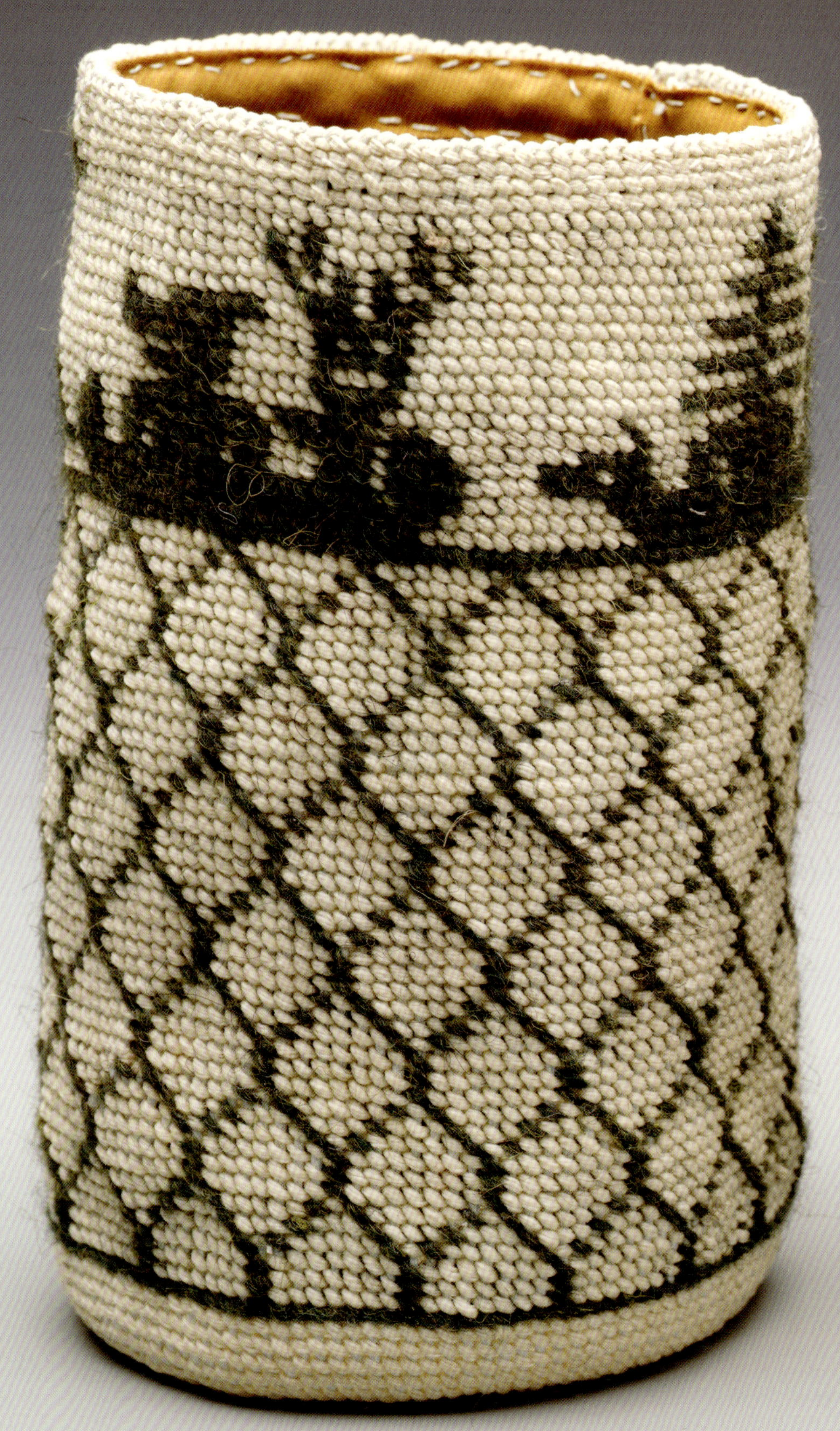

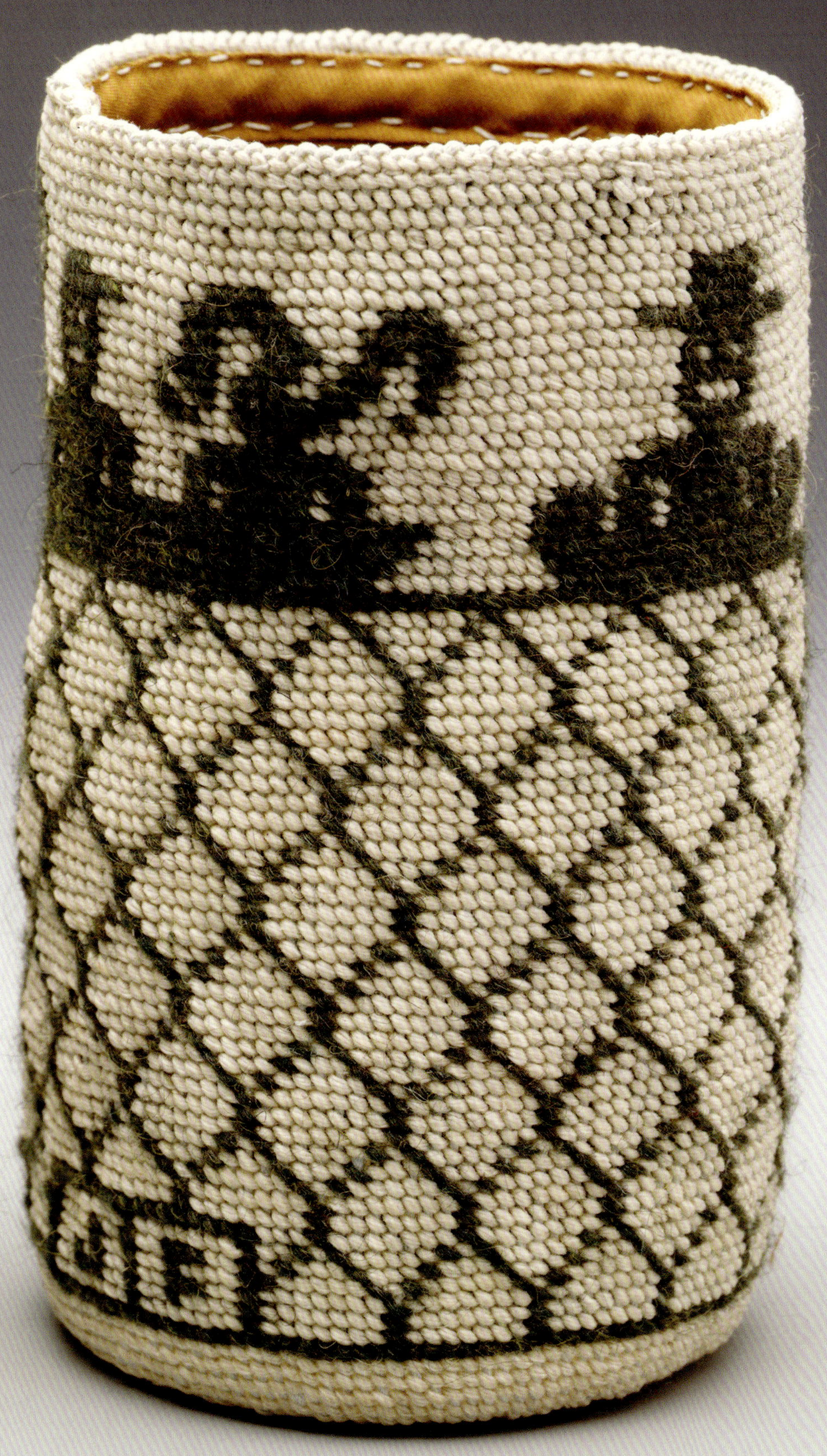

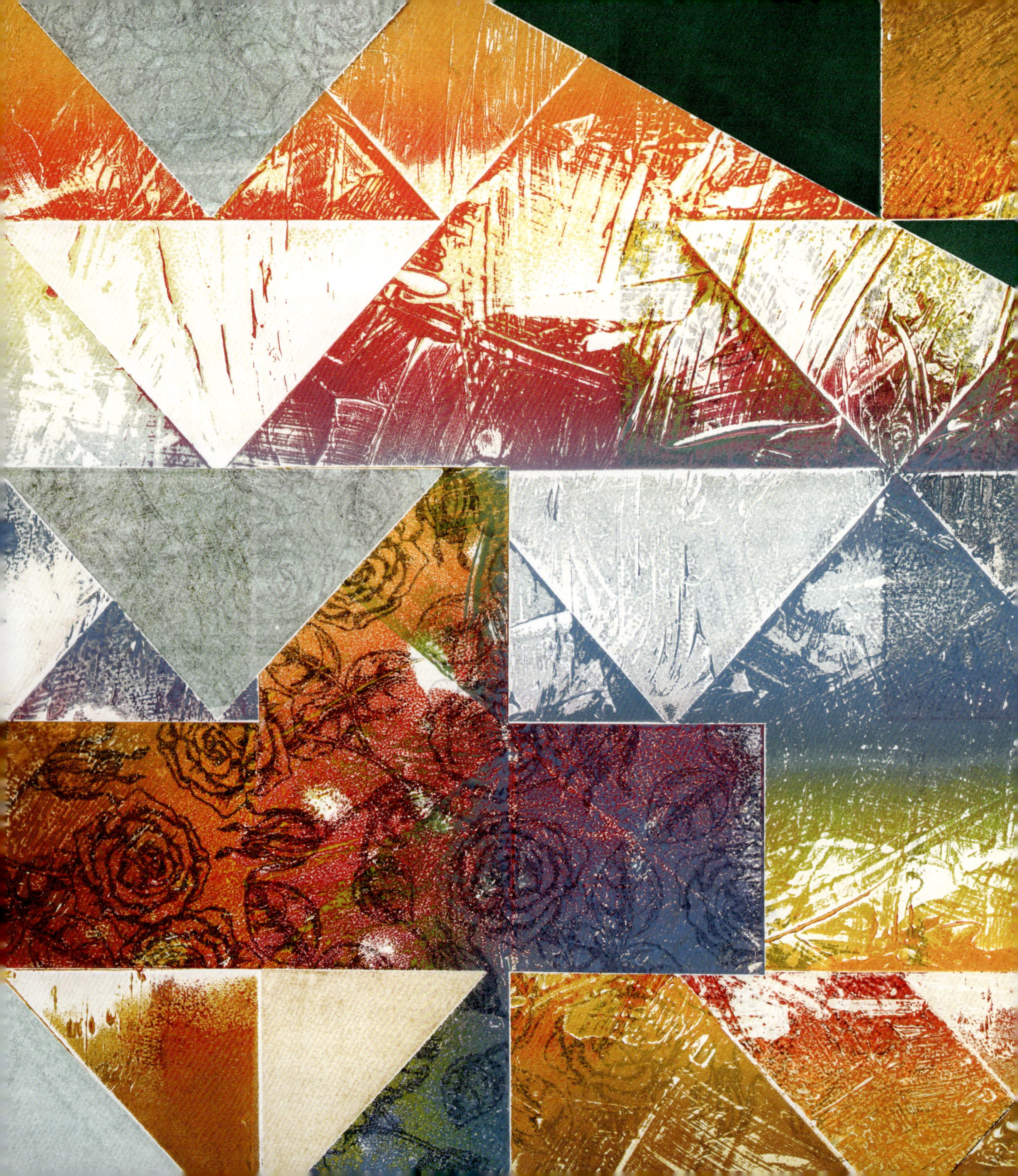

Selected Bibliography

Ackerman, Lillian A. *A Song to the Creator: Traditional Arts of Native American Women of the Plateau.* Norman: University of Oklahoma Press, 1996.

Adamson, Glenn, and Jen Padgett, eds. *Crafting America: Artists and Objects 1940 to Today*. Fayetteville: University of Arkansas Press, 2021.

ahtone, heather. "Cultural Paradigms of Contemporary Indigenous Art: As Found in the Work of Shan Goshorn, Norman Akers, Marie Watt, and Joe Feddersen." PhD diss. University of Oklahoma, 2018.

ahtone, heather. "Reading beneath the Surface: Joe Feddersen's Parking Lot." *Wicazo Sa Review* 27, no. 1 (2012): 73–84.

ahtone, heather. "Shifting the Paradigm of Art History: A Multi-sited Indigenous Approach." In *The Routledge Companion to Indigenous Art Histories in the United States and Canada*, edited by Heather Igloliorte and Carla Taunton, 42–52. New York: Routledge, 2023.

ahtone, heather, Rebecca J. Dobkins, and Prudence F. Roberts. *Crow's Shadow Institute of the Arts at 25.* Salem, OR: Hallie Ford Museum of Art, Willamette University, 2017.

Arnold, Laurie. *Bartering with the Bones of Their Dead: The Colville Confederated Tribes and Termination.* Seattle: University of Washington Press, 2012.

Askren, Mique'l Icesis. "Joe Feddersen." In *Manifestations: New Native Art Criticism*, 94–95. Santa Fe: IAIA Museum of Contemporary Native Arts, 2011.

Chambers, Letitia. *Clearly Indigenous: Native Visions Reimagined in Glass.* Santa Fe: Museum of New Mexico Press, 2021.

Dobkins, Rebecca J. "Critical Impressions: The Intersectional Space of Printmaking in Native Art." In *NATIVE ART NOW! Developments in Contemporary Native American Art Since 1992*, edited by Veronica Passalacqua and Kate Morris, compiled by James H. Nottage, 62–85. Indianapolis: Eiteljorg Museum of American Indians and Western Art, 2017.

Dobkins, Rebecca J. "Expect a Different Story: Portraying the Contemporary Plateau." *American Anthropologist* 102, no. 2 (2000): 330–36.

Dobkins, Rebecca J., Barbara Earl Thomas, and Gail Tremblay. *Joe Feddersen: Vital Signs.* Salem, OR: Hallie Ford Museum of Art, Willamette University, 2008.

Edwards, Julie A. *Weaving; Baskets and Stories.* Self-published, Blurb, Incorporated, 2021.

Feddersen, Joe, and Elizabeth Woody. "The Story as Primary Source: Educating the Gaze." In *Native American Art in the Twentieth Century: Makers, Meanings, Histories*, edited by W. Jackson Rushing III, 174–83. New York: Routledge, 1999.

García, Gloria Gonzáles, and Elizabeth A. Woody. *Joe Feddersen TERRAIN—A Survey*. Exhibition catalogue. Yakima, WA: Larson Gallery at Yakima Valley Community College, 2012.

Gilio-Whitaker, Dina. *As Long As Grass Grows: The Indigenous Fight for Environmental Justice, from Colonization to Standing Rock*. Boston: Beacon Press, 2020.

Harless, Susan E., ed. *Native Arts of the Columbia Plateau: The Doris Swayze Bounds Collection*. Bend, OR: High Desert Museum, 1998.

Jackson, Devon. "Joe Feddersen: Signs of the Times." *Southwest Art*, August 1, 2007.

Lippard, Lucy R. "Independent Identities." In *Native American Art in the Twentieth Century: Makers, Meanings, Histories*, edited by W. Jackson Rushing III, 134–48. New York: Routledge, 1999.

Lippard, Lucy R. *Mixed Blessings: New Art in a Multicultural America*. New York: The New Press, 1990.

Lippard, Lucy R. "The Color of the Wind." In *Our Land/Ourselves: American Indian Contemporary Artists*, edited by Jaune Quick-to-See Smith, 7–15. Albany, NY: University Art Gallery, University at Albany, 1990.

McFarland, Mack, and RYAN! Feddersen. "Two Generations: Joe Feddersen & Wendy Red Star." In *Cross-Platform Curation*, 7–55. Ashland, OR: Schneider Museum of Art, 2020.

Montiel, Anya. "Seeing the World Anew." In *Sharing Honors and Burdens: Renwick Invitational 2023*, 24–41. Washington, DC: Renwick Gallery of the Smithsonian American Art Museum, 2023.

Nahwooksy, Fred, and Richard Hill, Sr. *Who Stole the Tee Pee?* New York: National Museum of the American Indian, Smithsonian Institution, 2001.

Oral history interview with Joe Feddersen, 2021 April 29 and May 6. Archives of American Art, Smithsonian Institution.

Rushing, W. Jackson, III. "Joe Feddersen: Sacred Geometry." In *After the Storm: The Eiteljorg Fellowship for Native American Fine Art, 2001*, edited by W. Jackson Rushing III, 33–47. Indianapolis: Eiteljorg Museum of American Indians and Western Art, 2001.

Schlick, Mary Dodds. *Columbia River Basketry: Gift of the Ancestors, Gift of the Earth*. Seattle: University of Washington Press, 1994.

Wasserman, Abby. "Joe Feddersen." *Native Vision* 3, no. 2 (May/June 1986): 1–2.

Woody, Elizabeth. "Joe Feddersen: Geometric Abstraction—the Language of the Land." In *Continuum 12 Artists*. Washington, DC: National Museum of the American Indian, 2003.

Works in the Exhibition

All works by Joe Feddersen unless otherwise indicated. Works appear chronologically, then alphabetically within each year. Height precedes width precedes depth.

For unique prints: *Monotype* is used to describe a print made without a stable matrix where ink is applied in a way that is impossible or difficult to repeat. *Monoprint* describes a single print containing repeatable platemaking techniques. Platemaking techniques used in each monoprint are listed before the term, and other media are listed after.

Rainscape #2, 1983
Lithograph
Each: 44 × 33 in. (111.8 × 83.8 cm)
Collection of the artist; courtesy studio e gallery, Seattle, Washington
Plate 5

Self Portrait #1, 1983
Photograph
9½ × 8 in. (24.1 × 20.3 cm)
Hallie Ford Museum of Art, Willamette University, Salem, Oregon; gift of the artist 2008.043.027
Plate 2

Self Portrait #10, 1983
Photomontage
9½ × 8 in. (24.1 × 20.3 cm)
Hallie Ford Museum of Art, Willamette University, Salem, Oregon; gift of the artist 2008.043.028
Plate 2

Untitled (back of head), 1983
Photograph
7½ × 9½ in. (19.1 × 24.1 cm)
Hallie Ford Museum of Art, Willamette University, Salem, Oregon; gift of the artist 2008.043.026
Plate 2

Self Portrait #6, 1984
Collage of photography, paint, and glass
16 × 24 in. (40.6 × 61 cm)
Washington State Arts Commission, Olympia; direct purchase WSAC1985.058.000
Plate 3

Sheltered from Nightrain, 1984
Lithograph
33 × 90 in. (83.8 × 228.6 cm)
Washington State Arts Commission, Olympia; direct purchase WSAC1985.034.000
Plate 6

Inheritance Obscured by Neglect, 1989
Pastel, acrylic, and ink on paper
22 × 30 in. (55.9 × 76.2 cm)
Hallie Ford Museum of Art, Willamette University, Salem, Oregon; gift of the artist 2017.038.014
Plate 27

Two Blankets I, 1990
Relief monoprint
35½ × 37 in. (90.2 × 94 cm)
Collection of the artist
Plate 9

Blanket Series 5, 1991
Monotype
25½ × 38½ in. (64.8 × 97.8 cm)
Collection of the artist; courtesy studio e gallery, Seattle, Washington
Plate 7

Rainscape, 1993
Linocut monoprint
18½ × 23½ in. (47 × 59.7 cm)
Promised gift from private collection
Plate 4

Red Basket, 1993
Waxed linen, wool, fabric, and thread
6 × 4½ × 4½ in. (15.2 × 11.4 × 11.4 cm)
Collection of the artist; courtesy studio e gallery, Seattle, Washington
Plate 18

Plateau Geometrics #16, 1995
Aquatint and relief monoprint
Sheet: 26 × 20 in. (66 × 50.8 cm); image: 12 × 12 in. (30.5 × 30.5 cm)
Collection of the artist; courtesy studio e gallery, Seattle, Washington
Plate 53

Stairs and Stars, about 1995
Waxed linen, fabric, mother-of-pearl buttons, and thread
6 × 4½ × 4½ in. (15.2 × 11.4 × 11.4 cm)
Collection of the artist; courtesy studio e gallery, Seattle, Washington
Plate 39

Plateau Geometrics #48, 1996
Intaglio and relief monoprint
Sheet: 26 × 20 in. (66 × 50.8 cm); image: 12 × 12 in. (30.5 × 30.5 cm)
Collection of the artist; courtesy studio e gallery, Seattle, Washington
Plate 55

Plateau Geometrics #83, 1997
Siligraphy, drypoint, and relief monoprint with pearlescent powder
Sheet: 26 × 20 in. (66 × 50.8 cm); image: 12 × 12 in. (30.5 × 30.5 cm)
Collection of the artist; courtesy studio e gallery, Seattle, Washington
Plate 54

Plateau Geometrics #98, 1997
Siligraphy monoprint
Sheet: 26 × 20 in. (66 × 50.8 cm); image: 12 × 12 in. (30.5 × 30.5 cm)
Collection of the artist; courtesy studio e gallery, Seattle, Washington
Plate 59

Gauntlets, 1998
Toner print and glue on rice paper
Each: 13 × 10 × 3 in. (33 × 25.4 × 7.6 cm)
Northwest Museum of Arts and Culture, Spokane, Washington; gift of Joe Feddersen and Froelick Gallery 2020, 4450.1
Plate 108

Grandfather's Vest, 1998
Egg tempera and glue on rice paper and book pages
25 × 18½ × 4 in. (63.5 × 47 × 10.2 cm)
Northwest Museum of Arts and Culture, Spokane, Washington; museum purchase 1998, 3859.1
Plate 109

Pin Wheel, 1998
Relief print
Sheet: 26 × 20 in. (66 × 50.8 cm); image: 12 × 12 in. (30.5 × 30.5 cm)
Collection of the artist; courtesy studio e gallery, Seattle, Washington
Published by Sidereal Fine Art Press, Seattle, Washington
Plate 56

Plateau Geometrics #125, 1998
Siligraphy and drypoint monoprint
Sheet: 26 × 20 in. (66 × 50.8 cm); image: 12 × 12 in. (30.5 × 30.5 cm)
Collection of the artist; courtesy studio e gallery, Seattle, Washington
Plate 50

Plateau Geometrics #143, 1999
Siligraphy and relief monoprint
Sheet: 26 × 20 in. (66 × 50.8 cm); image: 12 × 12 in. (30.5 × 30.5 cm)
Collection of the artist; courtesy studio e gallery, Seattle, Washington
Plate 52

Plateau Geometrics #145, 1999
Siligraphy and relief monoprint
Sheet: 26 × 20 in. (66 × 50.8 cm); image: 12 × 12 in. (30.5 × 30.5 cm)
Collection of the artist; courtesy studio e gallery, Seattle, Washington
Plate 51

Target, 1999
Waxed linen, bias tape, and thread
4½ × 3½ × 3½ in. (11.4 × 8.9 × 8.9 cm)
Collection of the artist; courtesy studio e gallery, Seattle, Washington
Plate 18

Plateau Geometrics #195, 2000
Siligraphy and relief monprint
Sheet: 26 × 20 in. (66 × 50.8 cm); image: 12 × 12 in. (30.5 × 30.5 cm)
Collection of the artist; courtesy studio e gallery, Seattle, Washington
Plate 58

Interwoven Sign, 2001
Lithograph with chine collé
30 × 30 in. (76.2 × 76.2 cm)
Northwest Museum of Arts and Culture, Spokane, Washington; gift of Dr. and Mrs. Luis Vela 2021, 4458.1
Published by Rutgers Center for Innovative Print and Paper, Rutgers University, New Jersey
Plate 57

Plateau Geometrics, 2001
Lithograph
Sheet: 26 × 20 in. (66 × 50.8 cm); image: 16 × 16 in. (40.6 × 40.6 cm)
Collection of the artist; courtesy studio e gallery, Seattle, Washington
From the Lasting Impressions Portfolio
Printed by Jack Lemon
Published by the University of Arizona Foundation, Tucson
Plate 16

Tama 5, 2001
Collagraph, relief, stencil, aquatint, and drypoint monoprint
Sheet: 22½ × 30 in. (57.2 × 76.2 cm); image: 18¼ × 26 in. (46.4 × 66 cm)
Hallie Ford Museum of Art, Willamette University, Salem, Oregon; purchased with an endowment gift from the Confederated Tribes of Grand Ronde, through their Spirit Mountain Community Fund 2003.008.001
Plate 20

Untitled, 2001
Relief print
Sheet: 9 × 5½ in. (22.9 × 14 cm); image: 7 × 5 in. (17.8 × 12.7 cm)
Hallie Ford Museum of Art, Willamette University, Salem, Oregon; gift of the artist 2016.066.007
Plate 35

Bestiary, 2002
Edited by Joe Feddersen and Bill Ransom
Contributors: Rick Bartow, Ken Brewer, Corky Clairmont, Joe Feddersen, Samuel Green, Betty Moynahan, Bill Ransom, Gail Tremblay, Elizabeth Woody, Melanie Yazzie
Handbound book
9 × 7 in. (22.9 × 17.8 cm)
Hallie Ford Museum of Art, Willamette University, Salem, Oregon; gift of Joe Feddersen 2003.018
Published by Joe's Garage
Plates 104, 105

Cul-de-sac, 2002
Waxed linen, bias tape, and thread
6½ × 4½ × 4½ in. (16.5 × 11.4 × 11.4 cm)
Hallie Ford Museum of Art, Willamette University, Salem, Oregon; purchased with an endowment gift from the Confederated Tribes of Grand Ronde, through their Spirit Mountain Community Fund 2003.021
Plate 11

Parking Lot, from the *Urban Indian* series, 2002
Waxed linen, bias tape, and thread
6 × 4½ × 4½ in. (15.2 × 11.4 × 11.4 cm)
Collection of Preston Singletary
Plate 48

Barrier, 2003
Screenprint
Sheet: 20 × 15 in. (50.8 × 38.1 cm); image: 16½ × 12 in. (41.9 × 30.5 cm)
Hallie Ford Museum of Art, Willamette University, Salem, Oregon; gift of the artist 2008.0037.001e
Plate 37

Chain Link, 2003
Sandblasted blown glass
16½ × 12½ × 12½ in. (41.9 × 31.8 × 31.8 cm)
Hallie Ford Museum of Art, Willamette University, Salem, Oregon; The George and Colleen Hoyt Art Acquisition Fund 2004.024
Plate 47

Palouse Series, 2003
Relief and stencil monoprint
26 × 20 in. (66 × 51 cm)
Northwest Museum of Arts and Culture, Spokane, Washington; gift of Dr. and Mrs. Luis Vela 2021, 4458.2
Printed at the Department of Art, Washington State University, Pullman
Plate 46

Wyit View, 2003
Lithograph
40 × 30 in. (101.6 × 76.2 cm)
Hallie Ford Museum of Art, Willamette University, Salem, Oregon; Crow's Shadow Institute of the Arts Archive CSP 03–105
Printed by Frank Janzen
Published by Crow's Shadow Institute of the Arts
Plate 12

High Voltage Tower, 2004
Sandblasted blown glass
9 × 13 × 13 in. (22.9 × 33 × 33 cm)
Collection of Bill R. Roulette and Laura L. De Simone
Plate 74

Anthropomorphic Consciousness: Putting On the Skin of the Other, 2005
Edited by Joe Feddersen and Bill Ransom
Contributors: Jim Bodeen, Nellie Bridge, Anita Endrezze, Joe Feddersen, Marilyn Frasca, Tom Johnston, Alex McCarty, Bill Ransom, Barbara Thomas
Handbound book
9 × 7 in. (22.9 × 17.8 cm)
Hallie Ford Museum of Art, Willamette University, Salem, Oregon; gift of Rebecca Dobkins 2013.001
Published by Joe's Garage & Wordman Production Company
Plates 104, 106

Firehawk, 2005
Sandblasted blown glass
21½ × 9½ × 9½ in. (54.6 × 24.1 × 24.1 cm)
Collection of Jordan D. Schnitzer
Plate 19

Fish Trap II, 2005
Blown glass
14 × 22½ × 14 in. (35.6 × 57.2 × 35.6 cm)
Missoula Art Museum, Montana; purchased with gift from the Pleiades Foundation, 2010
Plate 76

Fish Trap IV, 2005
Blown glass
7 × 18 × 7 in. (17.8 × 45.7 × 17.8 cm)
Collection of the artist; courtesy studio e gallery, Seattle, Washington
Plate 75

Fish Trap V, 2005
Blown glass
13 × 17 × 13 in. (33 × 43.2 × 33 cm)
Collection of the artist; courtesy studio e gallery, Seattle, Washington
Plate 75

Rugged Trail 2, 2005
Blown glass
19 × 18½ × 18½ in. (48.3 × 47 × 47 cm)
Northwest Museum of Arts and Culture, Spokane, Washington; museum purchase, Works from the Heart Art Acquisition Fund 2011, 4266.1
Plate 17

Okanagan V, 2006
Relief on paper mounted on panels
Overall: 70 × 252 in. (177.8 × 640.1 cm); each panel: 14 × 14 in. (35.6 × 35.6 cm)
Hallie Ford Museum of Art, Willamette University, Salem, Oregon; gift of the artist and Froelick Gallery 2013.043
Plate 60

Stealth, 2006
Sandblasted blown glass
10 × 16 × 16 in. (25.4 × 40.6 × 40.6 cm)
Collection of the Jordan Schnitzer Family Foundation, from the Arlene and Harold Schnitzer Collection
Plate 10

Urban Vernacular: Communication Towers, 2008
Blown glass with silver mirroring and copper enamel
18½ × 14 × 14 in. (47 × 35.6 × 35.6 cm)
Collection of the Jordan Schnitzer Family Foundation, from the Arlene and Harold Schnitzer Collection
Plate 45

Cell Phone Tower, 2009
Sandblasted blown glass
22 × 8 × 8 in. (55.9 × 20.3 × 20.3 cm)
Collection of the artist; courtesy studio e gallery, Seattle, Washington
Plate 63

Cell Tower, 2009
Waxed linen, wool, bias tape, and thread
5½ × 3 × 3 in. (14 × 7.6 × 7.6 cm)
Collection of Bill R. Roulette and Laura L. De Simone
Plate 62

Clear-cut II, 2009
Sandblasted blown glass
19½ × 8 × 8 in. (49.5 × 20.3 × 20.3 cm)
Collection of the artist; courtesy studio e gallery, Seattle, Washington
Plate 44

Codex: Cell Tower, 2009
Sandblasted blown glass
16½ × 7 × 7 in. (41.9 × 17.8 × 17.8 cm)
Collection of the artist; courtesy studio e gallery, Seattle, Washington
Plate 61

Codex: Freeway with HOV, 2009
Sandblasted blown glass
18 × 9½ × 9½ in. (45.7 × 24.1 × 24.1 cm)
Collection of the artist; courtesy studio e gallery, Seattle, Washington
Plate 61

Codex: Lightning, 2009
Sandblasted blown glass
19 × 9½ × 9½ in. (48.3 × 24.1 × 24.1 cm)
Collection of the artist; courtesy studio e gallery, Seattle, Washington
Plate 61

Wild Cat, 2009
Waxed linen and brain-tanned deer hide
6½ × 4 × 4 in. (16.5 × 10.2 × 10.2 cm)
Collection of the artist; courtesy studio e gallery, Seattle, Washington
Plate 49

Gathering Under the Stars, 2010
Waxed linen, wool, fabric, and thread
8½ × 7½ × 7½ in. (21.6 × 19.1 × 19.1 cm)
Collection of the artist; courtesy studio e gallery, Seattle, Washington
Plate 21

Raising the Sky, 2011
Sandblasted blown glass
19 × 11 × 11 in. (48.3 × 27.9 × 27.9 cm)
Collection of Jordan D. Schnitzer
Plate 66

Changer 3, 2012
Sandblasted blown glass
22 × 9 × 9 in. (55.9 × 22.9 × 22.9 cm)
Eiteljorg Museum of American Indians and Western Art, Indianapolis; museum purchase from the Eiteljorg Contemporary Art Fellowship 2016.24.1
Plate 65

Changer 4, 2012
Sandblasted blown glass
24½ × 10½ × 10½ in. (62.2 × 26.7 × 26.7 cm)
Collection of the artist; courtesy studio e gallery, Seattle, Washington
Plate 64

Coyote Receives His Name, 2012
Waxed linen, bias tape, and thread
8½ × 7 × 7 in. (21.6 × 17.8 × 17.8 cm)
Hallie Ford Museum of Art, Willamette University, Salem, Oregon; The George and Colleen Hoyt Art Acquisition Fund 2013.016
Plate 97

Omak, 2012
Waxed linen, bias tape, and thread
9 × 6 × 6 in. (22.9 × 15.2 × 15.2 cm)
Collection of the artist; courtesy studio e gallery, Seattle, Washington
Plate 40

Tracks, 2012
Waxed linen, bias tape, and thread
8 × 5½ × 5½ in. (20.3 × 14 × 14 cm)
Collection of the artist; courtesy studio e gallery, Seattle, Washington
Plate 18

Wintermaster Plus, 2012
Waxed linen and brain-tanned deer hide
6 × 6 × 6 in. (15.2 × 15.2 × 15.2 cm)
Collection of the artist; courtesy studio e gallery, Seattle, Washington
Plate 49

Coyote Receives His Name, 2013
Carved blown glass
9 × 6½ × 6½ in. (22.9 × 16.5 × 16.5 cm)
Hallie Ford Museum of Art, Willamette University, Salem, Oregon; The George and Colleen Hoyt Art Acquisition Fund 2013.044
Plate 98

All Chiefs, 2014
Hand-engraved blown glass
9 × 7 × 7 in. (22.9 × 17.8 × 17.8 cm)
Collection of the artist; courtesy studio e gallery, Seattle, Washington
Plate 43

Coyote and Flying Geese, 2014
Waxed linen, bias tape, and thread
9½ × 7 × 7 in. (24.1 × 17.8 × 17.8 cm)
Collection of the artist; courtesy studio e gallery, Seattle, Washington
Plate 39

Fish Trap, 2014
Monotype
Overall: 30 × 67 in. (76.2 × 170.2 cm)
Missoula Art Museum, Montana; gift of Joe Feddersen
Published by MATRIX Press, University of Montana, Missoula
Plate 71

Fish Trap II, 2014
Monotype
Overall: 30 × 67 in. (76.2 × 170.2 cm)
Missoula Art Museum, Montana; gift of Joe Feddersen
Published by MATRIX Press, University of Montana, Missoula
Plate 70

Snipe Woman Steals Salmon, 2014
Waxed linen, bias tape, and thread
9 × 5½ × 5½ in. (22.9 × 14 × 14 cm)
Private collection
Plate 77

Terrain: Plateau Native Art & Poetry, 2014
Edited by Joe Feddersen
Contributors: Leo Adams, Sherman Alexie, Neal Ambrose, Gloria Bird, Ron Carraher, Vic Charlo, Corwin Clairmont, Cameron Decker, Alyne Watamet DeCoteau, Debra Earling, Vanessa Enos, Carly Feddersen, Joe Feddersen, RYAN! Feddersen, Jennifer Ferguson, Frank Finley, Ric Gendron, Cheryl Grunlose, Micheal Holloman, Van Holloman, Rochelle Kulei, James Lavadour, Miles Miller, Ramon Murillo, Ed Archie NoiseCat, William Passmore, Lilliam Pitt, Lawney Reyes, Susan Sheoships, Jaune Quick-to-See Smith, Kirby Stanton, Toma Villa, Ramona Wilson, Elizabeth Woody
Linocut, LaserJet, and mono-print on paper
10½ × 8 in. (26.7 × 20.3 cm)
Northwest Museum of Arts and Culture, Spokane, Washington; gift of the Longhouse Education & Cultural Center, The Evergreen State College, and Joe Feddersen 4316.1
Printed by Judith Bauman, Corwin Clairmont, Cameron Decker, Susan Sheoships, RYAN! Feddersen, William Passmore, Vanessa Enos, Ramon Murillo, Toma Villa, Ron Carraher, Miles Miller, Kirby Stanton, and Joe Feddersen
Printed at The Evergreen State College, Olympia, with Commercial Printing, Wenatchee, Washington
Plate 107

Voltage Tower, 2014
Monotype
Overall: 90 × 66 in. (228.6 × 167.6 cm)
Collection of the artist; courtesy studio e gallery, Seattle, Washington
Published by MATRIX Press, University of Montana, Missoula
Plate 72

Black Ghost, 2015
Relief, collagraph, and stencil monoprint with spray paint
30 × 22 in. (76.2 × 55.9 cm)
Collection of Jordan D. Schnitzer
Plate 68

Canoe Journey 1, 2015
Low-fire ceramic
13 × 27 × 12 in. (33 × 68.6 × 30.5 cm)
Collection of Jordan D. Schnitzer
Plate 95

Canoe Journey: Catamaran, 2015
Low-fire ceramic with gold leaf
8 × 7 × 15 in. (20.3 × 17.8 × 38.1 cm)
Collection of the artist; courtesy studio e gallery, Seattle, Washington
Plate 86

Geese Flying Over, 2015
Relief, collagraph, and stencil monoprint
30 × 22 in. (76.2 × 55.9 cm)
Collection of Jordan D. Schnitzer
Plate 69

Canoe Journey, 2016
Waxed linen, bias tape, and thread
6½ × 6 × 6 in. (16.5 × 15.2 × 15.2 cm)
Private collection
Plate 96

Canoe Journey: Capsized Canoe, 2016
Low-fire ceramic
8½ × 17 × 7½ in. (21.6 × 43.2 × 19.1 cm)
Collection of the artist; courtesy studio e gallery, Seattle, Washington
Plate 83

Canoe Journey: Coyote in Inner Tube, 2016
Low-fire ceramic
6½ × 7 × 7½ in. (16.5 × 17.8 × 19.1 cm)
Collection of the artist; courtesy studio e gallery, Seattle, Washington
Plate 92

Canoe Journey: Crow in Sturgeon Nose Canoe, 2016
Low-fire ceramic
8½ × 17 × 13 in. (21.6 × 43.2 × 33 cm)
Collection of the artist; courtesy studio e gallery, Seattle, Washington
Plate 82

Canoe Journey: Flat Screen and Hatted Man, 2016
Low-fire ceramic
8½ × 16 × 7 in. (21.6 × 40.6 × 17.8 cm)
Collection of the artist; courtesy studio e gallery, Seattle, Washington
Plate 90

Canoe Journey: Moon, 2016
Low-fire ceramic
10 × 13 × 17 in. (25.4 × 33 × 43.2 cm)
Collection of the artist; courtesy studio e gallery, Seattle, Washington
Plate 91

Canoe Journey: Person in Canoe, 2016
Low-fire ceramic
9 × 16 × 4 in. (22.9 × 40.6 × 10.2 cm)
Collection of the artist; courtesy studio e gallery, Seattle, Washington
Plate 84

Canoe Journey: Raft, 2016
Low-fire ceramic
11½ × 7 × 10 in. (29.2 × 17.8 × 25.4 cm)
Collection of the artist; courtesy studio e gallery, Seattle, Washington
Plate 89

Canoe Journey: Robot Rowing, 2016
Low-fire ceramic
9½ × 16 × 9½ in. (24.1 × 40.6 × 24.1 cm)
Collection of the artist; courtesy studio e gallery, Seattle, Washington
Plate 87

Canoe Journey: Snake and High Voltage Tower, 2016
Low-fire ceramic
11½ × 14 × 11½ in. (29.2 × 35.6 × 29.2 cm)
Collection of the artist; courtesy studio e gallery, Seattle, Washington
Plate 85

Canoe Journey: Troop, 2016
Low-fire ceramic
8 × 18 × 12 in. (20.3 × 45.7 × 30.5 cm)
Collection of the artist; courtesy studio e gallery, Seattle, Washington
Plate 93

Canoe Journey: Tulip, Parking Lot, Alien, 2016
Low-fire ceramic
9½ × 20 × 12 in. (24.1 × 50.8 × 30.5 cm)
Collection of the artist; courtesy studio e gallery, Seattle, Washington
Plate 88

Canoe Journey: Wolf, 2016
Low-fire ceramic
8½ × 14 × 9 in. (21.6 × 35.6 × 22.9 cm)
Collection of the artist; courtesy studio e gallery, Seattle, Washington
Plate 84

Drizzle, 2016
Relief and stencil monoprint with collage, staples, and spray paint
20½ × 18 in. (52.1 × 45.7 cm)
Collection of the artist; courtesy studio e gallery, Seattle, Washington
Plate 15

Elk at Spotted Lake, 2016
Relief monoprint with spray paint
19 × 14¾ in. (48.3 × 37.5 cm)
Hallie Ford Museum of Art, Willamette University, Salem, Oregon; gift of the artist 2019.009.005
Plate 14

Small Canoe Journey, 2016
Low-fire ceramic
duck and ram in inner tube, 4 × 5 × 3 in. (10.2 × 12.7 × 7.6 cm)
dog in canoe, 3 × 7 × 2 in. (7.6 × 17.8 × 5.1 cm)
parking lot in canoe, 4 × 4 × 2 in. (10.2 × 10.2 × 5.1 cm)
horse in canoe, 3½ × 6½ × 2 in. (8.9 × 16.5 × 5.1 cm)
fish in canoe, 2 × 4½ × 1½ in. (5.1 × 11.4 × 3.8 cm)
coyote on log, 4 × 5 × 2 in. (10.2 × 12.7 × 5.1 cm)
Collection of the artist; courtesy studio e gallery, Seattle, Washington
Plate 94

Red Urban Canoeing, 2017
Relief and stencil monoprint
Sheet: 25 × 40 in. (63.5 × 101.6 cm); image: 14½ × 19 in. (36.8 × 48.3 cm)
Collection of the artist; courtesy studio e gallery, Seattle, Washington
Plate 78

Small Bingo, 2017
Waxed linen, bias tape, and thread
6½ × 4 × 4 in. (16.5 × 10.2 × 10.2 cm)
Collection of the artist; courtesy studio e gallery, Seattle, Washington
Plate 110

Vivid Day, 2017
Relief and stencil monoprint with acrylic and collage
35½ × 23 in. (90.2 × 58.4 cm)
Collection of the artist; courtesy studio e gallery, Seattle, Washington
Plate 30

Yellow Urban Canoeing, 2017
Relief and stencil monoprint with collage
Sheet: 30 × 22½ in. (76.2 × 57.2 cm); image: 24 × 18 in. (61 × 45.7 cm)
Collection of the artist; courtesy studio e gallery, Seattle, Washington
Plate 79

Canoe Journey, 2018
Waxed linen, bias tape, and thread
7 × 10 × 10 in. (17.8 × 25.4 × 25.4 cm)
Collection of the artist; courtesy studio e gallery, Seattle, Washington
Plate 39

Eagle with High Voltage Towers, 2018
Waxed linen, wool, bias tape, and thread
6½ × 4 × 4 in. (16.5 × 10.2 × 10.2 cm)
Private collection
Plate 34

Elk at Canoe Race, 2018
Relief monoprint with collage, spray paint, acrylic, and graphite
24 × 18 in. (61 × 45.7 cm)
Washington State Arts Commission, Olympia, Washington; Direct purchase WSAC2020.024.001
Plate 67

Turn Lane, 2018
Waxed linen, bias tape, and thread
8 × 7 × 7 in. (20.3 × 17.8 × 17.8 cm)
Collection of the artist; courtesy studio e gallery, Seattle, Washington
Plate 49

Canoe Journey, 2019
Sandblasted blown glass
22 × 9½ × 9½ in. (55.9 × 24.1 × 24.1 cm)
Collection of the artist; courtesy studio e gallery, Seattle, Washington
Plate 80

Echo 3, 2019
Pigment inkjet, relief, and stencil monoprint
52½ × 35 in. (133.4 × 89 cm)
Collection of the artist; courtesy studio e gallery, Seattle, Washington
Printed with Matthew Letzelter
Published by Watershed Center for Fine Art Publishing & Research, Pacific Northwest College of Art, Portland, Oregon
Plate 25

Echo 6, 2019
Pigment inkjet, relief, and stencil monoprint
52½ × 35 in. (133.4 × 89 cm)
Collection of the artist; courtesy studio e gallery, Seattle, Washington
Printed with Matthew Letzelter
Published by Watershed Center for Fine Art Publishing & Research, Pacific Northwest College of Art, Portland, Oregon
Plate 26

Echo 11, 2019
Pigment inkjet, relief, and stencil monoprint
52½ × 35 in. (133.4 × 89 cm)
Collection of the artist; courtesy studio e gallery, Seattle, Washington
Printed with Matthew Letzelter
Published by Watershed Center for Fine Art Publishing & Research, Pacific Northwest College of Art, Portland, Oregon
Plate 24

Echo 12, 2019
Pigment inkjet, relief, and stencil monoprint
52½ × 35 in. (133.4 × 89 cm)
Collection of the artist; courtesy studio e gallery, Seattle, Washington
Printed with Matthew Letzelter
Published by Watershed Center for Fine Art Publishing & Research, Pacific Northwest College of Art, Portland, Oregon
Plate 23

Omak Lake 2, 2019
Relief and stencil monoprint with spray paint
Sheet: 26 × 19½ in. (66 × 49.5 cm); image: 19 × 14½ in. (48.3 × 36.8 cm)
Collection of the artist; courtesy studio e gallery, Seattle, Washington
Plate 29

River Road 9, 2019
Relief, toner print, and stencil monoprint with spray paint
Sheet: 19 × 15 in. (48.3 × 38.1 cm); image: 8 × 11 in. (20.3 × 27.9 cm)
Collection of the artist; courtesy studio e gallery, Seattle, Washington
Plate 28

Floating By, 2020
Blown glass with enamel
13 × 9¾ × 9¾ in. (33 × 24.8 × 24.8 cm)
Collection of the artist; courtesy studio e gallery, Seattle, Washington
Plate 13

Inhabited Landscapes 2, 2020
Collagraph, relief, and stencil monoprint
26 × 20 in. (66 × 50.8 cm)
Collection of the artist; courtesy studio e gallery, Seattle, Washington
Plate 32

Inhabited Landscapes 10, 2020
Collagraph, relief, and stencil monoprint
26 × 20 in. (66 × 50.8 cm)
Collection of the artist; courtesy studio e gallery, Seattle, Washington
Plate 33

Bestiary 1, 2021
Relief and stencil monoprint
Sheet: 44 × 30 in. (111.8 × 76.2 cm); image: 41 × 30 in. (104.1 × 76.2 cm)
Collection of Jordan D. Schnitzer
Printed at Corwin Clairmont's studio, Montana
Plate 100

Bestiary 7, 2021
Relief and stencil monoprint
Sheet: 44 × 30 in. (111.8 × 76.2 cm); image: 41 × 30 in. (104.1 × 76.2 cm)
Collection of the artist; courtesy studio e gallery, Seattle, Washington
Printed at Corwin Clairmont's studio, Montana
Plate 103

Bestiary 12, 2021
Relief and stencil monoprint with acrylic
Sheet: 44 × 30 in. (111.8 × 76.2 cm); image: 41 × 30 in. (104.1 × 76.2 cm)
Northwest Museum of Arts and Culture, Spokane, Washington; museum purchase 2021, 4460.1
Printed at Corwin Clairmont's studio, Montana
Plate 101

Bestiary 17, 2021
Relief and stencil monoprint
Sheet: 44 × 30 in. (111.8 × 76.2 cm); image: 41 × 30 in. (104.1 × 76.2 cm)
Collection of the artist; courtesy studio e gallery, Seattle, Washington
Printed at Corwin Clairmont's studio, Montana
Plate 102

Bestiary Basket 1, 2021
Sandblasted blown glass
15 × 8 × 8 in. (38.1 × 20.3 × 20.3 cm)
Collection of Jordan D. Schnitzer
Plate 99

Canoe Journey, 2021
Waxed linen, bias tape, and thread
7 × 5 × 5 in. (17.8 × 12.7 × 12.7 cm)
Colville Tribal Museum, Confederated Tribes of the Colville Reservation
Plate 38

Stripes, 2021
Blown glass
11½ × 9½ × 9½ in. (29.2 × 24.1 × 24.1 cm)
Collection of the artist; courtesy studio e gallery, Seattle, Washington
Plate 8

Elevator, 2022
Waxed linen, bias tape, and thread
9½ × 6 × 6 in. (24.1 × 15.2 × 15.2 cm)
Collection of the artist; courtesy studio e gallery, Seattle, Washington
Plate 41

Elevator, 2022
Sandblasted blown glass
9 × 6½ × 6½ in. (22.9 × 16.5 × 16.5 cm)
Collection of the artist; courtesy studio e gallery, Seattle, Washington
Plate 42

Snowing, 2022
Relief and stencil monoprint with acrylic
22 × 29½ in. (55.9 × 74.9 cm)
Collection of the artist; courtesy studio e gallery, Seattle, Washington
Plate 31

Okanogan Bestiary, 2023
Waxed linen, bias tape, thread, and wool yarn
8 × 8½ × 8½ in. (20.3 × 21.6 × 21.6 cm)
High Desert Museum, Bend, Oregon; museum commission, 2023
Plate 36

Black High Voltage Tower, 2023
Sandblasted blown glass
15 × 9 × 9 in. (38.1 × 22.9 × 22.9 cm)
Collection of the artist; courtesy studio e gallery, Seattle, Washington
Plate 73

Charmed (Bestiary), 2023
Fused glass and filament
120 × 180 × 10 in. (304.8 × 457.2 × 25.4 cm)
Collection of the artist; courtesy studio e gallery, Seattle, Washington
Plate 22

Fishing, 2023
Waxed linen, wool, bias tape, and thread
Each: 6½ × 3½ × 3½ in. (16.5 × 8.9 × 8.9 cm)
Northwest Museum of Arts and Culture, Spokane, Washington; museum purchase 2023, 4499.1
Plate 81

Self Portrait, 2023
Sandblasted blown glass
12½ × 7 × 7 in. (31.8 × 17.8 × 17.8 cm)
Collection of the artist; courtesy studio e gallery, Seattle, Washington
Plate 1

As of July 8, 2024

Not all works will be on view at all venues.

Contributors

heather ahtone, PhD (Choctaw/Chickasaw Nation), is director of curatorial affairs at First Americans Museum in Oklahoma City, Oklahoma. Her research examines the intersection between Indigenous cultural knowledge, art, and museum practice. Working in the Native arts community since 1993, she has curated numerous exhibits, publishes regularly, and continues to seek opportunities to broaden discourse on global contemporary Indigenous arts. In addition to her curatorial work, she serves the community through her membership on the boards of the *American Art* journal, Clara Luper Civil Rights Center, Association of Art Museum Curators, and the Native American Art Studies Association.

Rachel Allen (Nimiipuu [Nez Perce]) is a curator and PhD candidate. Before pursuing a PhD, Allen was an assistant curator at the Peabody Essex Museum, where she started as a curatorial fellow. Allen contributed to several major traveling exhibitions with publications while there, including *T.C. Cannon: At the Edge of America* and *Nature's Nation: American Art and Environment*. Additionally, Allen has worked with several other museums in various roles, including the Portland Museum of Art in Maine, the Eli and Edythe Broad Art Museum at Michigan State University, and the Missoula Art Museum in Montana.

Anya Montiel is a curator at the Smithsonian National Museum of the American Indian. She curated *Ancestors Know Who We Are* (2022), featuring the work of Black-Indigenous women artists, and co-curated *Pulse: Weavings and Paintings by Marlowe Katoney* at the University of Arizona Museum of Art (2023). She received her doctorate and master's degrees in American studies from Yale University and a bachelor's degree in Native American studies from the University of California, Davis. She has written for *American Indian* magazine, *Art in America*, *First American Art Magazine*, the *Journal of Modern Craft*, and *The Oxford Handbook of American Indian History*.

Index

All works are by Joe Feddersen unless otherwise indicated. Page numbers in **bold** refer to plates; those in *italics* refer to illustrations.

Credits

In reproducing the images contained in this publication, the Northwest Museum of Arts and Culture obtained the permission of the rights holders whenever possible. Reasonable efforts have been made to credit the copyright holders, photographers, and sources; if there are any errors or omissions, please contact the Northwest Museum of Arts and Culture so corrections can be made in any subsequent edition.

Front cover: *Black Ghost*, 2015, relief, collagraph, and stencil monoprint with spray paint. Collection of Jordan D. Schnitzer. Aaron Wessling Photography, Courtesy of Jordan Schnitzer Family Foundation

Back cover: *Canoe Journey: Coyote in Inner Tube*, 2016, low-fire ceramic. Collection of the artist and courtesy of studio e gallery. Dean Davis Photography

Plates 1–2, 4–5, 7–9, 11–18, 20–21, 23–35, 37–44, 46–64, 72–75, 77–94, 96–98, 101–110: Photo by Dean Davis
Plates 3, 6, 67: Photo courtesy of the artist and the Washington State Arts Commission
Plates 10, 19, 45, 66, 68–69, 95, 99–100: Aaron Wessling Photography, courtesy of Jordan Schnitzer Family Foundation
Plate 22: Photo by Albert Ting, courtesy of Smithsonian American Art Museum
Plate 36: Photo by Lindsey Brunsman, courtesy of the High Desert Museum, Bend, Oregon
Plate 65: Courtesy of the Eiteljorg Museum of American Indians and Western Art, Indianapolis
Plates 70–71: Photo by James Bailey, Courtesy of MATRIX Press
Plate 76: Photo by Chris Autio, courtesy of the Missoula Art Museum, Montana

pp. 2, 4, 6–7, 18–19, 35, 58, 67–68, 71, 76, 118, 120, 123, 125, 127, 130, 137, 158, 180–82: Photo by Dean Davis
p. 20: Photo by LaRonn Katchia (Warm Springs/Wasco/Paiute), courtesy of the High Desert Museum
p. 50: © Victor A. Charlo. Used by permission of the author. All rights reserved.
p. 60 (fig. 1): Photo by heather ahtone
p. 60 (fig. 2): Courtesy of the Amon Carter Museum of American Art, Fort Worth, Texas
p. 62: Photo by Joe Feddersen
p. 70: Photo by EG Schempf, courtesy of the Nerman Museum of Contemporary Art, Johnson County Community College, Overland Park, Kansas
p. 73: Photo by Albert Ting, courtesy of Smithsonian American Art Museum
p. 83: © Miles R. Miller. Used by permission of the author. All rights reserved.
p. 108: © Elizabeth A. Woody. Used by permission of the author. All rights reserved.
p. 122: Photo by Dominic Nieri
p. 126: Photo by Thomas Alix Johnston
p. 133: Photo by Aaron Wessling Photography, courtesy of Jordan Schnitzer Family Foundation
p. 152: © Ramona Wilson. Used by permission of the author. All rights reserved.

pp. 22–33: Maps by Alex Mann

This catalogue was produced on the occasion of the exhibition *Joe Feddersen: Earth, Water, Sky*, organized by the Northwest Museum of Arts and Culture, curated by heather ahtone, director of curatorial affairs, First Americans Museum, Oklahoma City, and Rachel Allen, special projects curator, Northwest Museum of Arts and Culture, Spokane, Washington.

Exhibition Itinerary:
Northwest Museum of Arts and Culture,
Spokane, Washington
September 28, 2024–January 5, 2025

High Desert Museum, Bend, Oregon
September 2025–January 2026

Missoula Art Museum, Montana
September 2026–December 2026

Joe Feddersen: Earth, Water, Sky was made possible through major support from the Henry Luce Foundation, the Terra Foundation for American Art, and the Andy Warhol Foundation for the Visual Arts.

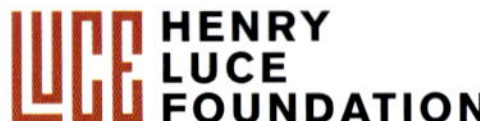

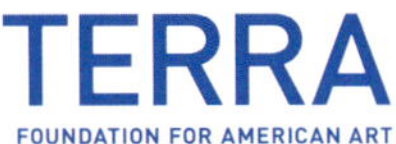

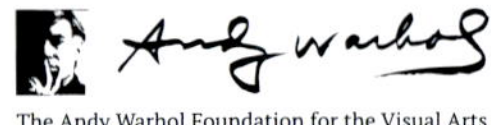

This project is supported in part by the National Endowment for the Arts and Mary and Cheney Cowles.

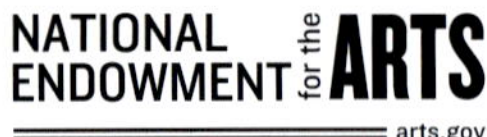

Library of Congress Control Number: 2024941341
ISBN 979-8-9879293-5-3

Northwest Museum of Arts and Culture
2316 W 1st Ave
Spokane, WA 99201
northwestmuseum.org

Distributed by University of Washington Press
uwapress.uw.edu

Produced by Marquand Books, Seattle
marquandbooks.com

Edited by Melissa Duffes
Designed by Ryan Polich
Typeset in Miller Text and Trade Gothic by Brynn Warriner
Proofread by Janice Lee
Indexed by Mylinh Hamlington
Color management by I/O Color, Seattle
Printed and bound in China by C & C Offset Printing Co.